CIMA

STRATEGIC

PAPER F3

FINANCIAL STRATEGY

T U D Y   T E X T

Our text is designed to help you study **effectively** and **efficiently**.

In this edition we:

- **Highlight** the **most important elements** in the syllabus and the **key skills** you will need

- **Signpost** how each chapter links to the syllabus and the learning outcomes

- Use **overview and summary diagrams** to develop understanding of interrelations between topics

- **Provide** lots of **exam alerts** explaining how what you're learning may be tested

- **Include examples** and **questions** to help you apply what you've learnt

- **Emphasise key points** in **section summaries**

- **Test your knowledge** of what you've studied in **quick quizzes**

- **Examine your understanding** in our **practice question bank**

SUITABLE FOR EXAMS IN 2018

PUBLISHED NOVEMBER 2017

BPP
LEARNING MEDIA

Fourth edition 2017

ISBN 9781509715831

e-ISBN 9781509715947

British Library Cataloguing-in-Publication Data
A catalogue record for this book
is available from the British Library

Published by

BPP Learning Media Ltd
BPP House, Aldine Place
London W12 8AA

www.bpp.com/learningmedia

Printed in the United Kingdom

Your learning materials, published by BPP
Learning Media Ltd, are printed on paper sourced
from sustainable, managed forests.

Contents

		Page

Introduction

How our Study Text can help you pass	iv
Features in our Study Text	v
Streamlined studying	vi
Syllabus and learning outcomes	vi
Studying F3	xiii
Assessment	xviii

Part A Formulation of financial strategy

1	Strategic financial objectives	3
2	Strategic financial management	19
3	Reporting issues	63

Part B Financing and dividend decisions

4	Dividend policy	97
5	Long-term debt finance	111
6	Managing the debt profile	135
7	Leasing	149
8	Equity finance	167
9	Capital structure	201

Part C Corporate finance

10	Strategic implications of acquisitions	223
11	Introduction to valuation techniques	243
12	Advanced valuation techniques	275
13	Post acquisition issues	293

Appendix 1: Discounted cash flow	323
Appendix 2: Mathematical tables and exam formulae	331
Practice question bank	337
Practice answer bank	365
Index	399

Review form

How our Study Text can help you pass

Streamlined studying	• We show you the best ways to study efficiently • Our Text has been designed to ensure you can easily and quickly navigate through it • The different features in our Text emphasise important knowledge and techniques
Exam expertise	• **Studying F3** on page xiii introduces the key themes of the syllabus and summarises how to pass • We highlight throughout our Text how topics may be tested and what you'll have to do in the exam • We help you see the complete picture of the syllabus, so that you can answer questions that range across the whole syllabus.
Regular review	• We frequently summarise the key knowledge you need • We test what you've learnt by providing questions and quizzes throughout our Text

Our other products

BPP Learning Media also offers these products for the Objective Test exams and the integrated case study (ICS) exams:

i-Pass	Providing computer-based testing in a variety of formats, ideal for self-assessment
Exam Practice Kit	Providing helpful guidance on how to pass the objective test and more question practice
Passcards	Summarising what you should know in visual, easy to remember, form
ICS Workbook	Providing help with exam skills and question practice for the integrated case study exam

You can purchase these products by visiting www.bpp.com/cimamaterials

Online Learning with BPP

BPP's online learning study modes provide flexibility and convenience, allowing you to study effectively, at a pace that suits you, where and when you choose.

Online Classroom Live	Through live interactive online sessions it provides you with the traditional structure and support of classroom learning, but with the convenience of attending classes wherever you are
Online Classroom	Through pre-recorded online lectures it provides you with the classroom experience via the web with the tutor guidance & support you'd expect from a face to face classroom

You can find out more by visiting www.bpp.com/cima

Features in our Study Text

Chapter Overview Diagrams illustrate the connections between the topic areas you are about to cover

 Section Introductions explain how the section fits into the chapter

 Key Terms are the core vocabulary you need to learn

KEY TERM

 Key Points are points that you have to know, ideas or calculations that will be the foundations of your answers

KEY POINT

 Exam Alerts show you how subjects are likely to be tested

 Exam Skills are the key skills you will need to demonstrate in the exam, linked to question requirements

 Exam formulae are formulae you will be given in the exam

EXAM

 Examples show how theory is put into practice

 Questions give you the practice you need to test your understanding of what you've learnt

 Case Studies link what you've learnt with the real-world business environment

CASE STUDY

 Links show how the syllabus overlaps with other parts of the qualification, including Knowledge Brought Forward that you need to remember from previous exams

 Website References link to material that will enhance your understanding of what you're studying

 Further Reading will give you a wider perspective on the subjects you're covering

 Chapter Summary Diagrams allow you to review each Chapter

*The format of the exam formulae in the Text may differ slightly to exam. For exam formulae in the CIMA format, please refer to the formulae table in Appendix 2.

Streamlined studying

What you should do	In order to
Read the Chapter and Section Introductions and look at the Chapter Overview Diagram	See why topics need to be studied and map your way through the chapter
Go quickly through the explanations	Gain the depth of knowledge and understanding that you'll need
Highlight the Key Points, Key Terms and Formulae	Make sure you know the basics that you can't do without in the exam
Focus on the Exam Skills and Exam Alerts	Know how you'll be tested and what you'll have to do
Work through the Examples and Case Studies	See how what you've learnt applies in practice
Prepare Answers to the Questions	See if you can apply what you've learnt in practice
Review the Chapter Summary Diagrams	Remind you of, and reinforce, what you've learnt
Answer the Quick Quiz	Find out if there are any gaps in your knowledge
Answer the Question(s) in the Practice Question Bank	Practise what you've learnt in depth

Should I take notes?

Brief notes may help you remember what you're learning. You should use the notes format that's most helpful to you (lists, diagrams, mindmaps).

Further help

BPP Learning Media's *Learning to Learn Accountancy* provides lots more helpful guidance on studying. It is designed to be used both at the outset of your CIMA studies and throughout the process of learning accountancy. It can help you **focus your studies on the subject and exam**, enabling you to **acquire knowledge, practise and revise efficiently and effectively**.

Syllabus and learning outcomes

Paper F3 Financial Strategy

The syllabus comprises:

Topic and Study Weighting

		%
A	Formulation of financial strategy	25
B	Financing and dividend decisions	35
C	Corporate finance	40

Learning Outcomes		
Lead	**Component**	**Syllabus content**
A Formulation of financial strategy		
1 Evaluate strategic financial and non-financial objectives of different types of entities.	(a) advise on the overall strategic financial and non-financial of objectives of different types of entities	(i) Overall strategic financial objectives (e.g. value for money, maximising shareholder wealth, providing a surplus) of different types of entities (e.g. incorporated, unincorporated, quoted, unquoted, private sector, public sector, for-profit and not-for-profit).
		(ii) Non-financial objectives (e.g. human, intellectual, natural, and social and relationship).
		(iii) Financial strategy in the context of international operations.
	(b) evaluate financial objectives of for-profit entities	(i) Financial objectives (e.g. earnings growth, dividend growth, gearing) and assessment of attainment.
		(ii) Sensitivity of the attainment of financial objectives to changes in underlying economic (e.g. interest rates, exchange rates, inflation) and business variables (e.g. margins, volumes).
	(c) advise on the use of sustainability and integrated reporting to inform stakeholders of relevant information concerning the interaction of a business with society and the natural environment.	(i) Limitations of financial statements for incorporated entities, prepared in accordance with International Accounting Standards (IAS), to reflect the value and stewardship of the non-financial capital base.
		(ii) Principles and scope of reporting social and environmental issues (e.g. Global Reporting Initiative's Sustainability Reporting Framework and International Integrated Reporting Council guidance).

Learning Outcomes		
Lead	**Component**	**Syllabus content**
2 Evaluate strategic financial management policy decisions.	(a) evaluate the interrelationship between investment, financing and dividend decisions for an incorporated entity	(i) Investment, financing and dividend decisions and the interrelationship between them in meeting the cash needs of the entity.
		(ii) Sensitivity of forecast financial statements and future cash position to investment, financing and dividend decisions.
		(iii) Consideration of the interests of shareholders and other stakeholders in investment, financing and dividend decisions (e.g. impact on investor and lender ratios, compliance with debt covenants and attainment of financial objectives).
		(iv) Determine financing requirements and cash available for payment of dividends based on the overall consideration of the forecast future cash flows arising from investment decisions, business strategy and forecast business and economic variables.
	(b) advise on the development of financial strategy for an entity taking into account taxation and other external influences	(i) Lenders' assessment of creditworthiness (e.g. business plans, liquidity ratios, cash forecasts, credit rating, quality of management).
		(ii) Financial strategy in the context of regulatory requirements (e.g. price and service controls exercised by industry regulators).
		(iii) Consideration of taxation regulations (domestic and international) in setting financial strategy.
	(c) evaluate the impact of the adoption of hedge accounting and disclosure of financial risk on financial statements and stakeholder assessment.	(i) The accounting treatment of hedge accounting (cash flow, fair value and net investment), IFRS 9 (or IAS 39, before effective date for IFRS 9).
		(ii) Impact of adoption of hedge accounting on financial statements and on stakeholder assessment.
		(iii) Disclosure of financial risk, including policies for managing such risk (*IFRS 7, Financial Instruments: Disclosures*).

Learning Outcomes		
Lead	**Component**	**Syllabus content**
B Financing and dividend decisions		
1 Evaluate the financing requirements of an entity and recommend a strategy for meeting those requirements.	(a) evaluate the impact of changes in capital structure for an incorporated entity on shareholders and other stakeholders	(i) Capital structure theories (traditional theory, Modigliani and Miller's (MM) theories with and without tax and practical considerations and calculations using MM formulae).
		(ii) Calculation of cost of equity or weighted average cost of capital (WACC) to reflect a change in capital structure.
		(iii) Modelling impact of choice of capital structure on financial statements and key performance measures (e.g. ratios of interest to investors and lenders and compliance with debt covenants).
		(iv) Structuring the debt/equity profile of group companies, including tax implications and thin capitalisation rules.
	(b) evaluate and compare alternative methods of raising long-term debt finance	(i) Criteria for selecting appropriate debt instruments (e.g. bank borrowings, bonds, convertible bonds, commercial paper).
		(ii) Target debt profile (e.g. interest, currency and maturity profile) to manage interest, currency and refinancing risk.
		(iii) Use of cross-currency swaps and interest rate swaps to change the currency or interest rate profile of debt.
		(iv) Tax considerations in the selection of debt instruments.
		(v) Procedures for issuing debt securities (private placement and capital market issues, role of advisers and underwriters).
		(vi) Debt covenants (e.g. interest cover, net debt/EBITDA, debt/debt and equity).
		(vii) The lease or buy decision (for both operating and finance leases).

Learning Outcomes		
Lead	**Component**	**Syllabus content**
	(c) evaluate and compare alternative methods of raising equity finance.	(i) Methods of flotation and implications for the management of the entity and for its stakeholders.
		(ii) Use of rights issues, including choice of discount rate, impact on shareholder wealth and calculation of the theoretical ex-rights price (TERP) and yield-adjusted TERP.
2 evaluate dividend policies for an incorporated entity that meet the needs and expectations of shareholders.	(a) evaluate alternatives to cash dividends and their impact on shareholder wealth and entity performance measures	(i) Impact of scrip dividends on shareholder value and entity value/financial statements/performance measures.
		(ii) Impact of share repurchase programmes on shareholder value and entity value/financial statements/performance measures.
	(b) recommend appropriate dividend policies, including consideration of shareholder expectations and the cash needs of the entity.	(i) Implications for shareholder value of alternative dividend policies including MM theory of dividend irrelevancy.
		(ii) Development of appropriate dividend policy, taking into account the interests of shareholders and the cash needs of the entity.
C Corporate finance		
1 Evaluate opportunities for acquisition, merger and divestment.	(a) evaluate the financial and strategic implications of proposals for an acquisition, merger or divestment, including taxation implications.	(i) Recognition of the interests of different stakeholder groups.
		(ii) Reasons for and against acquisitions, mergers and divestments (e.g. strategic position, synergistic benefits, Big Data opportunities, risks and tax implications).
		(iii) Taxation implications (group loss relief, differences in taxation rates, withholding tax, double tax treaties).
		(iv) Process and implications of a management buy-out, including potential conflicts of interest.
		(v) Role/function/implications of acquisition by private equity or venture capitalist
		(vi) Role and scope of competition authorities in relation to mergers and acquisitions.

Learning Outcomes		
Lead	**Component**	**Syllabus content**
2 Evaluate the value of entities.	(a) calculate the value of a whole entity (quoted or unquoted), a subsidiary entity or division using a range of methods including taxation	(i) Asset valuation (e.g. historic cost, replacement cost and realisable value).
		(ii) Forms of intangible asset (including intellectual property rights, brands etc) and methods of valuation.
		(iii) Share prices (quoted on stock market or private sale for non-quoted entities).
		(iv) Earnings valuation (e.g. price/earnings multiples and earnings yield).
		(v) Dividend valuation (e.g. dividend growth model, including estimating growth from past or forecast figures and including non-constant growth assumptions).
		(vi) Discounted free cash flow valuation (including taxation, risk-adjusted discount rate, foreign currency cash flows and sensitivity analysis).
		(vii) Ideas of diversifiable risk (unsystematic risk) and systematic risk.
		(viii) Capital asset pricing model (CAPM), including the meaning and derivation of the component, and the ability to gear and un-gear betas.
		(ix) Calculation of an appropriate cost of capital for use in discounted cash flow analysis (e.g. cost of equity or WACC) by reference to the nature of the transaction (e.g. division or an entire entity), including use of CAPM, dividend valuation model and MM WACC formula.
		(x) Efficient market hypothesis and its relevance for the valuation of quoted entities.
		(xi) Impact of government incentives on entity value (e.g. capital or revenue grants).
	(b) evaluate the validity of the valuation methods used and the results obtained in the context of a given scenario.	(i) Strengths and weaknesses of each valuation method.
		(ii) Validity of the results for use in decision making according to the nature of the target entity (e.g. a division, a whole entity, quoted or unquoted).

Learning Outcomes		
Lead	**Component**	**Syllabus content**
3 Evaluate pricing issues and post-transaction issues.	(a) evaluate alternative pricing structures and bid process including taxation implications	(i) Forms of consideration and terms for acquisitions (e.g. cash, shares, convertibles and earn-out arrangements), and their impact on shareholders, including taxation impact.
		(ii) Treatment of target entity debt (settlement, refinancing).
		(iii) Methods/implications of financing a cash offer and refinancing target entity debt.
		(iv) Bid negotiation (e.g. managing a hostile bid) including agency issues.
	(b) evaluate post-transaction issues.	(i) Potential post-transaction value for both acquirer and seller (e.g. taking into account synergistic benefits, forecast performance and market response).
		(ii) Integration of management/systems and effective realisation of synergistic benefits.
		(iii) Types of exit strategies and their implications.

Studying F3

1 What's F3 about

1.1 Formulation of financial strategy

In Part A of this book we examine the development of **financial strategy**. In Chapter 1 we are concerned with how **financial objectives** of different types of organisation are identified and achieved. Our starting point is the main financial objective of a profit making company – to **maximise shareholder wealth**. Throughout this Text we look at various **financial strategies** to achieve this objective. In this chapter we also look at the role of **stakeholders** in an organisation, and their influence on strategy. We also consider organisations' non-financial objectives in their overall strategy.

In Chapter 2, we look at how financial strategy is formulated from **investment, financing and dividend decisions**; their inter-relationships; and other influences on financial strategy such as economic and regulatory factors. We also cover the techniques of ratio analysis and forecasting. This enables a company to forecast whether or not it will achieve its financial objectives, and determine its future cash requirements, to make **financing decisions**.

Chapter 3 looks at the limitations of financial statements in not fully informing stakeholders of the impact an organisation's strategic objectives has on its value. This is being overcome by measures such as hedge accounting which reports the impact of hedging against financial risks; and disclosures of financial risk, which communicate an organisation's strategy for managing financial risks.

Performance measures of the achievement of a company's non-financial objectives are not required financial statements but will impact on the true value of an organisation (eg the impact it has on the environment). Integrated Reporting and Sustainability Reporting inform stakeholders of a more true value of an organisation by assessing its achievement of these objectives.

1.2 Financing and dividend decisions

In Part B of this book we consider various aspects of financing and dividend decisions, starting with a look in more detail at dividend decisions in Chapter 4.

In Chapters 5–9 we consider financing decisions, more specially, how a company can raise long-term finance. Companies can obtain long-term debt finance from the issue of bonds, or equity finance from the issue of shares, through capital markets. Leasing is also a common source of debt finance and the lease or buy decision evaluates the decision to lease (financing decision) or buy (investment decision).

In Chapter 9 we look at the financing decision of what proportion of debt and equity finance a company should have in its **capital structure**. We revisit calculation of the **weighted average cost of capital (WACC)** and examine theories which attempt to explain the effect of changes in capital structure on cost of capital, and therefore the market value of company.

1.3 Corporate finance

Part C of this book looks at mergers and acquisitions of companies and their valuation.

In Chapter 10 we look the strategic implications of acquisitions.

Chapters 11 and 12 look at various techniques of valuing a company, which can be applied to a merger and acquisition situation in Chapter 13.

Chapter 13 also looks at the financing decision of how to fund an acquisition (cash or paper offer); post-acquisition issues such as problems with integration; and different exit strategies an acquiror may take.

Part C carries the most weight of the syllabus and therefore draws on knowledge from earlier chapters, particularly Chapters 5–9.

2 What's required

You need to show understanding and ability to use techniques, and set your answers in context, above all in linking investment, financing and dividend decisions. Key higher level skills being tested are **analysis**, **evaluation** and **advice**.

The examiners are looking for:

- **Clear presentation** and **conclusions** (for the ICS)
- **Understanding** of the key issues and tools
- Ability to **analyse** data and information (going beyond a description of the issues for the ICS)
- Answers focused on the scenarios (for the ICS)

3 How to pass

3.1 Study the whole syllabus

You need to be comfortable with **all areas of the syllabus**, as questions in the objective test exam will cover all syllabus areas. **Wider reading** will help you understand the main risks businesses face, which will be particularly useful in the integrated case study exam.

3.2 Lots of question practice

You can **develop application skills** by attempting questions in the Practice Question Bank. While these might not be in the format that you will experience in your exam, doing the full question will enable you to answer the exam questions. For example, you will only be able to answer a question on an element of a WACC calculation if you know how to do the full calculation. Similarly, in the integrated case study exam you will have to answer questions that combine F3 syllabus areas with E3 and P3. However, by answering questions on F3 you will develop the technical knowledge and skills in order to answer those questions.

However, you should practice OT exam standard questions, which you will find in the BPP Exam Practice Kit.

4 Brought forward knowledge

The examiner may test knowledge or techniques you've learnt at lower levels. As F3 is part of the Financial pillar, the content of Papers F1 and F2 will be significant.

However, material from other papers may be relevant as well, including P2, P3 and E3.

5 The Integrated Case Study and links with E3 and P3

The integrated case study exam is based on the expectation that students are developing a pool of knowledge. When faced with a problem students can appropriately apply their knowledge from any syllabus. Students will avoid a historical problem of partitioning their knowledge and accessing, for example, their knowledge of IFRS only when faced with a set of financial statements.

- **Enterprise strategy decisions** will **impact** upon the financial objectives, sources of finance chosen, the investment decisions, the risks the organisation faces and the controls necessary to counter those risks.

- **Financial and performance strategies** must therefore fulfil the same criteria as enterprise strategy; for example they should be **acceptable, suitable and feasible.**

- At the same time **enterprise strategy** will be **constrained** by the finance available and the level of risks the organisation is prepared to bear.

- **Financial strategy decisions** will **impact** upon the **risks** the organisation bears and perhaps impose limitations on the controls the organisation can implement. Financial strategy will also be determined by the **financial risks** (some sources of finance may be thought too risky, the benefits of investment decisions too uncertain, risk may impact upon investment appraisal calculations).

- **Performance measurement** techniques such as ratio analysis may be useful in any paper. The **effectiveness of management accounting systems**, particularly the information provided and how useful they are as control mechanisms, could impact upon any of the papers.

6 What the examiner means

The table below has been prepared by CIMA to help you interpret the syllabus and learning outcomes and the meaning of questions.

You will see that there are five levels of Learning objective, ranging from Knowledge to Evaluation, reflecting the level of skill you will be expected to demonstrate. CIMA Certificate subjects only use levels 1 to 3, but in CIMA's Professional qualification the entire hierarchy will be used.

At the start of each chapter in your study text is a topic list relating the coverage in the chapter to the level of skill you may be called on to demonstrate in the exam.

Learning objectives	Verbs used	Definition
1 Knowledge		
What are you expected to know	• List	• Make a list of
	• State	• Express, fully or clearly, the details of/facts of
	• Define	• Give the exact meaning of
2 Comprehension		
What you are expected to understand	• Describe	• Communicate the key features of
	• Distinguish	• Highlight the differences between
	• Explain	• Make clear or intelligible/state the meaning or purpose of
	• Identify	
	• Illustrate	• Recognise, establish or select after consideration
		• Use an example to describe or explain something
3 Application		
How you are expected to apply your knowledge	• Apply	• Put to practical use
	• Calculate/ compute	• Ascertain or reckon mathematically
		• Prove with certainty or to exhibit by practical means
	• Demonstrate	
	• Prepare	• Make or get ready for use
	• Reconcile	• Make or prove consistent/compatible
	• Solve	• Find an answer to
	• Tabulate	• Arrange in a table
4 Analysis		
How you are expected to analyse the detail of what you have learned	• Analyse	• Examine in detail the structure of
	• Categorise	• Place into a defined class or division
	• Compare and contrast	• Show the similarities and/or differences between
	• Construct	• Build up or compile
	• Discuss	• Examine in detail by argument
	• Interpret	• Translate into intelligible or familiar terms
	• Prioritise	• Place in order of priority or sequence for action
	• Produce	• Create or bring into existence
5 Evaluation		
How you are expected to use your learning to evaluate, make decisions or recommendations	• Advise	• Counsel, inform or notify
	• Evaluate	• Appraise or assess the value of
	• Recommend	• Propose a course of action

Competency Framework

CIMA has developed a competency framework detailing the skills, abilities and competencies that finance professionals need. The CIMA syllabus has been developed to match the competency mix as it develops over the three levels of the professional qualification. The importance of the various competencies at the strategic level is shown below.

Assessment

The CIMA assessment is a two-tier structure with objective tests for each subject and an integrated case study at each level.

Objective test

The objective tests are computer based and can be taken on demand. The student exam preparation on the CIMA website (www.cimaglobal.com) has additional information and tools to help you become familiar with the test style. Make sure you check back regularly as more information may be added.

Integrated case study

Candidates must pass or receive exemptions from the three objective tests at each level, before attempting the integrated case study exam for that level.

The integrated case studies are available four times a year.

The integrated case study exams will combine the knowledge and learning from all the pillars. They will be set in the context of a preseen fictional organisation based on a real industry.

The strategic level will require long essays supported by calculations and analysis. The role of the candidate will be that of a senior manager reporting to the CFO and senior management team.

The focus from a F3 perspective will be in recommending alternative financial strategies.

FORMULATION OF FINANCIAL STRATEGY

Part A

STRATEGIC FINANCIAL OBJECTIVES

 In the first part of this Study Text, we are concerned with how the **financial objectives** of different types of organisations are identified and attained; the links between the investment, financing and dividend decisions; the external influences on formulating financial strategy; **non-financial objectives** and non-financial reporting; the analysis of the **performance of organisations**.

Remember the most important learning objective of this paper is that you should **recommend alternative financial strategies** for an organisation. What the first part of this Text provides you with are factors you should consider and tools you can use when formulating your recommendations.

In this chapter the key question is **what are we trying to achieve?** You need to understand what the most important objectives are and how you recognise that they have been achieved. However don't assume that you will always be asked about the financial objectives of profit-making companies. Questions may ask you to consider the objectives of non-commercial bodies or public sector bodies such as hospitals.

Topic list	learning outcomes	syllabus references	ability required
1 Objectives of companies	A(1)(a)	A(1)(a)(i)(ii)	advise
2 Stakeholders and objectives	A(1)(a)	A(1)(a)(i)	advise
3 Objectives of publicly owned and non-commercial bodies	A(1)(a)	A(1)(a)(i)	advise

Chapter Overview

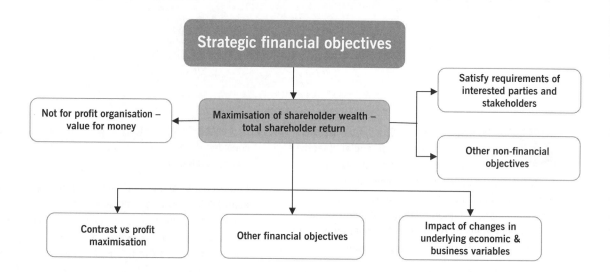

1   Objectives of companies

Introduction

In this section we identify the main objectives of an incorporated entity or company. **Profit maximisation** is often assumed to be the main objective of a **profit-making** company but shareholders may still be disappointed even when profits are rising. What other objectives are therefore also important?

1.1 Financial objectives of a company

KEY POINT

It is assumed that the main objective of a company should be to **maximise the wealth** of its **ordinary shareholders**.

A company is financed by ordinary shareholders, preferred shareholders, bond holders and other long-term and short-term payables. All surplus funds, however, belong to the legal owners of the company, its ordinary shareholders. Any retained profits represent the undistributed wealth of these equity shareholders.

1.2 Measuring wealth and value

If the financial objective of a company is to **maximise the value** of the company, and in particular the value of its ordinary shares, we need to be able to put values on a company and its shares. How do we do that?

Methods of company valuation	
Going concern basis	Based on the company's balance sheet (statement of financial position). Rising retained profits are an indication of potential dividends.
Break-up basis	Only of interest if company is threatened with insolvency, or if individual assets are being sold to raise cash.
Market values	Trading prices of stocks and shares, most relevant to financial objectives. Shareholder's return on investment comes from dividends received and increases in market value of shares (determined by expectations of future dividends).

When shares are in an **unquoted company**, it can be hard to measure their value as there is **no market price** available. However the priorities of unquoted shareholders will be the same, and therefore a company should be looking to maximise their wealth.

1.3 Increasing value

If a company's shares are **traded on a stock market**, the wealth of shareholders is increased when the **share price goes up**. The price of a company's shares should go up when the company is expected to make **additional profits**, which it will pay out as dividends or re-invest in the business to achieve future profit growth and dividend growth.

However, to increase the share price the company should achieve its profits without taking excessive **business risks** and **financial risks** that worry shareholders.

1.4 Financial targets

If there is an increase in earnings and dividends, management can hope for an increase in the share price too, so that shareholders benefit from both higher revenue (dividends) and also capital gains (higher share prices).

Management should set **financial targets** for factors which they can influence directly, such as cash flows, profits and dividend growth.

Examples of financial targets	
Increasing earnings per share	EPS should increase by 6% per annum.
Borrowing levels	Ratio of debt: equity shouldn't exceed 1:1 or finance costs shouldn't be higher than 25% of profit from operations.
Profit retention	Dividend cover (profit for the year: dividends) should exceed 2.5.
Profit from operations	Minimum return on capital employed of 20%.
Cash generation	Operating cash flow should increase by 2% more than inflation.

These financial targets are not primary targets, but they can act as **subsidiary targets** or constraints that should help a company to achieve its main financial objective without incurring excessive risks.

1.5 Short-term and long-term targets

In the **long term** companies should be looking to **maximise shareholder wealth**.

Short-term targets can encourage a company to pursue short-term objectives at the **expense** of long-term ones. For example, by deferring new capital investments, or spending only small amounts on research and development and on training.

1.6 Multiple financial targets

A major problem with setting a number of different financial targets, either primary targets or supporting secondary targets, is that they might not all be **consistent** with each other, and so might not all be achievable at the same time. When this happens, some **compromises** will have to be accepted.

Example: Evaluation of the attainment of financial objectives

Lion Grange Co has recently introduced a formal scheme of long-range planning. At a meeting called to discuss the first draft plans, the following estimates emerged:

(a)   Revenue in the current year reached £10,000,000, and forecasts for the next five years are £10,600,000, £11,400,000, £12,400,000, £13,600,000 and £15,000,000.

(b)   The ratio of profit for the year to revenues is 10%, and this is expected to continue throughout the planning period.

(c)   Total assets less current liabilities will remain at around 125% of sales. The current year equity is £8.75m.

It was also suggested that:

(d)   If profits rise, dividends should rise by at least the same percentage.

(e)   An earnings retention rate of 50% should be maintained.

(f)   The ratio of long-term borrowing to long-term funds (debt plus equity) is limited (by the market) to 30%, which happens also to be the current gearing level of the company.

Prepare a financial analysis of the draft long-range plan and suggested policies for dividends, retained earnings and gearing.

Solution

The draft financial plan for profits, dividends, assets required and funding can be drawn up in a table, as follows:

	Current year £m	Year 1 £m	Year 2 £m	Year 3 £m	Year 4 £m	Year 5 £m
Revenues	10.00	10.60	11.40	12.40	13.60	15.00
Profit for the year	1.00	1.06	1.14	1.24	1.36	1.50
Dividends (50% of profit after tax)	0.50	0.53	0.57	0.62	0.68	0.75
Retained earnings						
Total assets less current liabilities (125% of sales)	12.50	13.25	14.25	15.50	17.00	18.75
Equity (increased by retained earnings)	8.75	9.28	9.85	10.47	11.15	11.90
Maximum debt (30% of long-term funds)	3.75	3.98	4.22	4.49	4.78	5.10
	12.50	13.26	14.07	14.96	15.93	17.00
Funds available/(Shortfall in funds)*	0.00	0.01	(0.18)	(0.54)	(1.07)	(1.75)

* Given maximum gearing of 30% and no new issue of shares, this equals funds available minus total assets less current liabilities.

These figures show that the financial objectives of the company are not compatible with each other, and adjustments will have to be made.

(a) Given the assumptions about sales, profits, dividends and assets required, there will be an increasing shortfall of funds from year 2 onwards, unless new shares are issued or the gearing level rises above 30%.

(b) In years 2 and 3, the shortfall can be eliminated by retaining a greater percentage of profits, but this may have a serious adverse effect on the share price. In year 4 and year 5, the shortfall in funds cannot be removed even if dividend payments are reduced to nothing.

(c) The net asset turnover appears to be low. The situation would be eased if investments were able to generate higher revenues, so that fewer non-current assets and less working capital would be required to support the projected level of revenues.

(d) If net asset turnover cannot be improved, it may be possible to increase the profit to revenues ratio by reducing costs or increasing selling prices.

(e) If a new issue of shares is proposed to make up the shortfall in funds, the amount of funds required must be considered very carefully. Total dividends would have to be increased in order to pay dividends on the new shares. The company seems unable to offer prospects of suitable dividend payments, and so raising new equity might be difficult.

(f) It is conceivable that extra funds could be raised by issuing new debt, so that the level of gearing would be over 30%. It is uncertain whether investors would be prepared to lend money so as to increase gearing. If more funds were borrowed, profits would fall so that the share price might also be reduced.

1.6.1 Sensitivity of the attainment of financial objectives to changes in underlying economic and business variables

An entity's ability to meet it financial objectives will be sensitive to the following changes in **economic variables** and **business variables**:

Economic variables

Interest rates

When interest rates rise, consumer spending tends to fall because higher interest rates mean a higher cost of credit for customers, leading to less disposable income for spending. When assessing whether or not an entity will achieve its objectives, forecast sales figures may need to be revised downwards to allow for increases in interest rates. Increases in interest rates may also lead to higher costs of financing. Interest rates are covered in detail in Chapter 2.

Exchange rates

If a company's domestic currency increases in value against currencies of overseas customers, it will be harder for the company to export, since the cost to the overseas customers is higher. This could cause sales to fall if exports are significant.

Furthermore, if a company's domestic currency increases in value against currencies of overseas suppliers, costs will fall, since the cost of imports will be lower. Exchange rates are covered in detail in Chapter 2.

Inflation

A low stable rate of inflation, eg up to 3%, means fairly stable prices and potentially higher profits. High levels of inflation lead to a high level of uncertainty about prices and the level of investment returns, and therefore makes accurate forecasting difficult. Inflation is covered in detail in Chapter 2.

Business variables

Sales volumes and profit margins – in addition to changes in economic variables having an impact on sales, other factors can affect sales such as weather, seasonal changes, technology, location and demographics. These factors can also affect costs and therefore **profit margins** will be affected.

Exam alert

A possible exam scenario may be that you are presented with existing financial plans similar to the example in the previous section, and are required to calculate the impact of changes in economic and business variables, to assess the attainment of the entity's financial objectives.

1.7 Non-financial objectives

KEY POINT

Non-financial objectives such as quality measures, innovation measures and customer-based measures can also be important for a profit-making entity.

This is the balanced scorecard approach which is covered in the *E3 Strategic Management* paper.

A company's non-financial objectives may include the following:

Non-financial objectives		
Social and relationship	Customer satisfaction	A key target, because of the adverse financial consequences if customers take their business elsewhere
	Responsibilities to suppliers	Not exploiting power as buyer unscrupulously
Natural	Welfare of society	Concern for environment
Human	Welfare of employees	Competitive wages and salaries, comfortable and safe working conditions, good training and career development
	Welfare of management	High salaries, company cars, perks
Intellectual	Leadership in research and development	Failure to innovate may have adverse long-term financial consequences

Key performance indicators (KPIs) are often used by management to measure a company's performance against its non-financial objectives. Companies can also report on KPIs in their annual reports, in addition to the core financial statements. This is common for larger companies. Companies can also produce **sustainability reports**. The Global Reporting Initiative (GRI) provides guidelines on reporting economic, environmental and social performance indicators in sustainability reports. GRI guidelines are covered in Chapter 3.

Non-financial information can also be reported in an **integrated report,** which reports on how an entity creates value over time, particularly from non-financial factors eg human capital. Guidance on integrated reporting is produced by the International Integrated Reporting Council (IIRC). Integrated reporting is covered in Chapter 3.

Reporting of KPIs, sustainability reporting and integrated reporting are optional in most countries but mandatory for certain types of companies in certain counties.

1.8 Unincorporated entities

Unincorporated entities are not incorporated as companies. Unlike incorporated entities, they are not legally separate from their owners. They can be 'for profit' entities such as sole traders and limited liability partnerships (LLPs) whose key objective, as for incorporated entities, is to maximise profit. They also include 'not for profit' entities such as clubs and societies, whose key objective is often to achieve value for money. Not for profit organisations are discussed further in Section 3 of this chapter.

1.9 Quoted companies

A quoted company is one which has its shares quoted or listed on a stock exchange. This makes it easier for companies to raise finance. This is discussed further in Chapters 5 and 8.

Section summary

- In financial management of 'for-profit' companies, the key objective is the **maximisation of shareholders' wealth**.

- **Non-financial objectives** such as welfare, service provision and fulfilment of responsibilities are also important for businesses.

2 Stakeholders and objectives

Introduction

Many objectives and targets are set in terms of satisfying the requirements of interested parties or stakeholders. In this section we consider in more depth the importance of stakeholders and their role.

2.1 Stakeholder groups

KEY TERM

STAKEHOLDERS are those persons and organisations that have an interest in the strategy of an organisation. Stakeholders normally include shareholders, customers, staff and the local community.

(CIMA Official Terminology)

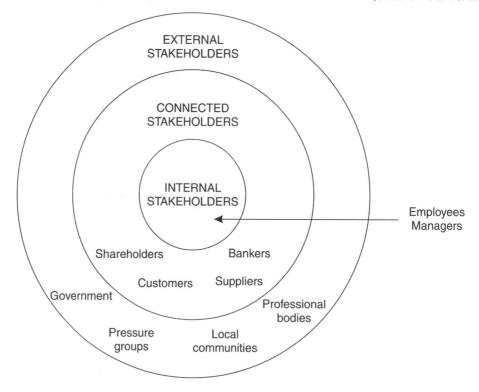

Exam skills

You may be told in a question that a company aims to respect the interests of stakeholders, and determines its policies in light of that aim. Even if you aren't, you will see at various times in this text circumstances when stakeholder interests become particularly important, for example in a merger and acquisition situation, or when a business is linking investments with customer desires.

2.2 Objectives of stakeholder groups

The various groups of stakeholders in a firm will have different goals which will depend in part on the situation of the organisation.

Stakeholder goals	
Shareholders	Providers of risk capital, aim to maximise wealth
Suppliers	Often other businesses, aim to be paid full amount by date agreed, but want to continue long-term trading relationship, and so may accept later payment

Stakeholder goals	
Long-term lenders	Wish to receive payments of interest and capital on loan by due date for repayment
Employees	Maximise rewards paid to them in salaries and benefits, also prefer continuity in employment
Government	Political objectives such as sustained economic growth and high employment (The effect of government policies on organisations will be discussed in Chapter 2)
Management	Maximising their own rewards

2.3 Stakeholder groups and strategy

The greater the power of stakeholders, the greater their influence will be. Each stakeholder group will have different expectations about what it wants, and the expectations of the various groups may conflict. Each group, however, will influence strategic decision making.

Question 1.1	Stakeholders

Learning outcome: A(1)(a)

Describe and discuss the significance of the main stakeholders of a supermarket.

2.4 The agency problem

KEY TERM

AGENCY THEORY is the hypothesis that attempts to explain elements of organisational behaviour through an understanding of the relationships between **principals** (such as shareholders) and **agents** (such as **company managers and accountants**).

A **conflict** may exist between the actions undertaken by agents in furtherance of their own self-interest, and those required to promote the interests of the principals. *(CIMA Official Terminology)*

The relationship between management and shareholders is sometimes referred to as an **agency relationship**, in which managers act as agents for the shareholders, using delegated powers to run the affairs of the company in the shareholders' best interests.

The agency relationship arising from the separation of ownership from management is sometimes characterised as the **agency problem**. For example, if managers hold none or very little of the equity shares of the company they work for, what is to stop them from:

- Working inefficiently?
- Not bothering to look for profitable new investment opportunities?
- Giving themselves high salaries and perks?

One power that shareholders possess is the **right to remove the directors from office**. However, shareholders have to take the initiative to do this, and in many companies, the shareholders lack the energy and organisation to take such a step.

2.5 Goal congruence

KEY TERM

In a control system, GOAL CONGRUENCE is the state which leads individuals or groups to take actions which are in their self-interest and also in the best interest of the entity. *(CIMA Official Terminology)*

Goal congruence may be better achieved, and the 'agency problem' better dealt with, by providing managers with incentives that are related to profits or share price, such as:

(a) **Performance related pay** either related to profit or a strategic performance measure

(b) Rewarding managers with **share options** (where selected employees are given a number of share options, each of which gives the holder the right after a certain date to subscribe for shares in the company at a fixed price)

In the UK, **corporate governance** regulations have been designed to monitor the actions of management (see Chapter 3: Reporting issues).

2.6 Social and environmental conflicts

Sometimes, strategies of companies to maximise shareholder wealth can have negative social and environmental effects.

Customers, the public and pressure groups are becoming more knowledgeable about the activities of companies and can put pressure them to act ethically and responsibly. Companies have to consider these factors in their decisions and this may conflict with maximising shareholder wealth.

Section summary

- One of the most important influences on strategy is the **goals of different interest groups**, or **stakeholder groups**.

  - **Internal**: managers, employees
  - **Connected**: shareholders, banks, customers, suppliers
  - **External**: government, pressure groups, local communities

- The **agency problem** arises when agents (managers) do not act in the best interests of their principals (shareholders).

- The system of corporate governance – which is the directors' responsibility – should seek to ensure **goal congruence** between the objectives of the organisation and those of its teams, departments or individual team members.

3 Objectives of publicly owned and non-commercial bodies

Introduction

Many organisations are **not for profit** and a more appropriate objective is to make sure the organisation is getting good **value for money.**

3.1 Not for profit organisations

Some organisations are set up with a prime objective which is not related to making profits. Charities and government organisations are examples. These organisations exist to pursue **non-financial aims**, such as providing a service to the community. However, there will be **financial constraints or finite resources** which limit what any such organisation can do.

(a) A not for profit organisation needs finance to pay for its operations, and the major financial constraint is the **amount of funds that it can obtain** from its donors (its 'customers').

(b)   Having obtained funds, a not for profit organisation will use the funds to help its 'clients', for example by alleviating suffering. It should seek to use the funds:

    (i)   **Economically**: not spending $2 when the same thing can be bought for $1
    (ii)   **Efficiently**: getting the best use out of what money is spent on
    (iii)   **Effectively**: spending funds so as to achieve the organisation's objectives

Value for money audits give assurance on whether organisations have achieved economy, efficiency and effectiveness in their operations.

 Value for money and the three E's are covered in Paper P3 *Risk Management.*

3.2 Government departments

Financial management in **government departments (public sector)** is different from financial management in an industrial or commercial company **(private sector)** for a number of reasons.

(a)   Government departments **do not operate to make a profit**, and the objectives of a department or of a programme of spending cannot be expressed in terms of maximising the return on capital employed.

(b)   Government services are provided **without the commercial pressure of competition**. There are no competitive reasons for controlling costs, being efficient, or, when services are charged for (such as medical prescriptions), keeping prices down.

(c)   Government departments have full-time professional civil servants as their **managers**, but decisions are also taken by **politicians**.

(d)   The government gets its money for spending from **taxes, other sources of income and borrowing** (such as issuing gilts). The nature of its fundraising differs substantially from fundraising by companies.

Since managing a government department is different from managing a company, a different framework is needed for planning and control. This is achieved by:

(a)   **Setting objectives** for each department
(b)   **Careful planning** of public expenditure proposals
(c)   Emphasis on getting **value for money**

In the UK, **internal markets** have been created in the health sector whereby purchasers are separated from providers of healthcare and the providers of hospital and other healthcare facilities compete for purchasers' funds. The idea is that those providing the best value for money will gain an increasing share of funds available.

3.3 The voluntary sector

This sector mostly comprises charities but also includes smaller groups such as community groups (eg, a local amateur dramatics group).

Charities are organisations that raise money for specific causes and aim to use the funds effectively to help these causes. Increasingly, charities are seeking to increase their funding by adopting similar strategies to profit-making commercial companies, such as trading and investing in profitable ventures.

 | **Question 1.2**   Voluntary sector

Learning outcome: A(1)(a)

Summarise the main strengths and weaknesses of a voluntary sector organisation.

3.4 Setting objectives

There are a number of issues to consider when objectives are set for not for profit organisations.

(a) **Who are the main stakeholders?**

There may be a complex mix of stakeholders, especially in the public sector. For example, a local government entity will be directed by a group of local politicians, controlled by the political party that won the last election. The local population will be the main stakeholders together with employees and central government.

(b) **Which are the most important objectives?**

Not for profit organisations tend to have **multiple objectives** so that even if they can all be clearly identified, it is impossible to say which is the overriding objective.

(c) **How will achievement of objectives be measured?**

Outputs can seldom be measured in a way that is generally agreed to be **meaningful.** (Are good exam results alone an adequate measure of the quality of teaching? How does one quantify the easing of pain following a successful operation?)

Bodies like local government and health services can **compare** their performance **against each other** and against the historical results of their predecessors.

Exam alert

You must always consider the specific needs of the organisation in a scenario.

Section summary

- The prime objective of publicly owned and non-commercial bodies will not be to make a profit but they will have to meet **financial targets and they are likely to be constrained by limited resources**.

- **Value for money** will be a more appropriate objective.

Chapter Summary

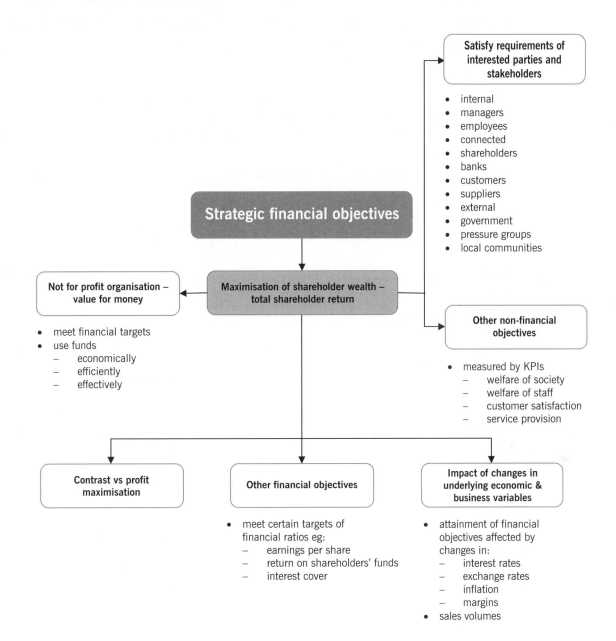

Quick Quiz

1   On what management objective is the theory of company finance primarily based?

2   Identify **three** non-financial and three financial objectives that might be pursued by a supermarket.

3   List six types of stakeholder group.

4   **Fill in the blanks:**

.... theory sees employees as individuals, each with their own objectives, the relationship between managers and shareholders being an .... relationship. If achieving individual and departmental objectives leads to achievement of the organisation's objectives, there is ....

5   Where external financing limits apply government-owned industries are not usually set financial targets.

True   ☐

False   ☐

6   To obtain value for money, a not for profit organisation should aim for the **three E's**, which are (**fill in the blanks**):

E ....

E ....

E ....

Answers to Quick Quiz

1   The objective of management is to maximise the market value of the enterprise and the shareholders' wealth.

2   Possible **non-financial objectives** that might be pursued by a supermarket include (choose any three):

   • Providing quality food at good value
   • Maintaining long-term relationships with suppliers
   • Reducing impact on the environment, eg reducing packaging
   • Creating more jobs and careers
   • Improving customer service
   • Improving range of products
   • Developing online shopping

   Possible **financial objectives** include (choose any three):

   • Revenue growth year-on-year
   • Stable earnings for the future
   • Increase dividends per share (or start paying dividends)
   • Containing costs

3   Any six from the following:

   Employees, managers, shareholders, bankers, customers, suppliers, government, local communities, pressure groups, professional bodies.

4   Agency; agency; goal congruence

5   False

6   Economy; efficiency; effectiveness

Answers to Questions

1.1 Stakeholders

(a)   **Customers**

Customers are very significant to a supermarket because this group directly provides **income** for the business.

(b)   **Employees**

This group looks to the supermarket to be a good employer, offering fair and continuing employment. This group is very significant to the company, as supermarkets are people-intensive businesses and good performance by employees can directly affect the customer shopping experience and hence company profitability.

(c)   **Suppliers**

Suppliers are key to a supermarket's supply chain in providing quality products that customers want, quickly. To achieve this, it is important for a supermarket to maintain good long-term relationships with suppliers.

(d)   **Government**

The government of a country may want to ensure that large supermarkets do not exploit their powers (eg putting pressure on small suppliers), by setting up a regulatory authority to oversee their conduct.

1.2 Voluntary sector

Strengths

- There are **no shareholders** who would expect a short-term return on their investment.

- There is less chance of **conflict** between social goals and profit goals.

- Voluntary organisations may be **trusted** more by users than a comparable private sector organisation, for whom users may be suspicious of the company's profit motives.

- There may be greater **dedication** from staff who share the voluntary organisation's vision.

- 'Staff' may be prepared to give their services for **free**.

Weaknesses

- The **absence** of a **profit motive** may lead to **unfocused** management whose results are difficult to monitor.
- There may be a reluctance to act in a **businesslike way**, thereby resulting in poor services to users.
- Users may **not** expect to **pay** for services provided, but overhead costs must still be covered.
- Voluntary workers may be **less committed** to their job as they will not lose pay for poor performance.

Now try the questions from the Practice Question Bank	**Question**	**Level**
	Section A: 1.1 – 1.5	Practice
	Section B: 1	Practice

STRATEGIC FINANCIAL MANAGEMENT

In this chapter we are concerned with creating a financial strategy to achieve an organisation's objectives. The start of this chapter deals with the interrelationships between the decisions concerning **investment, financing and dividends**. These links may be a central part of your answer as you consider how organisations finance their investments. We consider the influences on formulating financial strategy and the impact of changes or differences in external factors. The government can influence a market through **regulations**, eg using an industry regulator or a competition authority. **Economic**

influences on strategy are **inflation, interest rates** and **exchange rates.** We will also look at the influences on the strategies of companies that trade internationally.

We revise **ratio analysis** and other methods of **performance measurement**. You may be asked for example, to use ratio analysis to ascertain whether an organisation has **met its objectives.**

Cash forecasting is vital to ensure that **sufficient funds** will be **available** when they are needed to sustain the activities of an enterprise, at an acceptable cost.

Topic list	learning outcomes	syllabus references	ability required
1 Strategic financial management	A(2)(a)	A(2)(a)(i)	evaluation
2 Financial management decisions	A(2)(a)	A(2)(a)(i), (iii)	evaluation
3 Influences on financial strategy	A(2)(b)	A(2)(b)(i), (ii)	analysis
4 Regulatory bodies	A(2)(b)	A(2)(b)(ii)	analysis
5 Economic influences	A(1)(b), A(2)(b)	A(1)(b)(ii), A(2)(b)(i)	analysis
6 International influences	A(1)(a)	A(1)(a)(iii)	analysis
7 Impact of taxation on financial strategy	A(2)(b)	A(2)(b)(iii)	analysis
8 Performance analysis	A(1)(b)	A(1)(b)(i)	evaluation

Topic list	learning outcomes	syllabus references	ability required
9 Forecasts	A(2)(a)	A(2)(a)(ii), (iv)	evaluation
10 Sensitivity analysis and changes in variables	A(1)(b), A(2)(a)	A(1)(b)(ii), A(2)(a)(ii)	evaluation
11 Financing requirements	A(2)(a)	A(2)(a)(iv)	evaluation

Chapter Overview

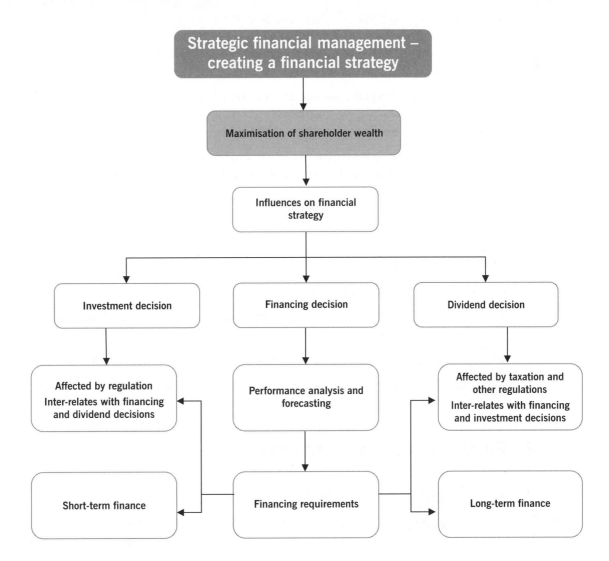

1 Strategic financial management

Introduction

In this section we define strategic financial management.

KEY TERM

STRATEGIC FINANCIAL MANAGEMENT is a framework of financial plans that aim to ensure that the entity's strategic financial objectives are met.

An obvious starting point is the identification and formulation of these objectives, which we looked at in Chapter 1. Here we saw that the main objective of a company is normally assumed to be the **maximisation of the wealth** of its **ordinary shareholders**.

In order to achieve this, a framework will be required to ensure that all areas of financial management are centred on the achievement of this primary objective. This framework is introduced in this chapter.

Section summary

Strategic financial management is:

- The identification of the possible strategies capable of maximising an organisation's net present value

- The allocation of scarce capital resources among the competing opportunities

- Monitoring of the chosen strategy so as to achieve stated objectives

2 Financial management decisions

Introduction

In this very important section we look at a framework for maximising shareholder wealth. An organisation must take sensible investment, financing and investment decisions. These decisions are **interrelated**.

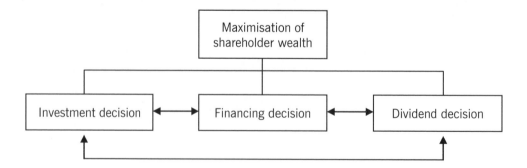

2.1 Investment decisions

The financial manager will need to **identify** investment opportunities, **evaluate** them and decide on the **optimum allocation of scarce funds** available between investments.

Investment decisions may be on the undertaking of **new projects** within the existing business, the **takeover** of, or the **merger** with, another company or the **selling off** of a part of the business.

Managers have to take decisions in the light of strategic considerations such as whether the business wants to **expand internally** (through investment in existing operations) or **externally** (through expansion).

2.2 Interaction of investment with financing and dividend decisions

Managers will need to consider whether **extra finance** will be required, and what will be the consequences of obtaining it. They will have to consider the demands of **providers of finance**, particularly of equity shareholders who require **dividends**. Will equity shareholders be content with projects that maximise their long-term returns, or will they require a minimum return or dividend each year?

2.3 Financing decisions

Financing decisions include those for both the long term (**capital structure**) and the short term (**working capital management**). The financial manager needs to determine the **source, cost** and **risk** of the possible sources of long-term finance. A balance between **profitability** and **liquidity** (ready availability of funds if required) must be taken into account when deciding on the optimal level of short-term finance.

2.4 Interaction of financing with investment and dividend decisions

When taking financial decisions, managers will have to fulfil the **requirements of the providers of finance**, otherwise finance may not be made available. This may be particularly difficult in the case of equity shareholders, since dividends are paid at the company's discretion. If equity shareholders do not receive the dividends they want, they will look to sell their shares, the share price will fall and the company will have more difficulty raising funds from share issues in future.

Although there may be risks in obtaining extra finance, the long-term risks to the business of **failing to invest** may be even greater and managers will have to balance these up. Investment may have direct consequences for decisions involving the **management of finance**. Extra working capital may be required if investments are made and sales expand as a consequence. Managers must be sensitive to this and ensure that a balance is maintained between receivables and inventory, and cash.

A further issue managers will need to consider is the **matching** of the **characteristics** of investment and finance. **Time** is a critical aspect; an investment which earns returns in the long term should be matched with finance which requires repayment in the long term.

The **financing of international investments** should also be considered. A company which expects to receive a substantial amount of income in a **foreign currency** will be concerned that this currency may weaken. **Short-term hedging strategies** can be used to deal with this risk.

Hedging and risk management is covered in Paper P3 *Risk Management.*

2.5 Dividend decisions

Dividend decisions may affect the view that shareholders have of the long-term prospects of the company, and thus the **market value of the shares**.

2.6 Interaction of dividend with investment and financing decisions

The amount of surplus cash paid out as **dividends** will have a direct impact on **finance** available for **investment**. Managers thus have a difficult decision to make. How much do they pay out to shareholders each year to keep them happy, and what level of funds do they retain in the business to invest in projects that will yield long-term income?

Funds available from **retained profits** may be needed if debt finance is likely to be unavailable, or if taking on more debt would expose the company to undesirable risks.

We will consider all of these decisions in more detail throughout this Study Text.

2.7 Consideration of shareholders and other stakeholders

In determining investment, dividend and financing decisions, management should consider the impact of these decisions on shareholders and other stakeholders.

Investment decisions

Shareholders

Investment decisions may mean that shareholders forego regular dividend payments in the short term in favour of long-term returns. An entity needs to consider whether shareholders will be content with this, or sell their shares, therefore decreasing the value of the company.

Employees

Investment decisions could affect employee morale. For example, investing in new projects could cause decreased morale due to increased workloads; a merger could cause concern among employees over potential job losses, restructuring of roles, or changes in management style and work culture.

Community

Investment decisions could have adverse affects on the environment, eg a local community may object to a new supermarket being built in their town.

Dividend decisions

Shareholders

As discussed above, management will need to consider the expectations of shareholders for dividend payments, in deciding how much to pay in dividends each year, and how much to retain for investment opportunities.

Employees

Decisions to pay regular dividends each year will mean less funds are available for pay and bonuses of employees. This could lead to decreased morale, or loss of talented employees.

Banks and lenders

Dividend decisions could mean that certain debt covenants required for lenders of debt finance are breached, entitling the lenders to ask for repayment or renegotiate the loan terms.

Financing decision

Banks and lenders

If the company seeks debt finance, banks and other lenders will need to be satisfied the company can meet its debts and not breach any debt covenants.

Suppliers

Repayments to providers of finance could affect cash flow and the ability to pay suppliers on time. This could lead to late payment fees, or worse still, suspension of supply.

Shareholders

Management need to consider if shareholders will be happy if the company is financed more from retained earnings over debt finance, as this will mean less funds are available for dividend payments.

2.8 Interrelationships between the three key decisions

As we have shown above, the three decisions covered are **interrelated**. Two typical interrelationships are shown below:

	Investment decision	Financing decisions	Dividend decision
High growth companies	High levels of capital investment	Low levels of debt finance	Low or zero dividend
Mature companies	Moderate to low levels of capital investment	High levels of debt finance	High dividend payouts

Exam alert

This area has been regularly examined in the previous syllabus and is therefore a potential area to be examined again. Any exam answer must always consider the specific entities involved.

Section summary

In seeking to maximise shareholder wealth, a financial manager has to make the following interrelated decisions:

- Investment
- Financing
- Dividends

A financial manager needs to consider the impact of these decision on various stakeholders including:

- Shareholders
- Banks and lenders
- Employees
- Community

3   Influences on financial strategy

Introduction

In this section we look at internal and external factors which affect an organisation's financial strategies. These factors include funding, investor relations, regulatory bodies and economic factors. We will look at the last two in more detail in Sections 4 and 5.

3.1 Funding constraints

Businesses may be reluctant to **obtain extra funds themselves** for a variety of reasons. In smaller non-listed companies, equity funding from the small group of owners will be a significant source of finance. However owners may not have the **financial resources** to provide significant equity injections, and may also require the company to pay them a regular source of income.

Larger companies listed on a stock exchange may be constrained when they are contemplating a share issue by fears that the issue **will not be fully taken up** or that they will have to issue shares at a **low price** in order to ensure full take-up.

Directors of companies of any size may be reluctant to obtain further **debt finance** because:

(a)   They fear that the company may be unable to **service the debt**, to make the required capital and interest payments on time.

(b)   The tax position is such that they will be unable to use the **tax shield**, to obtain any tax benefit from interest payments.

(c)   The company lacks the **asset base** to be able to **generate additional cash** if needed or provide **sufficient security**.

(d)   The company wishes to **maintain access** to the capital markets on **good terms**, and hence needs a good credit rating.

Smaller companies may be deterred from **obtaining debt finance** by lender requirements that the directors offer personal security.

3.1.1 Lenders' assessment of creditworthiness

If a company decides to obtain debt finance, the lender will assess the company's ability to repay the debt, usually from the following sources of information.

Business plan

A lender will ask for a business plan detailing the amount of loan required, what it is for, and the duration of the loan, the repayment period and any assets that can be used as security on the loan. This can be summarised using the mnemonic 'PARTS':

*   Purpose
*   Amount
*   Repayment
*   Time period
*   Security

Financial ratios

Lenders will perform ratio analysis on the company's financial statements, in particular, liquidity and gearing ratios. Interest cover ratio will give an indication of the ability of a firm to meet interest payments when profits are decreasing.

Gearing and investor ratios are analysed further in Chapter 9.

Stock market ratios such as P/E ratios give an indication of the risk of lending to a company as this measures how the company is perceived in the market.

Cash flow forecasts

Lenders will expect to see a cash flow forecast to demonstrate the company's liquidity and ability to meet repayments due. This is considered in Section 9.

Credit agencies

Independent credit rating agencies such as Standard and Poor's can be used by a lender to provide a credit rating on a company.

This rating provides an indication of the likelihood that a company will repay its debts. A 'triple A' rating is the best rating given by a credit agency. A company with such a high rating is considered to be a very low credit risk. Lenders generally charge lower rates of interest to companies with high credit ratings.

Credit agencies rate companies based on factors such as the quality of the management team, financial position, business plans and forecasts, financial ratios, political and regulatory risks, and industry strengths and trends.

3.2 Investor relations

Financial constraints are bound up with the need to **keep investors happy**. Investors need to be convinced that companies are investing in projects generating sufficient long-term returns, and that *en route* the company will also be able to generate enough dividends to satisfy investor requirements.

3.3 Agency theory

The ability of an entity to maximise shareholder wealth may be constrained by the actions of managers who sometimes have different objectives. This is the **agency problem** that we covered in Chapter 1.

3.4 Business strategy

Obviously a business's financial strategy is not independent of its overall business strategy. There may be occasions when an organisation departs from what appears to be the optimum financial strategy. It may for instance depart from its optimal capital structure to **raise funds** to seize a potentially **valuable investment opportunity**.

An entity may also suffer from a **shortage of key skills** or **limited production capacity**, both of which may limit its ability to operate to its maximum wealth-generating capacity.

Exam skills

An integrated case study scenario could give details of potential investments and you may need to discuss the internal and external influences and constraints affecting the investment decision. A fundamental problem with similar questions in the past has been the amount of material in the answers that appeared to have been lifted straight from study texts without applying that knowledge to the scenario provided.

Section summary

Influences on financial strategy include funding, investor relations, business strategy and economic factors.

4 Regulatory bodies

Introduction

A powerful **external influence** on the ability of a company to create wealth for its shareholders are local or overseas governments, or government regulators.

4.1 The impact of legislation

As you have seen in your earlier studies, legislation that affects entities includes:

- Companies Acts
- Health and safety regulations
- Consumer protection laws
- Contract and agency laws
- Employment law
- Protection of the environment laws

4.2 Compliance with legislation

Organisations need to consider carefully the financial aspects of compliance with the law. Compliance with legislation may involve **extra costs**, including the extra procedures and investment necessary to conform to safety standards, staff training costs and legal costs.

Higher costs of compliance, as well as costs of labour may mean that companies **relocate** to countries where costs and regulatory burdens are lower. However these costs may also act as a **significant barrier to entry**, benefiting companies that are already in the industry.

Businesses that fail to comply with the law run the risk of financial **penalties** and the financial consequences of accompanying **bad publicity**.

4.3 Corporate governance

The **corporate governance debate** impacts upon the way companies make decisions, their financial organisation and their relations with investors and auditors.

KEY TERM

CORPORATE GOVERNANCE is the system by which companies and other entities are directed and controlled. **Boards of directors** are responsible for the governance of their companies. The **shareholders'** role in governance is to appoint the directors and the **auditors** and to satisfy themselves that an appropriate governance structure is in place.

The responsibilities of the board include:

- Setting the company's **strategic aims**
- Providing the **leadership** to put them into effect
- Supervising the **management** of the business
- **Reporting** to shareholders on their stewardship

The board's actions are subject to laws, regulations and the shareholders in general meeting.

Corporate governance has emerged as a major issue in the last ten to fifteen years in the light of several high profile collapses. Guidance has been given because of the lack of confidence perceived in financial reporting and in the ability of auditors to provide the assurances required by the users of financial accounts.

Paper P3 *Risk Management* covers this area.

4.3.1 Impact of corporate governance requirements on businesses

The consequences of **failure to obey corporate governance regulations** should be considered along with failure to obey any other sort of legislation. In regimes where corporate governance rules are **guidelines** rather than regulations, businesses will consider what the consequences might be of non-compliance, in particular the **impact** on **share prices**.

Obedience to requirements or guidelines can also have consequences for businesses. For example increased disclosure regulations have highlighted **director remuneration packages** that investors have thought to be excessively generous.

4.4 Competition regulation

The government can influence a market through **regulations**, eg using an **industry regulator** or a **competition authority**.

4.4.1 Industry regulators

Where a market is not competitive, industry regulatory authorities have the role of ensuring that **consumers' interests** are not subordinated to those of other stakeholders, such as employees, shareholders and tax authorities.

The main methods used to regulate monopoly industries are as follows:

(a) **Price control**

The regulator **agrees the output prices** with the industry. Typically, the price is **progressively reduced** in **real terms** each year by setting price increases at a rate below that of inflation. This has been used with success by regulators in the UK but can be confrontational.

(b) **Profit control**

The regulator **agrees the maximum profit** which the industry can make. A typical method is to fix maximum profit at x% of capital employed, but this does not provide any incentive to making more efficient use of assets: the higher the capital employed, the higher the profit.

(c) **Service control**

The regulator **agrees a minimum standard of service** the industry should provide customers. For example, for gas companies – the minimum standard of service may be to restore customers' supply within a specific time period, following a network interruption.

In addition the regulator will be concerned with:

(a) Actively **promoting competition** by encouraging new firms in the industry and preventing unreasonable barriers to entry

(b) Addressing **quality** and **safety** issues and considering the **social implications** of service provision and pricing

4.4.2 Regulation of takeovers

Competition authorities such as the UK Competition and Markets Authority aim to protect competition within a market. It will make in-depth enquiries into mergers and markets to ensure that one company cannot dominate a market. Where a potential merger is **sufficiently large** to warrant an investigation, the competition authority will look at whether the merger will be **against the public interest** in terms of:

(a) **Effective competition** within the industry

(b) The interests of consumers, purchasers and users of the goods and services of that industry in respect of **quality**, **price** and **variety**

(c) The **reduction of costs** and the introduction of new products and techniques

We will look at the regulation of takeovers again in Chapter 10.

 Section summary

- A powerful **external influence** on the ability of a company to create wealth for its shareholders is local or overseas governments, or government regulators.

- The **corporate governance** debate impacts upon the way companies make decisions, their financial organisation and their relations with investors and auditors.

- The government can influence a market through **regulations**, eg using an industry regulator or a competition authority.

5 Economic influences

Introduction

Economic influences on strategy will be imposed by **inflation, interest rates** and **exchange rates**. You will be expected to have a good understanding of how economic factors can impact on an entity and be able to discuss the effect on financial strategies.

5.1 Effects of inflation

Inflation can affect all the financial areas of a business and impact upon its **profit performance** in a variety of ways.

(a)   The rate of inflation will **affect the prices** that a business must pay for all the factors of production and the prices that it is able to charge to its customers. It will therefore affect the level of reported profits.

(b)   When inflation is high, **regular price reviews** will be necessary so as to ensure that there is no erosion of real returns. In times of low inflation it may be difficult to achieve any price increases due to a reduced level of inflationary expectations.

(c)   Where there is a high level of inflation, there is also a **high level of uncertainty** about the future. This tends to make businesses wary of committing themselves to new long-term investments.

(d)   Inflation places **pressure on cash flow**, particularly where the prices of raw materials are rising ahead of prices charged to customers. Even where sales prices do keep up, additional cash will still be required to cover the increased payments to suppliers that will have to be made in advance of monies being received in respect of credit sales.

(e)   Companies may **increase their level of investment in inventory** as a hedge against anticipated price rises. This will also increase the amount of working capital required and restrict the funds available for new investment.

(f)   Different approaches may need to be taken to **financial reporting** and evaluation methods, such as current cost accounting techniques, which make it easier to understand the changing performance of a company over time.

(g)   The relationship between **inflation rates** and **interest rates** means that interest rates tend to rise during a period of inflation. This has implications both for the capital structure decisions and investment appraisal criteria used by companies.

5.2 Interest rates

Interest rates are an important element in the economic environment, and are of particular relevance for financial managers.

(a)   Interest rates **measure the cost of borrowing**. If a company wants to raise money, it must pay interest on its borrowing, and the rate of interest payable will be one which is 'current' at the time the borrowing takes place. When interest rates go up, companies will pay more interest on some of their borrowing (for example on bank overdrafts).

(b)   Interest rates in a country **influence the foreign exchange value** of the country's currency.

(c)   Interest rates act as a **guide to the sort of return** that a company's shareholders might want, and changes in market interest rates will affect share prices.

5.2.1 Nominal rates and real rates of interest

Nominal rates of interest are the actual rates of interest paid. **Real rates of interest** are rates of interest adjusted for the rate of inflation. The real rate is therefore a measure of the increase in the real wealth, expressed in terms of **buying power**, of the investor or lender.

The relationship between nominal rates and real rates of interest was originally explored by Fisher and can be expressed as follows:

EXAM

(1 + nominal rate of interest) = (1 + real rate of interest) × (1 + inflation rate)

This formula is often referred to as the **Fisher equation.**

The real rate of interest can be calculated as:

$$\text{Real rate of interest} = \frac{1 + \text{nominal rate of interest}}{1 + \text{rate of inflation}} - 1$$

If the nominal rate of interest is 12% and the rate of inflation is 8%, the real rate of interest would be 1.12/1.08 − 1 = 0.037 = 3.7%.

5.2.2 The general level of interest rates

Interest rates on any one type of financial asset will vary over time. In other words, the general level of interest rates might go up or down. The general level of interest rates is affected by several factors.

(a)   **Need for a real return**

Investors normally want to **earn a 'real' rate of return** on their investment. The appropriate real rate of return will depend on factors such as investment risk.

(b)   **Inflation**

Nominal rates of interest should be sufficient to **cover expected rates of inflation** over the term of the investment and to provide a real return.

(c)   **Uncertainty about future rates of inflation**

When investors are uncertain about inflation and therefore about what future nominal and real interest rates will be, they are likely to require **higher interest yields** to persuade them to take the risk of investing, especially in the longer term.

(d)   **Liquidity preference of investors and the demand for borrowing**

Higher interest rates have to be offered to persuade savers to invest their surplus money. When the demand to borrow increases, interest rates will rise.

(e)   **Balance of payments**

When a country has a continuing deficit on the current account of its balance of payments, and the authorities are unwilling to allow the exchange rate to depreciate by more than a certain amount, interest rates may have to be raised to **attract capital** into the country. The country can then finance the deficit by borrowing from abroad.

(f)   **Monetary policy**

Since mid 1997, decisions over UK interest rate policy have been made by the Monetary Policy Committee of the Bank of England. The Bank of England influences very short-term money market rates by means of **open market operations**. Usually longer-term money market rates, and then banks' base rates, will respond to the authorities' wish for interest rate changes. The purpose of influencing money market interest rates is to create a longer-term influence over the rate of inflation. One type of monetary policy is **quantitative easing**. In response to the 2008 financial crisis, the Bank of England adopted this policy which involves creating money to buy bonds from financial institutions. This aims to lower interest rates and therefore the cost of borrowing decreases, leading to increased spending, in order to bring inflation to a target rate.

(g)   **Interest rates abroad**

The rate of interest in one country will be influenced by **external factors**, such as interest rates in other countries and expectations about the exchange rate. When interest rates in overseas countries are high, interest rates on domestic currency investments must also be comparably high, to avoid capital transfers abroad and a fall in the exchange rate of the domestic currency.

5.2.3 Interest rates in different markets and market segments

(a)   **Risk**

Higher risk borrowers must pay higher rates on their borrowing, to compensate lenders for the greater risk involved.

(b)   **The need to make a profit on re-lending**

Financial intermediaries make their profits from re-lending at a higher rate of interest than the cost of their borrowing.

(c)   **The duration of the lending**

Normally, long-term loans will earn a higher yield than short-term loans. You should be familiar with the reasons for this term structure of interest rates as illustrated by the **yield curve**, from your previous studies; the main points are summarised below.

(d)   **The size of the loan**

Deposits above a certain amount with a bank or building society might attract higher rates of interest than smaller deposits.

(e)   **Different types of financial asset**

Different types of financial asset attract different rates of interest. This reflects the competition for deposits between different types of financial institution.

5.2.4 The term structure of interest rates: the yield curve

Interest rates depend on the **term to maturity** of the asset. For example, government bonds might be short-dated, medium-dated, or long-dated depending on when the bonds are to be redeemed and the investor repaid.

The **term structure of interest rates** refers to the way in which the yield on a security varies according to the term of the borrowing, as shown by the **yield curve**.

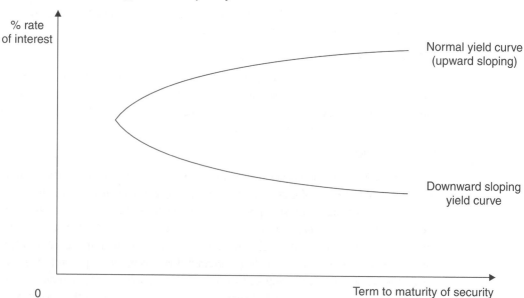

The reasons why, in theory, the yield curve will normally be upward sloping, so that long-term financial assets offer a higher yield than short-term assets, are as follows.

(a) **The investor must be compensated for tying up his money in the asset for a longer period of time**. The only way to overcome this **liquidity preference** of investors is to compensate them for the loss of liquidity; in other words, to offer a higher rate of interest on longer dated bonds.

(b) **There is a greater risk in lending long term than in lending short term**. To compensate investors for this risk, they might require a higher yield on longer dated investments.

A yield curve might **slope downwards**, with short-term rates higher than longer-term rates for a number of reasons.

(a) **Expectations**. When interest rates are expected to fall, short-term rates might be higher than long-term rates, and the yield curve would be downward sloping.

(b) **Government policy**. A policy of keeping interest rates relatively high might have the effect of forcing short-term interest rates higher than long-term rates.

(c) The **market segmentation theory**. The slope of the yield curve will reflect conditions in different segments of the market. This theory holds that the major investors are confined to a particular segment of the market and will not switch segment even if the forecast of likely future interest rates changes.

5.2.5 Interest rates and share prices

When interest rates change, the **return expected** by investors from shares will also change. For example, if interest rates fell from 14% to 12% on government bonds, and from 15% to 13% on company bonds, the return expected from shares (dividends and capital growth) would also fall. This is because shares and debt are alternative ways of investing money. **If interest rates fall, shares become more attractive to buy**. As demand for shares increases, their prices rise too, and so the dividend return gained from them falls in percentage terms.

5.2.6 Changes in interest rates and financing decisions

Interest rates are important for financial decisions by companies.

(a) **When interest rates are low**, it might be financially prudent:

    (i) To **borrow more**, preferably at a fixed rate of interest, and so increase the company's gearing

    (ii) To **borrow for long periods** rather than for short periods

    (iii) To **pay back loans which incur a high interest rate**, if it is within the company's power to do so, and take out new loans at a lower interest rate

(b) **When interest rates are higher:**

    (i) A company might decide to **reduce the amount of its debt finance**, and to substitute equity finance, such as retained earnings.

    (ii) A company which has a large surplus of cash and liquid funds to invest might switch some of its **short-term investments** out of equities and into interest-bearing securities.

    (iii) A company might opt to raise new finance by borrowing short-term funds and debt at a **variable interest rate** (for example on overdraft) rather than long-term funds at fixed rates of interest, in the hope that interest rates will soon come down again.

5.2.7 Interest rates and new capital investments

When interest rates go up, and so the cost of finance to a company goes up, **the minimum return** that a company will require on its own new capital investments will go up too. Some new capital projects might be in the pipeline, with purchase contracts already signed with suppliers, and so there will often be a time lag before higher interest rates result in **fewer new investments**.

A company's management should give close consideration, when interest rates are high, to keeping **investments in assets**, particularly unwanted or inefficient non-current assets, inventories and receivables, down **to a minimum**, in order to reduce the company's need to borrow.

5.3 Exchange rates

KEY TERM

EXCHANGE RATE is the rate at which a national currency exchanges for other national currencies, being set by the interaction of demand and supply of the various currencies in the foreign exchange markets (**floating** exchange rate) or by government intervention in order to maintain a constant rate of exchange (**fixed** exchange rate).

Exchange rates between different currencies on the world's foreign exchange markets are continually changing, and often by large amounts.

Foreign exchange rates are important for a business and its financial management because they affect:

- The cost of imports
- The value of exports
- The costs and benefits of international borrowing and lending

5.3.1 Impact of changes in exchange rates

Changes in the value of a currency will affect the cost of goods from abroad. For example, if a consignment of goods is shipped from the US to Germany and the invoice price is US$420,000:

- If the euro-dollar exchange rate is €1 = $1.50, the cost of the imports would be €280,000
- If the euro fell in value to €1 = $1.25, the cost of the imports would be higher, at €336,000

Changes in the value of a currency affect buying costs, companies and households alike, because a large proportion of the raw materials, components and finished goods that we consume is imported.

Exchange rates affect **exporting companies**, for similar reasons, because changes in exchange rates affect the price of exported goods to foreign buyers.

(a) **When the local currency, say the yen, goes up in value**, goods sold abroad by Japanese exporters, and invoiced in yen, will cost more to the foreign buyers (who must purchase yens with their own currency in order to pay).

(b) **When the yen falls in value,** goods sold abroad by Japanese exporters and invoiced in yen will become cheaper to foreign buyers.

To the extent that demand is influenced by price, the demand for exports will therefore vary with changes in the exchange rate.

Similarly if you are going on holiday or on a shopping trip abroad you will be interested in movements in the exchange rate. When you are buying currency, you want your own currency to appreciate as this means you will get more of the foreign currency for every unit of your own currency. For example, if £1 is worth $1.5066 and you purchased £500 worth of dollars, you would receive $753.30. However if sterling appreciated to £1 = $1.5300, you would receive $765.

When you are exchanging foreign currency into your home currency, you want your home currency to depreciate. For example, if you came back from holiday with $50 and £1 = $1.5300, you would receive £32.68 ($50/$1.5300). If sterling depreciated to £1 = $1.5066, you would receive £33.19.

Exchange rate risk is covered in Paper P3 *Risk Management* and you should use your knowledge from this paper if it is appropriate.

5.4 Forecasting exchange rates

The value of a currency may change for many reasons. One key reason is inflation. High foreign inflation means that the purchasing power of this foreign currency is reduced. Over time this may cause the value of this foreign currency to devalue (this can be predicted by using the formula for purchasing power parity theory shown below).

Purchasing power parity

$$S1 = So \times \frac{[1 + r_{var}]}{[1 + r_{base}]}$$

where

r_{base} = base currency annual inflation rate r_{var} = variable currency annual inflation rate

S1 = spot exchange rate in 1 year   So = spot exchange rate today

---

Example: Forecasting exchange rates

The \$/£ exchange rate in January 20X0 was 0.645 (that is, \$1 = £0.645); and the forecast for the annual rate of inflation in the US was 2.6% and 3.4% in the UK, for each of the next three years.

Required

Calculate the forecast spot \$/£ exchange rate in January 20X0 for each of the next three years, January 20X1, January 20X2 and January 20X3.

Solution

Year 1: 0.645 × 1.034/1.026 = 0.650

Year 2: 0.650 × 1.034/1.026 = 0.655

Year 3: 0.655 × 1.034/1.026 = 0.660

Exam alert

In the exam, if you are given an exchange rate of US\$/£0.89 this means that US\$1 = £0.89.

Question 2.1

Learning outcome: C(1)(b)

The £/€ exchange rate in April 20X0 was £/€1.138 (that is, £1 = €1.138). At this date, the expected annual rate of inflation for the next three years was 1.5% for the eurozone and 3.7% for the UK.

Required

Calculate the spot rate that would have been forecast in April 20X0, using PPP theory, for April in each of the next three years, 20X1 – 20X3.

5.4.1 An alternative approach

You may be given an exchange rate and told that one of the currencies is appreciating/depreciating against the other. The way you calculate the new rates depends on which currency is appreciating/depreciating. It is important to identify the **base currency**.

Example: Appreciating/depreciating currencies

The currency exchange rate £/$ is £1 = $1.55.

Suppose you are told that the $ will appreciate against the £ by 3% for each of the next two years.

The $ is not the base currency (that is, it is not quoted as $1 = £X), therefore you do not multiply the current spot rate by 1.03, but instead you **divide** by 1.03 (to indicate that it now takes 3% fewer $ to purchase £1).

Year	Exchange rate
0	£1 = $1.55
1	£1 = $1.55/1.03 = $1.505
2	£1 = $1.505/1.03 = $1.461

If you changed the exchange rate to be expressed as $1 = £1/1.55 = 0.645. It would then be correct to multiply this spot rate by 1.03 to forecast future rates.

Alternatively, you could multiply the original spot rate of £1 = $1.55 by 0.97 to get an estimate of future exchange rates. These would be marginally different to those future rates calculated above, but the difference would be small. As these future rates are estimates, these differences would be immaterial in the exam.

5.4.2 Interest rate parity

Another factor affecting the value of a currency is the level of nominal interest rates in a country. High nominal interest rates in a foreign currency indicate that **inflation** is high in that country.

Interest rate parity theory shows that the **forward rate** of exchange can be found by adjusting the spot rate of exchange to reflect the differential in interest rates between the two countries.

If **interest rates** are given, you can use the following formula:

EXAM

> **Interest rate parity**
>
> $$Fo = So \times \frac{[1 + r_{var}]}{[1 + r_{base}]}$$

> where
>
> r_{base} = base currency annual nominal interest rate
>
> r_{var} = variable currency annual nominal interest rate
>
> Fo = forward exchange rate in 1 year
>
> So = spot exchange rate today

Example: Interest rate parity

Company A is a company based in country A with the A$ as its functional currency. It makes some sales to country B denominated in B$.

The financial director of Company A is attempting to estimate the likely exchange rate in 6 months' time, so that she can assess the likely value of the entity's foreign income from country B. Company A has a sales objective to generate A$8.2 million in revenue from sales to country B in 6 months' time.

Sales to country B in 6 months' time are expected to be B$20 million.

The spot rate of exchange is A$1 = B$2.41. Interest rates in Country B and Country A are expected to be 2% and 4% respectively next year.

Required

What is the forecast forward rate in 6 months' time and will Company A achieve its sales objective?

Solution

To forecast the 6 month forward rate, 6 month interest rates should be used.

The 6 month interest rate for country A is 4% x 6/12 = 2%

The 6 month interest rate for country B is 2% x 6/12 = 1%

Forecast forward rate = 2.41 x (1.01/1.02) = 2.39

Income from country B = B$20 million/2.39 = A$ 8.37 million, therefore meeting their sales objective.

Exam skills

Examiners have commented that the calculation of forward rates and conversion of currencies has been surprisingly poor. Make sure you are confident with these calculations as they are likely to be required in your exam.

Exchange rate risk is covered in Paper P3 *Risk Management* and you should use your knowledge from this paper if it is appropriate.

Section summary

Economic influences on strategy will be imposed by inflation, interest rates and exchange rates.

6 International influences

Introduction

A scenario may concern an entity which trades internationally. You need to be able to discuss the particular factors that will impact on such an entity's financial strategy, such as the risks of interference in its business.

6.1 Why invest overseas?

We can summarise the reasons for overseas investment using 5 Cs:

The 5 Cs	Explanation
Company	An expansion strategy may create economies of scale as the company gets bigger.
Country	The company could locate near to high quality local supplies or access cheaper labour or government grants.
Customer	The company could locate closer to its end customers to enable shorter delivery times.
Competition	Overseas markets may have weaker competition.
Currency	International investments can create costs which can be matched against revenues from that country and help to manage exchange rate risk.

6.2 Constraints of trading abroad

Compared with companies that trade entirely within one country, companies that trade overseas will have to deal with a variety of international constraints.

6.2.1 Foreign exchange influences

As we have already seen, any company that exports or imports faces the risk of **higher costs** or **lower revenues** because of adverse movements in foreign exchange rates. A company that owns assets in different countries (subsidiaries abroad) faces the risk of accounting losses due to adverse movements in exchange rates causing a fall in the value of those assets, as expressed in domestic currency. Currency risks can be categorised into the following risks.

Currency risks	
Transaction risk	Changes in the spot exchange rate between the time that a transaction is made and the time that it is paid for
Translation risk	Changes to values of foreign assets and liabilities arising from re-translation at different exchange rates at the year end in the statement of financial position
Economic risk	Effect of exchange rate movements on the international competitiveness of the organisation

One of the techniques used to hedge **against** currency risk is **the use of** currency swaps. **Currency swaps** are discussed in Chapter 6. Hedge accounting is discussed in **Chapter** 3.

Currency risk is covered in detail in Paper P3 *Risk Management*.

6.2.2 Political issues

A company which trades abroad can face risks of **economic or political measures** being taken by governments, affecting the operations of its subsidiaries abroad. An example of this is import restrictions imposed by Russia on certain products from the EU and US in 2014, in retaliation for EU and US sanctions imposed against Russia following Russia's annexation of Crimea from Ukraine.

Political risk is covered in detail in Paper P3 *Risk Management*.

6.2.3 Geographical separation

The **geographical separation** of the **parent company** from its subsidiaries adds to the problems of management control of the group of companies as a whole. Separation may enhance problems caused by **language** and **cultural differences**.

6.2.4 Litigation

The risk of litigation varies in different countries and to minimise this risk, attention should be paid to **legislation** and **regulations** covering the products sold in different countries. Care should be taken to comply with contract terms.

6.3 Multinationals

KEY TERM

A MULTINATIONAL COMPANY or enterprise is one which owns or controls production facilities or subsidiaries or service facilities outside the country in which it is based. Thus, a company does not become 'multinational' simply by virtue of exporting or importing products – **ownership and control of facilities abroad** is involved.

Examples of multinational companies include:

Food and drink	Hospitality and leisure	Car manufacturers	Technology	Pharmaceuticals
Coca Cola	Hilton	Ford	Microsoft	GlaxoSmithKline
McDonald's	Marriott	Toyota	Dell	Pfizer

6.3.1 Foreign subsidiaries

The basic structure of multinationals consists of a parent company (a holding company) with subsidiaries in various countries. The subsidiaries may be wholly owned or just partly owned, and some may be owned through other subsidiaries.

6.3.2 The purpose of setting up subsidiaries abroad

The following are some reasons why a parent company might want to set up subsidiary companies in other countries.

- The location of markets
- The need for a sales organisation
- The opportunity to produce goods more cheaply
- The need to avoid import controls
- The need to obtain access to raw materials
- The availability of grants and tax concessions

Exam skills

It is essential to ensure that any discussion concerning a multinational entity recognises its size and complexity. For example, potential losses from unfavourable tax rates or exchange rate movements are immaterial for a large multinational group. Also, the impact of exchange rate movements relating to a

project could be largely immaterial to group gearing levels due to the small size of the project in relation to the size of the group.

Section summary

Entities which trade **internationally** must be aware of additional external factors such as foreign exchange risk, political risk, geographical separation and litigation.

7 Impact of taxation on financial strategy

Introduction

Tax regulations are an important factor to consider in setting financial strategy. As part of maximising shareholder wealth, companies can take advantage of tax relief schemes, and have subsidiaries in countries with lower tax rates. Tax liabilities are an important factor in cash flow forecasts.

7.1 Domestic and international tax considerations

DOMESTIC

Payment of taxes

The deadlines for payment of taxes needs to be factored into cash flow forecasts to ensure the entity has enough cash to meet the deadlines and avoid penalties. This will have an effect on a company's working capital management.

Tax relief incentives

Companies can reduce their tax bill by taking advantages of tax relief schemes. For example, capital allowances (ie tax allowable depreciation) on purchases of equipment are deductible from a company's taxable profits.

Tax relief is also available for interest payments on debt finance, but not equity finance. This will be a factor in a company's financing decisions.

INTERNATIONAL

Multinational companies will have the following tax considerations in setting financial strategy.

Tax regime and dividend payments

Tax considerations are thought to be the primary reason for the dividend policies inside a multinational firm. For example, the parent company may reduce its overall tax liability by receiving larger amounts of dividends from subsidiaries in countries where undistributed earnings would otherwise be taxed.

Tax havens

Tax havens are countries with lenient tax rules or relatively low tax rates, which are often designed to attract foreign investment.

Multinational companies may decide to **shift profits** to these low tax regimes for example, by exploiting transfer pricing, which is discussed below.

Transfer pricing

Transfer pricing is charging for goods and services traded between group companies. This can be structured in such a way that reduces tax, whereby a company in the low tax regime charges fees,

arguably at unrealistically high rates, to another group company in a higher tax jurisdiction to effectively shift profits to the lower tax jurisdiction.

For example, some companies have exploited the use of management charges and royalties between group companies to reduce tax. Company B in a low tax rate country could charge a high management fee to another group Company A in a high tax rate country. This effectively shifts profits from Company A to Company B, resulting in a lower tax charge on the profits. Many tax authorities have imposed limits on transfer prices to prevent these being exploited for tax.

In a similar way, another example of profit shifting is intercompany loans. Company B in a low tax rate country could lend to Company A in a high tax rate country. Company B could charge a high rate of interest to Company A. Not only does this shift profits from Company A to Company B, it also means Company A can claim tax relief on interest payments (see **thin capitalisation** below).

 Transfer pricing is covered in P2 *Advanced Management Accounting.*

Thin capitalisation

Excessive tax relief on interest payments is a result of **thin capitalisation**. A company that has a significantly higher level of debt compared to equity (normally from intra-group borrowings) than it could achieve on its own is described as **thinly capitalised.** This means that in theory, it can claim excessive tax relief on interest payments. However there are rules in many tax jurisdictions that limit the amount of interest that can be claimed for tax relief. Thin capitalisation is covered in Chapter 9.

Taxation issues

If a company makes investments abroad it will be liable to income tax in the home country on the profits made, the taxable amount being before the deduction of any foreign taxes. The profits may be any of the following.

- **Profits of an overseas branch** or agency
- **Income from foreign securities**, for example debentures in overseas companies
- **Dividends from overseas subsidiaries**
- **Gains** made on disposals of foreign assets

In many instances, a company will be potentially subject to overseas taxes as well as to local income tax on the same profits. However, this can be reduced by double taxation relief (DTR).

7.1.1 Double taxation relief (DTR)

KEY TERM

A DOUBLE TAXATION AGREEMENT is an agreement between two countries whereby tax payable on profits made by an overseas subsidiary, including withholding tax, may be deductible against tax on the same profits in another country.

Typical provisions of double taxation agreements are as follows.

(a)   DTR is given to taxpayers in their **country of residence** by way of a credit for tax suffered in the country where income arises. This may be in the form of relief for withholding tax only or, given a holding of specified size in a foreign company, for the underlying tax on the profits out of which dividends are paid.

(b)   **Total exemption from tax** is given in the country where income arises in the hands of, for example:

(i)   Visiting diplomats
(ii)   Teachers on exchange programmes

(c)   **Preferential rates of withholding tax** are applied to, for example, payments of rent, interest and dividends. The usual rate is frequently replaced by 15% or less.

(d)   There are **exchange of information** clauses so that tax evaders can be chased internationally.

(e)   There are **rules to determine** a person's residence and to prevent dual residence (tie-breaker clauses).

(f)   There are **clauses** which render certain profits taxable in only one rather than both of the contracting states.

(g)   There is a **non-discrimination clause** so that a country does not tax foreigners more heavily than its own nationals.

Example: Double taxation relief

Suppose the tax rate on profits in the Federal West Asian Republic is 20%, the UK company tax is 30%, and there is a double taxation agreement between the two countries.

A subsidiary of a UK firm operating in the Federal West Asian Republic earns the equivalent of £1 million in profit, and therefore pays £200,000 in tax on profits. When the profits are remitted to the UK, the UK parent can claim a credit of £200,000 against the full UK tax charge of £300,000, and hence will only pay £100,000.

Section summary

Taxation will have an impact on strategy. Tax relief schemes can reduce a company's tax bill. Multinational companies can also take advantage of low tax regimes through transfer pricing or switching production from one country to another.

8   Performance analysis

Introduction

In Chapter 1 we looked at financial objectives. The aim of this section is to determine whether an entity will **meet** its objectives and to consider the impact of financial decisions on an organisation's results. Ratios provide a means of systematically analysing financial statements. You will have covered much of this section in your earlier studies so the material here is designed to refresh your memory.

8.1 Uses of ratio analysis

The key to obtaining meaningful information from ratio analysis is **comparison**: comparing ratios over time within the same business to establish whether the business is **improving** or **declining**, and comparing ratios between similar businesses to see whether the company you are analysing is better or worse than average within its own business sector.

A vital element in effective ratio analysis is understanding the needs of the person for whom the ratio analysis is being undertaken.

(a)   **Investors** will be interested in the **risk and return** relating to their investment, so will be concerned with dividends, market prices, level of debt vs equity etc.

(b) **Suppliers** and **loan creditors** are interested in receiving the payments due to them, so will want to know how liquid the business is. Lenders of finance to a company can impose limits on financial ratios as part of the debt agreement. These are known as **debt covenants** and are discussed further in Chapter 5.

(c) **Managers** are interested in ratios that indicate how well the business is being run, and also how the business is doing in relation to its **competitors**.

Exam alert

Exam questions may ask you to use ratio analysis to assess whether financial objectives have been met. Furthermore, questions may require you to assess the impact of investment, financing and dividend decisions on financial ratios.

8.2 Limitations of ratio analysis

Although ratio analysis can be a very useful technique, it is important to realise its limitations.

(a) **Availability of comparable information**

When making comparisons with other companies in the industry, industry averages may hide **wide variations** in figures. Figures for 'similar' companies may provide a better guide, but then there are problems identifying which companies are similar, and obtaining enough detailed information about them.

(b) **Use of historical/out-of-date information**

Comparisons with the previous history of a business may be of limited use, if the business has recently undergone, or is about to undergo, **substantial changes**.

(c) **Ratios are not definitive**

'Ideal levels' vary industry by industry, and even they are not definitive. Companies may be able to exist without any difficulty with ratios that are rather worse than the industry average.

(d) **Need for careful interpretation**

For example, if comparing two businesses' liquidity ratios, one business may have higher levels. This might appear to be 'good', but further investigation might reveal that the higher ratios are a result of higher inventory and receivable levels which are a result of poor working capital management by the business with the 'better' ratios.

(e) **Manipulation**

Any ratio including profit may be distorted by **choice of accounting policies**. For smaller companies, working capital ratios may be distorted depending on whether a big customer pays, or a large supplier is paid, before or after the year end.

(f) **Other information**

Ratio analysis on its own is not sufficient for interpreting company accounts, and there are other items of information that should be looked at. We shall consider this further below.

Exam skills

Bear these limitations in mind when calculating and interpreting ratios, as examiners' reports give many examples of misapplication of ratio analysis, and over-simplistic and misleading interpretations.

8.2.1 Use of financial statements for financial analysis

When assessing the performance of a company, the most readily available information to many stakeholders is the annual report.

Analysis using financial statements is not a precise science. The nature of accounting information means that distortions and differences will always exist between sets of accounts not only from entity to entity but also over time.

Information in published accounts is generally summarised information and detailed information may be needed to make informed decisions. Many items in the accounts will be included at their historic cost. Historic cost information may not be the most appropriate for the decision for which the analysis is being undertaken. Always remember that 'profit' and 'net assets' are fairly arbitrary figures and can be affected by manipulation.

Different firms **use different accounting policies** and have different methods of estimating balances. This means statements from two organisations may not be comparable. In addition, comparability may be impaired where estimates and judgements are used.

A further complication is using accounting loopholes to allow an organisation to obtain finance without it needing to be reported in the statement of financial position.

8.3 Categorisation of ratios

You may remember that ratios can be grouped into the following four categories:

- Profitability and return
- Debt and gearing
- Liquidity: control of cash and other working capital items
- Shareholders' investment ratios (or 'stock market ratios')

8.4 Profitability and return

Knowledge brought forward from earlier studies

Return on capital employed

$$ROCE = \frac{PBIT}{Capital\ employed}\% = \frac{Profit\ from\ operations}{Total\ assets\ less\ current\ liabilities}\%$$

Where capital employed = shareholders' funds + long-term debt finance

When **interpreting** ROCE look for the following.

- How risky is the business?
- How capital intensive is it?
- What ROCE do similar businesses have?
- How does it compare with current market borrowing rates, is it earning enough to be able to cover the costs of extra borrowing?

Problems: which items to consider to achieve comparability:

- Revaluation of assets
- Accounting policies, eg goodwill, research and development
- Whether a bank overdraft is classified as a short or long-term liability

---

Return on equity (return on net assets)

$$ROE = \frac{\text{Profit after interest and tax}}{\text{Book value of shareholders' funds}}\%$$

This gives a more **restricted view** of capital than ROCE, but the same principles apply.

ROCE = Asset turnover × Profit margin

Asset turnover

$$\text{Asset turnover} = \frac{\text{Sales}}{\text{Capital employed}} \quad \text{or} \quad \frac{\text{Sales}}{\text{Total assets less current liabilities}}$$

This measures how efficiently the assets have been used. Amend to just non-current assets for capital intensive businesses.

Profit margin

$$\text{Operating profit margin} = \frac{\text{PBIT}}{\text{Sales}}\% \qquad\qquad \text{Gross profit margin} = \frac{\text{Gross profit}}{\text{Sales}}\%$$

PBIT = Profit before Interest and Tax. This is also referred to as Operating profit.

Gross profit = Sales – Cost of sales

Another measure of profit is Earnings before interest, tax, depreciation and amortisation **(EBITDA).**

It is useful to compare profit margin to gross profit % to investigate movements which do not match.

Gross profit margin

$$\frac{\text{Sales}}{\text{Capital employed}}$$

- Sales prices, sales volume and sales mix
- Purchase prices and related costs (discount, carriage etc)
- Production costs, both direct (materials, labour) and indirect (overheads both fixed and variable)
- Inventory levels and valuation, including errors, cut-off and costs of running out of goods

Net profit margin

- Sales expenses in relation to sales levels
- Administrative expenses, including salary levels
- Distribution expenses in relation to sales levels

8.5 Debt and gearing

Knowledge brought forward from earlier studies

Debt ratio

$$\text{Debt ratio} = \frac{\text{Current and non}-\text{current liabilities}}{\text{Current and non}-\text{current assets}}\% \ (>50\%=\text{high})$$

Debt/equity

$$\text{Debt/equity ratio} = \frac{\text{Interest bearing net debts}}{\text{Shareholders' funds}}\% \ (> 100\% = \text{high})$$

Or simply $\dfrac{\text{Value of debt}}{\text{Value of equity}}$

The formula for gearing used most frequently in the exam and in the real world is

$$\dfrac{\text{Value of debt}}{\text{Value of Debt} + \text{Value of equity}}$$

Operating gearing (leverage)

$$\text{Gearing} = \dfrac{\text{Contribution (sales minus variable cost of sales)}}{\text{PBIT}}$$

This demonstrates the relationship between cost operating structure and profitability and is an indication of business risks from rises or falls in volume.

Interest cover

$$\text{Interest cover} = \dfrac{\text{PBIT (incl int receivable)}}{\text{Interest payable}} \text{ or } \dfrac{\text{Profit from operations}}{\text{Finance costs}}$$

Is this a better way to measure gearing? Companies must generate enough profit to cover interest. Certainly it's important to bankers and lenders.

We shall consider gearing and investor ratios further in Chapter 9.

8.6 Liquidity

Knowledge brought forward from earlier studies

Current ratio

$$\text{Current ratio} = \dfrac{\text{Current assets}}{\text{Current liabilities}}$$

Assume assets are realised at book level, therefore theoretical. Is 2:1 acceptable? 1.5:1? It depends on the industry. Remember that excessively large levels can indicate excessive receivables and inventories, and poor control of working capital.

Quick ratio

$$\text{Quick ratio (acid test)} = \dfrac{\text{Current assets} - \text{inventory}}{\text{Current liabilities}}$$

Eliminates illiquid and subjectively valued inventory. Care is needed: it could be high if **overtrading** with receivables, but no cash. Is 1:1 okay? Many supermarkets operate on 0.3, as inventories of goods are very liquid and inventory turnover is very fast.

Receivables collection period (receivables days)

$$\text{Average collection period} = \dfrac{\text{Trade receivables}}{\text{Credit sales}} \times 365$$

Is it **consistent** with quick/current ratio? If not, investigate.

Inventory days

$$\text{Inventory days} = \dfrac{\text{Inventory}}{\text{Cost of sales}} \times 365$$

Note that cost of sales excludes depreciation of any production equipment.

Is the quicker the turnover the better? But remember:

- Lead times
- Seasonal fluctuations in orders
- Alternative uses of warehouse space
- Bulk buying discounts
- Likelihood of inventory perishing or becoming obsolete

Payables payment period (payables days)

$$\text{Payables payment period} = \frac{\text{Trade payables}}{\text{Purchases}} \times 365$$

Use **cost of sales (excluding depreciation)** if purchases are not disclosed.

Cash operating cycle

=   Average time raw materials are in inventory

−   Period of credit taken from suppliers

+   Time taken to produce goods

+   Time taken by customers to pay for goods

Reasons for changes in liquidity

- Credit control efficiency altered
- Altering payment period of suppliers as a source of funding
- Reducing inventory holdings to maintain liquidity

8.7 Shareholder investor ratios

Knowledge brought forward from earlier studies

Dividend yield

$$\text{Dividend yield} = \frac{\text{Dividend per share}}{\text{Market price per share}} \%$$

- **Low yield**: the company retains a large proportion of profits to reinvest
- **High yield**: this is a risky company or slow-growing

Dividend yield is generally less than interest yield. Shareholders will expect price rises, and wish for return (dividends + capital gains) to exceed the return investors get from fixed interest securities.

Earnings per share (EPS)

$$\text{EPS} = \frac{\text{Profits distributable to ordinary shareholders}}{\text{Number of ordinary shares issued}}$$

Investors look for growth; earnings levels need to be sustained to pay dividends and invest in the business. In order for comparisons over time to be valid, there must be a consistent basis of calculation. EPS can be manipulated.

Consider the possibility of dilution through exercise of warrants or options, or conversion of bonds.

Dividend cover

$$\text{Dividend cover} = \frac{\text{EPS}}{\text{Dividend per share}}$$

This shows **how safe the dividend is**, or the extent of profit retention. Variations are due to maintaining dividend when profits are declining.

The converse of dividend cover is the **dividend payout ratio**.

$$\text{Dividend payout ratio} = \frac{\text{Dividend per share}}{\text{EPS}}$$

P/E ratio

$$\text{P/E ratio} = \frac{\text{Market price per share}}{\text{EPS}}$$

The **higher the better** here: it reflects the confidence of the market in high earnings growth and/or low risk. A rise in EPS will cause an increase in P/E ratio, but maybe not to same extent.

P/E ratio will be affected by interest rate changes; a rise in rates will mean a fall in the P/E ratio as shares become less attractive. P/E ratio also depends on market expectations and confidence.

Earnings yield

$$\text{Earnings yield} = \frac{\text{EPS}}{\text{Market price per share}} \; \%$$

This shows the dividend yield if there is no retention of profit. It allows you to compare companies with **different dividend policies**, showing growth rather than earnings.

Net assets per share

$$\text{Net assets per share} = \frac{\text{Net assets}}{\text{No. of shares}}$$

This is a crude measure of value of a company, liable to distortion.

Return on shareholders' funds

$$\text{Return on shareholders' funds (equity)} = \frac{\text{Earnings}}{\text{Shareholders' funds}} \times 100$$

Earnings are after interest, tax and any preference dividends. A high return on shareholders' funds suggests that the company is profitable and has more funds available for equity shareholders.

Total shareholder return

Total shareholder return = dividend yield + capital gain

As the name suggests, this is a measure of the total return to shareholders over a one-year period.

Other factors

Investors are also interested in current market price, past and future returns and security of investment.

We shall look at the major investor ratios again in Chapter 9.

8.8 Other information

As well as ratios, other **financial** and **non-financial information** can give valuable indicators of a company's performance and position.

(a) **The revaluation of non-current assets**

Non-current assets may be stated in the statement of financial position at cost less accumulated depreciation. They may also be revalued from time to time to a current market value, which will lead to an increased depreciation charge.

(b) **Share capital and reserves**

The nature of any increase in share capital and accumulated profits will be of interest including **share issues** and **substantial profit retentions**. If a company has **issued shares in the form of a dividend**, are there obvious reasons why this should be so? For example, does the company need to retain capital within the business because of poor trading in the previous year, making the directors reluctant to pay out more cash dividend than necessary?

(c)   **Loans and other liabilities**

Two aspects to look out for are whether or not loans are **secured** and the **redemption dates** of loans.

(d)   **Contingencies**

Contingencies are conditions which exist at the balance sheet date where the outcome will be confirmed only on the occurrence or non-occurrence of one or more uncertain future events. For example, a pending lawsuit.

(e)   **Events after the statement of financial position date**

Significant events occurring after statement of financial position date include mergers and acquisitions or the purchase and sales of major non-current assets and investments. Knowledge of such events allows the analyst to 'update' the latest published figures by taking account of their potential impact.

Section summary

Ratios provide a means of systematically analysing financial statements. They can be grouped under the headings **profitability**, **liquidity**, **gearing** and **shareholders' investment**.

---

9   Forecasts

Introduction

Forecasting is used to set shareholder expectations, for performance evaluation and to analyse financing requirements. In the exam you could be expected to complete a section of a forecast statement of comprehensive income, a forecast statement of financial position and/or a cash flow forecast. Alternatively, you may be presented with completed forecasts. In both cases you may be required to use the data to evaluate:

- Whether or not the company will meets its financial objectives
- The sensitivity of the forecasts to investment, financing and dividend decisions
- The sensitivity of the objectives to changes in economic and business variables
- Cash available for dividends and financing requirements

In this section we look at how to put together a forecast statement position, and how to derive a cash flow forecast from a forecast statement of financial position and a forecast statement of comprehensive income.

Exam alert

The nature of the Objective Test (OT) questions and Integrated Case Study (ICS) questions means it is unlikely you will have to construct full forecasts. However, you will need to know the principles behind putting forecasts together to be able to answer a question that includes forecasting.

9.1 Cash budgets

KEY TERM

A CASH BUDGET (or FORECAST) is a detailed budget of estimated cash inflows and outflows incorporating both revenue and capital items.   *(CIMA Official Terminology)*

Cash forecasts (or budgets) provide an early warning of liquidity problems, by estimating:

- How much cash is required
- When it is required
- How long it is required for
- Whether it will be available from anticipated sources

A company must know **when** it might need to borrow and **for how long**, not just **what amount** of funding could be required.

9.2 Estimating a future statement of financial position

Statement of financial position based forecasts can be used to assess the scale of funding requirements or cash surpluses expected over time, and to act as a check on the realism of cash flow based forecasts.

This forecast calls for some prediction of the amount/value of each item in the company's statement of financial position, **excluding cash and short-term investments**, as these are what we are trying to predict. A forecast is prepared by taking each item in the statement of financial position, and estimating what its value might be at the future date. The assumptions used are critical, and the following guidelines are suggested.

(a) **Intangible non-current assets and long term investments**

If there are any, they should be taken at their current value unless there is good reason for another treatment.

(b) **Property, plant and equipment**

Some estimate of **asset purchases** (and disposals) will be required. Revaluations can be ignored as they are not cash flows.

(c) **Current assets**

Estimates of **inventory** and **receivables** are sometimes based on fairly simple assumptions, such as the following:

(i) **Same** as current amounts; this is unlikely if business has boomed

(ii) **Increase by a certain percentage**, to allow for growth in business volume – for example, the volume of receivables might be expected to increase by a similar amount

(iii) **Decrease by a certain percentage**, to allow for tighter management control over working capital

(iv) Assume to be a **certain percentage** of the company's estimated **annual sales revenue** for the year

(v) Assume that the **operating cycle** will more or less **remain the same**

In other words, if a firm's customers take two months to pay, this relationship can be expected to continue. Therefore, if total annual sales are $12m and customers take two months to pay, receivables at the year end will be $^2/_{12} \times \$12m = \$2m$.

If revenue increases to $18m, and the collection period stays at two months, receivables will amount to $^2/_{12} \times \$18m = \$3m$. Similar relationships might be plotted for inventory and hence purchases and suppliers.

(d) **Current liabilities**

Some itemising of current liabilities will be necessary, because no single set of assumptions can accurately estimate them collectively.

(i) **Trade payables and accruals** can be estimated in a similar way to current assets, as indicated above.

(ii)   Current liabilities include **bank loans** due for repayment within 12 months. These can be identified individually.

(iii)   **Bank overdraft facilities**. Often there will be no overdraft in the forecast balance sheet. Any available overdraft facility can be considered when the company's overall cash needs are identified.

(iv)   **Taxation**. Any tax on profits payable should be estimated from anticipated profits and based on an estimated percentage of those profits.

(v)   **Dividends payable**. Any ordinary dividend payable should be estimated from anticipated profits, and any preference dividend payable can be predicted from the coupon rate of dividend for the company's preference shares.

(vi)   **Other creditors** can be included if required and are of significant value.

(e)   **Non-current creditors**

Non-current creditors are likely to consist of non-current loans, bonds and any other non-current finance debt. Unless the company has already arranged further non-current borrowing, this item should include just existing long-term debts, minus debts that will be repaid before the statement of financial position date (or debts transferred from long-term to short-term creditors).

(f)   **Share capital and reserves**

With the exception of accumulated profits (retained earnings), the estimated figures for share capital and other reserves should be the same as their current amount, unless it is expected or known that a new issue of shares will take place, in which case the total amount raised (net of issue expenses) should be added to the share capital/other reserves total.

(g)   **Accumulated profits**

An estimate is required of the change in the company's **accumulated profits** in the period up to the statement of financial position date. This reserve should be calculated as:

(i)   The existing value of the retained earnings

(ii)   **Plus** further retained profits anticipated in the period to the statement of financial position date (ie post tax profits minus estimated dividends)

9.3 Compiling a statement of financial position

The various estimates should now be brought together into a statement of financial position. The figures on each side will not be equal, and there will be one of the following.

(a)   A surplus of share capital and reserves over net assets (total assets minus total liabilities). If this occurs, the company will be forecasting a **cash surplus**.

(b)   A surplus of net assets over share capital and reserves. If this occurs, the company will be forecasting a **funding deficit**.

Alpha has an existing statement of financial position and an estimated forecast in one year's time **before the necessary extra funding is taken into account**, as follows.

	Existing		*Forecast after one year*	
	€'000	€'000	€'000	€'000
ASSETS				
Non-current assets		100		180
Current assets		90		100
Total assets		190		280

	Existing		Forecast after one year	
	€'000	€'000	€'000	€'000
EQUITY AND LIABILITIES				
Share capital and reserves				
€1 ordinary shares	50		50	
Other reserves	20		20	
Accumulated profits	30		50	
		100		120
Non-current liabilities				
5% bonds	20		20	
Deferred tax	10		10	
		30		30
Current liabilities		60		90
Total equity and liabilities		190		240

The company is expecting to increase its total assets in the next year by €90,000 (€280,000 – €190,000) but expects accumulated profits for the year to be €20,000 (€50,000 – €30,000) and current liabilities to increase by €30,000. There is an excess of net assets over share capital and reserves amounting to €40,000 (€280,000 – €240,000), which is a **funding deficit**. The company must consider ways of obtaining extra cash (eg by borrowing) to cover the deficit. If it cannot, it will need to keep its assets below the forecast amount, or to have higher short-term payables.

A revised projected statement of financial position can then be prepared by introducing these new sources of funds. This should be checked for realism (eg by **ratio analysis**) to ensure that the proportion of the statement made up by non-current assets and working capital, etc is sensible.

9.4 Deriving cash flow from statement of comprehensive income and statement of financial position information

The previous paragraphs concentrated on preparing a forecast statement of financial position, with estimated figures for receivables, payables and inventory. Cash requirements might therefore be presented as the 'balancing figure'. However, it is possible to derive a forecast figure for cash flows using both the statement of comprehensive income and statement of financial position. The profit from operations is adjusted first of all for items not involving cash, such as depreciation. This is further adjusted for changes in the levels of working capital (eg receivables and payables) to arrive at operational cash flows.

This is illustrated in the example below. For the time being, assume that there is no depreciation. The task is to get from profit to operational cash flow, by taking into account movements in working capital.

	Profit	Operational cash flow
	$	$
Sales	200,000	200,000
Opening receivables (∴ received in year)		15,000
Closing receivables (outstanding at year end)		(24,000)
Cash in		191,000
Cost of sales	170,000	170,000
Closing inventory (purchased, but not used, in year)		21,000
Opening inventory (used, but not purchased, in year)		(12,000)
Purchases in year		179,000
Opening payables (∴ paid in year)		11,000
Closing payables (outstanding at year end)		(14,000)
Cash out		176,000
Profit/operational cash flow	30,000	15,000

This may be summarised as:

		$	$
Profit			30,000
(Increase)/Decrease in inventory	Opening	12,000	
	Closing	(21,000)	
			(9,000)
(Increase)/Decrease in receivables	Opening	15,000	
	Closing	(24,000)	
			(9,000)
Increase/(Decrease) in payables	Closing	14,000	
	Opening	(11,000)	
			3,000
Operational cash flow			15,000

Question 2.2   Forecast financial statements

Learning outcome: A(2)(a)

Triassic produces smoke alarms for residential and office premises. As a result of recent changes in government legislation, it has been predicted that the market for smoke alarms will increase significantly in the short term. The directors of Triassic are planning to expand the business significantly in order to exploit these new market conditions. The following forecasts for the forthcoming year have been prepared by the directors.

TRIASSIC

FORECAST STATEMENT OF COMPREHENSIVE INCOME FOR THE YEAR TO 30 NOVEMBER 20X3

	€m	€m
Revenue		300.0
Cost of sales		210.0
Gross profit		90.0
Expenses	54.6	
Depreciation of buildings	1.0	
Depreciation of plant and machinery	16.4	
		72.0
Profit before taxation		18.0
Taxation (30%)		5.4
Profit after taxation		12.6
Dividend (50%)		6.3
Retained profit		6.3

TRIASSIC

FORECAST STATEMENT OF FINANCIAL POSITION AS AT 30 NOVEMBER 20X3

	€m	€m	€m
Non-current assets			
Freehold buildings at cost		24.4	
Less accumulated depreciation		5.4	
			19.0
Plant and machinery at cost		94.9	
Less accumulated depreciation		29.3	
			65.6
			84.6
Current assets			
Inventory		21.0	
Trade receivables		75.0	
		96.0	

	€m	€m	€m
Payables: amounts falling due within one year			
Bank overdraft	19.2		
Trade payables	24.0		
Taxation payable	5.4		
Dividend payable	6.3		
		54.9	
			41.1
			125.7
Payables: amounts falling due after more than one year			
Loan			31.4
Total net assets			94.3
Share capital and reserves			
Ordinary shares of €1			20.0
Accumulated profits			74.3
Total equity and reserves			94.3

The most recent statement of financial position of the company is set out below.

STATEMENT OF FINANCIAL POSITION AS AT 30 NOVEMBER 20X2

	€m	€m	€m
Non-current assets			
Freehold buildings at cost		24.4	
Less: accumulated depreciation		4.4	20.0
Plant and machinery at cost		37.9	
Less: accumulated depreciation		12.9	25.0
			45.0
Current assets			
Inventory	39.0		
Trade receivables	20.0		
Bank	8.3	67.3	
Less: payables: amounts falling due within one year			
Trade payables	12.0		
Taxation	4.5		
Dividends	7.8	24.3	
			43.0
			88.0
Capital and reserves			
			€m
Ordinary €1 shares			20.0
Accumulated profits			68.0
			88.0

Required

Comment briefly on the financial performance and position of the business using the forecast financial statements.

Section summary

- **Cash forecasting** should ensure that sufficient funds will be available when needed, to sustain the activities of an enterprise at an acceptable cost.

- **Statement of financial position-based forecasts** can be used to assess the scale of funding requirements or cash surpluses expected over time, and to act as a check on the realism of cash flow based forecasts.

Exam alert

In the Integrated Case Study, if a question has a forecasting element, it is likely to be discursive.

10 Sensitivity analysis and changes in variables

Introduction

As part of a business's risk analysis, different forecasts should be prepared with **changing financial** or **business variables**. The links between these variables and the figures in the forecasts may not be straightforward.

10.1 Sensitivity analysis

In a well-designed forecast a great number of **'what-if'** questions can be asked and answered quickly by carrying out **sensitivity analysis** and changing the relevant data or variables. In a cash flow forecast model, managers may wish to know the cash flow impact if sales growth per month is nil, $\frac{1}{2}$%, 1%, $1\frac{1}{2}$%, $2\frac{1}{2}$% or minus 1% and so on.

Changes in any of the key elements of financial strategy (investment, financing, dividend decisions) can significantly impact financial forecasts and may influence a company's ability to achieve its stated financial objectives.

Businesses will also want to estimate the magnitude of changes in sales and ultimately profits if economic or business variables change. This will be more problematic.

10.2 Changes in economic variables

Businesses need to be aware of likely changes in inflation, interest rates and so on. Governments and central banks issue regular updates and forecasts, and the financial press is also helpful.

However businesses will also need to forecast:

- How the **predicted changes** will **affect demand**. The links may not be easy to forecast. Businesses should consider separately the effect of major increases on each type of product.

- How the **business** will **respond to changes in variables**. For example will the business automatically adjust prices upwards by the rate of inflation, or will it try to hold prices? What will its competitors do? If raw material prices increase, will the business try to change suppliers? What effect will this have on payment patterns?

10.3 Changes in business variables

Economic variables will clearly impact upon business variables such as **sales volumes** or **profit margins**. Businesses need to be aware of the other factors, such as changes in the competitive environment that could affect these variables and how this effect might work.

The original forecast should itself have been based on **demand forecasts,** determined by **market surveys** and **statistical models** based on past changes in demand. However if factors such as taste change, businesses need to recognise this might not just require marginal changes in forecasts, but a re-visiting of the base data, since the changes will ultimately render the previous surveys or models redundant.

CASE STUDY

Singapore Airlines provide sensitivity analysis in their annual reports. For example, an extract from their 2016/17 annual report shows the sensitivity of passenger revenue to changes in key variables.

Sensitivity of passenger revenue to a one percentage point change in passenger load factor and a one percentage point change in passenger yield is as follows:

	$m
1.0% point change in passenger load factor, if yield and seat capacity remain constant	95.4
1.0% point change in passenger yield, if passenger traffic remains constant	75.4

A change in the price of fuel of one USD per barrel affects the Singapore Airline's annual fuel cost by about $43 million.

Section summary

- Current and forecast information can be evaluated taking account of variation in **economic** (eg interest rates) and **business** (eg volume and margins) factors.

- The **sensitivity** of changes in expected values in the forecasts can be analysed.

11 Financing requirements

Introduction

Cash deficits will be funded in different ways, depending on whether they are short or long term. Sources of finance are covered in Paper F2 *Advanced Financial Reporting*, and revisited in Chapters 5 and 8 of this Study Text. Businesses should also have procedures for investing surpluses with appropriate levels of risk and return.

11.1 Deficiencies

Any forecast **deficiency** of cash will have to be funded.

(a) **Borrowing**. If borrowing arrangements are not already secured, a source of funds will have to be found. If a company cannot fund its cash deficits it could be wound up.

(b) The firm can make arrangements to **sell any short-term marketable financial investments** to raise cash.

(c) The firm can delay payments to suppliers, or pull in payments from customers. This is sometimes known as **leading and lagging**.

Because cash forecasts cannot be entirely accurate, companies should have **contingency funding**, available from a surplus cash balance and liquid investments, or from a bank facility. The approximate size of contingency margin will vary from company to company, according to the cyclical nature of the business and the approach of its cash planners.

Forecasting gives management **time** to arrange its funding. If planned in advance, instead of a panic measure to avert a cash crisis, a company can more easily choose when to borrow, and will probably obtain a lower interest rate.

11.2 Cash surpluses

If a **cash surplus** is forecast, having an idea of both its size and how long it will exist could help decide how best to invest it.

In some cases, the amount of **interest** earned from surplus cash could be significant for the company's earnings. The company might then need a forecast of its interest earnings in order to indicate its prospective **earnings per share** to stock market analysts and institutional investors.

The entity must have procedures for investing surpluses which consider both **risk** and **return**.

11.2.1 Motives for holding cash surpluses

One of the main financing decisions is the level of cash reserves to retain for unforeseen costs. If cash reserves are low, a company could face liquidity issues. On the other hand, retaining excess cash reserves has an opportunity cost of that cash not being used for investments and generating a return.

There are three different motives for an organisation to hold cash reserves:

The **precautionary motive** – a company holds on to surplus cash to maintain a safety net in case there is unexpected cash expenditure in the near future, or an unexpected fall in cash receipts.

The **speculative motive** – a company holds cash in order to be able to take advantage of opportunities such as buying assets at temporarily favourable prices or making an acquisition.

The **transaction motive** – a company needs to hold enough cash to meet its day-to-day obligations.

Section summary

Once a cash forecast has been prepared, decisions on **financing** can then be made.

Chapter Summary

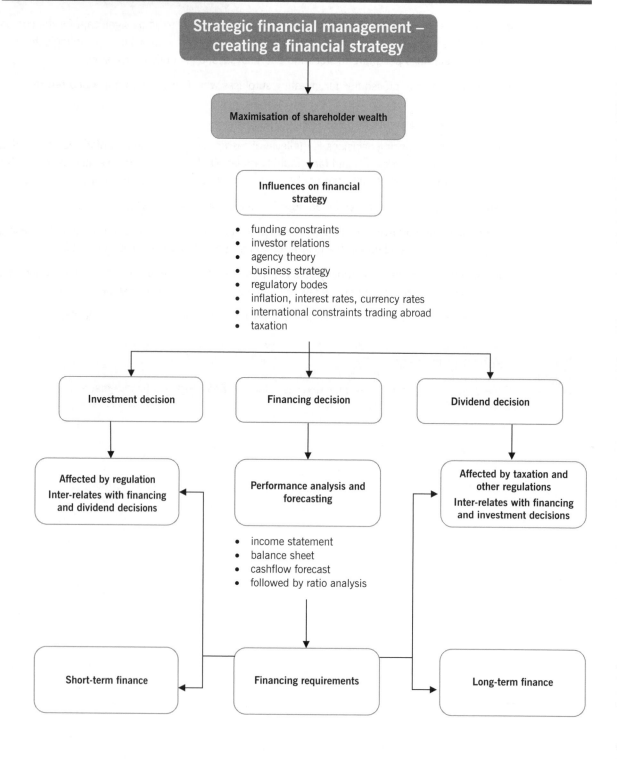

Strategic financial management – creating a financial strategy

Maximisation of shareholder wealth

Influences on financial strategy

- funding constraints
- investor relations
- agency theory
- business strategy
- regulatory bodes
- inflation, interest rates, currency rates
- international constraints trading abroad
- taxation

Investment decision

Financing decision

Dividend decision

Affected by regulation
Inter-relates with financing and dividend decisions

Performance analysis and forecasting

Affected by taxation and other regulations
Inter-relates with financing and investment decisions

- income statement
- balance sheet
- cashflow forecast
- followed by ratio analysis

Short-term finance

Financing requirements

Long-term finance

Quick Quiz

1   **Fill in the blanks:**

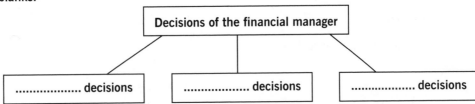

2   .... is a course of action, including the specification of resources required, to achieve a specific objective.

3   List two principal methods of regulating a monopoly industry.

4   Draw a 'normal' yield curve, labelling axes.

5   Fill in the following at (A), (B) and (C) in the equation below.

- Nominal rate of interest
- Real rate of interest
- Rate of inflation

$$\frac{1+(A)}{1+(B)} - 1 = (C)$$

6   **Fill in the blank:**

Corporate governance is ....

7   What are the main limitations of ratio analysis?

8   Return on equity = ?

Answers to Quick Quiz

1   Investment; financing; dividend

2   Strategy

3   Price control; profit control.

4

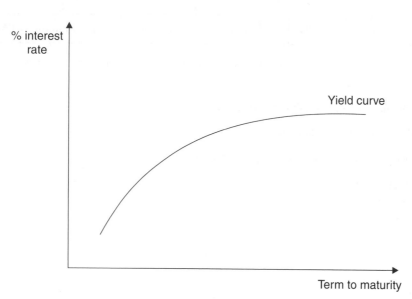

5   (A)   Nominal rate of interest
     (B)   Rate of inflation
     (C)   Real rate of interest

6   The system by which companies are directed and controlled.

7   •   Lack of comparable industry information
     •   Historical information used for comparison may be out-of-date
     •   Ratio levels may not indicate situation fairly
     •   Ratios need careful interpretation
     •   Ratios can be manipulated
     •   Some ratios can be calculated in different ways
     •   Ratios shouldn't be used in isolation

8    $\text{Return on equity} = \dfrac{\text{Profit after interest and tax}}{\text{Book value of shareholders' funds}} \times 100\%$

Answers to Questions

2.1 Forecasting exchange rates

$1.138 \times 1.015/1.037 = 1.114$

$1.114 \times 1.015/1.037 = 1.090$

$1.090 \times 1.015/1.037 = 1.067$

Note: The exchange rate is quoted as £ to € so the € inflation rate is divided by the £ inflation rate.

2.2 Forecast financial statements

The profit after tax next year will be €12.6 million, giving a return on equity of (12.6/94.3) 13.4% and a profit margin on sales of (12.6/300) 4.2%. In the previous year, the profit after tax was €15.6 million (double the dividend), with a ROE of (15.6/88) 17.7% and a profit/sales ratio of (15.6/240) 6.5%.

The forecast profit is therefore lower, with a lower ROE and a lower profit/sales ratio, despite a 25% increase in sales.

Liquidity is also expected to deteriorate. The company is forecasting a bank overdraft of €19.2 million at the end of November 20X3, compared to a positive cash balance the previous year. The company will have to ensure that bank overdraft facilities are available if it goes ahead with its plan to increase sales.

The company will also have some long-term debt capital, having been ungeared in the year to 30 November 20X2.

On the basis of the forecasts, it is questionable whether there is any financial benefit to be obtained from expanding sales, and the company management should review its plans urgently, before implementing them.

Now try the questions from the Practice Question Bank	**Question** Section A: 2.1 – 2.3	**Level** Practice

REPORTING ISSUES

 Various developments in corporate reporting are helping to improve the information available to stakeholders about a company.

We start by looking at how certain financial risks have become more transparent in financial statements with the adoption of hedge accounting and the disclosure requirements for financial instruments.

However, financial statements do not provide a full picture of the risks and opportunities facing a company from external factors. We will also look at how voluntary reporting such as sustainability reporting and integrated reporting show how factors such as society and environment can affect long-term value.

Topic list	learning outcomes	syllabus references	ability required
1 Hedge accounting	A2(c)	A2(c)(i),(ii)	evaluation
2 Disclosure of financial instruments	A2(c)	A2(c)(iii)	evaluation
3 Management commentary	A1(c)	A1(c)(i),(ii)	analysis
4 Sustainability	A1(c)	A1(c)(i),(ii)	analysis
5 Integrated reporting	A1(c)	A1(c)(i),(ii)	analysis

Chapter Overview

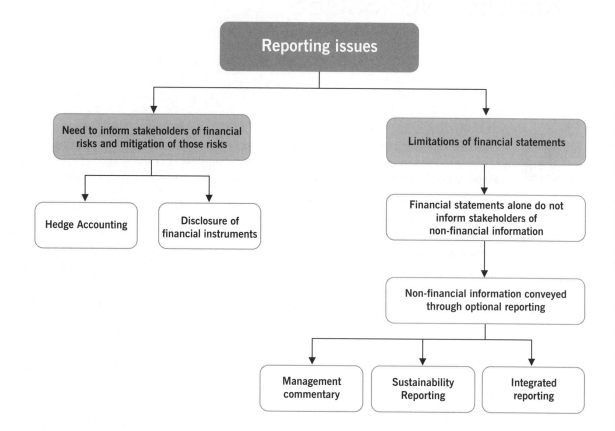

1   Hedge accounting

Introduction

Stakeholders need to be informed about the financial risks faced by a company. One way to do this is through International Accounting Standard IAS 39 which **requires hedge accounting** where there is a **designated hedging relationship** between a hedging instrument and a hedged item.

1.1 Purpose of hedge accounting

Hedge accounting comes under International Accounting Standard IAS 39 *Financial Instruments: Recognition and Measurement*. The purpose of hedge accounting is to **match** the loss or gain made by a **hedged item** to the gain or loss made by a **hedged instrument** (or vice versa), in the same accounting period, reducing overall risk.

The hedged item is an item that exposes an entity to changes in value or cash flows. The hedged instrument is designed to offset those changes in value or cash flows.

1.2 Definitions

KEY TERMS

HEDGING, for accounting purposes, means designating one or more hedging instruments so that their change in fair value is an offset, in whole or in part, to the change in fair value or cash flows of a hedged item.

A HEDGED ITEM is an asset, liability, firm commitment, or forecasted future transaction that:

(a)   Exposes the entity to risk of changes in fair value or changes in future cash flows
(b)   Is designated as being hedged

A HEDGING INSTRUMENT is a designated derivative or (in limited circumstances) another financial asset or liability whose fair value or cash flows are expected to offset changes in the fair value or cash flows of a designated hedged item.

(A non-derivative financial asset or liability may be designated as a hedging instrument for hedge accounting purposes only if it hedges the risk of changes in foreign currency exchange rates.)*

HEDGE EFFECTIVENESS is the degree to which changes in the fair value or cash flows of the hedged item attributable to a hedged risk are offset by changes in the fair value or cash flows of the hedging instrument.   (*IAS 39*)

* for example, a foreign currency loan

A **DERIVATIVE** is a financial instrument that **derives** its value from the price or rate of an underlying item. Common **examples** of derivatives include:

(a)   **Forward contracts**: agreements to buy or sell an asset at a fixed price at a fixed future date

(b)   **Futures contracts**: similar to forward contracts except that contracts are standardised and traded on an exchange

(c)   **Options**: rights (but not obligations) for the option holder to exercise at a pre-determined price

(d)   **Swaps**: agreements to swap one set of cash flows for another (normally interest rate or currency swaps – the use of swaps as instruments to hedge against currency risk and interest rate risk is covered in Chapter 6)

The **standard** identifies three types of **hedging relationship**.

KEY TERMS

FAIR VALUE HEDGE: These hedge against the change in value of an asset or liability that could affect the profit or loss (eg hedging the fair value of fixed rate debentures due to changes in interest rates).

CASH FLOW HEDGE: These hedge against the risk of a change in value of future cash flows that could affect profit or loss (eg hedging a variable rate interest income stream).

HEDGE OF A NET INVESTMENT IN A FOREIGN OPERATION: These hedge against changes in the value of an entity's investment in a foreign operation.

IAS 21 defines a net investment in a foreign operation as the amount of the reporting entity's interest in the net assets of that operation.

(IAS 39)

In simple terms, entities hedge to reduce their exposure to risk and uncertainty, such as changes in prices, interest rates or foreign exchange rates. Hedge accounting recognises hedging relationships by allowing (for example) losses on a hedged item to be offset against gains on a hedging instrument.

1.3 Conditions for hedge accounting

Adopting the hedge accounting provisions of IAS 39 is mandatory where a transaction qualifies as a hedge. In order to qualify, the relationship needs to show that it satisfies the following conditions:

(a)   It was **designated at its inception** as a hedge with full documentation of how this hedge fits into the company's strategy.

(b)   The hedge has been and is expected to be **'highly effective'** (ie the ratio of the gain or loss on the hedging instrument compared to the loss or gain on item being hedged is within the ratio of 80% to 125%).

(c)   The hedge effectiveness can be **reliably measured**.

1.4 Accounting treatment

1.4.1 Fair value hedges

The **gain or loss** resulting from **remeasuring** the hedging instrument at fair value is **recognised in the statement of profit or loss**.

The gain or loss on the hedged item attributable to the **hedged risk** should **adjust the carrying amount** of the hedged item and be **recognised in the statement of profit or loss**.

1.4.2 Example: fair value hedge

On 1 July 20X6 Joules Ltd acquired 10,000 ounces of a material which it held in its inventory. This cost $200 per ounce, for a total of $2 million. Joules was concerned that the price of this inventory would fall, so on 1 July 20X6 he entered a contract to sell 10,000 ounces in the futures market for $210 per ounce for delivery on 30 June 20X7. On 1 July 20X6 the conditions for hedge accounting were all met.

At 31 December 20X6, the end of Joules' reporting period, the fair value of the inventory was $220 per ounce while the futures price for 30 June 20X7 delivery was $227 per ounce. On 30 June 20X7 the trader sold the inventory and closed out the futures position at the then spot price of $230 per ounce.

Required

Set out the accounting entries in respect of the above transactions.

Solution

At 31 December 20X6 the increase in the fair value of the inventory was $200,000 (10,000 × ($220 – $200)) and the increase in the forward contract liability was $170,000 (10,000 × ($227 – $210)). Hedge effectiveness was 85% (170,000 as a percentage of 200,000), so hedge accounting was still permitted.

31 December 20X6	Debit $	Credit $
Profit or loss	170,000	
Financial liability		170,000
(To record the loss on the forward contract)		
Inventories	200,000	
Profit or loss		200,000
(To record the increase in the fair value of the inventories)		

At 30 June 20X7 the increase in the fair value of the inventory was another $100,000 (10,000 × ($230 – $220)) and the increase in the forward contract liability was another $30,000 (10,000 × ($230 – $227)).

30 June 20X7	Debit $	Credit $
Profit or loss	30,000	
Financial liability		30,000
(To record the loss on the forward contract)		
Inventories	100,000	
Profit or loss		100,000
(To record the increase in the fair value of the inventories)		
Profit or loss	2,300,000	
Inventories		2,300,000
(To record the inventories now sold)		
Cash	2,300,000	
Profit or loss – revenue		2,300,000
(To record the revenue from the sale of inventories)		
Financial liability	200,000	
Cash		200,000
(To record the settlement of the net balance due on closing the financial liability)		

Note that because the fair value of the material rose, Joules made a profit of only £100,000 on the sale of inventories. Without the forward contract, the profit would have been £300,000 (2,300,000 – 2,000,000). In the light of the rising fair value, the trader might in practice have closed out the futures position earlier, rather than waiting until the settlement date.

1.4.3 Cash flow hedges

The portion of the gain or loss on the hedging instrument that is determined to be an **effective** hedge (ie, the extent to which the gain or loss offsets the loss or gain on the hedging instrument) shall be **recognised in other comprehensive income (OCI)**.

The **ineffective portion** of the gain or loss on the hedging instrument should be **recognised in profit or loss**.

When a hedging transaction results in the recognition of an asset or liability, changes in the value of the hedging instrument recognised in equity either:

(a)   Are adjusted against the carrying value of the asset or liability, or

(b)   Affect the profit or loss at the same time as the hedged item (for example, through depreciation or sale)

1.4.4 Example: Cash flow hedge

Bets Co signs a contract on 1 November 20X1 to purchase an asset on 1 November 20X2 for €60,000,000. Bets reports in US$ and hedges this transaction by entering into a forward contract to buy €60,000,000 on 1 November 20X2 at US$1: €1.5. Beta Co's year end is 31 December 20X1.

Spot and forward exchange rates at the following dates are:

	Spot	Forward (for delivery on 1.11.X2)
1.11.X1	US$1: €1.45	US$1: €1.5
31.12.X1	US$1: €1.20	US$1: €1.24
1.11.X2	US$1: €1.0	US$1: €1.0 (actual)

Required

Show the double entries relating to these transactions at 1 November 20X1, 31 December 20X1 and 1 November 20X2.

Solution

Entries at 1 November 20X1

The value of the forward contract at inception is zero so no entries are recorded (other than any transaction costs), but risk disclosures will be made.

The contractual commitment to buy the asset would be disclosed if material (IAS 16).

Entries at 31 December 20X1

Fair value of forward contract:

	$
Rate agreed at 31.12.X1 (€60,000,000/1.24)	48,387,096
Rate agreed at 1.11.X1 (€60,000,000/1.5)	40,000,000
Fair value of forward contract	8,387,096

Compare to movement in value of asset (unrecognised):

Increase in $ cost of asset

(€60,000,000/1.20 – €60,000,000/1.45) $8,620,690

As this is higher, the hedge is deemed fully effective at this point:

DEBIT Financial asset (Forward contract) $8,387,096

CREDIT OCI $8,387,096

Entries at 1 November 20X2

Additional gain on forward contract

	$
Value of contract at 1.11.X2 (€60,000,000/1.0)	60,000,000
Value of contract at 31.12.X1 (€60,000,000/1.24)	48,387,096
Gain on contract	11,612,904

Compare to movement in value of asset (unrecognised):

Additional increase in $ cost of asset

(€60,000,000/1.0 – €60,000,000/1.2) $10,000,000

Therefore, the hedge is highly effective (and hence hedge accounting can be used):

$10,000,000/ $11,612,904 = 86% which is within the 80% – 125% bandings.

DEBIT Financial asset (Forward contract)	$11,612,904	
CREDIT OCI		$10,000,000
CREDIT Profit or loss		$1,612,904

Purchase of asset at market price

DEBIT Asset (€60,000,000/1.0)	$60,000,000	
CREDIT Cash		$60,000,000

Settlement of forward contract

DEBIT Cash	$20,000,000	
CREDIT Financial asset (Forward contract)		$20,000,000

Realisation of gain on hedging instrument

The cumulative gain of $18,387,096 recognised in equity:

- Is transferred to profit or loss as the asset is used, ie over the asset's useful life, or
- Adjusts the initial cost of the asset (reducing future depreciation)

1.4.5 Hedge of a net investment in a foreign operation

When an entity has an investment in a foreign operation, eg a foreign subsidiary, the net assets of the foreign subsidiary should be translated into the functional currency of the parent company at the closing rate of exchange each year end. Any exchange gains or losses from retranslation should be recognised in **other comprehensive income**. This is in accordance with IAS 21 *The Effects of Changes in Foreign Exchange Rates.*

Suppose that the entity **hedged** against exchange rate movements in the foreign operation by using a loan in the same currency as the foreign subsidiary.

Under normal circumstances, exchange gains/losses on a foreign loan are recognised in **profit or loss**. However, where the loan is **designated as a hedge**, hedge accounting applies and the loan should be treated as follows.

The **effective portion** of exchange gains or losses from retranslation of the loan should also be recognised in **other comprehensive income**. This is in order to **match** the gain/loss on the **hedged item** (net assets of foreign subsidiary) with the loss/gain on the **hedged instrument** (foreign currency loan).

The **ineffective portion** of the gain or loss on the hedging instrument should be **recognised in profit or loss**.

1.4.6 Example: Hedge of a net investment in a foreign operation

On 1 January 20X6, Company A, whose functional currency is $, had partly financed an investment of €800,000 in a foreign company via the use of a borrowing of €700,000 taken out on 1 January 20X6. The following additional financial information is available:

	01/01/X6	*31/12/X6*
Spot rate	US$1: €1.45	US$1: €1.50

Required

Show the impact of the net investment hedge on the financial statements of Company A at 31 December 20X6. Assume that the € loan was designated as a hedge at 1 January 20X6.

Solution

Both the investment and borrowing will initially be translated at the historic rate and re-translated at the closing rate at the year end.

Gain on retranslation of borrowing

	$
Borrowing at 1.01.X6 (€700,000/1.45)	482,759
Borrowing at 31.12.X6 (€700,000/1.50)	466,667
Gain on retranslation	16,092

Loss on retranslation of investment

	$
Investment at 1.01.X6 (€800,000/1.45)	551,724
Investment at 31.12.X6 (€800,000/1.50)	533,333
Loss on retranslation	18,391

This gives a hedge effectiveness of $16,092 ÷ $18,391 = 87%. The hedge is therefore **highly effective** as the hedge effectiveness is between 80% and 120%. Furthermore, the borrowing was designated as a hedge at inception, so the conditions for hedge accounting to apply to the gain on the borrowing have been met.

The gain and loss are off-set against each other in OCI.

1.4.7 Impact of hedge accounting on stakeholder assessment

Hedge accounting matches the hedged item and the hedged instrument. If a loss arises on a hedged item, if the hedging is effective, then an opposite gain will arise on the hedging instrument and vice versa.

Without hedge accounting, stakeholders (eg investors, lenders, customers and suppliers) cannot see hedges entered into from financial statements. Hedge accounting allows stakeholders to make more informed decisions about a company, eg to lend to, invest in, or do business with a company.

Section summary

- **Hedge accounting** means designating one or more instruments so that their change in fair value is **offset** by the change in fair value or cash flows of another item.

- **Hedge accounting** is permitted in certain circumstances, provided the hedging relationship is **designated at inception**, **measurable** and **highly effective**.

- There are three types of hedge: **fair value** hedge; **cash flow** hedge; hedge of a **net investment in a foreign operation**.

- The accounting treatment of a hedge **depends on its type**.

2 Disclosure of financial instruments

Introduction

The IASB maintains that users of financial instruments need information about an entity's exposures to risks and how those risks are managed, as this information can **influence a user's assessment of the financial position and financial performance of an entity** or of the amount, timing and uncertainty of its **future cash flows**.

There have been new techniques and approaches to measuring risk management, which highlighted the need for guidance.

Accordingly, IFRS 7 *Financial instruments: Disclosures* was issued in 2005.

2.1 Objective

The objective of IFRS 7 is to require entities to provide disclosures in their financial statements that enable users to evaluate:

(a)   The **significance** of financial instruments for the entity's financial position and performance

(b)   The **nature and extent of risks** arising from financial instruments, and how the entity manages those risks

The principles in IFRS 7 complement the principles for recognising, measuring and presenting financial assets and financial liabilities in IAS 32 *Financial instruments: presentation* and IAS 39 *Financial instruments: recognition and measurement*.

2.2 Classes of financial instruments and levels of disclosure

The entity must group financial instruments into classes **appropriate to the nature of the information presented**. An entity must decide, based on its circumstances, how much detail it provides. Sufficient information must be provided to permit reconciliation to the line items presented in the statement of financial position.

2.2.1 Statement of financial position

The following must be disclosed:

(a)   **Carrying amount** of financial assets and liabilities (by IAS 39 category)

(b)   Special disclosures about financial assets and financial liabilities designated to be measured **at fair value through profit and loss**, including disclosures about credit risk and market risk, changes in fair values attributable to these risks and the methods of measurement

(c)   **Reason for any reclassification** of financial instruments from one category to another

(d)   The **carrying amount** of financial assets the entity has **pledged as collateral** for liabilities or contingent liabilities and the associated terms and conditions

(e)   Reconciliation of movement in the allowance account for credit losses (bad debts) by class of financial assets

(f)   The **existence of multiple embedded derivatives**, where compound instruments contain these

(g)   Defaults on loans payable

2.2.2 Statement of profit or loss and other comprehensive income

The entity must disclose the following items of **income, expense, gains or losses**, either on the face of the financial statements or in the notes:

(a)   **Net gains/losses** on financial instruments recognised in profit or loss by IAS 39 category (broken down as appropriate: eg interest, fair value changes, dividend income)

(b)   Total effective **interest income/expense** (for items **not** held at fair value through profit or loss)

(c)   Impairments losses by class of financial asset

2.2.3 Other disclosures

Other disclosures must be made relating to **hedge accounting**, as follows:

(a)   Accounting policy for the measurement basis of financial instruments

(b)   Description of each hedge

(c)   Description of each financial instrument designated as **hedging instruments** and their fair value at the reporting date

(d)   The **nature of the risks** being hedged

(e)   For **cash flow hedges**, periods **when the cash flows will occur** and when they will affect profit or loss

(f)   For fair value hedges, details of fair value changes of the hedging instrument and the hedged item

(g)   The **ineffectiveness recognised in profit or loss** arising from cash flow hedges and net investments in foreign operations

Disclosures must be made relating to **fair value** by class of financial instrument, in a way that allows comparison to statement of financial position value in the statement of financial position. (Financial assets and liabilities may only be offset to the extent that their carrying amounts are offset in the statement of financial position.)

Example: fair value disclosures

Background

On 1 January 20X1 an entity purchases financial assets for $15 million that are not traded in an active market. The entity has only one class of such financial assets.

The transaction price of $15 million is the fair value at initial recognition.

After initial recognition, the entity will apply a valuation technique to establish the financial assets' fair value. This valuation technique includes variables other than data from observable markets.

At initial recognition, the same valuation technique would have resulted in an amount of $14 million, which differs from fair value by $1 million.

The entity has existing differences of $5 million at 1 January 20X1.

Solution

Application of requirements

The entity's 20X2 disclosure would include the following:

Accounting policies

The entity uses the following valuation technique to determine the fair value of financial instruments that are not traded in an active market: [description of technique, not included in this example]. Differences may arise between the fair value at initial recognition (which, in accordance with IAS 39, is generally the transaction price) and the amount determined at initial recognition using the valuation technique. Any such differences are [description of the entity's accounting policy].

In the notes to the financial statements

As discussed in note X, the entity uses [name of valuation technique] to measure the fair value of the following financial instruments that are not traded in an active market. However, in accordance with IAS 39, the fair value of an instrument at inception is generally the transaction price. If the transaction price differs from the amount determined at inception using the valuation technique, that difference is

[description of the entity's accounting policy]. The differences yet to be recognised in profit or loss are as follows:

	31 Dec 20X2	31 Dec 20X1
	$m	$m
Balance at beginning of year	5.3	5.0
New transactions		1.0
Amounts recognised in profit or loss during the year	(0.7)	(0.8)
Other increases		0.2
Other decreases	(0.1)	(0.1)
Balance at end of year	4.5	5.3

Disclosures of fair value are **not required** if carrying value is a reasonable approximation to fair value, or if fair value cannot be measured reliably.

2.3 Nature and extent of risks arising from financial instruments

In undertaking transactions in financial instruments, an entity may assume or transfer to another party one or more of **different types of financial risk** as defined below. The disclosures required by the standard show the extent to which an entity is exposed to these different types of risk, relating to both recognised and unrecognised financial instruments.

Credit risk	The risk that one party to a financial instrument will cause a financial loss for the other party by failing to pay for its obligation.
Liquidity risk	The risk that an entity will encounter difficulty in paying its financial liabilities. (Loans payable are financial liabilities, other than short-term trade payables on normal credit terms.)
Market risk	The risk that the fair value or future cash flows of a financial instrument will fluctuate because of changes in market prices.

2.3.1 Qualitative disclosures

For each type of risk arising from financial instruments, an entity must disclose:

(a)   The **exposures to risk** and how they arise

(b)   Its objectives, policies and processes for managing the risk and the methods used to measure the risk; for example, a company's policy to manage interest rate risk and currency risk might be to use derivatives such as interest rate swaps and currency swaps to hedge against these risks (the use of interest rate swaps and currency swaps is covered in chapter 6)

(c)   Any **changes** in (a) or (b) from the previous period

2.3.2 Quantitative disclosures

For each financial instrument risk, **summary quantitative data** about risk exposure must be disclosed. This should be based on the information provided internally to key management personnel. More information should be provided if this is unrepresentative.

Information about **credit risk** must be disclosed by class of financial instrument:

(a)   Maximum exposure at the year end

(b)   Any collateral pledged as security

(c)   In respect of the amount disclosed in (b), a description of collateral held as security and other credit enhancements

(d)   Information about the credit quality of financial assets that are neither **past due** nor impaired

(e)   Financial assets that are past due or impaired, giving an age analysis and a description of collateral held by the entity as security

(f)   Collateral and other credit enhancements obtained, including the nature and carrying amount of the assets and policy for disposing of assets not readily convertible into cash

For **liquidity risk** entities must disclose:

(a)   A maturity analysis of financial liabilities
(b)   A description of the way risk is managed

Disclosures required in connection with **market risk** are:

(a)   Sensitivity analysis, showing the effects on profit or loss of changes in each market risk
(b)   Additional information if the sensitivity analysis is not representative of the entity's risk exposure

2.4 Capital disclosures

Certain disclosures about **capital** are required. An entity's capital does not relate solely to financial instruments, but has more general relevance. Accordingly, those disclosures are included in IAS 1, rather than in IFRS 7.

Section summary

IFRS 7 specifies the **disclosures** required for financial instruments. The standard requires qualitative and quantitative disclosures about exposure to risks arising from financial instruments and specifies minimum disclosures about credit risk, liquidity risk and market risk.

3   Management commentary

Introduction

Financial statements do not provide a full picture of an organisation's performance. Recent proposals have been put forward for a **Management Commentary** to supplement and complement the financial statements. We will look at this in the section below. In Sections 5 and 6, we will look at **Sustainability Reporting** and **Integrated Reporting**, which supplement financial statements by reporting on non-financial factors such as social and environmental factors, that contribute to an entity's performance.

3.1 Limitations of financial statements

Financial statements do not provide a full picture of an entity's ability to create value. Under International Accounting Standards (IAS), not all 'assets' of a business are recognised on the balance sheet (statement of financial position). For example, human resource assets cannot be recognised in financial statements under IAS 38 *Intangible assets*. However, human capital is an important asset to an organisation in its ability to create value. This limitation is overcome with **Integrated Reporting**, which reports on how an entity creates value over time, particularly from non-financial factors. This is covered in Section 6.

Furthermore, financial statements alone do not provide information on **economic, environmental and social factors** that affect an entity. For example, if a company is involved in projects which give back to communities, this will enhance the reputation of the company. **Sustainability reporting** aims to report on these factors. The Global Reporting Initiative (GRI) provides guidelines on sustainability reporting. This is covered in Section 5.

In addition to these limitations, financial statements alone are not considered sufficient without an **accompanying explanation of the performance**, eg highlighting a restructuring that has reduced profits or

the cost of developing a new business channel in the current period which will generate profits in the future. Financial statements can be enhanced through the adoption of **management commentary**.

3.2 Management commentary

A good management commentary not only talks about the past position and performance, but how this will translate **into future financial position** and performance. It should also address the **risks and issues** facing the organisation that may not be apparent from a review of the financial statements, and how they will be addressed.

In December 2010, the IASB published the practice statement *Management Commentary* which gives a non-binding framework for the presentation of management commentary in financial statements prepared in accordance with IFRS.

3.2.1 Principles for the preparation of a management commentary

Management commentary should follow these principles:

(a)   To provide **management's view** of the entity's performance, position and progress

(b)   To **supplement and complement** information presented in the financial statements

(c)   To include **forward-looking information**

(d)   To include information that possesses the **qualitative characteristics** described in IASB's *Conceptual framework for financial reporting*

3.2.2 Elements of management commentary

While acknowledging that the nature of management commentary would vary between entities, the IASB has provided a table of five essential elements of information that should be included to meet the needs of the primary users of a management commentary (existing and potential investors, lenders and creditors).

Element	User needs
Nature of the business	The knowledge of the business in which an entity is engaged and the external environment in which it operates
Objectives and strategies	To assess the strategies adopted by the entity and the likelihood that those strategies will be successful in meeting management's stated objectives
Resources, risks and relationships	A basis for determining the resources available to the entity as well as obligations to transfer resources to others; the ability of the entity to generate long-term sustainable net inflows of resources; and the risks to which those resource-generating activities are exposed, both in the near term and in the long term
Results and prospects	The ability to understand whether an entity has delivered results in line with expectations and, implicitly, how well management has understood the entity's market, executed its strategy and managed the entity's resources, risks and relationships
Performance measures and indicators	The ability to focus on the critical performance measures and indicators that management uses to assess and manage the entity's performance against stated objectives and strategies

3.2.3 Advantages and disadvantages of management commentary

Advantages	Disadvantages
Entity	**Entity**
• Promotes the entity, ie attracts investors, lenders, customers and suppliers	• Costs of production may outweigh benefits
• Creates an image of transparency and accountability to stakeholders	• If compulsory, could encourage companies to de-list to avoid requirement to produce MC
• Communicates management plans and outlook	• Risk that investors may ignore the financial statements
• Provides an opportunity to explain financial trends and results which might be perceived negatively	
Users	**Users**
• Enables users to make more informed decisions based on a fuller understanding of financial and non-financial information	• Subjective, potential for management to be selective about the information they present
• Provides forward-looking information as well as historical information	• Not normally audited
• Highlights risks	• The lack of specific disclosure requirements reduces comparability with other entities
• Useful for making comparisons with other entities	• Risk of over-reliance on management commentary, to the exclusion of a closer analysis of the financial statements
• Can offer a concise summary of complex information	

Section summary

The **management commentary** supplements the financial statements with forward-looking information about the entity's prospects and risks.

4 Sustainability

Introduction

Pressure is mounting for companies to **widen** their **scope for corporate public accountability**. Many companies are responding by measuring and disclosing their social impacts.

4.1 What is sustainability?

The term **sustainability** is often defined as development that meets the needs of the present without compromising the ability of future generations to meet their own needs.

Sustainable development recognises that without the environment, businesses and society could not exist and that businesses have a **corporate responsibility** to take the needs of their wider stakeholders into account.

Increasingly the concept of corporate responsibility recognises that organisations which consider their **social and environmental impacts**, may end up improving shareholder wealth by having a positive effect on their economic performance.

Examples of **social measures** or issues include: philanthropic donations, employee satisfaction levels and remuneration issues, community support and stakeholder consultation information.

Environmental measures might consider: levels of waste and pollution, use of natural resources, compliance with environmental legislation.

Sustainability reporting often goes beyond environmental and social reporting to include the **economic element** of sustainability (such as wages, taxes and core financial statistics) and involves integrating environmental, social and economic performance data and measures.

4.2 The Global Reporting Initiative (GRI)

The Global Reporting Initiative is an international not-for-profit organisation whose mission is to make sustainability reporting standard practice by providing guidance and support to organisations.

It has pioneered and developed a sustainability reporting framework with the ultimate aim of helping organisations to make their operations more sustainable through the setting of goals, measuring performance and managing change.

4.3 GRI guidelines

The GRI guidelines (updated in May 2013) offer two options to an organisation: the **Core option** and the **Comprehensive option**.

The Core option contains the essential elements of a sustainability report. It provides the background against which an organisation communicates the impacts of its economic, environmental, and social and governance performance.

The Comprehensive option builds on the Core option by requiring additional standard disclosures of the organisation's strategy and analysis, governance, and ethics and integrity. In addition, the organisation is required to communicate its performance more extensively by reporting all indicators related to identified material aspects.

An organisation can choose the option that best enables it to meet its stakeholders' information needs.

4.3.1 Reporting principles

Section 4 of the Guidelines outlines the following principles which define the content of reports:

Stakeholder inclusive – the entity should identify its stakeholders and explain how it responds to their expectations and interests.

Sustainability context – the report should present the organisation's performance in the wider context of sustainability.

Materiality – materiality is the threshold at which aspects become sufficiently important that they should be reported. Relevant topics for inclusion in the report are those that reflect the entities economic, environmental and social impacts, or influence the decision of stakeholders.

Completeness – the report should cover material aspects and their boundaries, in order to reflect significant economic, environmental and social impacts, and to allow stakeholders to assess the entity's performance in the reporting period.

Non-disclosures – in exceptional circumstances, if it is not possible for an entity to disclose certain required information, the report should clearly identify the omitted information and explain why it has been omitted. The following reasons for omission should also be provided:

- A standard disclosure, part of a standard disclosure or an indicator is not applicable – the entity should also explain why it is not applicable.

- The information is subject to confidentiality constraints – the entity should disclose these constraints.

- The existence of legal prohibitions – the entity should disclose these prohibitions.

- The information is currently unavailable – the entity should also disclose the steps being taken to obtain the information and the timeframe for doing so.

Section 4 of the Guidelines also outlines the following principles for defining report quality:

Balance – both positive and negative aspects of an entity's performance should be reported on to enable a reasoned assessment of performance.

Comparability – the entity should report information consistently. Reports should present information in a way that allows stakeholders to analyse changes over time and to compare to other organisations.

Timeliness – entities should report on a regular basis and be timely enough to allow stakeholders to make informed decisions.

Clarity – information should be understandable and accessible.

Reliability – the entity should report information in a way that can be examined and that establishes the quality and materiality of the information.

4.3.2 Standard disclosures

Two different types of disclosures are required per Section 5 of the Guidelines:

- General standard disclosures
- Specific standard disclosures

The general standard disclosures cover seven areas (for both the Core and Comprehensive options). The detail below is for the Core option with *additional disclosures for the Comprehensive option added in italics.*

GRI Report content	Detail of GRI requirements
1 Strategy and analysis	A statement from the most senior decision maker of the organisation about the relevance of sustainability to the organisation and the organisation's strategy for addressing sustainability. *A description of key impacts, risks and opportunities.*
2 Organisational Profile	An overview of the organisational characteristics including the name of the organisation; primary brands, products and services; location of its headquarters; number of and names of countries where it operates; nature of ownership and legal form; markets served; scale (including employee numbers); supply chain; significant changes during the period and commitment to external initiatives.
3 Identified Material Aspects and Boundaries	An overview of the process that the organisation has followed to define the report content, the identified material aspects and their boundaries, and restatements.
4 Stakeholder engagement	An overview of the organisation's stakeholder engagement during the period including a list of stakeholder groups; the basis for identification and selection of stakeholders; the organisation's approach to stakeholder engagement and the key topics and concerns raised through stakeholder engagement.
5 Report profile	An overview of the basic information about the report, the GRI content index and the approach to seeking external assurance, including the reporting period, the date of the most recent report and the reporting cycle (eg annual, biennial).

GRI Report content		Detail of GRI requirements
6	Governance	An overview of the governance structure and composition *including the role of the highest governance body in setting organisation's purpose/values/strategy, in risk management, in sustainability reporting and in evaluating economic, environmental and social performance. The competencies and performance evaluation of this body should also be covered as well as remuneration and incentives.*
7	Ethics and integrity	An overview of the organisations values, principles and norms; *internal and external mechanisms for seeking advice on ethical and lawful behaviour; internal and external mechanisms for reporting concerns about unethical or unlawful behaviour and matters of integrity.*

The **specific standard disclosures** cover two areas:

GRI Report content		Detail of GRI requirements
1	Disclosures on management approach	These disclosures give the organisation an opportunity to explain how the economic, environmental and social impacts related to material aspects are managed. Material aspects are those that reflect the organisation's significant economic, environmental and social impacts; or that substantively influence the assessment and decisions of stakeholders.
		The disclosures provide narrative information on how an organisation identifies, analyses and responds to its actual and potential material economic, environmental and social impacts. They also provide context for the performance reported by indicators.
2	Indicators	Indicators give information on the economic, environmental and social performance or impacts of an organisation related to its material aspects. More detail is provided below.

4.4 Indicators in the GRI framework

GRI structures performance indicators according to a hierarchy of category, aspect and indicator. The indicators are grouped in terms of the three categories of the conventional definition of sustainability – **economic, environmental and social**.

The **economic dimension** concerns the organisation's impact on the economic conditions of its stakeholders and on national and global economic systems, **not** the financial condition of the organisation.

The **environmental dimension** concerns the organisation's impact on living and non-living natural systems including land, air, water and ecosystems.

The **social dimension** concerns the impacts the organisation has on the social systems in which it operates. Within the social category there are a number of sub-categories (set out below).

Entities choosing the **Core option** have to disclose at least one indicator related to each material aspect. **Material aspects** are those relating to the organisation's **significant** economic, environmental and social impacts.

Entities choosing the **Comprehensive option** have to disclose all indicators related to each identified material aspect.

The categories and aspects are listed below:

	Category	Aspects
Economic	**Economic**	• Economic performance • Market presence • Indirect economic impacts • Procurement practices
Environmental	**Environmental**	• Materials • Energy • Water • Biodiversity • Emissions • Effluents and waste • Products and services • Compliance • Transport • Overall • Supplier environmental assessment • Environmental grievance mechanisms
Social	**Labour practices and decent work**	• Employment • Labour and management relations • Occupational health and safety • Training and education • Diversity and equal opportunity • Equal remuneration for women and men • Supplier assessment for labour practices • Labour practices grievance mechanisms
	Human rights	• Investment • Non-discrimination • Freedom of association and collective bargaining • Child labour • Forced or compulsory labour • Security practices • Indigenous rights • Assessment • Supplier human rights assessment • Human rights grievance mechanisms
	Society	• Local communities • Anti-corruption • Public policy • Anti-competitive behaviour • Compliance • Supplier assessment for impacts on society • Grievance mechanisms for impacts on society
	Product responsibility	• Customer health and safety • Product and service labelling • Marketing communications • Customer privacy • Compliance

For each aspect, the GRI set out indicators that can be used to report an organisation's performance in that area. For example:

Economic: Market presence – percentage of senior management at significant locations hired from local community

Environmental: Energy – total fuel consumption from non-renewable resources; reduction in energy consumption achieved as a result of efficiency initiatives

Social: Training and education – average hours of training employees have undertaken during the reporting period by gender and employee category

4.4.1 Impact of revised guidelines

The GRI published **revised guidelines, the G4 Sustainability Guidelines,** in May 2013.

The guidelines are available at the GRI website, www.globalreporting.org.

The revised guidelines (which have been described in Sections 4.2 – 4.4) placed more emphasis on **focussing** on aspects that are material. This requires an organisation to explain their process for establishing which aspects are material, and may result in shorter sustainability reports.

Companies must now disclose how they manage economic, environmental and social issues in their **supply chain**.

New disclosure requirements have been introduced in relation to **governance and ethics** eg the number and nature of critical concerns communicated to the highest governance body, and the ratio of the pay of the highest paid individual to the median employee.

4.5 Criticism of GRI

The GRI framework has been criticised by some businesses for being burdensome and costly. It has also been criticised by environmental campaigners for failing to define what norms of environmental behaviour are actually required for an organisation's impacts to be regarded as sustainable.

CASE STUDY

PUMA, the sportswear company, was among the pioneers of sustainability reporting. Included in its key sustainability targets are the following (source: Puma AG annual report, 2015):

Social Target

Factory audits are used to ensure that PUMA's suppliers comply with PUMA's Code of Conduct. PUMA aim for 90% of their PUMA's suppliers to receive an audit rating of A or B+ by 2015 (PUMA uses an A, B+, B-, C and D grading criteria to rate performance).

Environmental Targets

Targets for PUMA (offices, stores and warehouses) and their key suppliers include:

- Electricity consumption
- Consumption of natural gas
- Consumption of fuel for company cars
- Water consumption
- Paper consumption
- % waste that is recycled, and % of cardboard that is from recycled sources

---

Section summary

Make sure you understand the influence of the GRI Sustainability Reporting Guidelines.

5 Integrated reporting

Introduction

Integrated reporting aims to combine financial, environmental, social and governance reporting in a single report.

5.1 Definition of an integrated report

'An integrated report is a concise communication about how an organisation's strategy, governance, performance and prospects, in the context of its external environment, lead to the creation of value in the short, medium and long term.'

Source: International Integrated Reporting Council, www.theiirc.org

The International Integrated Reporting Council (IIRC) is a global coalition of regulators, investors, companies, standard setters, and the accounting profession. They share the view that communication about value creation should be the next step in the evolution of corporate reporting. Although integrated reporting does give prominence to sustainability issues, the focus is often more on helping investors to make **financial decisions**.

Integrated reporting aims to address the limitations of financial statements in assessing how the value of an organisation is affected by its interaction with its external environment and society over time.

Financial statements do not provide a full picture of an organisation's performance, as they do not fully reflect the value and stewardship of its non-financial capital base. This is the non-financial resources and relationships used and affected by an organisation to create value over time, referred to as 'capitals'.

For example, as mentioned in Section 3, human resource assets cannot be recognised in financial statements under IAS 38 *Intangible Assets*. However, human capital is an important asset to an organisation in its ability to create value and integrated reporting allows a company to report this.

5.2 Categories of capitals

The integrated reporting framework classifies capitals, both financial and non-financial, as:

Capital	Comment
Financial capital	The pool of funds that is: • Available to an organisation for use in the production of goods or the provision of services • Obtained through financing, such as debt, equity or grants, or generated through operations or investments
Manufactured capital	Manufactured physical objects (as distinct from natural physical objects) that are available to an organisation for use in the production of goods or the provision of services, including: • Buildings • Equipment • Infrastructure (such as roads, ports, bridges and waste and water treatment plants) Manufactured capital is often created by other organisations, but includes assets manufactured by the reporting organisation for sale or when they are retained for its own use.

Capital	Comment
Intellectual capital	Organisational knowledge-based intangibles, including: • Intellectual property, such as patents, copyrights, software, rights and licences • 'Organisational capital' such as tacit knowledge, systems, procedures and protocols
Human capital	People's competencies, capabilities and experience, and their motivations to innovate, including their: • Alignment with and support for an organisations governance framework, risk management approach and ethical values • Ability to understand, develop and implement an organisation's strategy • Loyalties and motivations for improving processes, goods and services, including their ability to lead, manage and collaborate
Natural capital	All renewable and non-renewable environmental resources and processes that provide goods and services that support the past, current or future prosperity of an organisation. It includes: • Air, water, land, minerals and forests • Biodiversity and ecosystem health
Social and relationship capital	The institutions and the relationships within and between communities, groups of stakeholders and other networks, and the ability to share information to enhance individual and collective wellbeing. Social and relationship capital includes: • Shared norms and common values and behaviours • Key stakeholder relationships and the trust and willingness to engage that an organisation developed and strives to build and protect with external stakeholders • Intangibles associated with the brand and reputation that an organisation has developed • An organisations social licence to operate

Source: International Integrated Reporting Council, www.theiirc.org

These categories of capital are not mandatory for integrated reporting, and an organisation can choose to report only on capitals felt to be most relevant in communicating performance. Key performance indicators are effective in communicating performance.

Integrated reporting should not only show how value is created but how value is lost through capitals. Best practice in integrated reporting requires organisations to report on both positive and negative movements in capital.

Integrated reporting is not aimed at attaching a monetary value to every aspect of an organisation's operations; rather, it is fundamentally concerned with evaluating value creation through the communication of qualitative and quantitative performance measures.

Capitals continually interact with one another. An increase in one capital can decrease another. For example, a decision to purchase a new IT system would improve an organisation's manufactured capital while decreasing its financial capital in the form of its cash reserves.

CASE STUDY

Marks and Spencer describe their approach to delivering long-term value in terms of a sustainable value creation model based on six key resources and relationships:

- generating stakeholder returns through effective management of **financial resources**

- **manufactured resources**: maintaining supply chain infrastructure

- creation and protection of **intellectual properties**: to strengthen their core brand

- **human resources**: developing people and their knowledge

- **natural resources**: sourcing responsibly and using natural resources efficiently

- **social & relationship**: building relationships with customers and suppliers and in the communities in which they operate

(Source: delivering plan A, M&S website, 2016)

5.3 Guiding principles and content of an integrated report

The International Integrated Reporting Council (IIRC) provides the following framework of guiding principles and content elements in the preparation of an integrated report. This is available from its website:

www.theiirc.org

GUIDING PRINCIPLES

The following guiding principles underpin the preparation of an integrated report, informing the content of the report and how information is presented:

- Strategic focus and future orientation: an integrated report should provide insight into the organisation's strategy, and how it relates to the organisation's ability to create value in the short, medium and long term, and to its use of and effects on the capitals.

- Connectivity of information: an integrated report should show a holistic picture of the combination, interrelatedness and dependencies between the factors that affect the organisation's ability to create value over time.

- Stakeholder relationships: an integrated report should provide insight into the nature and quality of the organisation's relationships with its key stakeholders, including how and to what extent the organisation understands, takes into account and responds to their legitimate needs and interests.

- Materiality: an integrated report should disclose information about matters that substantively affect the organisation's ability to create value over the short, medium and long term.

- Conciseness: an integrated report should be concise.

- Reliability and completeness: an integrated report should include all material matters, both positive and negative, in a balanced way and without material error.

- Consistency and comparability: the information in an integrated report should be presented: (a) on a basis that is consistent over time; and (b) in a way that enables comparison with other organisations to the extent it is material to the organisation's own ability to create value over time.

CONTENT ELEMENTS

An integrated report includes eight Content Elements that are fundamentally linked to each other and are not mutually exclusive:

- Organisational overview and external environment: what does the organisation do and what are the circumstances under which it operates?

- Governance: how does the organisation's governance structure support its ability to create value in the short, medium and long term?

- Business model: what is the organisation's business model?

- Risks and opportunities: what are the specific risks and opportunities that affect the organisation's ability to create value over the short, medium and long term, and how is the organisation dealing with them?

- Strategy and resource allocation: where does the organisation want to go and how does it intend to get there?

- Performance: to what extent has the organisation achieved its strategic objectives for the period and what are its outcomes in terms of effects on the capitals?

- Outlook: what challenges and uncertainties is the organisation likely to encounter in pursuing its strategy, and what are the potential implications for its business model and future performance?

- Basis of presentation: how does the organisation determine what matters to include in the integrated report and how are such matters quantified or evaluated?

Exam skills

Sustainability and integrated reporting are current important topics in the business world. These could be areas to come up in the integrated case study. A question may require you to discuss how reporting such as sustainability and integrated reporting have advantages over traditional financial statements in informing stakeholders of a company's interaction with society and the environment. It will be helpful to look at recent real life sustainability and integrated reports.

5.4 Examples of companies adopting integrated reporting

Adoption of integrated reporting is voluntary. However, in South Africa, listed companies are required to submit integrated reports on a comply or explain basis.

CASE STUDY

Case study: Woolworths Holdings Ltd (WHL)

Have a look at the integrated report for the Woolworths Holdings Limited (WHL), a South African-based group of retail companies in the food and clothing sectors. This is available at the following URL:

www.woolworthsholdings.co.za/investor/annual_reports/ar2013/WHL_IR_2013.pdf?v=1.1

(accessed on 11 March 2015)

The intentions of the report are made clear at the outset:

'This report provides a holistic view of our group's business, strategy and performance for the year, including highlights from our Good Business Journey that pertain to particular business operational segments. We also set out our governance structures and remuneration philosophy'.

Key elements from WHL's integrated report

Business model

The following extract shows the group's business model and how they add value:

OUR BUSINESS MODEL AND HOW WE ADD VALUE

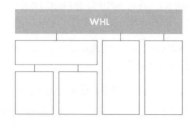

WHL GROUP

RETAIL PRESENCE

Extensive store footprint

Combination of store formats in addition to online offerings aimed at customer convenience

Focused expansion strategies in place

Developing presence in selected African countries

TRUSTED BRANDS

Key focus on quality and innovation through strong and well-defined premium private label brands

Leader in ethical, sustainable and environmentally aware sourcing

FINANCIAL PERFORMANCE

A 10-year compounded growth rate:

- HEPS + 18.7%
- Dividend payout + 23.2%

A 10-year annual growth in shareholder return of 34%

Return on equity of 50.7% is the result of strong focus on growth, profitability, asset management and the ability to maintain strong cash flows

BUSINESS RESILIENCE

Defensive food and clothing product mix and rand hedge through geographic spread

Opportunities to further penetrate market segments

GOVERNANCE

Board with strong commitment to governance, deep experience in global industries and key focus on King III

Values-driven business integrated into employee performance management system

Included in the JSE SRI Index as well as the Dow Jones World Sustainability Index

The WHL Group aims to create value by growing sales through differentiation, improving profitability and being a good business. We believe that this aim is supported by key strengths, which enable us to deliver on our vision:

TO BE A WORLD LEADER IN RETAIL BRANDS THAT APPEAL TO PEOPLE WHO CARE ABOUT QUALITY, INNOVATION AND SUSTAINABILITY.

Strategic focus and risk

The following extract reports on the performance of the group in achieving one of its strategic objectives, to become an omnichannel business. It also reports on the risk of not achieving this objective and how the group is dealing with this risk:

BECOME AN OMNI-CHANNEL BUSINESS

STRATEGIC IMPERATIVE

Internationally, retailers are striving to achieve a seamless customer experience between stores and online, an omni-channel experience. Mobile devices are increasingly the favoured way to access the internet, a trend apparent in South Africa and in the developed world.

In Australia, online shopping has taken an enormous leap forward and now represents 7% of retail sales. All four Country Road brands are available online and sales are growing quickly.

While South African online retail sales are still a way off the levels seen in the UK, US and Australia, online spend is growing and investment in new online offerings continues unabated. Woolworths online comprises predominantly food sales – however, Clothing and General merchandise are growing rapidly.

Our omni-channel vision is to offer any WHL Group product or service at a time and place convenient to the customer – regardless of channel. We want to

grow loyalty to our brands and enrich our relationships with customers through a seamless experience. Our investment in this objective is measured and focused on consistency, optimising our offering and seeking efficiencies as we scale the business.

Key success factors in achieving this are our website, mobile compatibility of all our communication, nationwide delivery and single customer sign-on abilities.

OBJECTIVES	ACHIEVEMENTS
Create a simple, consistent user experience	The refreshed Woolworths website was launched in July 2013. Responsive design allows for customer access on all electronic mobile devices
Improve our fulfilment and reach	Established the order fulfilment processes to ensure excellent customer service and greater efficiency
Optimise products and services	Integration of online into merchandise cycle timelines

RISK	MITIGATION
Technology advances require substantial investment	We continue to monitor developments both locally and abroad to ensure that if there are substantial shifts in the way technology is being used, we are well positioned to react to these changes and offer a service that is market leading

Value creation

In addition to the traditional reporting of financial performance the report also details those capitals regarded as being important in creating value over the long term.

The following extract shows how human capital or 'people' create value over time:

SOCIAL SUSTAINABILITY

People are at the core of the WHL Group and create value for stakeholders through the application of their skills, competencies, knowledge and experience – thereby delivering products and services according to the WHL Group's long-term strategy.

Our strategic intent is to establish and drive an employment value proposition (EVP) that will continue to attract, engage and retain the best, diverse talent.

PEOPLE ARE AT THE CORE OF THE WHL GROUP AND CREATE VALUE FOR STAKEHOLDERS

People management at Woolworths focuses on the following:

* Attract, develop and retain talent
* Create a future fit business
* Continue our commitment to diversity
* Build a high-performance culture
* Create a values-based culture

We boast a wide range of in-house and external training and development programmes that are designed to help employees deliver our business strategies, foster talent and equip our employees with vital skills and experience.

We are deeply committed to transformation and extend opportunities to learners from disadvantaged backgrounds. There was a significant increase in the number of unemployed graduates that were offered workplace experience across our business, the total number of tertiary students that were offered the opportunity to complete their practicals with us and the total number of unemployed South Africans that were offered bursaries.

During 2013, we also partnered with Western Cape-based FET college lecturers to expose them to the retail industry to create an understanding of the skills required by our sector.

Country Road Group is committed to attracting, developing and retaining an inspired, high performance workforce and providing a safe and healthy workplace.

Fig 18: Our employee demographics

	2013	2012
Total employees WHL Group	26 955	27 053
Total Woolworths	23 585	25 693
Total Country Road	3 370	1 360
Woolworths % male	34.5%	34.5%
Woolworths % female	65.5%	65.5%
Woolworths % with disabilities	1.79%	1.83%
Woolworths health and safety – number of injuries on duty	682	778

Fig 19: Woolworths Key social indicators

	2013	2012
Overall BEE level	Level 3 80.45	Level 2 72.93
Equity ownership	7.63	7.89
Management control	9.75	9.7
Employment equity	10.87	12.32
Skills development	13.21	11.00
Preferential procurement	18.99	14.62
Enterprise development	15	12.4
Socio-economic development	5	5
Total CSI contribution	R500.1m	R438m
Surplus product distributed	R448m	R393m
MySchool contribution	R41m	R35m
No of employees trained	24 531	22 538

The extracts in this case study are from *Woolworths Holdings Limited 2013 Integrated Report*. Copyright © 2014 by Woolworths. Reprinted by permission of Woolworths.

Question 3.1   Integrated reporting

Learning outcome: A(1)(c)

Discuss what is meant by 'integrated reporting', highlighting how it differs from traditional performance reporting.

Section summary

Integrated reporting allows stakeholders to see the bigger picture of an organisation's value over time, in the context of its external environment, which financial statements alone do not show.

Chapter Summary

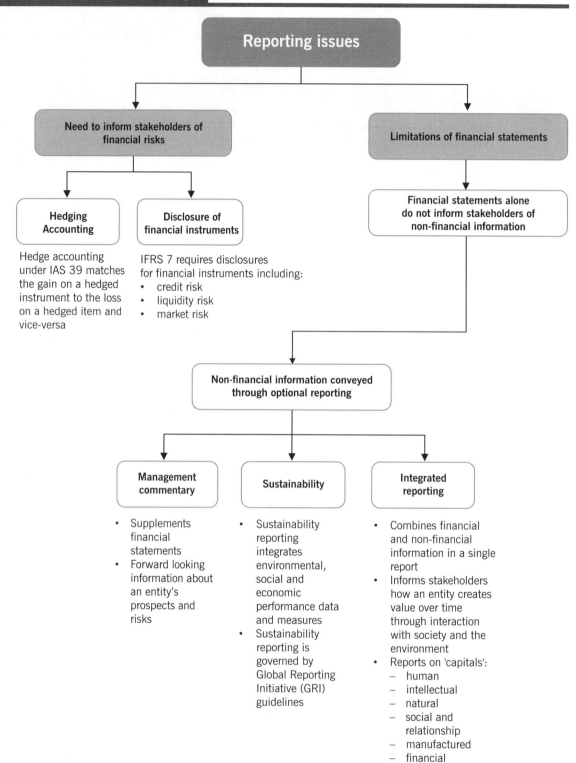

Reporting issues

Need to inform stakeholders of financial risks

Limitations of financial statements

Hedging Accounting

Disclosure of financial instruments

Financial statements alone do not inform stakeholders of non-financial information

Hedge accounting under IAS 39 matches the gain on a hedged instrument to the loss on a hedged item and vice-versa

IFRS 7 requires disclosures for financial instruments including:
- credit risk
- liquidity risk
- market risk

Non-financial information conveyed through optional reporting

Management commentary

Sustainability

Integrated reporting

- Supplements financial statements
- Forward looking information about an entity's prospects and risks

- Sustainability reporting integrates environmental, social and economic performance data and measures
- Sustainability reporting is governed by Global Reporting Initiative (GRI) guidelines

- Combines financial and non-financial information in a single report
- Informs stakeholders how an entity creates value over time through interaction with society and the environment
- Reports on 'capitals':
  - human
  - intellectual
  - natural
  - social and relationship
  - manufactured
  - financial

Quick Quiz

1   What is hedging?

2   Name the three types of hedging relationship identified by IAS 39.

3   What objectives might a company have in relation to wider society?

4   An entity is preparing a sustainability report under GRI Guidelines and is unable to report on a piece of required information for legal reasons. What should the company disclose in relation to the omitted information?

5   What is an integrated report?

6   State three non-financial capitals that might be reported on in an integrated report.

Answers to Quick Quiz

1   Hedging, for accounting purposes, means designating one or more hedging instruments so that their change in fair value is an offset, in whole or in part, to the change in fair value or cash flows of a hedged item.

2   Fair value hedge; cash flow hedge; hedge of a net investment in a foreign operation

3   Contingent liabilities   Management commentary or Operating and financial review comments
    Exceptional charges   Profit and capital expenditure forecasts

4   The entity should clearly identify the omitted information and explain why it has been omitted. The entity should also state that the information was omitted due to legal prohibitions and state what the prohibitions are.

5   A concise communication about how an organisation's strategy, governance, performance and prospects, in the context of its external environment, lead to the creation of value in the short, medium and long term.

6   Any three of:

    Human capital

    Intellectual capital

    Natural capital

    Social and relationship capital

    Manufactured capital

Answers to Questions

3.1 Integrated reporting

Wider performance appraisal

Integrated reporting is concerned with conveying a wider message on an entity's performance. It is not solely centred on profit and the company's financial position but aims to focus on how the organisation's activities interact to create value over the short, medium and long term. It is thought that by producing a holistic view of organisational performance that this will lead to improved management decision making as business decisions are not taken in isolation.

Value creation

In the context of integrated reporting an organisation's resources are referred to as 'capitals'. The International Integrated Reporting Council have identified six capitals which can be used to assess value creation. Increases or decreases in these capitals indicate the level of value created or lost over a period. Capitals cover various types of resources found in a standard organisation. These may include financial capitals, such as the entity's financial reserves, through to its intellectual capital which is concerned with intellectual property and staff knowledge.

Performance evaluation of the six capitals is central to integrated reporting. Throughout time these capitals continually interact with one another, an increase in one may lead to a decrease in another. A decision to purchase a new IT system would improve an entity's 'manufactured' capital while decreasing its financial capital. By contrast the decision to purchase a patent for a new production technology would increase intellectual capital and may also boost financial capital if it reduces costs and increases output. It is important to note that due to the voluntary nature of integrated reporting, organisations are free to report only on those 'capitals' felt to be most relevant.

Short term v long term

In many ways, integrated reporting forces management to balance its short-term objectives against its longer term plans. Business decisions which are solely dedicated to the pursuit of increasing profit (financial capital) at the expense of building good relations with key stakeholders such as customers (social capital) are likely to hinder value creation in the longer term.

Performance measures

Integrated reporting is not aimed at attaching a monetary value to every aspect of the organisation's operations. It is fundamentally concerned with evaluating value creation, and uses qualitative and quantitative performance measures to help stakeholders assess how well an organisation is creating value.

The use of KPIs to convey performance is an effective way of reporting. For example when providing detail on customer satisfaction, this can be communicated as the number of customers retained compared to the previous year. Best practice in integrated reporting requires organisations to report on both positive and negative movements in 'capital'. This ensures the entity's performance is fully communicated and not just those favourable movements. Stakeholders are likely to be as interested (if not more so) in understanding what an organisation has not done well as opposed to only considering the entity's achievements. Integrated reporting ensures that a balanced view of performance is presented.

Now try the questions from the Practice Question Bank	**Question** Section A: 3.1 – 3.5	**Level** Practice

FINANCING AND DIVIDEND DECISIONS

Part B

DIVIDEND POLICY

The dividend decision is an important decision for financial managers. You should be able to **recommend alternative dividend policies** for an organisation.

Dividend policy is a key element in overall financial strategy. In this chapter we consider dividend policy in depth, in particular whether the amounts of profits that a company distributes has much or little impact on shareholders.

Topic list	learning outcomes	syllabus references	ability required
1 Dividend policy	B(2)(b)	B(2)(b)(i)	evaluation
2 Theories of dividend policy	B(2)(b)	B(2)(b)(ii)	evaluation
3 Scrip dividends	B(2)(a)	B(2)(a)(i),(ii)	evaluation
4 Share repurchase	B(2)(a)	B(2)(a)(i),(ii)	evaluation

Chapter Overview

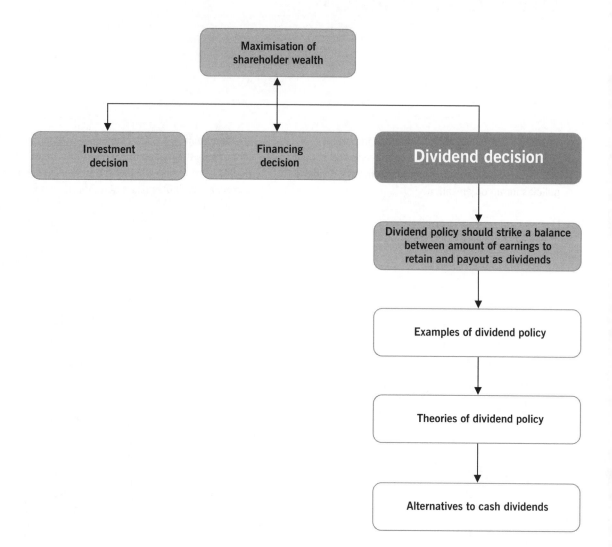

1   Dividend policy

Introduction

In Chapter 2, we identified the three main types of decisions facing financial managers – investment decisions, financing decisions and dividend decisions. In this section we are going to look in more detail at the dividend decision.

KEY TERM

A DIVIDEND is a distribution of profits to the holders of equity investments in proportion to their holdings of a particular class of capital.   *(CIMA Official Terminology)*

1.1 Dividend payments

Shareholders normally have the power to vote to **reduce** the size of the dividend at the AGM, but not the power to **increase** the dividend. The directors of the company are therefore in a strong position, with regard to shareholders, when it comes to determining dividend policy. For practical purposes, shareholders will usually be obliged to accept the dividend policy that has been decided on by the directors, or otherwise to sell their shares.

1.2 Dividend payout policy

Senior management have to decide on a suitable payout policy that reflects the **expectations** and **preferences** of investors.

The focus of all financial management decisions should be on the **primary objectives** of the company. If shareholders expect dividends to be paid, then senior management must balance the dividend payment and retention policies to meet these expectations while ensuring sufficient funds are available to finance profitable investment opportunities and fulfil the objective of maximising shareholder value.

You will often find that shareholders in a particular company have **similar expectations** and preferences regarding dividends. Those investing in a company that is not paying dividends will not be expecting dividends (or actually want them) whereas other investors expect dividends and newer shareholders may have purchased shares with this expectation in mind. The attraction of particular types of investors to particular companies because of their policies (such as dividend policy) is known as the **clientele effect**. Companies should have a consistent dividend policy in order to meet the expectations of their shareholders.

1.3 Factors influencing dividend policy

In Chapter 2, we looked at the interaction between the investment, financing and investment decisions. The amount of surplus cash paid out as dividends will have a **direct impact** on **finance available for investment**.

When deciding upon the dividends to pay out to shareholders, one of the main considerations of the directors will be the amount of earnings they wish to retain to meet **financing needs**.

Question 4.1   Retained earnings

Learning outcome: B(2)(b)

What are the major reasons for using the cash from retained earnings to finance new investments, rather than to pay higher dividends and then raise new equity funds for the new investments?

As well as future financing requirements, the decision on how much of a company's profits should be retained, and how much paid out to shareholders, will be influenced by:

(a)   The **need to remain profitable** (dividends are paid out of profits, and an unprofitable company cannot for ever go on paying dividends out of retained profits made in the past)

(b)   The **law on distributable profits**

(c)   Any **dividend restraints** that might be imposed by debt covenants in loan agreements

(d)   The **effect of inflation**, and the need to retain some profit within the business just to maintain its operating capability unchanged

(e)   The company's **gearing level** (if the company wants extra finance, the sources of funds used should strike a balance between equity and debt finance)

(f)   The company's **liquidity position** (dividends are a cash payment, and a company must have enough cash to pay the dividends it declares)

(g)   The need to **repay debt** in the near future

(h)   The ease with which the company could raise **extra finance** from sources other than retained earnings (see below re life cycle issues)

(i)   The **signalling effect** of dividends to shareholders and the financial markets in general (see below)

1.4 Examples of dividend policies

Possible dividend policies include:

- **Stable:** this is a constant annual dividend payment, or a dividend payment that increases at a constant rate each year **(constant growth).**

- **Constant percentage of annual earnings:** a constant percentage of earnings is paid out each year.

- **Special or extra dividend**: a one-off dividend is paid outside of normal dividend distributions, usually arising from exceptional earnings.

- **Residual:** dividend payments come out of the residual or leftover equity only after investment opportunities have been exhausted.

- **Zero:** no dividends are paid. Instead, profits are re-invested profits in the business. This is common in high growth technology companies.

- **Ratchet:** this is a form of stable dividend policy with an increasing dividend per share.

1.5 Life cycle issues

Young companies usually have a **residual** dividend policy which means they choose to rely on internally generated equity to finance any new projects. As a result, dividend payments can come out of the residual or leftover equity only after all project capital requirements are met; therefore, dividends are **rarely paid**.

Mature companies usually have a **stable growth** dividend policy. They have less need to invest in new projects and investments can and should be financed by **debt.**

1.6 Dividends as a signal to investors

The ultimate objective in any financial management decisions is to **maximise shareholders' wealth**. This wealth is basically represented by the **current market value** of the company, which should largely be determined by the **cash flows arising from the investment decisions** taken by management.

Although the market would **like** to value shares on the basis of underlying cash flows on the company's projects, such information is **not readily available to investors**. But the directors do have this information.

The dividend declared can be interpreted as a **signal** from directors to shareholders about the strength of underlying project cash flows.

Investors usually expect a **consistent dividend policy** from the company, with stable dividends each year or, even better, **steady dividend growth**. A large rise or fall in dividends in any year can have a marked effect on the company's share price. Stable dividends or steady dividend growth are usually needed for share price stability. A cut in dividends may be treated by investors as signalling that the future prospects of the company are weak. Thus, the dividend which is paid acts, possibly without justification, as a **signal** of the future prospects of the company.

The signalling effect of a company's dividend policy may also be used by management of a company which faces a possible **takeover**. The dividend level might be increased as a defence against the takeover: investors may take the increased dividend as a signal of improved future prospects, thus driving the share price higher and making the company more expensive for a potential bidder to take over.

1.7 Clientele effect

Another advantage of a **consistent dividend policy** is that shareholders will be attracted by the type of dividend policy that they prefer (whether this is a high dividend or a low dividend intended to create capital gain). If a company pursues a **consistent dividend policy**, it will attract a clientele of shareholders that prefer that type of dividend policy; this is often called the **clientele effect**. It is therefore difficult for a company to change its policy without alienating its shareholders.

Exam skills

You should show, whenever relevant in exam answers, that you appreciate the signalling effect of dividends. However, it won't be relevant for a private company.

Section summary

- **Retained earnings** are the most important single source of finance for companies, and financial managers should take account of the proportion of earnings that are retained as opposed to being paid as dividends.

- Companies generally **smooth out dividend payments** by adjusting only gradually to changes in earnings: large fluctuations might **undermine investors' confidence**.

- The dividends a company pays may be treated as a **signal** to investors. A company needs to take account of different **clientele** of shareholders in deciding what dividends to pay.

2 Theories of dividend policy

Introduction

In this section, we look at Modigliani and Miller's irrelevance theory, to examine the effect dividend policy has on shareholder wealth.

2.1 Irrelevance theory

Modigliani and Miller (MM) proposed that in a tax-free world, shareholders are **indifferent** between dividends and capital gains, and the value of a company is determined solely by the 'earning power' of its assets and investments. This is sometimes referred to as **dividend irrelevancy theory** (Modigliani & Miller, 1961).

MM argued that if a company with attractive investment opportunities **decides to pay a dividend**, so that it requires external finance to fund some or all of its investments, the shortfall in funds will be made up by **obtaining additional funds** from outside sources. As a result of obtaining outside finance there will be a loss in the value of the firm to the original shareholders. The loss in value will be equal to the amount of dividend paid, so shareholders have not lost out overall.

Alternatively, if the dividend policy is cut to finance attractive (+NPV) projects, then **this does not matter** to shareholders because if shareholders do require cash, they can **manufacture dividends** by selling shares (which will have risen in value because of the investment). The increase in the value of the shares compensates for the loss of dividend.

So, according to this theory, dividend policy is irrelevant to shareholders.

2.1.1 Assumptions of MM dividend irrelevancy theory

MM make a number of assumptions:

(a)   **No taxes exist** (corporate or personal).

(b)   **Capital markets are perfectly efficient:** for example, funds will always be made available to finance attractive (ie + net present value) investments.

(c)   There are **no transactions costs:** for example, in issuing new shares, or taking out a bank loan, or selling shares.

(d)   All **information is fully and freely available** to shareholders.

2.2 The case in favour of the relevance of dividend policy (and against MM's views)

There are strong arguments **against** MM's view that dividend policy is irrelevant as a means of affecting shareholder's wealth. These reflect the unrealistic nature of the assumptions in MM dividend irrelevancy theory (see section 2.1.1).

(a)   **Impact of taxation**

     Differing rates of **taxation** on **dividends** and **capital gains** can create a **preference** for either a **high dividend** or one for **high earnings retention**. This is of the key reasons why different clientele are attracted by different dividend policies (see **clientele effect** section 1.7).

(b)   **Capital markets are not perfectly efficient**

     Companies may find that funds are **not** always available to finance attractive investments. Where capital rationing is an issue, **dividend retention** may be **preferred** by companies.

(c)   **Impact of transactions costs**

Because of **transaction costs** on the sale of shares, investors who want some cash from their investments will prefer to receive **dividends** rather than to sell some of their shares to get the cash they want.

(d)   **Imperfect information**

If markets are do not price shares accurately, based on all available information, then shareholders may face a possible difficulty in selling shares easily at a fair price (to manufacture a dividend), in this case shareholders might need **dividends** in order to have funds to **invest** in **opportunities** outside the company.

Shareholders are often not fully aware of the **future investment plans** and **expected profits** of their company. Even if management were to provide them with profit forecasts, these forecasts would not necessarily be accurate or believable unless backed up with a signal of confidence in the form of a rising dividend (see section 1.6). So shareholders may prefer a current dividend to future capital gains (or deferred dividends) because the future is more uncertain. This is known as the **bird-in-the-hand** theory.

Exam skills

For the integrated case study, even if you accept that dividend policy may have some influence on share values, there may be other, more important, influences. Don't be tempted to regurgitate chunks of theory in the exam; you must focus on the entities involved.

| Question 4.2 | Dividend policy |

Learning outcome: B(2)(b)

Ochre is a company that is still managed by the two individuals who set it up 12 years ago. In the current year the company was launched on the stock market. Previously, all of the shares had been owned by its two founders and certain employees. Now, 40% of the shares are in the hands of the investing public. The company's profit growth and dividend policy are set out below. Will a continuation of the same dividend policy as in the past be suitable now that the company is quoted on the stock market?

Year	Profits	Dividend	Shares in issue
	£'000	£'000	
4 years ago	176	88	800,000
3 years ago	200	104	800,000
2 years ago	240	120	1,000,000
1 year ago	290	150	1,000,000
Current year	444	222 (proposed)	1,500,000

Section summary

- Modigliani and Miller's (MM) **irrelevance theory** proposes that in a tax-free world, dividend policy is irrelevant to shareholder wealth, however there are strong arguments against this theory.

3 Scrip dividends

Introduction

In this section we look at scrip dividends as an alternative to cash dividends, their advantages and disadvantages, and their impact on shareholder wealth.

KEY TERM

SCRIP DIVIDEND is a dividend paid by the issue of additional company shares, rather than by cash.

(CIMA Official Terminology)

A scrip dividend effectively converts retained earnings into **issued share capital**. When the directors of a company would prefer to retain funds within the business but consider that they must pay at least a certain amount of dividend, they might offer equity shareholders the choice of a **cash dividend** or a **scrip dividend**. Each shareholder would decide separately which to take.

3.1 Advantages of scrip dividends

(a) They can **preserve** a company's **cash position** if a substantial number of shareholders take up the share option.

(b) Investors may be able to obtain **tax advantages** if dividends are in the form of shares.

(c) Investors looking to **expand their holding** can do so **without incurring** the **transaction costs** of buying more shares.

(d) A small scrip issue will **not dilute the share price significantly.** If however cash is not offered as an alternative, empirical evidence suggests that the share price will tend to fall.

3.2 Disadvantages of scrip dividends

(a) Assuming that dividend per share is maintained or increased, the total cash required to pay future dividends will increase.

(b) Scrip dividends may be seen as a negative signal by the market ie the company is experiencing cash flow issues.

(c) Scrip dividends incur more administrative costs than paying no dividend at all.

(d) By converting retained earnings to share capital, reserves are moved from distributable to non-distributable, reducing the reserves available for distribution at a future date.

Example: Scrip dividends

Mongoose plc has 100,000 ordinary shares in issue. Assume that today's market price is £1.10 per share.

Evaluate the effect of the following dividend policies on the value of Mongoose plc, and the wealth of a shareholder with 1,000 shares.

(1) Pay a cash dividend of 10p per share.
(2) Issue a scrip dividend giving shareholders 1 new share for every 10 held.

Solution

(1)

Value of Mongoose plc before cash dividend	= 100,000 × £1.10	= £110,000
Less: cash dividend paid	= 100,000 × £0.10	= (£10,000)
Value of Mongoose plc after cash dividend	=	= £100,000
Share price after cash dividend	= £100.000 ÷ 100,000	= £1.00

Shareholder wealth before cash dividend	= 1,000 × £1.10	=	£1,100
Shareholder wealth after cash dividend:			
shares	= 1,000 × £1.00	=	£1,000
cash received	= 1,000 × £0.10	=	£100
		=	£1,100

Shareholder wealth is the same before and after the cash dividend. This supports the Modigliani and Miller irrelevance theory of dividend policy.

(2)

Value of Mongoose plc	= 100,000 × £1.10	= £110,000
New shares issued	= 10,000	
Value of Mongoose plc after share issue	=	= £110,000
(total value is unchanged, since no cash is paid out)		
Share price after share issue	= £110.000 ÷ 110,000	= £1.00
Shareholder wealth before share issue	= 1,000 × £1.10	= £1,100
New shares received (1 for every 10 held)	= 100	
Shareholder wealth after share issue	= 1,100 × £1.00	= £1,100

Shareholders should be indifferent between no dividend, a cash dividend and a scrip dividend (dividend policy irrelevance). The entity value of Mongoose plc is reduced by £10,000 if it pays a cash dividend, but will remain unchanged if it pays no dividend, or issues a scrip dividend.

Section summary

- **Scrip dividends** are dividends in the form of issue of additional shares rather than cash.

- **Advantages** of scrip dividends include:

    - preserving a company's cash position
    - decreasing its gearing which can enhance its borrowing capacity

- **Disadvantages** of scrip dividends include:

    - higher future dividend payments if dividends per share is to be maintained
    - an indication that the company may have cash issues

4 Share repurchase

Introduction

In this section we look at **share repurchases** (also known as **share buybacks**) as an alternative to dividends, their advantages and disadvantages, and their impact on shareholder wealth.

In many countries companies have the right to **buy back shares from shareholders** who are willing to sell them, subject to certain conditions.

For a **smaller company** with few shareholders, the reason for buying back the company's own shares may be that there is no immediate willing purchaser at a time when a shareholder wishes to sell shares.

For a **public company**, share repurchase could provide a way of withdrawing from the share market and 'going private'.

4.1 Benefits of a share repurchase scheme

(a)   It finds a **use for surplus cash**, which may be a 'dead asset'.

(b)   **It increases earnings per share** through a reduction in the number of shares in issue. This should lead to a higher share price than would otherwise be the case, and the company should be able to increase dividend payments on the remaining shares in issue.

(c)   **It increases gearing**. Repurchase of a company's own shares allows debt to be substituted for equity, so raising gearing. This will be of interest to a company wanting to increase its gearing without increasing its total long-term funding.

(d)   It r**eadjusts the company's equity base** to more appropriate levels, for a company whose business is in decline.

(e)   It possibly **prevents a takeover** or enables a quoted company to withdraw from the stock market.

4.2 Drawbacks of a share repurchase scheme

(a)   It can be **hard to arrive at a price** that will be fair both to the vendors and to any shareholders who are not selling shares to the company.

(b)   A repurchase of shares could be seen as an **admission** that the company **cannot make better use of the funds** than the shareholders.

(c)   Some shareholders may suffer from being **taxed on a capital gain** following the purchase of their shares rather than receiving dividend income.

CASE STUDY

In 2012, Apple's Board of Directors authorised a $10 billion share repurchase programme, over three years, to commence from September 2012. Tim Cook, the CEO, stated this was a use of surplus cash and that there was plenty of cash remaining to run the business.

Example: Share repurchase

KTP has 100,000 ordinary shares in issue. Assume that today's market price is £2 per share.

Evaluate the effect of the following options on the value of KTP, and the wealth of a shareholder who holds 10% of the company's shares.

(1)   Pay a cash dividend of 10p per share.

(2)   Make a distribution of £10,000 to shareholders through a share buyback of 5,000 shares.

Solution

(1)

Value of KTP before cash dividend	= 100,000 × £2.00	= £200,000
Less: cash dividend paid	= 100,000 × £0.10	= (£10,000)
Value of KTP after cash dividend	=	= £190,000
Share price after cash dividend	= £190,000 ÷ 100,000	= £1.90
Shareholder wealth before cash dividend	= 10,000 × £2.00	= £20,000
Shareholder wealth after cash dividend:		
shares	= 10,000 × £1.90	= £19,000
cash dividend received	= 10,000 × £0.10	= £1,000
		= £20,000

(2)

Value of KTP before share buyback	= 100,000 × £2	= £200,000
Shares bought back	= 5,000 × £2	= (£10,000)
Value of KTP after share buyback	=	= £190,000
Share price after distribution	= £190,000 ÷ 95,000	= £2
Shareholder wealth before distribution	= 10,000 × £2	= £20,000
Shareholder wealth after distribution		
shares	= 9500 × £2	= £19,000
cash received for shares bought back	= 500 × £2	= £1,000
		= £20,000

In both cases the shareholder wealth remains unchanged (dividend policy irrelevance). The entity value of KTP falls by paying a cash dividend or share buyback. In (2) the number of shares in isssue is reduced and earnings per share will increase.

Exam alert

In the previous syllabus, exam questions have asked for a discussion of the comparative advantages of a share repurchase *versus* a one-off dividend payment.

Section summary

- A company with cash available for dividend payments may choose instead to repurchase issued shares from shareholders, in the form of **share buybacks**.

- **Advantages** of share buybacks include:
    - finding a use for surplus cash
    - increasing earnings per share

- **Disadvantages** of share buybacks include:
    - the difficulty of arriving at a price that will be fair both to the vendors and to any shareholders who are not selling shares to the company
    - indicating that the company cannot make better use of funds than shareholders

Chapter Summary

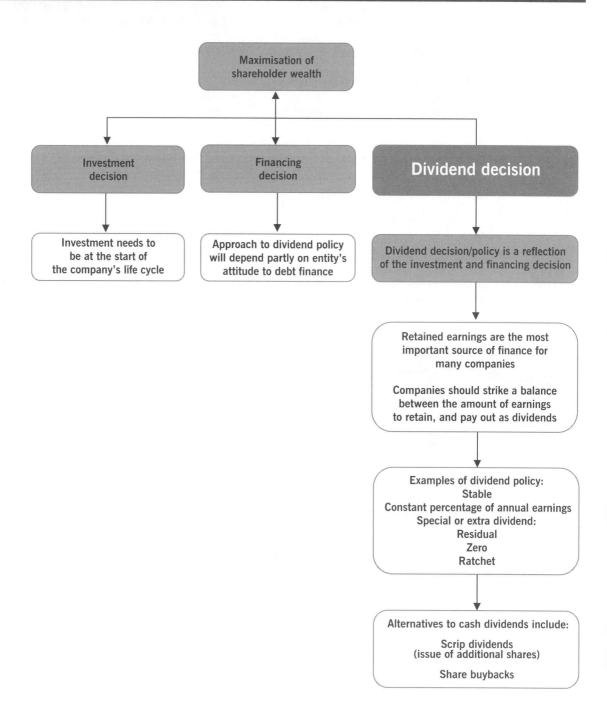

Maximisation of
shareholder wealth

Investment
decision

Financing
decision

Dividend decision

Investment needs to
be at the start of
the company's life cycle

Approach to dividend policy
will depend partly on entity's
attitude to debt finance

Dividend decision/policy is a reflection
of the investment and financing decision

Retained earnings are the most
important source of finance for
many companies

Companies should strike a balance
between the amount of earnings
to retain, and pay out as dividends

Examples of dividend policy:
Stable
Constant percentage of annual earnings
Special or extra dividend:
Residual
Zero
Ratchet

Alternatives to cash dividends include:

Scrip dividends
(issue of additional shares)

Share buybacks

Quick Quiz

1 **Fill in the blank:**

   Particular companies may attract particular types of shareholders. This is called the ....
   effect.

2 Give a definition of 'signalling' in the context of dividends policy.

3 **Fill in the blank:**

   A .... is a dividend payment which takes the form of new shares instead of cash.

4 Why might shareholders prefer a current dividend to a future capital gain?

5 Why would a company buy back shares from shareholders?

Answers to Quick Quiz

1   Clientele

2   The use of dividend policy to indicate the future prospects of an enterprise

3   Scrip dividend

4   Tax advantages or because the future capital gain will be uncertain

5   • To find a use for surplus cash
     • To increase EPS
     • To increase gearing
     • To readjust the equity base to more appropriate levels
     • To prevent a takeover
     • To withdraw from the stock market

 ## Answers to Questions

4.1 Retained earnings

(a)   The dividend policy of a company is in practice often determined by the directors. From their standpoint, funds from retained earnings are an attractive source of finance because investment projects can be undertaken without involving either the shareholders or any outsiders.

(b)   The use of retained earnings as opposed to new shares or debentures avoids issue costs.

(c)   The use of funds from retained earnings avoids the possibility of a change in control resulting from an issue of new shares.

4.2 Dividend policy

Year	Dividend per share pence	Dividend as % of profit
4 years ago	11.0	50%
3 years ago	13.0	52%
2 years ago	12.0	50%
1 year ago	15.0	52%
Current year	14.8	50%

The company appears to have pursued a dividend policy of paying out half of after-tax profits in dividend. This policy is only suitable when a company achieves a stable EPS or steady EPS growth. Investors do not like a fall in dividend from one year to the next, and the fall in dividend per share in the current year is likely to be unpopular, and to result in a fall in the share price.

The company would probably serve its shareholders better by paying a dividend of at least 15p per share, possibly more, in the current year, even though the dividend as a percentage of profit would then be higher.

Now try the questions from the Practice Question Bank	Question	Level
	Section A: 4.1 – 4.5	Practice
	Section B: 3	Practice

LONG-TERM DEBT FINANCE

The topic of sources of long-term finance has moved to Paper F2 *Advanced Financial Reporting*. However you will be required to draw on this knowledge to evaluate and compare alternative methods of raising long-term finance.

We look in this chapter at the most important forms of long-term debt finance. We examine the **practical factors** that determine whether lenders provide finance, how much they provide and on what terms. Remember that you may need to use the detail in this chapter to explain **why** organisations choose particular sources of finance.

Some of the content in this chapter revisits key points covered in Paper F2 *Advanced Financial Reporting*.

You must always make recommendations that are suitable for the **specific type of entity** so the specific financing for multinationals and small entities are also examined in this chapter.

5

Topic list	learning outcomes	syllabus references	ability required
1 Procedures for issuing debt finance	B(1)(b)	B(1)(b)(v)	evaluation
2 Factors influencing the choice of debt finance	B(1)(b)	B(1)(b)(i)	evaluation
3 Short and medium-term debt finance	B(1)(b)	B(1)(b)(i)	evaluation
4 Long-term debt finance	B(1)(b)	B(1)(b)(i),(iv),(vi)	evaluation
5 Convertible securities	B(1)(b)	B(1)(b)(i)	evaluation
6 Warrants	B(1)(b)	B(1)(b)(i)	evaluation
7 International debt finance	B(1)(b)	B(1)(b)(i)	evaluation
8 Small and medium-sized entities	B(1)(b)	B(1)(b)(i)	evaluation
9 Cost of capital	C(2)(a)	C(2)(a)(ix)	evaluation
10 The cost of debt	C(2)(a)	C(2)(a)(ix)	evaluation

Chapter Overview

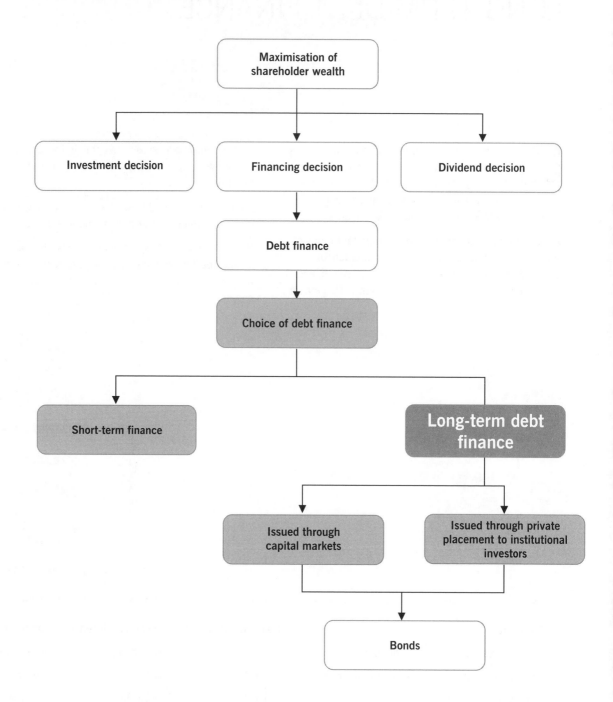

1   Procedures for issuing debt finance

Introduction

In this section we look at the procedures for issuing long-term debt finance.

1.1 Capital markets

Companies can raise long-term debt finance by issuing debt securities (eg bonds) to investors through capital markets. A debt security is effectively a loan from an investor to the issuing company in return for the right to receive interest payments and repayment of the principal loan amount upon maturity.

Capital markets are a source of both **debt** and **equity finance**. We will look at equity finance in Chapter 8. In the UK, the principle markets are the Stock Exchange and the AIM (Alternative Investment Market).

The various participants in the capital markets are summarised in the diagram below:

Capital markets

Demand for funds comes from ...	◄————	*Intermediaries*	◄————	*Suppliers of funds*
INDIVIDUALS (eg housing/consumer goods finance)	————	Banks	————	INDIVIDUALS (as savers and investors)
		Building societies		
FIRMS (share capital; loans)	————	Insurance companies and pension funds	————	FIRMS (with long-term funds to invest)
		Unit trust/investment trust companies		
GOVERNMENT (budget deficit)	————	Stock exchanges Venture capital organisations	————	GOVERNMENT (budget surplus)

In order to trade on capital markets, companies need to obtain a **stock market listing**. Obtaining a listing is a long and costly process and will require **advisers** such as investment banks and stockbrokers. This is covered in Chapter 8.

Debt and equity securities issued on capital markets may be **underwritten** by financial institutions. Underwriting is the process whereby financial institutions agree to buy securities from the issuer that have not been taken up by investors. Underwriters therefore bear the risk of not all of the issued securities being sold.

1.2 Private placement of debt

Debt securities can also be issued by private placement. This is the process whereby a company sells debt securities to specific institutional investors rather than issuing debt securities to the public through capital markets.

KEY TERM

INSTITUTIONAL INVESTORS are institutions which have large amounts of funds which they want to invest, and they will invest in bonds and shares or any other assets which offer satisfactory returns and security.

The institutional investors are now the biggest investors on many stock markets. The major institutional investors in the UK are pension funds, insurance companies, investment trusts, unit trusts, private equity and venture capital organisations.

Private placement does not have the high costs of issuing debt to public investors, and finance can be raised more quickly and without the onerous requirements of obtaining a stock market listing.

Section summary

Capital markets such as the Stock Exchange and the AIM in the UK, enable companies to raise finance by issuing debt securities to public investors.

Private placement of debt is a process whereby debt securities are issued to specific institutional investors rather than the public and has advantages over capital markets of a quicker and less costly form of raising finance.

2   Factors influencing the choice of debt finance

Introduction

In this section we look at the criteria for choosing different types of long-term debt finance (eg bank borrowings, bonds, convertibles).

Generally, the following considerations influence what type of debt finance is sought:

(a)   **Availability**

Only listed companies will be able to make a public issue of bonds on a stock exchange. With a 'public issue' the bonds are listed on a stock market, although most bond trading is off-exchange. Most investors will not invest in bonds issued by small companies. Smaller companies are only able to obtain significant amounts of debt finance from a bank.

(b)   **Credit rating**

Large companies may prefer to issue bonds if they have a strong credit rating. Credit ratings are given to bond issues by credit rating agencies such as Standard & Poor's and Moody's. The credit rating given to a bond issue affects the interest yield that investors will require. If a company's bonds would only be given a sub-investment grade rating ('junk bond' rating), the company may prefer to seek debt finance from a bank loan as it will be less expensive.

(c)   **Amount**

Bond issues are usually for large amounts. If a company wants to borrow only a small amount of money, a bank loan would be appropriate.

(d)   **Duration**

If loan finance is sought to buy a particular asset to generate revenues for the business, the length of the loan should **match** the length of time that the asset will be generating revenues.

(e)   **Fixed or floating rate**

Expectations of interest rate movements will determine whether a company chooses to borrow at a fixed or floating rate. Fixed rate finance may be more expensive, but the business runs the risk of adverse upward rate movements if it chooses floating rate finance. Banks may refuse to lend at a fixed rate for more than a given period of time.

(f)   **Security and covenants**

The choice of finance may be determined by the assets that the business is willing or able to offer as **security**, also on the restrictions in **covenants** that the lenders wish to impose.

Section summary

The following factors should be considered in the choice of debt finance:

- Availability
- Credit rating
- Amount
- Duration
- Fixed or floating interest rate
- Security and covenants

3 Short and medium-term debt finance

Introduction

In this section we look at the different types of short and medium-term debt finance available.

3.1 Commercial paper

Commercial paper is **short-term unsecured corporate debt** with a maturity date of anywhere between one week and one year. The typical term of this debt is about 30 days. Commercial paper can only be issued by large organisations with good credit ratings, normally to fund short-term expenditure. The debt is issued at a discount that reflects the prevailing interest rates. When one issue of commercial paper matures, another can be issued, effectively making it a medium-term source of finance in this case.

3.2 Bank borrowings

Banks often provide term loans as medium or long-term financing for customers. The customer borrows a fixed amount and pays it back with interest over a period or at the end of it. This contrasts with an overdraft facility when a customer, through their current account, can borrow money on a short-term basis up to a certain amount. Overdrafts are repayable on demand.

The **advantages** of a term loan are as follows:

(a)   They are easy and quick to negotiate and arrange.
(b)   Flexible repayment schedules may be offered by banks.
(c)   They are particularly useful for small entities who can have problems raising capital.

3.3 Mezzanine finance

This describes unsecured loans that rank after secured debt but ahead of equity in a liquidation. It is commonly used for **management buy-outs** (see Chapter 13), where there is a need to **bridge the gap** between the amount of loans that banks are prepared to make and the amount of equity funding available.

It is **higher risk** lending than bank loans so tends to attract a **higher rate of interest**. There may also be warrants attached (see Section 6) entitling the holder to subscribe for future equity.

3.4 Creditworthiness

From the lender's viewpoint, the interest rate charged on loan finance will normally reflect the **risk** associated with the loan and an assessment of a company's creditworthiness will be made. Lenders' assessment of creditworthiness is discussed in Chapter 2.

Section summary

- Commercial paper is a source of short-term debt finance, typically maturing between a week and a year.

- Bank loans tend to be a **source** of **medium or long-term finance**, linked with the purchase of specific assets. Interest and repayments will be set in advance.

4 Long-term debt finance

Introduction

In this section we look at the appropriateness of different types of long-term debt finance.

4.1 Bonds

The term **bonds** describes various forms of long-term debt a company may issue. A bond is effectively a loan from an investor for a defined period at a fixed interest rate. Bonds are also referred to as debentures, loan notes or loan stock.

Bonds come in various forms, including redeemable, irredeemable, floating rate, zero coupon and convertible.

Bonds have a **nominal value**, which is the debt owed by the company, and interest is paid at a stated **'coupon'** on this amount. For example, if a company issues 10% bonds, the coupon will be 10% of the nominal value of the bonds, so that £100 of bonds will receive £10 interest each year. The rate quoted is the gross rate, before tax.

Unlike shares, debt is often issued **at par**, ie with £100 payable per £100 nominal value. Where the coupon rate is fixed at the time of issue, it will be set according to prevailing market conditions given the credit rating of the company issuing the debt. Subsequent changes in market (and company) conditions will cause the **market value of the bond to fluctuate**, although the coupon will stay at the **fixed percentage** of the nominal value.

4.1.1 Debentures

KEY TERM

A DEBENTURE is a written acknowledgement of a debt by a company, usually given under its seal and normally containing provisions as to payment of interest and the terms of repayment of principal. A bond may be secured on some or all of the assets of the company or its subsidiaries.

Debentures are defined as the written acknowledgement of a debt incurred by a company, normally containing provisions about the payment of interest and the eventual repayment of capital. The terms of the bond are set out in a **trust deed**.

4.1.2 Security

Bonds will often be secured. **Security** may take the form of either a **fixed charge** or a **floating charge.**

(a) **Fixed charge**

Security would be related to a **specific asset** or group of assets, typically land and buildings. The company would be unable to dispose of the asset without providing a substitute asset for security, or without the lender's consent.

(b)   **Floating charge**

With a floating charge on **certain assets** of the company (for example inventory or receivables), the lender's security in the event of a default of payment is whatever assets of the appropriate class the company then owns (provided that another lender does not have a prior charge on the assets). The company would be able, however, to dispose of its assets as it chose until a default took place. In the event of default, the lender would probably appoint a receiver to run the company rather than lay claim to a particular asset.

Not all bonds are secured. Investors are likely to expect a **higher yield** with **unsecured bonds** to compensate them for the extra risk. The rate of interest on unsecured bonds may be around 1% or more higher than for secured debt.

4.1.3 Deep discount bonds

KEY TERM

A Deep discount bond is a bond offered at a large discount on the face value of the debt so that a significant proportion of the return to the investor comes by way of a capital gain on redemption, rather than through interest payment.   *(CIMA Official Terminology)*

Deep discount bonds will be redeemable at par (or above par) when they eventually mature. For example a company might issue £1,000,000 of bonds in 20X2, at a price of £50 per £100, and redeemable at par in the year 20Y7. For a company with specific cash flow requirements, the **low servicing costs** during the currency of the bond may be an attraction, coupled with a high cost of redemption at maturity.

Investors might be attracted by the **large capital gain** offered by the bonds, which is the difference between the issue price and the redemption value. However, deep discount bonds will carry a much **lower rate of interest** than other types of bonds. The only tax advantage is that the gain gets taxed (as **income**) in one lump on maturity or sale, not as amounts of interest each year.

4.1.4 Zero coupon bonds

KEY TERM

A Zero coupon bond is a bond offering no interest payments, all investor return being gained through capital appreciation.   *(CIMA Official Terminology)*

Zero coupon bonds are bonds that are issued at a discount to their redemption value, but no interest is paid on them. The investor gains from the difference between the issue price and the redemption value, and there is an implied interest rate in the amount of discount at which the bonds are issued (or subsequently resold on the market).

(a)   The advantage for borrowers is that zero coupon bonds can be used to **raise cash immediately**, and there is no cash repayment until redemption date. The cost of redemption is known at the time of issue, and so the borrower can plan to have funds available to redeem the bonds at maturity.

(b)   The advantage for lenders is restricted, unless the rate of discount on the bonds **offers a high yield**. The only way of obtaining cash from the bonds before maturity is to sell them, and their market value will depend on the remaining term to maturity and current market interest rates.

The tax advantage of zero coupon bonds is the same as that for deep discount bonds.

4.1.5 The redemption of bonds

Bonds are usually **redeemable**. They are issued for a term of ten years or more, and perhaps 25 to 30 years. At the end of this period, they will 'mature' and become redeemable (at par or possibly at a value above par).

KEY TERM

Redemption is repayment of the principal amount (for example a bond) at the date of maturity.   *(CIMA Official Terminology)*

Some redeemable bonds have an earliest and a latest redemption date. For example, 12% Loan Notes 20X4/X6 are redeemable at any time between the earliest specified date (in 20X4) and the latest date (in 20X6). The issuing company can choose the date. The decision by a company when to redeem a debt will depend on **how much cash** is available to the company to repay the debt, and on the **nominal rate of interest** on the debt.

Some bonds do not have a redemption date, and are **'irredeemable'** or **'undated'**. Undated bonds might be redeemed by a company that wishes to pay off the debt, but there is no obligation on the company to do so.

4.1.6 Tax relief on loan interest

As far as companies are concerned, debt capital is a potentially attractive source of finance compared to a new issue of shares because:

(a)   Interest charges reduce the profits chargeable to corporation tax.

(b)   Companies might wish to avoid dilution of shareholding and may prefer to increase gearing in order to improve their earnings per share.

4.2 Debt covenants

Debt finance often comes with certain debt covenants from the lender. Debt covenants are agreements between a lender and the borrower to not breach certain limits of financial ratios and to abide by other restrictions, for example:

Restrictions on dividend payments: this is to safeguard the company's future cash flows and ability to meets its debts.

Financial ratio limits: certain financial ratios cannot fall below specified levels, eg interest cover, net debt/EBIDTA, debt/debt and equity.

Restrictions of additional debt: lenders may restrict the type and amount of additional debt a company can take on or the nature of charges over assets that the company can issue.

Breaches of debt covenants usually entitle the lender to demand full repayment of the loan. However in practice this is unlikely; rather, the debt is renegotiated.

Exam alert

An exam question may require you to assess whether a company will breach a certain debt convenant(s) if a particular investment, financing or dividend decision is made (eg a company that has existing debt and is considering increasing its borrowings).

Section summary

- The term **bonds** describes various forms of long-term debt a company may issue. Bonds come in various forms, including redeemable, irredeemable, floating rate, zero coupon and convertible.

- Lenders of debt can require that borrowers do not breach certain **debt covenants** such as limits on financial ratios and restrictions on dividend payments.

5 Convertible securities

Introduction

Convertible securities are a **hybrid** of debt and equity. They can be converted to ordinary shares at a future date.

5.1 Convertible bonds

KEY TERM

CONVERTIBLE DEBT is a liability that gives the holder the right to convert into another instrument, normally ordinary shares, at a predetermined price/rate and time.   *(CIMA Official Terminology)*

Conversion terms often vary over time. For example, the conversion terms of convertible bonds might be that on 1 April 20X0, £2 of bonds can be converted into one ordinary share, whereas on 1 April 20X1, the conversion price will be £2.20 of bonds for one ordinary share. Once converted, convertible securities cannot be converted back into the original fixed return security.

5.2 The conversion value and the conversion premium

The current market value of ordinary shares into which a unit of bonds may be converted is known as the conversion value. The **conversion value** will be below the value of the bonds at the date of issue, but will be expected to increase as the date for conversion approaches on the assumption that a company's shares ought to increase in market value over time.

Conversion value = Conversion ratio × market price per ordinary share

Conversion premium = Current market value of convertible − current conversion value

Question 5.1	Convertible debt

Learning outcome: B(1)(b)

The 10% convertible bonds of Starchwhite are quoted at $142 per $100 nominal. The earliest date for conversion is in four years' time, at the rate of 30 ordinary shares per $100 nominal. The share price is currently $4.15. Annual interest on the bonds has just been paid.

Required

(a)   Calculate the current conversion value.
(b)   Calculate the conversion premium and comment on its meaning.

5.3 The issue price and the market price of convertible bonds

A company will aim to issue bonds with the **greatest possible conversion premium** as this will mean that, for the amount of capital raised, it will, on conversion, have to issue the lowest number of new ordinary shares. The premium that will be accepted by potential investors will depend on the company's growth potential, and so on prospects for a sizeable increase in the share price.

Convertible bonds issued at par normally have a **lower coupon rate of interest** than straight debt. This lower yield is the price the investor has to pay for the conversion rights. It is, of course, also one of the reasons why the issue of convertible bonds is attractive to a company, particularly one with tight cash flows around the time of issue, but an easier situation when the notes are due to be converted.

When convertible bonds are traded on a stock market, their **minimum market price** or **floor value** will be the price of straight bonds with the same coupon rate of interest. If the market value falls to this minimum, it follows that the market attaches no value to the conversion rights.

The actual market price of convertible bonds will depend on:

- The **price of straight debt**
- The **current conversion value**
- The **length of time** before conversion may take place
- The **market's expectation** as to future equity returns and the risk associated with these returns

Most companies issuing convertible bonds expect them to be **converted**. They view the notes as **delayed equity**. They are often used either because the company's ordinary share price is considered to be particularly depressed at the time of issue or because the issue of equity shares would result in an immediate and significant drop in earnings per share. There is no certainty, however, that the security holders will exercise their option to convert; therefore the bonds may run their full term and need to be redeemed.

Example: Convertible bonds

CD wants to issue 50,000 units of convertible bonds, each with a nominal value of $100 and a coupon rate of interest of 10%, payable yearly. Each $100 of convertible bonds may be converted into 40 ordinary shares of CD in three years' time. Any bonds not converted will be redeemed at 110 (that is, at $110 per $100 nominal value of bond).

Estimate the likely current market price for $100 of the bonds, if investors in the bonds now require a pre-tax return of only 8%, and the expected value of CD ordinary shares on the conversion day is:

(a) $2.50 per share
(b) $3.00 per share

Solution

(a)   Shares are valued at $2.50 each.

If shares are only expected to be worth $2.50 each on conversion day, the value of 40 shares will be $100, and investors in the debt will presumably therefore redeem their debt at 110 instead of converting them into shares.

The market value of $100 of the convertible debt will be the discounted present value of the expected future income stream.

Year		Cash flow $	Discount factor 8%	Present value $
1	Interest	10	0.926	9.26
2	Interest	10	0.857	8.57
3	Interest	10	0.794	7.94
3	Redemption value	110	0.794	87.34
				113.11

The estimated market value is $113.11 per $100 of debt. This is also the floor value.

(b)   Shares are valued at $3 each.

If shares are expected to be worth $3 each, the debt holders will convert their debt into shares (value per $100 of stock = 40 shares × $3 = $120) rather than redeem their debt at 110.

Year		Cash flow/value	Discount factor	Present value
		$	8%	$
1	Interest	10	0.926	9.26
2	Interest	10	0.857	8.57
3	Interest	10	0.794	7.94
3	Value of 40 shares	120	0.794	95.28
				121.05

The estimated market value is $121.05 per $100 of debt.

Thus the higher the expected share price, the more finance CD will be able to raise as investors will be prepared to pay more for future conversion rights.

5.4 Advantages of convertibles

(a)   Convertibles serve as a **sweetener** for debt by allowing the investor to participate in increases in price of share capital.

(b)   The issuer can pay **lower interest** than on straight debt. This may be significant if funds are tight during the early years of issue of the bonds. They are usually issued by **high growth companies** who do not want the burden of high interest payments.

(c)   The **attractions of the conversion rights**, the possibility of a significant capital gain and the hedge against risk (the right to have the debt repaid if conversion is not worthwhile), should mean the lender is willing to accept fewer other conditions.

(d)   Convertibles may provide a means of issuing equity ultimately at a **higher price** than **current** market price.

(e)   If the company issued straight bonds initially and then equity to redeem the bonds, two lots of issue costs would be paid, whereas with convertible debt, issue costs would only be **paid once**.

(f)   The **debt ratio** is **reduced** if conversion takes place.

5.5 Disadvantages of convertibles

(a)   If the company had waited for funds, and the **market price increases significantly** above the conversion price, it would be better off issuing shares at a higher price, rather than having to issue shares at the lower conversion terms.

(b)   The company has to **repay the debt** if the share price does not increase.

(c)   Some borrowers may be reluctant to invest because of the **lower yield** on convertible shares compared with securities not having conversion rights.

Section summary

- **Convertible debt** can, at the holder's option, be converted to ordinary shares at some future date instead of being held to maturity.

- Convertibles are **debt sweeteners** as they allow a lower rate of interest to be paid on the debt.

6 Warrants

Introduction

Share warrants are another form of debt sweetener which give their holder the right to apply for new shares at a specified exercise price in the future.

6.1 Purpose of warrants

A **warrant** is a right given by a company to an investor, **allowing them** to **subscribe** for new shares at a future date at a fixed, predetermined price (the **exercise price**).

Warrants are usually issued as part of a package with unsecured bonds; an investor who buys bonds will also acquire a certain number of warrants. The purpose of warrants is to make the bonds more attractive.

Once issued, warrants are detachable from the bonds and can be sold and bought separately before or during the 'exercise period' (the period during which the right to use the warrants to subscribe for shares is allowed). The market value of warrants will depend on expectations of actual share prices in the future.

6.2 Advantages of warrants

(a) Warrants themselves **do not involve** the **payment** of any **interest or dividends**. Furthermore, when they are initially attached to bonds, the interest rate on the bonds will be lower than for a comparable straight debt.

(b) Warrants make a bond issue more attractive and may make an issue of unsecured bonds possible where **adequate security is lacking**.

(c) Warrants provide a means of **generating additional equity** funds in the future without any immediate dilution in earnings per share. The cost will be the right that warrants holders to buy at the **possibly reduced exercise price**.

6.3 Disadvantages of warrants

The disadvantages of warrants are:

(a) When exercised, they will result in the **dilution** of **share capital**.

(b) Warrants may be exercised when a business **does not need additional capital**.

(c) The company has **less control** over the exercise of warrants than it does over the exercise of share capital.

Section summary

Share warrants give their holder the right to apply for new shares at a specified exercise price in the future. They can be issued as an 'add-on' to a new issue of bonds.

7 International debt finance

Introduction

Large companies with excellent credit ratings use the euromarkets to borrow in any foreign currency using unregulated markets organised by merchant banks.

7.1 International borrowing

Borrowing markets are becoming increasingly internationalised, particularly for larger companies. Large companies which have an excellent credit rating are able to borrow funds on the **eurocurrency (money) markets** and on the markets for **eurobonds**. These markets are collectively called **euromarkets**. Large companies can also borrow on the **syndicated loan market** where a syndicate of banks provides medium to long-term currency loans.

If a company is receiving income in a foreign currency or has a long-term investment overseas, it can try to **limit the risk** of adverse exchange rate movements by **matching**. It can take out a long-term loan and use the foreign currency receipts to repay the loan.

7.2 Eurocurrency markets

KEY TERMS

Eurocurrency is currency which is held by individuals and institutions outside the country of issue of that currency.

Eurodollars are US dollars deposited with, or borrowed from, a bank outside the USA.

(CIMA Official Terminology)

A UK company might borrow money from a bank or from the investing public, in sterling. However it might also borrow in a foreign currency, especially if it trades abroad, or if it already has assets or liabilities abroad denominated in a foreign currency. When a company borrows in a foreign currency, the loan is known as a **eurocurrency loan**. (As with euro-equity, it is not only the euro that is involved, and so the 'euro' prefix is a misnomer.) Banks involved in the eurocurrency market are **not subject to central bank reserve requirements** or regulations in respect of their involvement.

The eurocurrency markets involve the **depositing of funds** with a **bank outside the country** of the currency in which the funds are denominated and **relending these funds for a fairly short term**, typically three months, normally at a floating rate of interest.

Eurocredits are medium to long-term international bank loans which may be arranged by individual banks or by **syndicates of banks**. Syndication of loans increases the amounts available to hundreds of millions, while reducing the exposure of individual banks.

7.3 Eurobonds (international bonds)

KEY TERM

A eurobond is a bond sold outside the jurisdiction of the country in whose currency the bond is denominated.   *(CIMA Official Terminology)*

In recent years, a strong market has built up which allows very large companies to borrow in this way, long-term or short-term. Again, the market is not subject to national regulations.

Eurobonds are **long-term loans raised by international companies** or other institutions and **sold to investors in several countries** at the same time. Eurobonds are normally repaid after 5–15 years, and are for major amounts of capital ie $10 million or more. This market is much bigger than the market for domestic bonds.

Exam alert

Don't make the common mistake of thinking that eurobonds are issued in Europe or only denominated in euros.

7.3.1 How are eurobonds issued?

 A lead manager is appointed from a major merchant bank; the lead manager liaises with the credit rating agencies and organises a **credit rating** of the eurobond.

 The lead manager organises an **underwriting syndicate** (of other merchant banks) who agree the terms of the bond (eg interest rate, maturity date) and buy the bond.

 The underwriting syndicate then organise the sale of the bond; this normally involves **placing** the bond with **institutional investors**.

7.3.2 Advantages of eurobonds

(a)   Eurobonds are '**bearer instruments**', which means that the owner does not have to declare his identity.

(b)   Interest is paid gross and this has meant that eurobonds have been used by investors to avoid tax.

(c)   Eurobonds create a liability in a foreign currency to **match** against a foreign currency asset.

(d)   They are often **cheaper** than a foreign currency bank loan because they can be sold on by the investor, who will therefore accept a lower yield in return for this greater liquidity.

(e)   They are also extremely **flexible**. Most eurobonds are fixed rate but they can be floating rate or linked to the financial success of the company.

(f)   They are typically issued by companies with excellent credit ratings and are normally **unsecured**, which makes it easier for companies to raise debt finance in the future.

(g)   Eurobond issues are not normally advertised because they are **placed** with institutional investors and this reduces issue costs.

7.3.3 Disadvantages of eurobonds

Like any form of debt finance there will be **issue costs** to consider (approximately 2% of funds raised in the case of eurobonds) and there may also be problems if gearing levels are too high.

A borrower contemplating a eurobond issue must consider the **foreign exchange risk** of a long-term foreign currency loan. If the money is to be used to purchase assets which will earn revenue in a currency different to that of the bond issue, the borrower will run the risk of exchange losses if the currency of the loan strengthens against the currency of the revenues out of which the bond (and interest) must be repaid.

 Exam skills

Since eurobonds are a major source of finance, they may feature in exam questions. For example, you may be required to compare euro bank loans and a euro-denominated eurobond or to examine the advantages and disadvantages of different methods of funding, including a euro-denominated eurobond.

 Section summary

Large companies will have access to international debt such as **eurobonds (international bonds)**.

8   Small and medium-sized entities

Introduction

In this exam you must always suggest suitable finance for the specific needs of the entity in the scenario. Small and medium-sized entities have specific problems obtaining finance which are very different to large, multinational entities.

The options open to small and medium-sized enterprises (SMEs) may be particularly limited. They face **competition** for funds, as investors have opportunities to invest in all sizes of organisation, also overseas and government debt. In this competition they are handicapped by the problem of **uncertainty**.

(a)   Whatever the details provided to potential investors, SMEs do not have the **business** history **or track record** of larger organisations.

(b)   Larger enterprises are subject by law to **more public scrutiny**; their accounts have to contain more detail and be audited, they receive more press coverage and so on.

(c)   Because of the uncertainties involved, banks often use **credit scoring** systems to **control exposure.**

(d)   **The costs of monitoring** small businesses may be **excessive for banks**, particularly if they are **facing difficult conditions themselves**.

(e)   Banks face **regulatory pressures** with regulators classifying **lending to the small business sector** as being a **higher risk investment**.

A common problem is often that banks will be **unwilling** to increase **loan funding** without an increase in **security given** (which the owners may be unwilling or unable to give), or an increase in **equity funding** (which may be difficult to obtain).

Certain trends in various countries may be more helpful for small businesses.

(a)   The **development of the non-bank sector**, with some organisations specialising in lending to small businesses.

(b)   **Government aid** includes loan guarantee schemes, grants and enterprise capital funds.

Exam alert

In the integrated case study, make sure that your financing recommendations are suitable for the type of entity in the scenario and not just a 'brain-dump' of types of finance.

You are not expected to have knowledge of any specific government scheme but you may gain credit in the exam for relevant discussion of available schemes in your own country, if this comes up in the integrated case study.

Section summary

Small and medium-sized entities often find it difficult to obtain finance due to the **risks** involved for lenders.

9 Cost of capital

Introduction

In F2 *Advanced Financial Reporting* you will have covered the cost of debt finance, a component of the cost of capital. In Section 10, we will revisit the cost of debt. Firstly in this section we will recap the main points of the cost of capital.

From the perspective of the providers of debt or equity finance, the cost of capital is the **rate of return** that the entity must pay to satisfy the providers of funds, and it reflects the **riskiness** of the finance used.

9.1 The cost of capital

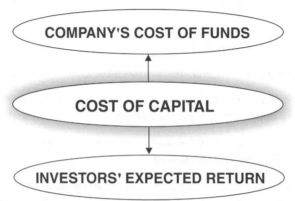

It is thus the **minimum return** that a company should make on its own investments, to earn the cash flows out of which investors can be paid their return.

KEY TERM

COST OF CAPITAL is the minimum acceptable return on an investment, generally computed as a discount rate for use in investment appraisal exercises. The computation of the optimal cost of capital can be complex, and many ways of determining this opportunity cost have been suggested.

(CIMA Official Terminology)

9.2 The cost of capital as an opportunity cost of finance

The cost of capital, however it is measured, is an **opportunity cost of finance,** because it is the minimum return that investors require. If they do not get this return, they will transfer some or all of their investment somewhere else. Here are two examples:

(a)   If a bank offers to lend money to a company, the interest rate it charges is the **yield** that the bank wants to receive from **investing** in the company, because it can get just as good a return from lending the money to someone else. In other words, the interest rate is the **opportunity cost** of lending for the bank.

(b)   When shareholders invest in a company, the returns that they can expect must be sufficient to persuade them not to sell some or all of their shares and invest the money somewhere else. The yield on the shares is therefore the **opportunity cost** to the shareholders of not investing somewhere else.

9.3 The cost of capital and risk

The cost of capital has three elements.

Risk-free rate of return +
Premium for business risk +
Premium for financial risk

COST OF CAPITAL

(a) **Risk-free rate of return**

This is the return which would be required from an investment if it were completely free from risk. Typically, a risk-free yield would be the **yield on government securities**.

(b) **Premium for business risk**

This is an increase in the required rate of return due to the existence of **uncertainty about** the future and about a **firm's business prospects**. The actual returns from an investment may not be as high as they are expected to be. Business risk will be higher for some firms than for others, and some types of project undertaken by a firm may be more risky than other types of project that it undertakes.

(c) **Premium for financial risk**

This relates to the danger of high debt levels (high gearing). For ordinary shareholders, financial risk is evident in the variability of earnings after deducting payments to holders of debt capital. The higher the gearing of a company's capital structure, the greater will be the financial risk to ordinary shareholders, and this should be reflected in a higher risk premium and therefore a higher cost of capital.

Because different companies are in different types of business (varying **business risk**) and have different capital structures (varying **financial risk**) the cost of capital applied to one company may differ radically from the cost of capital of another.

Section summary

The cost of capital is the **cost of funds** that a company raises and uses, and is the **minimum return** it should make on its investments.

10 The cost of debt

Introduction

As mentioned in the previous section, the cost of debt is a component of a company's cost of capital. The cost of debt is covered in F2 *Advanced Financial Reporting*.

10.1 The cost of debt capital

Debt finance offers a **higher degree of security** as interest has to be paid, there may be a security for the debt and it will be repaid ahead of equity in a liquidation. Interest also attracts **tax relief** so the cost of debt will be **lower** than the cost of equity.

10.2 Irredeemable debt capital

Cost of irredeemable debt capital (k_d), paying interest i in perpetuity, and having a current ex-div price P_0:

$$k_d = \frac{i}{P_0}$$

Example: Cost of debt (no tax)

Lepus has issued bonds of $100 nominal value with annual interest of 9% per year, based on the nominal value. The current market price of the bonds is $90. What is the cost of the bonds?

Solution

$k_d = {}^9/_{90} = 10\%$

10.3 Redeemable debt capital

If the debt is **redeemable** then in the year of redemption the interest payment will be received by the holder as well as the amount payable on redemption, so:

$$P_0 = \frac{i}{(1+k_{d\,net})} + \frac{i}{(1+k_{d\,net})^2} + \quad ..... \quad + \frac{i+p_n}{(1+k_{d\,net})^n}$$

The above equation cannot be simplified, so 'r' will have to be calculated by trial and error, as an **internal rate of return (IRR)**.

You will find it helpful to lay out the cash flows so they look like a project:

Time	Cash flow
0	(Market value)
1–n	Interest
N	Redemption value

To calculate the IRR:

 Calculate the net present value using a trial discount rate eg 10%.

 Calculate the NPV using a second discount rate.

(a)   If the NPV is **positive**, use a second rate that is **greater** than the first rate.
(b)   If the NPV is **negative**, use a second rate that is **less** than the first rate.

 Use the two NPV values to **estimate the IRR**. The formula to apply is as follows.

$$IRR \approx a + \left(\left(\frac{NPV_a}{NPV_a - NPV_b} \right)(b-a) \right)\%$$

Where $\quad$ a $\quad = \quad$ the lower of the two rates of return used
$\quad\quad\quad$ b $\quad = \quad$ the higher of the two rates of return used
$\quad\quad\quad NPV_a = \quad$ the NPV obtained using rate a
$\quad\quad\quad NPV_b = \quad$ the NPV obtained using rate b

10.4 Debt capital and taxation

The interest on debt capital is likely to be an allowable deduction for purposes of taxation and this **tax relief on interest** must be recognised in computations. The after-tax cost of irredeemable debt capital is:

$$k_{d\,net} = \frac{i(1-t)}{P_0}$$

Where $\quad k_{d\,net}$ $\quad$ is the cost of debt capital

$\quad\quad\quad$ i $\quad$ is the annual interest payment

$\quad\quad\quad P_0$ $\quad$ is the current market price of the debt capital ex interest (that is, after payment of the current interest)

$\quad\quad\quad$ t $\quad$ is the rate of corporation tax

Therefore if a company pays $10,000 a year interest on irredeemable debt with a nominal value of $100,000 and a market price of $80,000, and the rate of tax is 30%, the cost of the debt would be:

$$\frac{10,000}{80,000} (1 - 0.30) = 0.0875 = 8.75\%$$

The higher the rate of tax is, the greater the tax benefits in having debt finance will be compared with equity finance. In the example above, if the rate of tax had been 50%, the cost of debt would have been, after tax:

$$\frac{10,000}{80,000} (1 - 0.50) = 0.0625 = 6.25\%$$

In the case of **redeemable debt**, the capital repayment is not allowable for tax. To calculate the cost of the debt capital to include in the weighted average cost of capital, it is necessary to calculate an internal rate of return which takes account of tax relief on the interest.

Example: Cost of redeemable debt (with tax)

Goodies Co has €100,000 6% redeemable bonds in issue. Interest is paid annually on 31 December. The ex-interest market value of the bonds on 1 January 20X5 is €93 and the bonds are redeemable at a 10% premium on 31 December 20X9. The effective rate of tax is 30%.

What is the cost of debt?

Solution

Year		Cash flow	Discount factor @ 10%	PV	Discount factor @ 5%	PV
		€		€		€
0	Market value	(93)	1.000	(93.00)	1.000	(93.00)
1–5	Interest after tax	6 × (1 – 0.3)	3.791	15.92	4.329	18.18
5	Capital repayment	110	0.621	68.31	0.784	86.24
				(8.77)		11.42

The approximate cost of redeemable debt capital is, therefore:

$$5 + \left[\frac{11.42}{(11.42 - -8.77)} \right] \times 5 = 7.82\%$$

10.5 The cost of floating rate debt

If a firm has variable or **'floating rate' debt**, then the cost of an equivalent fixed interest debt should be substituted. 'Equivalent' usually means fixed interest debt with a similar term to maturity in a firm of similar standing, although if the cost of capital is to be used for project appraisal purposes, there is an argument for using debt of the same duration as the project under consideration.

10.6 The cost of bank loans

The cost of funds such as bank loans and overdrafts is the **current interest** being charged on such funds.

Section summary

The **cost of debt** is the return an enterprise must pay to its lenders.

- For **irredeemable debt**, this is the (post-tax) interest as a percentage of the ex-interest market value of the bonds.

- For **redeemable debt**, the cost is given by the internal rate of return of the cash flows involved.

Chapter Summary

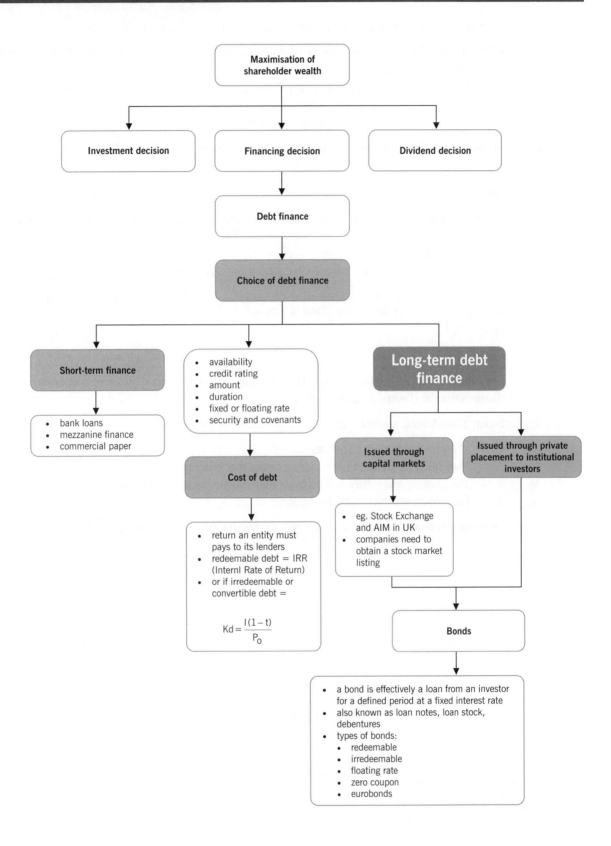

Quick Quiz

1   State two ways a company can issue debt securities to raise long-term debt finance.

2   Which of the following comparisons between bonds and preference shares is not a true statement?

    A   Bonds are cheaper to service since interest is tax-deductible.
    B   Bonds are more attractive to investors because they are secured against assets.
    C   Bonds holders rank above preference shareholders in the event of a liquidation.
    D   Bonds are more similar to equity than preference shares.

3   Holders of bonds are long-term receivables of the company.

    True   ☐

    False   ☐

4   A company has 12% bonds in issue, which have a market value of $135 per $100 nominal value. What is:

    (a)   The coupon rate?
    (b)   The amount of interest payable per annum per $100 nominal?

5   An investor has the option of redeeming a company's 11% loan notes 20X3/20X5 at any date between 1 January 20X3 and 31 December 20X5 inclusive.

    True   ☐

    False   ☐

6   Convertible securities are fixed return securities that may be converted into zero coupon bonds/ordinary shares/warrants. (Delete as appropriate.)

7   Which of the following statements about convertible securities is false?

    A   They are fixed return securities.
    B   They must be converted into shares before the redemption date.
    C   The price at which they will be converted into shares is predetermined.
    D   Issue costs are lower than for equity.

8   Do borrowers benefit from floating rate bonds when interest rates are rising or falling?

Answers to Quick Quiz

1   Capital markets and private placement

2   D

3   False. They are long-term payables of the company.

4   (a)   12%
     (b) $12

5   False. The company will be able to choose the date of redemption.

6   Ordinary shares

7   B   The holder has the option to convert, but he will only convert if it is advantageous for him to do so. If the share price falls, the bonds may run their full term and need to be redeemed in the same way as other forms of debt.

8   Falling

Answers to Questions

5.1 Convertible debt

(a)   Conversion ratio is $100 bond = 30 ordinary shares

       Conversion value = 30 × $4.15 = $124.50

(b)   Conversion premium = $(142 – 124.50) = $17.50

       or $\frac{17.50}{124.50} \times 100\% = 14\%$

       The share price would have to rise by 14% before the conversion rights became attractive.

Now try the questions from the Practice Question Bank	**Question** Section A: 5.1 – 5.5	**Level** Practice

MANAGING THE DEBT PROFILE

In this chapter we look at how a company should structure its debt profile to ensure that risks associated with debt finance such as refinancing risk, interest rate risk and currency risk are mitigated. This includes structuring the maturity profile so that debts mature at different times, and using derivatives such as interest rate swaps and currency swaps to hedge against adverse fluctuations in interest rates and exchange rates.

Topic list	learning outcomes	syllabus references	ability required
1 Managing the debt profile	B1(b)	B1(b)(ii)(iii)	evaluation
2 Managing currency risk	B1(b)	B1(b)(ii)(iii)	evaluation
3 Managing interest rate risk	B1(b)	B1(b)(ii)(iii)	evaluation

Chapter Overview

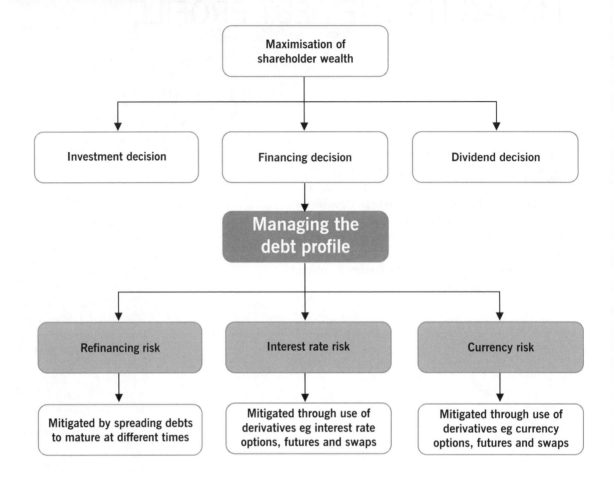

1 Managing the debt profile

Introduction

A company's debt profile is its mix of different types of debt finance. Management will be responsible for structuring the debt profile to reduce the risks associated with debt finance, such as refinancing risk, currency risk and interest rate risk.

1.1 Refinancing risk

This is the risk that a company cannot repay or refinance existing debts. This risk is reduced if its maturity profile (ie the timing of maturity of debts) is spread so that the debts mature at different times. This enables the company to put in place a schedule of refinancing and ensure there is adequate cash available to pay off debts when they mature.

1.2 Currency risk

A company can face higher costs if it borrows in a currency for which exchange rates move adversely against the company's domestic currency. Management should seek to match the currency of the loan with the currency of the underlying operations or assets that generate revenue to pay interest or repay the loans. Currency swaps can be used to hedge against currency risk from long-term borrowings in a different currency. Currency swaps are discussed in Section 2.

1.3 Interest rate risk

This is the risk of interest payments increasing due to fluctuating interest rates. A company that has fixed interest debt may end up paying more than it needs to if interest rates fall. However the company runs the risk of adverse increases in interest rates if it chooses floating rate debt. Interest rate swaps can be used to hedge against interest rate risk from long-term borrowings. Interest rate swaps are discussed in Section 3.

Section summary

- **Refinancing risk** is the risk that a company cannot repay or refinance existing debts. This can be mitigated by spreading debts to mature at different times.

- **Currency risk** is the risk of higher costs resulting from adverse exchange rate movements. This can be mitigated through the use of derivatives.

- **Interest rate risk** is the risk of interest rate payments increasing due to fluctuating interest rates. This can be mitigated through the use of derivatives.

2 Managing currency risk

Introduction

Techniques for managing currency risk are covered in detail in Paper P3 *Risk Management*. In this section we will briefly recap these techniques and then look at currency swaps in more detail as a technique for managing currency risk.

2.1 Foreign currency risk

Multinational corporations are affected by movements in exchange rates. Generally, exposure to foreign exchange risk can be categorised as **transaction** exposure, **translation** exposure and **economic** exposure.

Transaction risk is the risk of adverse exchange rate movements occurring in the course of normal international trading transactions.

Translation exposure occurs in multinational corporations that have foreign subsidiaries with assets and liabilities denominated in foreign currency. Translation exposure occurs because the value of these accounts must eventually be stated in domestic currency for reporting purposes in the company's financial statements. In general, as exchange rates change, the home currency value of the foreign subsidiaries' assets and liabilities will change. Such changes can result in translation losses or gains which will be recognised in financial statements. The nature and structure of the subsidiaries' assets and liabilities determine the extent of translation exposure to the parent company.

Economic risk is the risk that the present value of a company's future cash flows might be reduced by adverse fluctuations in exchange rates.

To reduce economic exposure a foreign subsidiary can be financed, as far as possible, with a loan in the currency of the country in which the subsidiary operates. A depreciating currency results in reduced income but also reduced loan service costs. A multinational will try to match assets and liabilities in each country as far as possible. This will also reduce the impact of translation risk as it minimises the net balance to be translated.

Methods of reducing currency risk include the following:

- **Leading and lagging payments** – making payments in advance (leading) or delaying payments (lagging) to take advantage of foreign exchange rate movements

- **Matching receipts and payments in the same currency** – a company that expects to make payments and have receipts in the same foreign currency should plan to offset its payments against its receipts in the currency

- **Matching assets and liabilities in the same currency** – a company which has a long-term foreign investment, for example an overseas subsidiary, should try to match its foreign assets (property, plant etc) with a long-term loan in the foreign currency

- **Currency futures** – standardised contracts to buy or sell a fixed amount of currency at a fixed rate at a fixed future date

- **Forward exchange contracts** – non-standardised contracts with a bank for a specific amount of foreign currency to be delivered at an agreed date at an exchange rate agreed now

- **Currency options** – agreements involving a right, but not an obligation, to buy or sell a certain amount of currency at a stated rate of exchange (the exercise price) at some time in the future

- **Currency swaps** (see below)

2.2 Currency swaps

In a **currency swap**, the parties agree to swap equivalent amounts of currency for a period. This effectively involves the exchange of debt from one currency to another. Liability on the main debt (the principal) is not transferred and the parties are liable to **counterparty risk**: if the other party defaults on the agreement to pay interest, the original borrower remains liable to the lender. In practice, most currency swaps are conducted between banks and their customers. An agreement may only be necessary if the swap were for longer than, say, one year.

Example

Consider a US company X with a subsidiary Y in France, which owns vineyards. Assume a spot rate of $1 = €0.7062. Suppose the parent company X wishes to raise a loan of €1.6 million for the purpose of buying another French wine company. At the same time, the French subsidiary Y wishes to raise $1 million to pay for new up-to-date capital equipment imported from the US. The US parent company X could borrow the $1 million and the French subsidiary Y could borrow the €1.6 million, each effectively borrowing on the other's behalf. They would then swap currencies.

2.2.1 Benefits of currency swaps

(a) **Flexibility**

Swaps are **easy to arrange** and are **flexible** since they can be arranged in any size and are reversible.

(b) **Cost**

Transaction costs are low, only amounting to legal fees, since there is no commission or premium to be paid.

(c) **Market avoidance**

The parties can **obtain the currency they require** without subjecting themselves to the **uncertainties** of the foreign exchange markets.

(d) **Access to finance**

The company can gain **access to debt finance in another country** and currency where it is little known, and consequently has a poorer credit rating, than in its home country. It can therefore take advantage of lower interest rates than it could obtain if it arranged the currency loan itself.

(e) **Financial restructuring**

Currency swaps may be used to restructure the currency base of the company's liabilities. This may be important where the company is trading overseas and receiving revenues in foreign currencies, but its borrowings are denominated in the currency of its home country. Currency swaps therefore provide a means of reducing exchange rate exposure.

(f) **Conversion of debt type**

At the same time as exchanging currency, the company may also be able to **convert fixed rate debt** to **floating rate or vice versa**. Thus it may obtain some of the benefits of an interest rate swap in addition to achieving the other purposes of a currency swap.

(g) **Liquidity improvement**

A currency swap could be used to **absorb excess liquidity** in one currency which is not needed immediately, to create funds in another where there is a need.

2.2.2 Disadvantages of currency swaps

(a) **Risk of default by the other party to the swap (counterparty risk)**

If one party became **unable to meet its swap payment obligations**, this could mean that the other party risked having to make them itself.

(b) **Position or market risk**

A company whose main business lies outside the field of finance should **not increase financial risk** in order to make **speculative gains**.

(c)   **Sovereign risk**

There may be a risk of **political disturbances or exchange controls** in the country whose currency is being used for a swap.

(d)   **Arrangement fees**

Swaps have arrangement fees payable to third parties. Although these may appear to be cheap, this is because the intermediary accepts **no liability** for the swap. (The third party does however suffer some spread risk, as they warehouse one side of the swap until it is matched with the other, and then undertake a temporary hedge on the futures market.)

Example

 Edted, a UK company, wishes to invest in Germany. It borrows £20 million from its bank and pays interest at 5%. To invest in Germany, the £20 million will be converted into euros at a spot rate of €1.5 = £1. The earnings from the German investment will be in euros, but Edted will have to pay interest on the swap. The company arranges to swap the £20 million for €30 million with Gordonbear, a company in the euro currency zone. Gordonbear is thus the counterparty in this transaction. Interest of 6% is payable on the €30 million. Edted can use the €30 million it receives to invest in Germany.

 Each year when interest is due:

(a)   Edted receives from its German investment cash remittances of €1.8 million (€30 million × 6%).

(b)   Edted passes this €1.8 million to Gordonbear so that Gordonbear can settle its interest liability.

(c)   Gordonbear passes to Edted £1 million (£20 million × 5%).

(d)   Edted settles its interest liability of £1 million with its lender.

 At the end of the useful life of the investment the original payments are reversed with Edted paying back the €30 million it originally received and receiving back from Gordonbear the £20 million. Edted uses this £20 million to repay the loan it originally received from its UK lender.

 Section summary

- **Currency swaps** can be to hedge against adverse foreign currency movements.

- **Currency swaps** effectively involve the exchange of debt from one currency to another.

3 Managing interest rate risk

 Introduction

Techniques for managing interest rate risk are covered in detail in Paper P3 Risk Management. In this section we will briefly recall these techniques and then look at interest rate swaps in more detail as a technique for managing interest rate risk.

3.1 Interest rate risk management

If the organisation faces interest rate risk, it can seek to **hedge the risk**. Alternatively where the magnitude of the risk is **immaterial** in comparison with the company's overall cash flows or appetite for risks, one option is to **do nothing**. The company then accepts the effects of any movement in interest rates which occur.

The company may also decide to do nothing if **risk management costs are excessive**, both in terms of the costs of using derivatives and the staff resources required to manage risk effectively. **Appropriate products** may not be available and of course the company may consider hedging unnecessary as it believes that the **chances of an adverse movement** are **remote**.

Methods of reducing interest rate risk include the following:

- **Netting** – aggregating all positions, assets and liabilities, and hedging the net exposure

- **Smoothing** – maintaining a balance between fixed and floating rate borrowing

- **Matching** – matching assets and liabilities to have a common interest rate

- **Forward rate agreement (FRA)** – a binding contract that fixes an interest rate for short-term lending, investing or short-term borrowing, for an interest rate period that begins at a future date

- **Interest rate futures** – can be used to hedge against interest rate changes between the current date and the date at which the interest rate on the lending or borrowing is set (borrowers **sell futures** to hedge against **interest rate rises;** lenders buy futures to hedge against **interest rate falls)**

- **Interest rate options** – an **interest rate option** grants the buyer of it the right, but **not the obligation**, to deal at an agreed interest rate (strike rate) at a future maturity date

- **Interest rate swaps** (see below)

Exam skills

Bear in mind the possibility that a company may take the decision to do nothing to reduce interest rate risk – it is a situation you should consider when answering exam questions.

3.2 Interest rate swaps

A **swap** is an arrangement whereby two organisations contractually agree to exchange payments on different terms, for example one interest payment at a fixed rate and the other at a floating rate, or in different currencies.

Interest rate swaps can act as a means of **switching** from paying one type of interest to another, allowing an organisation to obtain **less expensive loans** and **securing better** deposit **rates**.

3.2.1 Swap procedures

Interest rate swaps involve two parties agreeing to exchange interest payments with each other over an agreed period. In practice, however, the major players in the swaps market are banks and many other types of institution can also become involved, for example national and local governments and international institutions.

In the simplest form of interest rate swap, party A agrees to pay the interest on party B's loan, while party B reciprocates by paying the interest on A's loan. If the swap is to make sense, **the two parties must swap interest which has different characteristics**. Assuming that the interest swapped is in the same currency, the most common motivation for the swap is to switch from paying floating rate interest to fixed interest or *vice versa*. This type of swap is known as a '**plain vanilla**' or **generic** swap.

An example is illustrated below.

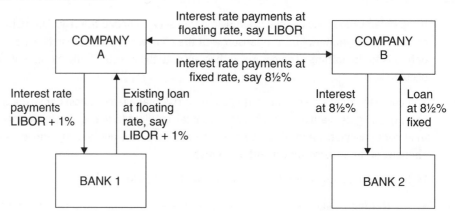

Interest rate swap

In this example, company A can use a swap to change from paying interest at a floating rate of LIBOR + 1% (or 100 basis points) to one of paying fixed interest of (8½% + 1%) = 9½%.

Bonds, debentures and loan stock usually have a fixed rate of interest, whereas bank loans and overdrafts usually have a variable or floating rate of interest, quoted as a % above a benchmark rate (eg the base rate or LIBOR).

LIBOR or the London interbank offered rate is the rate of interest at which banks borrow from each other in the London interbank market.

A swap may be arranged with a bank, or a counterparty may be found through a bank or other financial intermediary. Fees will be payable if a bank is used. However a bank may be able to find a **counterparty more easily**, and may have **access to more counterparties** in **more markets** than if the company seeking the swap tried to find the counterparty itself.

Swaps are generally terminated by agreeing a **settlement interest rate**, generally the current market rate.

 Question 6.1   Interest rate swaps

Learning outcome: B(1)(b)

Goodcredit has been given a high credit rating. It can borrow at a fixed rate of 11%, or at a variable interest rate equal to LIBOR, which also happens to be 11% at the moment. It would like to borrow at a variable rate.

Secondtier is a company with a lower credit rating, which can borrow at a fixed rate of 12½% or at a variable rate of LIBOR plus ½%. It would like to borrow at a fixed rate.

Required

Design a swap that allows both companies to gain by equal amounts.

3.2.2 Why bother to swap?

Obvious questions to ask are:

- Why do the companies bother swapping interest payments with each other?

    The swap makes use of the fact that different businesses will have different preferences for risk and different credit ratings and sources of finance available. So a business that wants a fixed rate loan but can only obtain cheap variable rate finance can swap with one that has access to cheap fixed rate finance but would prefer floating rate. The bank acts as an intermediary to effect this.

- Why don't they just terminate their original loan and take out a new one?

  The answer is that **transaction costs** may be too high. Terminating an original loan early may involve a significant termination fee and taking out a new loan will involve issue costs. Arranging a swap can be significantly cheaper, even if a banker is used as an intermediary. Because the banker is simply acting as an agent on the swap arrangement and has to bear no default risk, the arrangement fee can be kept low.

3.2.3 Advantages and disadvantages of interest rate swaps

Advantages

(a) **Flexibility and costs**

As with currency swaps, interest rate swaps are **flexible**, since they can be arranged in any size, and they can be **reversed** if necessary. **Transaction costs are low**, particularly if no intermediary is used, and are potentially much lower than the costs of terminating one loan and taking out another.

(b) **Credit ratings**

Companies **with different credit ratings** can **borrow in the market** that offers each the best deal and then swap this benefit to reduce the mutual borrowing costs. This is an example of the principle of **comparative advantage**.

(c) **Capital structure**

Swaps allow **capital restructuring** by changing the nature of interest commitments without renegotiating with lenders.

(d) **Risk management**

Swaps can be used to **manage interest rate risk** by swapping floating for fixed rate debt if rates are expected to rise. Swaps can also be used to swap a variable rate for a fixed rate investment if interest rates are expected to fall.

(e) **Convenience**

As with currency swaps, interest rate swaps are relatively **easy to arrange**.

(f) **Predictability of cash flows**

If a company's future cash flows are uncertain, it can use a swap to ensure it has **predictable fixed rate commitments**.

Disadvantages

(a) **Additional risk**

The swap is subject to **counterparty risk:** the risk that the other party will default leaving the first company to bear its obligations. This risk can be avoided by using an intermediary.

(b) **Movements in interest rates**

If a company takes on a floating rate commitment, it may be vulnerable to **adverse movements in interest rates**. If it takes on a fixed rate commitment, it won't be able to **take advantage of favourable movements in rates**.

(c) **Lack of liquidity**

The **lack of a secondary market in swaps** makes it **very difficult to liquidate a swap contract**.

Section summary

- **Interest rate swaps** can be used to hedge against adverse interest rate movements.

- A **swap** is an arrangement whereby two organisations contractually agree to exchange payments on different terms, for example one interest payment at a fixed rate and the other at a floating rate.

Chapter Summary

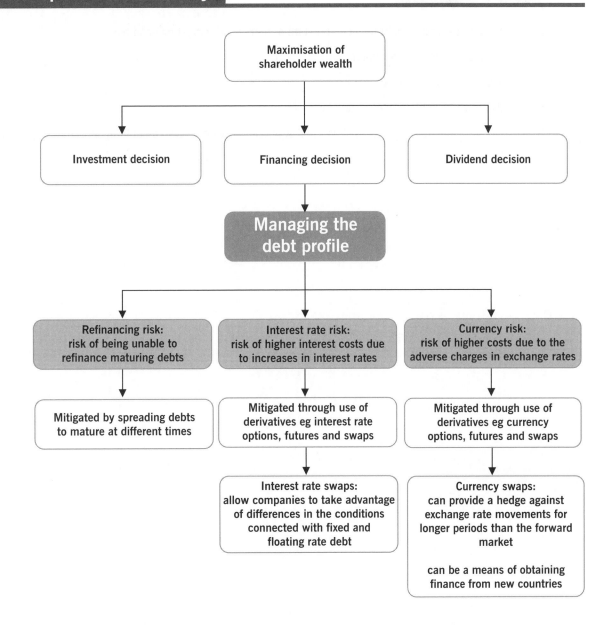

Quick Quiz

1   Name three risks of debt finance and state a method for mitigating each risk.

2   What is an interest rate swap?

3   What is a currency swap?

4   Give three uses of an interest rate swap.

5   .... risk is the risk of one party on a swap defaulting on the arrangement.

Answers to Quick Quiz

1. Refinancing risk: mitigated by spreading debts to mature at different times.

    Interest rate risk: mitigated by using derivatives such as interest rate swaps.

    Currency risk: mitigated by using derivates such as currency swaps.

2   An interest rate swap is an arrangement whereby two organisations contractually agree to exchange interest payments on different terms, ie one interest payment at a fixed rate and the other at a floating rate.

3   A currency swap is where two parties agree to swap equivalent amounts of currency for a period.

4   Any three of:

    (a) Switching from paying one type of interest to another

    (b) Raising less expensive loans

    (c) Securing better deposit rates

    (d) Acting as a cost-effective method of managing interest rate risk

    (e) Avoiding charges for early termination of loans

    (f) Accessing a type of finance that could not be accessed directly

5   Counterparty

Answers to Questions

6.1 Interest rate swaps

	Goodcredit	Secondtier	Sum total
Company wants	Variable	Fixed	
Would pay (no swap)	(LIBOR)	(12.5%)	(LIBOR + 12.5%)
Could pay	(11%)	(LIBOR + 0.5%)	(LIBOR + 11.5%)
Potential gain			1%
Split evenly	0.5%	0.5%	
Expected outcome	(LIBOR – 0.5%)	(12%)	(LIBOR + 11.5%)
Swap terms			
Pay interest that could pay	(11%)	(LIBOR + 0.5%)	(LIBOR + 11.5%)
Swap floating	(LIBOR)	LIBOR	
Swap fixed (Working)	11.5%	(11.5%)	
Net paid	(LIBOR – 0.5%)	(12%)	(LIBOR + 11.5%)
Would pay	(LIBOR)	(12.5%)	(LIBOR + 12.5%)
Gain	0.5%	0.5%	1%

Workings

The floating interest swapped is the amount paid by Secondtier.

Given that the gains are split equally, the fixed interest swap is designed to achieve a situation where each party gains by 0.5%. To achieve LIBOR – 0.5% for Goodcredit, the fixed rate must be 11.5%.

The results of the swap are that Goodcredit ends up paying variable rate interest, but at a lower cost than it could get from a bank, and Secondtier ends up paying fixed rate interest, also at a lower cost than it could get from investors or a bank.

Tutorial note: reason for gain

If both parties ended up paying interest at a lower rate than was obtainable from the bank, where did this gain come from? To answer this question, set out a table of the rates at which both companies could borrow from the bank.

	Goodcredit	*Secondtier*	*Difference*
			%
Can borrow at fixed rate	11%	12.5%	1.5
Can borrow at floating rate	LIBOR	LIBOR + 0.5%	0.5
Difference between differences			1.0

Goodcredit has a better credit rating than Secondtier in both types of loan market, but its advantage is comparatively higher in the fixed interest market. The 1% differential between Goodcredit's advantage in the two types of loan may represent a market imperfection or there may be a good reason for it. Whatever the reason, it represents a potential gain which can be made out of a swap arrangement. For a gain to happen:

(a) Each company must borrow in the loan market in which it has **comparative advantage**. Goodcredit has the greatest advantage when it borrows fixed interest. Secondtier has the least disadvantage when it borrows floating rate.

(b) The parties must actually **want** interest of the opposite type to that in which they have comparative advantage. Goodcredit wants floating and Secondtier wants fixed.

Once the target interest rate for each company has been established, there is an infinite number of swap arrangements which will produce the same net result. The example illustrated above is only one of them.

Now try the questions from the Practice Question Bank	**Question** Section A: 6.1 – 6.4	**Level** Practice

LEASING

 In this chapter we consider the option of
leasing an asset.

As well as looking at the **advantages** and **disadvantages**
of different types of lease compared with **other forms of
credit finance**, we shall be discussing the tax and cash
flow implications of leasing. You need to know how to
determine whether an organisation should **lease** or **buy**
an asset.

Topic list	learning outcomes	syllabus references	ability required
1 Leasing as a source of finance	B(1)(b)	B(1)(b)(vii)	evaluation
2 Lease or buy decisions	B(1)(b)	B(1)(b)(vii)	evaluation

Chapter Overview

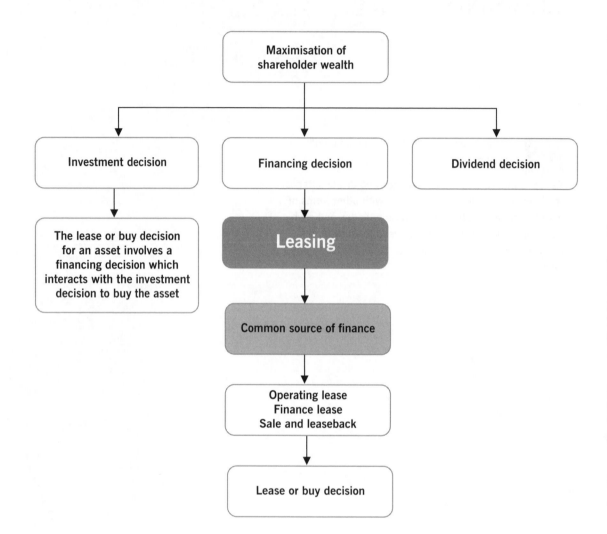

1   Leasing as a source of finance

Introduction

Lease accounting is covered in Paper F2 *Advanced Financial Reporting*. Leasing is a commonly used source of finance, especially for small or medium-sized entities. It is a form of debt finance that can be very useful where capital is rationed.

1.1 The nature of leasing

Rather than buying an asset outright, using either available cash resources or borrowed funds, a business may lease an asset.

KEY TERM

LEASING is a contract between lessor and lessee for hire of a specific asset selected from a manufacturer or vendor of such assets by the lessee.

(a)   The **lessor** retains ownership of the asset.

(b)   The **lessee** has possession and use of the asset on payment of specified rentals over a period.

(c)   Many lessors are **financial intermediaries** such as banks and insurance companies.

(d)   The **range of assets leased** is wide, including office equipment and computers, cars and commercial vehicles, aircraft, ships and buildings.

1.2 Operating leases

Operating leases are rental agreements between the user of the leased asset (the lessee) and a provider of finance (the lessor) whereby:

(a)   The **lessor supplies the equipment** to the lessee.

(b)   The **lessor** is **responsible** for **servicing and maintaining the leased equipment.**

(c)   The **period of the lease** is fairly **short**, **less** than the **expected economic life** of the asset, so that at the end of one lease agreement, the lessor can either lease the same equipment to someone else, and obtain a good rent for it, or sell the equipment second-hand.

With an operating lease, the lessor, often a finance house, purchases the equipment from the manufacturer and then leases it to the user (the lessee) for the agreed period.

1.3 Finance leases

KEY TERM

FINANCE LEASE is a lease agreement that transfers substantially all the risks and rewards incidental to ownership of an asset from the lessor to the lessee.   *(CIMA Official Terminology)*

Finance leases are lease agreements between a **lessor** and **lessee**, for most or all of the asset's expected useful life.

Suppose that a company decides to obtain a company car and to finance the acquisition by means of a finance lease. A **car dealer** will **supply the car**. A finance house will agree to act as lessor in a finance leasing arrangement, and so will purchase the car from the dealer and lease it to the company. The company will take possession of the car from the car dealer, and make regular payments (monthly, quarterly, six monthly or annually) to the finance house under the terms of the lease.

There are other important characteristics of a finance lease.

(a) The **lessee** is normally **responsible** for the **upkeep**, servicing and maintenance of the asset. For a car this would mean repairs and servicing, road tax insurance and garaging. The lessor is not involved in this at all.

(b) The **lease** has a **primary period**, which covers all or most of the useful economic life of the asset. At the end of this primary period, the lessor would not be able to lease the asset to someone else, because the asset would be worn out. The lessor must therefore ensure that the lease payments during the primary period pay for the full cost of the asset as well as providing the lessor with a suitable return on his investment.

(c) The lessee may be able to continue to lease the asset for an **indefinite secondary period**, in return for a very low nominal rent, sometimes called a 'peppercorn rent'. Alternatively, the lessee might be allowed to sell the asset on a lessor's behalf (since the lessor is the owner) and to keep most of the sale proceeds, paying only a small percentage (perhaps 10%) to the lessor.

Example: Finance lease

On 1 January 20X0, Gordon Co leased an asset with a fair value of $38 million. The lease term was five years and the interest rate implicit in the lease was 10%. The company is required to make five annual instalments of $10 million on 31 December, with the first payment on 31 December 20X0.

Solution

Interest is calculated as 10% of the outstanding **capital** balance at the beginning of each year. The outstanding capital balance reduces each year by the capital element comprised in each instalment. The outstanding capital balance at 1 January 20X0 is the $38 million fair value at which both the asset and liability are initially recorded.

	$m
Balance 1 January 20X0	38.0
Interest 10%	3.8
Instalment 31 December 20X0	(10.0)
Balance outstanding 31 December 20X0	31.8
Interest 10% (rounded)	3.2
Instalment 31 December 20X1	(10.0)
Balance outstanding 31 December 20X1	25.0
Interest 10%	2.5
Instalment 31 December 20X2	(10.0)
Balance outstanding 31 December 20X2	17.5
Interest 10% (rounded)	1.7
Instalment 31 December 20X3	(10.0)
Balance outstanding 31 December 20X3	9.2
Interest 10% (rounded)	0.8
Instalment 31 December 20X4	(10.0)
	–

1.4 Attractions of leasing

The attractions of leases to the supplier of the equipment, the lessee and the lessor are as follows:

(a) The **supplier** of the **equipment** is **paid in full** at the **beginning**. The equipment is sold to the lessor, and apart from obligations under guarantees or warranties, the supplier has no further financial concern about the asset.

(b) The **lessor invests finance** by **purchasing assets** from suppliers and makes a return out of the lease payments from the lessee. Provided that a lessor can find lessees willing to pay the amounts he wants to make his return, the lessor can make good profits. He will also get capital allowances on his purchase of the equipment.

(c) **Leasing** might be **attractive** to the **lessee**:

   (i) If the lessee does not have enough cash to pay for the asset, and would have difficulty obtaining a bank loan to buy it, and so has to rent it in one way or another if they are to have use of it at all

   (ii) If finance leases are **cheaper** than **bank loans;** surveys suggest that this is a major reason why leases are used (the logic is that the lessor is prepared to **lend** at a **lower cost** because he possesses greater security ie the ownership of the asset)

   (iii) Leases, once negotiated, are **legally binding** and **cannot be withdrawn** with immediate effect in the way an overdraft facility might be.

   (iv) The lessee may find the **tax relief** available advantageous.

Operating leases have these further advantages.

(a) The leased equipment does **not** have to be **shown** in the **lessee's published balance sheet**, and so the lessee's balance sheet shows no increase in its gearing ratio.

(b) The **equipment** is **leased** for a **shorter period** than its expected useful life. In the case of high-technology equipment, if the equipment becomes out of date before the end of its expected life, the lessee does not have to keep on using it, and it is the lessor who must bear the risk of having to sell obsolete equipment second-hand.

(c) The lessor deals with **servicing**, **maintenance** and **administration**.

Not surprisingly perhaps, a major growth area in operating leasing has been in computers and office equipment (such as photocopiers and fax machines) where technology is continually improving.

CASE STUDY

The aircraft leasing industry has come to the fore after several aviation downturns in recent years. Lessors' ownership of the world's civil aircraft fleet has increased from 12 per cent in 1990 to 36 per cent in 2010, according to Boeing, the plane maker.

Some aircraft lessors are predicting their share of the global fleet will rise to as much as 50 per cent by 2015, partly because some airlines may find it harder to secure financing for their jets due to economic circumstances. Lessors make most of their money through the charges paid by airlines that use their jets.

(Source: Financial Times 17 January 2012)

1.5 Allocating the finance charge – the actuarial method

The actuarial method of allocating the finance charge uses a periodic interest rate to calculate interest on the outstanding amount of the lease.

At the beginning of the lease, the capital invested is equal to the fair value of the asset (less any initial deposit paid by the lessee).

This amount reduces as each instalment is paid. Interest is charged on the reducing balance of the capital. It follows that the interest accruing is greatest in the early part of the lease term and gradually reduces as capital is repaid. The example below illustrates this point.

Example: Actuarial method

On 1 January 20X5 Jennifer Co acquired a machine from Alice Co under a finance lease. The cash price of the machine was $7,710 while the minimum payments in the lease agreement totalled $10,000. The agreement required the immediate payment of a $2,000 deposit with the balance being settled in four equal annual instalments commencing on 31 December 20X5. The finance charge of $2,290 represents interest of 15% per annum, calculated on the remaining balance of the liability during each accounting period. Depreciation on the plant is to be provided for at the rate of 20% per annum on a straight line basis assuming a residual value of nil.

Required

Show the breakdown of each instalment between interest and capital, using the actuarial method.

Solution

Interest is calculated as 15% of the outstanding **capital** balance at the beginning of each year. The outstanding capital balance reduces each year by the capital element included in each instalment. The outstanding capital balance at 1 January 20X5 is $5,710 ($7,710 fair value less $2,000 deposit).

	Total $	Capital $	Interest $
Capital balance at 1 Jan 20X5		5,710	
1st instalment (interest = $5,710 × 15%)	2,000	1,144	856
Capital balance at 1 Jan 20X6		4,566	
2nd instalment (interest = $4,566 × 15%)	2,000	1,315	685
Capital balance at 1 Jan 20X7		3,251	
3rd instalment (interest = $3,251 × 15%)	2,000	1,512	488
Capital balance at 1 Jan 20X8		1,739	
4th instalment (interest = $1,739 × 15%)	2,000	1,739	261
	8,000	–	2,290
Capital balance at 1 Jan 20X9			

1.6 Allocating the finance charge – the sum of digits method

The **sum of digits** method splits the total interest (without reference to a rate of interest) in such a way that the greater proportion falls in the earlier years. This method is quicker and easier to calculate than the actuarial method. The procedure is as follows:

Assign a digit to each instalment. The digit 1 should be assigned to the final instalment, 2 to the penultimate instalment and so on.

Add the digits. A quick method of adding the digits is to use the formula $n(n+1)/2$ where n is the number of periods of borrowing.

Calculate the interest charge included in each instalment. Do this by multiplying the total interest accruing over the lease term by the fraction:

$$\frac{\text{Digit applicable to the payment}}{\text{Sum of the digits}}$$

Example: Sum of digits method

Using the same information as the previous example of Jennifer Co:

Required

Show the interest payments in each year, using the sum of digits method.

Solution

Assign digits to the borrowing periods:

20X5   4
20X6   3
20X7   2
20X8   1

Add the digits:

1 + 2 + 3 + 4 = 10

Or (4 × 5)/2 = 10

Calculate the interest charge:

The total interest paid is $10,000 – $7,710 = $2,290. The amount charged to each year is:

20X5   4/10 × $2,290 = $916
20X6   3/10 × $2,290 = $687
20X7   2/10 × $2,290 = $458
20X8   1/10 × $2,290 = $229

1.7 Sale and leaseback arrangements

A company which owns its own premises can obtain finance by selling the property to an insurance company or pension fund for immediate cash and renting it back, usually for at least 50 years with rent reviews every few years.

A company would raise more cash from a **sale and leaseback agreement** than from a mortgage, but it should only make such an agreement if it cannot raise sufficient funds any other way.

Disadvantages of sale and leaseback are as follows:

(a)   The company **loses ownership** of a valuable asset which is almost certain to appreciate over time.

(b)   The **future borrowing capacity** of the firm will be reduced, since the property if owned could be used to provide security for a loan.

(c)   The company is **contractually committed** to occupying the property for many years ahead, and this can be restricting.

(d)   The **real cost** is likely to be high, particularly as there will be frequent rent reviews.

1.8 Hire purchase

Hire purchase is a **vendor credit arrangement** similar to leasing, with the exception that ownership of the goods passes to the hire purchase customer on payment of the final credit instalment, whereas a lessee never becomes the owner of the goods.

Learning outcome: B(1)(b)

Explain the cash flow characteristics of a finance lease, and compare it with the use of a bank loan. Your answer should include some comment on the significance of a company's anticipated tax position on lease *versus* buy decisions.

Section summary

Leasing is a commonly used source of finance. Major types of leases are **operating leases** (**lessor** responsible for maintaining asset), **finance leases** (**lessee** responsible for maintenance), and **sale and leaseback** arrangements.

2 Lease or buy decisions

Introduction

Leasing as a source of debt finance needs to be carefully analysed against other forms of debt finance using discounted cash flow techniques.

Discounted cash flow techniques are revised in the appendix: discounted cash flow. We will also be using these techniques in Chapter 11.

2.1 Lease or buy calculations

The decision whether to buy or lease an asset is made once the **decision to invest** in the asset has been made.

Discounted cash flow techniques are used to evaluate the lease or buy decision so that the **least-cost financing option** can be chosen.

The cost of capital that should be applied to the cash flows for the financing decision is the **cost of borrowing**. We assume that if the organisation decided to purchase the equipment, it would finance the purchase by borrowing funds (rather than out of retained funds). We therefore compare the **cost of borrowing** with the **cost of leasing** by applying this cost of borrowing to the financing cash flows.

The cost of borrowing **does not include the interest repayments on the loan** as this is dealt with via the cost of capital.

2.2 A simple example

Brown Co has decided to invest in a new machine which has a ten-year life and no residual value. The machine can either be purchased now for $50,000, or it can be leased for ten years with lease rental payments of $8,000 per annum payable at the end of each year.

The cost of capital to be applied is 9% and taxation should be ignored.

Solution

Present value of leasing costs

PV = Annuity factor at 9% for 10 years × $8,000
= 6.418 × $8,000
= $51,344

If the machine was purchased now, it would cost $50,000. The purchase is therefore the least-cost financing option.

2.3 An example with taxation

Mallen and Mullins Inc has decided to install a new milling machine. The machine costs $20,000 and it would have a useful life of five years with a trade-in value of $4,000 at the end of the fifth year. A decision has now to be taken on the method of financing the project.

(a) The company could purchase the machine for cash, using bank loan facilities on which the current rate of interest is 13% before tax.

(b) The company could lease the machine under an agreement which would entail payment of $4,800 at the end of each year for the next five years.

The rate of tax is 30%. If the machine is purchased, the company will be able to claim a tax depreciation allowance of 100% in Year 1. Tax is payable with a year's delay.

Solution

Cash flows are discounted at the after-tax cost of borrowing, which is at 13% × 70% = 9.1%, say 9%.

The present value (PV) of purchase costs

Year	Item	Cash flow $	Discount factor @ 9%	PV $
0	Equipment cost	(20,000)	1.000	(20,000)
2	Tax savings from allowances (30% × $20,000)	6,000	0.842	5,052
5	Trade-in value	4,000	0.650	2,600
6	Balancing charge arising from trade-in value (30% × $4,000)	1,200	0.596	(715)
			NPV of purchase	(13,063)

The PV of leasing costs

It is assumed that the lease payments are fully tax-allowable.

Year		Lease payment $	Savings in tax (30%) $	Discount factor @ 9%	PV $
1–5		(4,800) pa		3.890	(18,672)
2–6			1,440 pa	3.569 (W)	5,139
				NPV of leasing	(13,533)

Working

	$
6 year cumulative present value factor 9%	4.486
1 year present value factor 9%	(0.917)
	3.569

The cheapest option would be to purchase the machine.

An alternative method of making lease or buy decisions is to carry out a single financing calculation with the payments for one method being negative and the receipts being positive, and vice versa for the other method.

Year	0	1	2	3	4	5	6
	$m	$m	$m	$m	$m	$m	$m
Saved equipment cost	20,000						
Lost trade-in value						(4,000)	
Tax on trade-in value							1,200
Lost tax savings from allowances			(6,000)				
Lease payments		(4,800)	(4,800)	(4,800)	(4,800)	(4,800)	
Tax allowances			1,440	1,440	1,440	1,440	1,440
Net cash flow	20,000	(4,800)	(9,360)	(3,360)	(3,360)	(7,360)	2,640
Discount factor 9%	1.000	0.917	0.842	0.772	0.708	0.650	0.596
PV	20,000	(4,402)	(7,881)	(2,594)	(2,379)	(4,784)	1,573
NPV	(467)						

The **negative NPV** indicates that the **lease is unattractive** and the **purchasing decision is better**, as the net costs of leasing exceed the purchase price saved.

Exam skills

In this exam, speed is of the essence and you may find it much quicker to do a single calculation, especially if you then have to do a sensitivity analysis.

2.4 A more complicated example with taxation

Using the information from Example 2.3 (apart from the tax payment date) now assume that the company can claim tax depreciation allowances of 25%, on a reducing balance basis over the machine's five year life, if it is purchased.

Depreciation is tax deductible and Mallen and Mullins Inc uses straight line depreciation in its accounts. The interest element of the lease payments is also tax deductible.

The rate of tax is 30%, payable in the year of the relevant profits.

Exam skills

Tax treatment of leases varies in different countries and you need to read the information in an exam question very carefully. The examiners have commented that the tax aspects of these calculations have caused difficulties.

Solution

Tax depreciation allowances

Year	Value at start of year	25% depreciation	30% tax allowance
	$	$	$
1	20,000	5,000	1,500
2	15,000	3,750	1,125
3	11,250	2,813	844
4	8,437	2,109	633
5	8,437 – 2,109 – 4,000	Balance 2,328	698

Present value of purchase costs

Year	0	1	2	3	4	5
	$	$	$	$	$	$
Purchase cost	(20,000)					
Tax allowances		1,500	1,125	844	633	698
Trade-in value						4,000
Net cash flow	(20,000)	1,500	1,125	844	633	4,698
Discount factor 9%	1.000	0.917	0.842	0.772	0.708	0.650
PV	(20,000)	1,376	947	652	448	3,054
Total	(13,523)					

Leasing cost

$$\text{Depreciation costs} = \frac{20,000 - 4,000}{5} = \$3,200$$

Tax relief @ 30% = 960

In order to calculate the **interest implicit** in the lease, we need to calculate the implicit interest rate by using an IRR calculation:

Year		Cash flow	Discount factor @ 6%	PV	Discount factor @ 7%	PV
		$		$		$
0	Purchase cost	(20,000)	1.000	(20,000)	1.000	(20,000)
1–5	Lease payments	4,800	4.212	20,218	4.100	19,680
				218		(320)

$$\text{IRR} = 6\% + \frac{218}{(218 - 320)} \times 1 = 6.4\%$$

Opening balance	Implicit interest at 6.4%	End of year debt	Repayment	Closing balance
$	$	$	$	$
20,000	1,280	21,280	4,800	16,480
16,480	1,055	17,535	4,800	12,735
12,735	815	13,550	4,800	8,750
8,750	560	9,310	4,800	4,510
4,510	289	4,799	4,800	(1)

Rounding means that the final closing balance does not exactly equal zero.

NPV of leasing costs

	Year 1 $	Year 2 $	Year 3 $	Year 4 $	Year 5 $
Lease payments	(4,800)	(4,800)	(4,800)	(4,800)	(4,800)
Tax relief on depreciation	960	960	960	960	960
Tax relief on implicit interest	384	317	245	168	87
Net cash flows	(3,456)	(3,523)	(3,595)	(3,672)	(3,753)
Discount factor @ 9%	0.917	0.842	0.772	0.708	0.650
PV	(3,169)	(2,966)	(2,775)	(2,600)	(2,439)
Total	(13,949)				

2.5 Evaluating a lease or buy decision

Lease or buy decisions are not purely a matter of calculations. We discussed above why leasing might be attractive to a business; the following issues are also relevant to a lease or buy decision.

(a) **Effect on cash flow**

The organisation's liquidity at the time the **decision** is made may be **important**. If the business is suffering cash flow difficulties, lease payments may offer a smoother cash flow than one big lump sum.

(b) **Cost of capital**

The decision on whether to **obtain use** of the asset may be **dependent upon the appraisal method or cost of capital used**. A decision not to invest taken using the company's overall cost of capital may be reversed if a significantly lower cost of leasing is used in the cash flow.

(c) **Running expenses**

Lease or buy calculations normally assume that the **running costs** are the **same** under each alternative. This may not be so. **Expenses like maintenance and insurance** may differ between the alternatives.

(d) **Trade-in value**

The organisation will gain the (uncertain) benefits of a **trade-in value** if it chooses the purchase option.

(e) **Effect on reported profits**

Annual profits are reported on an **accruals basis**, after the deduction of depreciation. The effect of the alternatives on reported profits should be considered since this could, if significant, affect **dividend policy** and the **valuation of shares**.

(f) **Alternative uses of funds**

Lease or buy decisions will not be taken in **isolation**. If the business has limited funds available, there may be **better uses** for those funds than obtaining the asset, even if the asset does yield net positive cash flows.

2.6 The position of the lessor

So far, we have looked at examples of leasing decisions from the viewpoint of the lessee. You might be asked to evaluate a leasing arrangement from the position of the **lessor**. This is rather like a **mirror image** of the lessee's position.

Assuming that it is purchasing the asset, the lessor will receive capital allowances on the expenditure, and the lease payments will be taxable income.

2.7 Example: lessor's position

Continuing the same case of Mallen and Mullins from Example 2.3, suppose that the lessor's required rate of return is 12% after tax. The lessor's cash flows will be as follows.

	Cash flow $	Discount factor @ 12%	PV $
Purchase costs (see above)			
Year 0	(20,000)	1.000	(20,000)
Year 5 trade-in	4,000	0.567	2,268
Tax savings			
Year 2	6,000	0.797	4,782
Lease payments: years 1–5	4,800	3.605	17,304
Tax on lease payments: years 2–6			
(discount factor = 4.111 – 0.893)	(1,440)	3.218	(4,634)
NPV			(280)

Conclusion. The leasing payments proposed are not justifiable for the lessor if it seeks a required rate of return of 12%, since the resulting NPV is negative.

Question 7.2	Lease or buy

Learning outcome: B(1)(b)

The management of a company has decided to acquire Machine X which costs $63,000 and has an operational life of four years. The expected scrap value would be zero. Tax is payable at 30% on operating cash flows one year in arrears. Capital allowances are available at 100% in Year 1.

Suppose that the company has the opportunity either to purchase the machine or to lease it under a finance lease arrangement, at an annual rent of £20,000 for four years, payable at the end of each year. The company can borrow to finance the acquisition at 10%. Should the company lease or buy the machine?

Section summary

- The decision whether to **lease or buy** an asset is a **financing decision** which interacts with the investment decision to buy the asset.

- Identify the **least-cost financing option** by comparing the cash flows of purchasing and leasing. The cash flows are discounted at an **after-tax cost of borrowing**.

Chapter Summary

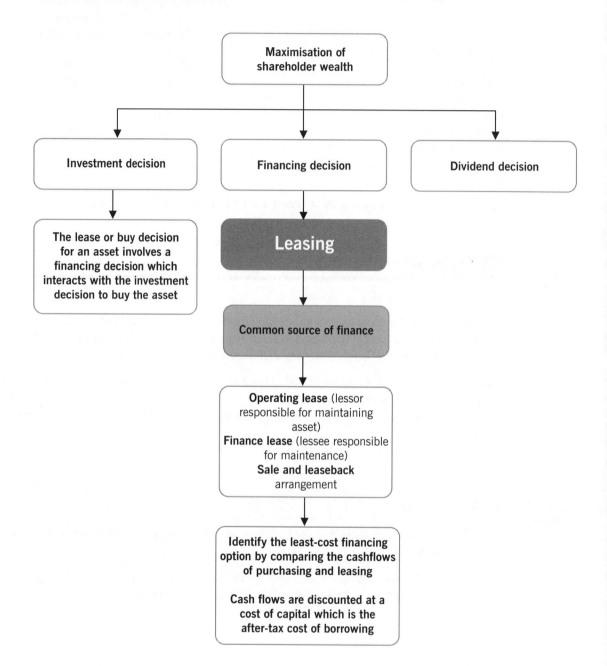

Quick Quiz

1   Operating leases and finance leases are distinguished for accounting purposes. Which of the following statements is not true of an operating lease?

A   The lessor supplies the equipment to the lessee.
B   The period of the lease is less than the expected economic life of the asset.
C   The lessee is normally responsible for servicing and maintaining the leased equipment.
D   The lessor retains most of the risks and rewards of ownership.

2   Who is responsible for the servicing of a leased asset in the case of:

(a)   An operating lease?
(b)   A finance lease?

    | The lessee | or | The lessor |

3   Why should operating leases be popular for users of high-technology equipment?

4   A hire purchase contract is a contract for the hire of an asset that contains a provision giving the hirer an option to acquire legal title to the asset upon the fulfilment of certain conditions stated in the contract.

True   ☐

False   ☐

Answers to Quick Quiz

1. C   The lessor is normally responsible for maintaining the equipment.

2. (a)   The lessor
   (b)   The lessee

3. Because such equipment may soon become obsolete

4. True

Answers to Questions

7.1 Lease v loan

A finance lease is an agreement between the user of the leased asset and a provider of finance that covers the majority of the asset's useful life. Key features of a finance lease are as follows:

(a) The provider of finance is usually a **third party finance house** and not the original provider of the equipment.

(b) The **lessee is responsible for the upkeep**, servicing and maintenance of the asset.

(c) The lease has a **primary period**, which covers all or most of the useful economic life of the asset. At the end of the primary period the lessor would not be able to lease the equipment to someone else because it would be worn out.

(d) It is common at the end of the primary period to allow the lessee to continue to lease the asset for an indefinite **secondary period**, in return for a very low nominal rent, sometimes known as a 'peppercorn' rent.

The cash flow implications of this form of lease are therefore as follows:

(a) **Regular payments** to the **lessor**, which comprise interest and principal. This can be very useful to the lessee from a cash flow management point of view.

(b) **Costs of maintenance** and so on, which may be less predictable in terms of both timing and amount.

(c) **Tax-allowable depreciation** cannot be claimed on the purchase cost of the equipment, but the lease payments are fully allowable for tax purposes. This may be of benefit to a company that is unable to make full use of its tax-allowable depreciation.

If the equipment is acquired using a **medium-term bank loan**, the cash flow patterns would be similar to those that would arise using a finance lease. However, if the loan were subject to a **variable rate of interest**, this would introduce a further source of variability into the cash flows. The main difference between the two approaches would be that the company could claim **tax-allowable depreciation** on the purchase cost of the equipment. The **interest element** of the repayments would also be allowable against tax, but the repayments of principal would not.

7.2 Lease or buy

The financing decision will be appraised by discounting the relevant cash flows at the after-tax cost of borrowing, which is $10\% \times 70\% = 7\%$.

(a)   **Purchase option**

Year	Item	Cash flow $	Discount factor 7%	Present value $
0	Cost of machine	(63,000)	1.000	(63,000)
2	Tax saved from tax-allowable depreciation			
	30% × £63,000	18,900	0.873	16,500
				(46,500)

(b)   **Leasing option**

It is assumed that the lease payments are tax-allowable in full.

Year	Item	Cash flow $	Discount factor 7%	Present value $
1–4	Lease costs	(20,000)	3.387	(67,740)
2–5	Tax savings on lease costs (×30%)	6,000	3.165	18,990
				(48,750)

The purchase option is cheaper, using a cost of capital based on the after-tax cost of borrowing. On the assumption that investors would regard borrowing and leasing as equally risky finance options, the purchase option is recommended.

> **Now try the questions from the Practice Question Bank**

Question	Level
Section A: 7.1 – 7.5	Practice
Section B: 5	Practice

EQUITY FINANCE

The topic of sources of long-term finance is covered in paper F2 *Advanced Financial Reporting*. However, you will be required to draw on this knowledge to evaluate and compare alternative methods of raising long-term finance.

In this chapter, we shall look at the methods of raising equity finance and describe the different forms of share.

We look at the process of floatation which a company must go through in order to issue shares on stock markets. As well as issues of new shares, we look at rights issues to existing shareholders.

Some of the content in this chapter revisits key points covered in F2 *Advanced Financial Reporting*.

Topic list	learning outcomes	syllabus references	ability required
1 Methods of raising equity finance	B(1)(b)(c)	B(1)(b)(v), (c)(i)	evaluation
2 Rights issues	B(1)(c)	B(1)(c)(ii)	evaluation
3 Share prices and investment returns	B(1)(c), C(2)(a)	B(1)(c)(i), C2(a)(iii)	evaluation
4 The dividend valuation model	C(2)(a)	C(2)(a)(v), C(2)(a)(ix), C(2)(a)(viii)	evaluation
5 The Capital Asset Pricing Model (CAPM)	C(2)(a)	C(2)(a)(viii)	evaluation

Chapter Overview

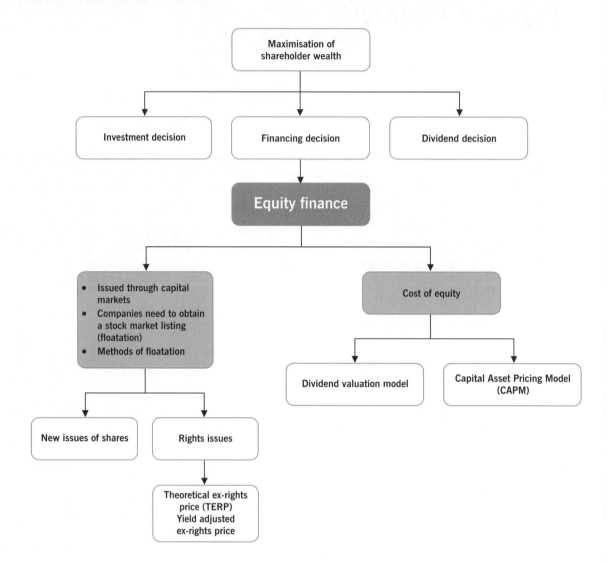

1   Methods of raising equity finance

Introduction

Companies can raise equity finance by issuing shares on capital markets. In this section we look at the different forms of share and the process of obtaining a stock market listing, which is required to trade on capital markets.

1.1 Ordinary (equity) shares

KEY TERMS

EQUITY is share capital, retained earnings and other reserves of a single entity, plus minority interests in a group, representing the investment made in the entity by the owners.

EQUITY SHARE CAPITAL is a company's issued share capital less capital which carries preferential rights. Equity share capital normally comprises ordinary shares.

Ordinary (equity) shares are those of the owners of a company.

The ordinary shares of UK companies have a **nominal** or 'face' value, typically £1. Outside the UK it is not uncommon for a company's shares to have no nominal value.

The market value of a quoted company's shares bears **no relationship** to their **nominal value**, except that when ordinary shares are issued for cash, the issue price must be equal to or (more usually) more than the nominal value of the shares.

1.2 Preference shares

KEY TERMS

PREFERENCE SHARES are shares carrying a fixed rate of dividends, the holders of which, subject to the conditions of issue, have a prior claim to any company profits available for distribution. They are an example of prior charge capital.

Preferred shareholders may also have a prior claim to the repayment of capital in the event of winding up.

PRIOR CHARGE CAPITAL is capital which has a right to the receipt of interest or of preferred dividends in precedence to any claim on distributable earnings on the part of the ordinary shareholders. On winding up, the claims of holders of prior charge capital also rank before those of ordinary shareholders.

1.2.1 Types of preference shares

Cumulative preference shares are preference shares where, if the company fails to pay a preference dividend, the arrears of dividend are carried forward and remain payable. When eventually the company decides to pay a dividend, the cumulative preference shareholders are entitled to all their arrears before ordinary shareholders are paid a dividend.

Participating preference shares are shares that have an additional entitlement to dividend over and above their specified fixed rate. Participating preferred shareholders are entitled to participate along with ordinary shareholders in available profits, normally once the ordinary shareholders have themselves received a specified level of dividend.

Convertible preference shares are shares that can be converted into ordinary shares.

1.2.2 Advantages and disadvantages of preference shares

From the company's point of view, preference shares have some positive features.

- Dividends do **not have** to be **paid** in a year in which **profits are poor**, while this is not the case with interest payments on long-term debt.

- Since they do not normally carry voting rights, preference shares **avoid diluting** the **control** of existing shareholders while an issue of equity shares would not.

- Unless they are redeemable, issuing preference shares will **lower** the company's **gearing**. Redeemable preference shares are normally treated as debt when gearing is calculated, but irredeemable preference shares are included in equity for the purpose of measuring gearing.

- The issue of preference shares does **not restrict** the company's **borrowing power**, at least in the sense that preference share capital is not secured against assets of the business.

- The non-payment of dividend does **not give** the preference shareholders the **right** to **appoint a receiver**, a right which is normally given to debenture holders.

From the point of view of the investor, preference shares are less attractive than loan stock because:

- They **cannot be secured** on the company's assets

- The **dividend yield** traditionally offered on preferred dividends has been much **too low** to provide an attractive investment compared with the interest yields on loan stock, in view of the additional risk involved.

- **Dividend payments on preference shares may not be tax-deductible** in the way that interest payments on debt are. Furthermore, for preference shares to be attractive to investors, the dividend yield needs to be higher than the interest yield on debt, to compensate for the additional risks.

1.3 Capital markets

In addition to long-term debt finance (see Chapter 5), equity finance can be raised on capital markets. Capital markets serve the following main purposes:

(a) **Primary markets**

As **primary markets** they enable organisations to **raise new finance**, by issuing new shares or debt securities. Capital markets make it easier for companies to raise new long-term finance than if they had to raise funds privately by contacting investors individually.

(b) **Secondary markets**

Secondary markets enable existing investors to sell their investments, should they wish to do so. They also allow investors to buy securities that have already been issued. The **marketability** of securities is a very important feature of the capital markets, because investors are more willing to buy investments if they know that they could sell them easily, should they wish to.

(c) **Realisation of value**

When a company comes to the stock market for the first time, and 'floats' its shares on the market, the **owners** of the company can **realise** some of the **value** of their shares in cash, because they will offer a proportion of their personally-held shares for sale to new investors.

(d) **Takeovers by means of share exchange**

When one company wants to take over another, it is common to do so by issuing shares to finance the takeover. Takeovers by means of a share exchange are only feasible if the shares that are offered can be readily traded on a stock market, and so have an identifiable market value.

1.4 Obtaining a stock market listing

In order for companies to raise finance on capital markets they need to obtain a stock market listing.

Some of the main requirements for obtaining a stock market listing are as follows.

- Three years of successful trading history
- Compliance with the corporate governance rules of the Combined Code
- Minimum 25% of shares in public hands

1.5 Advantages of a stock market listing

1.6 Disadvantages of a stock market listing

The owners of a company seeking a stock market listing must take the following disadvantages into account:

(a)   There will be significantly greater **public regulation, accountability** and **scrutiny.** The legal requirements the company faces will be greater, and the company will also be subject to the rules of the stock exchange on which its shares are listed.

(b)   A **wider circle of investors** with more exacting requirements will hold shares. There may be pressure to deliver short-term profits or certain levels of dividend.

(c)   There will be additional costs involved in making share issues, including **brokerage commissions** and **underwriting fees, as well as ongoing stock exchange membership fees**.

(d)   Listing may make the company a target for takeover.

1.7 Methods of obtaining a listing/flotation

The process of making shares available to investors by obtaining a quotation on a stock exchange is called **flotation**.

An unquoted company can obtain a listing on the stock market by means of:

- **Offer for sale**
- **Prospectus issue**
- **Placing**
- **Introduction**

Of these, an offer for sale or a placing are the most common.

Flotation has an impact on stakeholders as follows:

*   **Customers and suppliers** will have more faith in a company that has gone through the due diligence process and is governed by stock exchange rules.

*   **Employees** can benefit from receiving shares in the company.

*   Existing **shareholders** can exit at flotation.

*   Flotation is a very lengthy process and requires a lot of **management** time.

1.8 Initial public offer

KEY TERM

An INITIAL PUBLIC OFFER (IPO) is an invitation to the public to apply for shares in a company based on information contained in a prospectus.

An Initial Public Offer (IPO) is a means of selling the shares of a company to the public at large. When companies 'go public' for the first time, a **large** issue will probably take the form of an IPO. Subsequent issues are likely to be **placings** or **rights issues**, described later.

An IPO entails the **acquisition by an issuing house** of a large block of shares of a company, with a view to offering them for sale to the public.

An **issuing house** is usually an investment bank (or sometimes a firm of stockbrokers). It may acquire the shares either as a direct allotment from the company or by purchase from existing members. In either case, the issuing house publishes an invitation to the public to apply for shares, either at a fixed price or on a tender basis. The issuing house **accepts responsibility** to the public, and gives the support of its own reputation and standing to the issue.

CASE STUDY

In March 2017 the owners of Snapchat launched an IPO at $17. After briefly rising to over $24 in the early days of trading, doubts over its growth prospects caused a fall in its share price in the following weeks and months. In October 2017 the share price was $14.60.

1.8.1 Offers for sale by tender

It is often very difficult to decide upon the price at which the shares should be offered to the general public. One way of trying to ensure that the issue price reflects the value of the shares as perceived by the market is to make an **offer for sale by tender.** A **minimum price** will be fixed and subscribers will be invited to tender for shares at prices equal to or above the minimum. The shares will be **allotted at the highest price** at which they will **all be taken up**. This is known as the **striking price**.

Example: Offer for sale by tender

Byte Henderson is a new company that is making its first public issue of shares. It has decided to make the issue by means of an offer for sale by tender. The intention is to issue up to 4,000,000 shares (the full amount of authorised share capital) at a minimum price of 300 pence. The money raised, net of issue costs of £1,000,000, would be invested in projects which would earn benefits with a present value equal to 130% of the net amount invested.

The following tenders have been received. (Each applicant has made only one offer.)

Price tendered per share £	Number of shares applied for at this price
6.00	50,000
5.50	100,000
5.00	300,000
4.50	450,000
4.00	1,100,000
3.50	1,500,000
3.00	2,500,000

(a) How many shares would be issued, and how much in total would be raised, if Byte Henderson chooses:

    (i)   To maximise the total amount raised?

    (ii)   To issue exactly 4,000,000 shares?

(b) Harvey Goldfinger, a private investor, has applied for 12,000 shares at a price of £5.50 and has sent a cheque for £66,000 to the issuing house that is handling the issue. In both cases (a)(i) and (ii), how many shares would be issued to Mr Goldfinger, assuming that any partial acceptance of offers would mean allotting shares to each accepted applicant in proportion to the number of shares applied for? How much will Mr Goldfinger receive back out of the £66,000 he has paid?

Solution

(a) We begin by looking at the cumulative tenders.

Price £	Cumulative number of shares applied for	Amount raised if price is selected, before deducting issue costs £
6.00	50,000	300,000
5.50	150,000	825,000
5.00	450,000	2,250,000
4.50	900,000	4,050,000
4.00	2,000,000	8,000,000
3.50	3,500,000	12,250,000
3.00	6,000,000 (4,000,000 max)	12,000,000

    (i)   To maximise the total amount raised, the issue price should be £3.50. The total raised before deducting issue costs would be £12,250,000.

    (ii)   To issue exactly 4,000,000 shares, the issue price must be £3.00. The total raised would be £12,000,000, before deducting issue costs.

(b)   (i)   Harvey Goldfinger would be allotted 12,000 shares at £3.50 per share. He would receive a refund of 12,000 × £2 = £24,000 out of the £66,000 he has paid.

    (ii)   If 4,000,000 shares are issued, applicants would receive two thirds of the shares they tendered for. Harvey Goldfinger would be allotted 8,000 shares at £3 per share and would receive a refund of £42,000 out of the £66,000 he has paid.

1.9 Prospectus issue

Issues where the issuing firm sells shares directly to the general public tend to be quite rare on many stock exchanges, and the issues that are made tend to be quite large. These issues are sometimes known as **offers by prospectus**. This type of issue is very risky, because of the lack of guarantees that all shares will be taken up.

1.10 A placing

A **placing** is an arrangement whereby the shares are not all offered to the public, but instead, the sponsoring market maker arranges for most of the issue to be bought by a **small number of investors**, usually institutional investors such as pension funds and insurance companies.

1.10.1 The choice between an offer for sale and a placing

Is a company likely to prefer an offer for sale of its shares, or a placing?

(a) **Placings** are much **cheaper**. Approaching institutional investors privately is a much cheaper way of obtaining finance, and thus placings are often used for smaller issues.

(b) Placings are likely to be **quicker**.

(c) Placings are likely to involve **less disclosure** of **information.**

(d) However, most of the shares will be placed with a **relatively small number of (institutional) shareholders**, which means that most of the shares are **unlikely to be available for trading** after the flotation, and that **institutional shareholders** will have control of the **company**.

(e) When a company first comes to the market in the UK, the **maximum proportion of shares** that can be **placed** is **75%**, to ensure some shares are available to a wider public.

1.11 An introduction

By this method of obtaining a quotation, no shares are made available to the market, neither existing nor newly created shares; nevertheless, the stock market grants a quotation. This will only happen where shares in a large company are already widely held, so that a market can be seen to exist. A company might want an **introduction** to obtain **greater marketability** for the shares, a known share valuation for inheritance tax purposes and easier access in the future to additional capital.

1.12 The role of advisers

Advisers will be required if a company wishes to obtain a listing. The key adviser is the sponsor, usually an **investment bank** who will lead a team of other advisers in carrying out the flotation process.

An investment bank will:

• Advise on the best method (placing or offer for sale)

• Advise on the suitability of the directors

• Advise on stock exchange requirements

• Be responsible for the prospectus, and for assuring investors that the regulatory requirements have been fulfilled

• Advise on the issue price and act as an underwriter (see Section 1.13 below).

Other advisers include accountants, brokers and lawyers. A broker will represent the company to investors to stimulate interest, and to advise on the timing of the issue; often the sponsor is the broker.

Accountants will prepare a detailed report on the company's finances, forecasts and financial controls to assess the suitability of a company for flotation. Lawyers will ensure compliance with all the legal requirements of the flotation.

1.13 Underwriting

In the same way as debt securities issues, a company about to issue equity securities might decide to have the issue underwritten. **Underwriters** are financial institutions which agree (in exchange for a fixed fee, perhaps 2.25% of the finance to be raised) to buy at the issue price any securities which are **not subscribed** for by the investing public.

Underwriters **remove** the **risk** of a share issue being undersubscribed, but at a cost to the company issuing the shares. It is not compulsory to have an issue underwritten. Ordinary offers for sale are most likely to be underwritten although rights issues may be as well.

1.14 Costs of share issues on stock market

Companies may incur the following costs when issuing shares:

- Underwriting costs
- Stock market listing fee (the initial charge) for the new securities
- Fees of the issuing house, solicitors, auditors and public relations consultant
- Charges for printing and distributing the prospectus
- Advertising in national newspapers

1.15 Pricing shares for a stock market launch

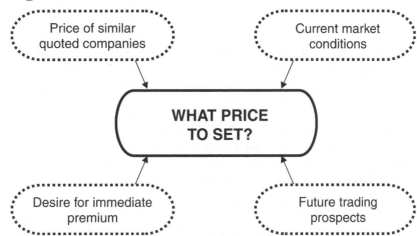

Companies will be keen to avoid **overpricing an issue**, which could result in the **issue** being **undersubscribed**, leaving underwriters with the unwelcome task of having to buy up the unsold shares. On the other hand, if the **issue price** is **too low** then the issue will be **oversubscribed** and the company would have been able to raise the required capital by issuing fewer shares.

The share price of an issue is usually advertised as being based on a certain P/E ratio, the ratio of the price to the company's most recent earnings per share figure in its audited accounts. The issuer's P/E ratio can then be compared by investors with the P/E ratios of similar quoted companies.

1.16 Venture capital

KEY TERM

VENTURE CAPITAL is risk capital, normally provided in return for an equity stake.

Venture capital companies (such as 3i group) make funding available to **young, unquoted companies** to help them to expand.

The requirements are **very high growth potential** and **very high returns** (in excess of 30% per annum). This return arises when the company that has been financed is **floated** on the stock market or **sold**.

Venture capitalists have been accused of **short-termism** by requiring early reported profits and an early exit. Failure to hit targets set by the venture capitalist can lead to an **equity ratchet** where extra shares are transferred to their ownership at no additional cost to the venture capitalist.

When a company's directors look for help from a venture capital institution, they must recognise that:

(a) The institution will want an **equity stake** in the company.

(b) It will need convincing that the company can be successful (management buyouts of companies which already have a record of **successful trading** have been increasingly favoured by venture capitalists in recent years).

(c) It may want to have a **representative** appointed to the company's board, to look after its interests, or an **independent director** (the 3i group runs an Independent Director Scheme).

1.17 Private equity

Private equity describes a group of companies that raises funds from investors, typically pension funds, and uses the money to buy companies which they **run privately**.

Private equity deals are much bigger than venture capitalists' and typically use a **high proportion of debt** when making acquisitions. This debt is placed on the balance sheet of the acquired company. Once a private equity firm has owned a company for six months or a year, it will **refinance** all the debt and pay some cash back to its investors. The private equity firm makes a series of often drastic changes to improve the business such as new management, cutting jobs and getting rid of loss-making divisions.

In the same way as venture capitalists, exit involves sale or flotation three to five years later.

1.18 Business angels

Business angels are like venture capitalists. They are wealthy individuals or groups of individuals who invest directly in small businesses. They are prepared to take **high risks** in the hope of **high returns**.

The main problem with business angel financing is that it is **informal** in terms of a market and can be difficult to set up. However, informality can be a strength. There may be less need to provide business angels with **detailed information** about the company, since business angels generally have prior knowledge of the industry. Surveys suggest that business angels are often more patient than providers of other sources of finance. However, the money available from individual business angels may be limited, and large sums may only be available from a consortium of business angels.

CASE STUDY

Investors in private equity are increasingly turning to emerging markets to generate their returns.

Private equity (PE) investment is increasing in global growth markets, especially in Southeast Asia outside China, sub-Saharan Africa and Latin America outside Brazil. That's good news for entrepreneurs in international markets or hoping to expand there, because PE investors provide key capital for expansion.

Over the past 15 years, private equity funds, most of which are U.S.-based, have gradually been increasing their investments in emerging markets as more of the world's growth comes from markets like Nigeria, the Philippines and Mexico.

(Source: Forbes, 29 April 2015)

Section summary

- Equity finance can be raised on **capital markets**. In order to trade on capital markets, a company needs to obtain a stock market listing.

- A company can obtain a stock market listing through an **offer for sale**, a **prospectus issue**, a **placing** or an **introduction.**

- **Venture capital** and **private equity** are also sources of equity finance.

2 Rights issues

Introduction

A **rights issue** is a way for a company to raise funds from existing shareholders. You will need to understand how it works and be able to do the necessary price calculations.

KEY TERMS

A RIGHTS ISSUE is the raising of new capital by giving existing shareholders the right to subscribe to new shares in proportion to their current holdings. These shares are usually issued at a discount to market price. A shareholder not wishing to take up a rights issue may sell the rights.

A DILUTION is the reduction in the earnings and voting power per share caused by an increase or potential increase in the number of shares in issue.   (*CIMA Official Terminology*)

2.1 Advantages of rights issues

(a)   Rights issues are **cheaper** than offers for sale to the general public. This is partly because no **prospectus** is generally required (provided that the issue is for less than 10% of the class of shares concerned), partly because the **administration** is **simpler** and partly because the cost of underwriting will be less.

(b)   Rights issues are **more beneficial** to **existing shareholders** than issues to the general public. New shares are issued at a **discount** to the current market price, to make them attractive to investors. A rights issue secures the discount on the market price for existing shareholders, who may either keep the shares or sell them if they wish.

(c)   **Relative voting rights** are **unaffected** if shareholders all take up their rights.

(d)   The finance raised may be used to **reduce gearing** in book value terms by increasing share capital and/or to pay off long-term debt which will reduce gearing in market value terms.

2.2 Disadvantages of rights issues

(a)   The **amount of finance** that can be **raised** by rights issues of unquoted companies is limited by the funds available to existing shareholders.

(b)   **Choosing the best issue price** may **be problematic**. If the price is considered too high, the issue may not be fully subscribed; if too low, the company will not have raised all the funds it conceivably could have done.

(c)   During the time between the **announcement of the rights issue** and the **date of subscription** the **market price of shares** may **fall**, and the issue price of rights will be above the market price, with the result that the rights issue will fail.

(d)   Rights issues **can't be used** to **widen the base** of shareholders.

2.3 Pricing a rights issue

A company making a rights issue must set a price which is low enough to **secure the acceptance** of shareholders, who are being asked to provide extra funds, but not so low that earnings per share are excessively diluted. Other possible problems include getting the issue **underwritten** and an excessive **fall** in the **share price.**

Rights issues are commonly priced at a discount of 20%–30% of the market price of shares.

Exam alert

A question might ask for discussion on the effect of a rights issue as well as calculations, eg of the effect on EPS.

If you want to read more on the practicalities of rights issues you can do so at www.thisismoney.co.uk/money/investing/article-2412182/What-shareholders-rights-issue.html

Example: Rights issue (1)

Seagull can achieve a profit after tax of 20% on the capital employed. At present its capital structure is as follows:

	£
200,000 ordinary shares of £1 each	200,000
Retained earnings	100,000
	300,000

The directors propose to raise an additional £126,000 from a rights issue. The current market price is £1.80.

Required

(a) Calculate the number of shares that must be issued if the rights price is:
£1.60; £1.50; £1.40; £1.20.

(b) Calculate the dilution in earnings per share in each case.

Solution

The earnings at present are 20% of £300,000 = £60,000. This gives earnings per share of 30p. The earnings after the rights issue will be 20% of £426,000 = £85,200.

Rights price £	No. of new shares (£126,000 ÷ rights price)	EPS (£85,200 ÷ total no of shares) Pence	Dilution Pence
1.60	78,750	30.6	+ 0.6
1.50	84,000	30.0	–
1.40	90,000	29.4	– 0.6
1.20	105,000	27.9	– 2.1

Note that at a high rights price the earnings per share are increased, not diluted. The breakeven point (zero dilution) occurs when the rights price is equal to the capital employed per share:

£300,000 ÷ 200,000 = £1.50.

2.4 The market price of shares after a rights issue: the theoretical ex-rights price (TERP)

After the announcement of a rights issue, **share prices generally fall**. This temporary fall is due to **uncertainty in the market about** the consequences of the issue, with respect to future profits, earnings and dividends. After the issue has actually been made, the market price per share will normally fall, because there are more shares in issue and the new shares were issued at a discount price.

When a rights issue is announced, all existing shareholders have the **right to subscribe for new shares**, and so there are **rights attached to the existing shares**. The shares are therefore described as being

traded as 'cum rights'. On the first day of dealings in the newly issued shares, the rights no longer exist and the old shares are now 'ex rights' (without rights attached).

In theory, the new market price will be the consequence of an adjustment to allow for the discount price of the new issue, and a **theoretical ex-rights price (TERP)** can be calculated (the shares are ex rights because the new shares have been issued and the rights no longer exist).

Example: Rights issue (2)

Fundraiser has 1,000,000 ordinary shares of £1 in issue, which have a market price on 1 September of £2.10 per share. The company decides to make a rights issue, and offers its shareholders the right to subscribe for one new share at £1.50 each for every four shares already held. After the announcement of the issue, the share price fell to £1.95, but by the time just prior to the issue being made, it had recovered to £2 per share. This market value just before the issue is known as the cum rights price. What is the theoretical ex-rights price?

Solution

Value of the portfolio for a shareholder with 4 shares before the rights issue:

	£
4 shares @ £2.00	8.00
1 share @ £1.50	1.50
	9.50

so the value per share after the rights issue (or TERP) is: $\dfrac{£9.50}{5}$ = £1.90

EXAM

An alternative method would be to use the formula given to you in the exam.

Theoretical ex-rights price = $\dfrac{1}{N+1}\left((N \times \text{cum rights price}) + \text{issue price}\right)$

where N = number of shares required to buy one new share.

Theoretical ex-rights price = $\dfrac{1}{4+1}((4 \times £2) + £1.50)$ = $\dfrac{£9.50}{5}$ = £1.90

2.5 Yield-adjusted ex-rights price

We have assumed so far that the additional funds raised by the rights issue will generate the **same rate** of **return as existing funds**. If the new funds are likely to earn a **different return** from what is currently being earned, the **yield-adjusted** theoretical ex-rights price should be calculated. The yield-adjusted price demonstrates how the market will view the rights issue, and what will happen to the market value.

EXAM

Yield-adjusted theoretical ex-rights price = $\left[\dfrac{\text{Cum rights price} \times N}{(N+1)}\right] + \left[\dfrac{\text{Issue price}}{(N+1)} \times \dfrac{\text{Yield on new funds}}{\text{Yield on existing funds}}\right]$

Example: Rights issue (3)

Using the same data for Fundraiser as above, with the additional information that rate of return on new funds = 12%, and on existing funds = 8%, calculate the yield-adjusted theoretical ex-rights price.

Solution

$$\text{Yield-adjusted theoretical ex-rights price} = \left[\frac{2\times4}{5}\right] + \left[\frac{1.50}{5}\times\frac{0.12}{0.08}\right] = \pounds2.05$$

Exam skills

An exam question may give you the net present value of the project which the rights issue has been raised for. The yield-adjusted ex-rights price will then simply be:

$$\frac{\text{Original market capitalisation of the company} + \text{NPV of the project} + \text{proceeds of rights issue}}{\text{New number of shares in issue}}$$

2.6 The value of rights

$$\text{Value of a right} = \frac{\text{Theoretical ex-rights price} - \text{Issue price}}{\text{N}}$$

Where N = the number of rights required to buy one share

Using the above example:

$$\text{Value of a right} = \frac{2.00 - 1.50}{5} = \frac{1.90 - 1.50}{4} = 10p$$

This means that the value of a right attaching to each **existing** share is 10p. If a holder of four existing shares exercises his rights to buy one new share, and then sells it, his gain will be $1.90 - 1.50 = 40p$, in other words $(4 \times 10p)$ or the difference between the theoretical ex-rights price and the rights issue price.

The value of rights is the **theoretical gain** a shareholder would make by exercising his rights.

Question 8.1	Effects of rights issue

Learning outcome: B(1)(c)

Devonian has the following long-term capital structure as at 30 November 20X3.

	$m
Ordinary shares 25c fully paid	50.0
General reserve	22.5
Retained profit	25.5
	98.0

The company has no long-term loans.

In the year to 30 November 20X3, the profit from operations (net profit before interest and taxation) was $40m and it is expected that this will increase by 25% during the forthcoming year. The company is listed on a major stock exchange and the current share price is $2.10.

The company wishes to raise $72m in order to re-equip one of its factories and is considering making a one-for-five rights issue at a discounted price of $1.80 per share. It is expected that the price earnings (P/E) ratio will remain the same for the forthcoming year.

Assume a tax rate of 30%.

Required

(a) Assuming the rights issue of shares is made, calculate:

    (i)   The theoretical ex-rights price of an ordinary share in Devonian

    (ii)   The value of the rights for each original ordinary share

(b) Calculate the price of an ordinary share in Devonian in one year's time assuming a rights issue is made.

2.7 Shareholder options

Possible courses of action open to shareholders:

(a) **'Take up' or 'exercise' the rights**

This means buying the new shares at the rights price. Shareholders who do this will maintain their percentage holdings in the company by subscribing for the new shares.

(b) **'Renounce' the rights and sell them on the market**

Shareholders who do this will have lower percentage holdings of the company's equity after the issue than before the issue, and the total value of their shares will be less (on the assumption that the actual market price after the issue is close to the theoretical ex-rights price).

(c) **Renounce part of the rights and take up the remainder**

For example, a shareholder may sell enough of his rights to enable him to buy the remaining rights shares he is entitled to with the sale proceeds, and so keep the total market value of his shareholding in the company unchanged.

(d) **Do nothing**

Shareholders may be protected from the consequences of their inaction because rights not taken up are sold on a shareholder's behalf by the company. The Stock Exchange rules state that if new securities are not taken up, they should be sold by the company to new subscribers for the benefit of the shareholders who were entitled to the rights.

The decision by individual shareholders as to whether they take up the offer will therefore depend on:

(a) The **expected rate of return** on the investment (and the risk associated with it)

(b) The **return obtainable** from other investments (allowing for the associated risk)

Question 8.2	Rights issue

Learning outcome: B(1)(c)

Gopher has issued 3,000,000 ordinary shares of £1 each, which are at present selling for £4 per share. The company plans to issue rights to purchase one new equity share at a price of £3.20 per share for every three shares held. A shareholder who owns 900 shares thinks that he will suffer a loss in his personal wealth because the new shares are being offered at a price lower than market value. On the assumption that the actual market value of shares will be equal to the theoretical ex-rights price, what would be the effect on the shareholder's wealth if:

(a) He sells all the rights?

(b) He exercises half of the rights and sells the other half?

(c) He does nothing at all?

Exam skills

Make sure you practise the calculations in this chapter so that you can do them competently and quickly if required.

Section summary

A **rights issue** is an offer to existing shareholders for them to buy more shares, usually at lower than the current share price.

3   Share prices and investment returns

Introduction

In this section we look at how share prices are determined. As we shall see, there are various theories which seek to explain share price movements.

3.1 Book value *versus* market value

The **book value** of equity is the ordinary share capital in the balance sheet plus the value of shareholders' reserves. The book value is a **historical figure** which reflects accounting adjustments and procedures.

The book value may be very different to the **market value** of the shares. This is the share price multiplied by the number of shares in issue which reflects **investors' expectations of future earnings**.

3.2 Theories of share price behaviour

There are the following differing views about share price movements:

- The fundamental analysis theory
- Technical analysis (chartist theory)
- Random walk theory

These different theories about how share prices are reached in the market, especially fundamental analysis, have important consequences for financial management.

3.3 The fundamental analysis theory of share values

The fundamental theory of share values is based on the theory that the 'realistic' market price of a share can be derived from a **valuation of estimated future dividends** (the dividend valuation model). The value of a share will be the discounted present value of all future expected dividends on the share, discounted at the shareholders' cost of capital.

KEY TERM

FUNDAMENTAL ANALYSIS is the analysis of external and internal influences that directly affect the operations of a company with a view to assisting in investment decisions. Information accessed might include fiscal/monetary policy, financial statements, industry trends, competitor analysis, etc.

(CIMA Official Terminology)

In general terms, fundamental analysis seems to be valid. This means that if an investment analyst can foresee before anyone else that:

(a)   A **company's future profits** and **dividends** are going to be different from what is currently expected

(b)   **Shareholders' cost of capital** will **rise or fall** (for example in response to interest rate changes)

then the analyst will be able to predict a future share price movement, and so recommend clients to buy or sell the share before the price change occurs.

In practice however, share price movements are affected by **day to day fluctuations**, reflecting:

- Supply and demand in a particular period
- Investor confidence
- Market interest rate movements

Investment analysts want to be able to predict these fluctuations in prices, but fundamental analysis might be inadequate as a technique.

3.4 Charting or technical analysis

Chartists or '**technical analysts**' attempt to predict share price movements by assuming that past price patterns will be repeated. There is no real theoretical justification for this approach, but it can at times be spectacularly successful. Studies have suggested that the degree of success is greater than could be expected merely from chance.

KEY TERM

TECHNICAL ANALYSIS is the analysis of past movements in the prices of financial instruments, currencies, commodities etc, with a view to, by applying analytical techniques, predicting future price movements.

(CIMA Official Terminology)

Chartists do not attempt to predict every price change. They are primarily interested in trend reversals, for example when the price of a share has been rising for several months but suddenly starts to fall.

One of the main problems with chartism is that it is often difficult to see a **new trend** until **after it has happened**. By the time the chartist has detected a signal, other chartists will have as well, and the resulting mass movement to buy or sell will push the price so as to eliminate any advantage.

With the use of sophisticated computer programs to simulate the work of a chartist, academic studies have found that the results obtained were **no better or worse** than those obtained from a simple 'buy and hold' strategy of a **well diversified portfolio** of shares.

3.5 Random walk theory

Random walk theory is consistent with the fundamental theory of share values. It accepts that a share should have an intrinsic price dependent on the fortunes of the company and the expectations of investors. One of its underlying assumptions is that **all relevant information about a company is available to all potential investors** who will act upon the information in a **rational** manner.

The key feature of random walk theory is that although share prices will have an **intrinsic or fundamental value**, this value will be altered as new information becomes available, and that the behaviour of investors is such that the actual share price will fluctuate from day to day around the intrinsic value.

Section summary

- **Fundamental analysis** is based on the theory that share prices can be derived from an analysis of **future dividends**.

- **Technical analysts** or **chartists** work on the basis that past price patterns will be repeated.

- **Random walk theory** is based on the idea that share prices will alter when **new information** becomes **available**.

4 The dividend valuation model

Introduction

In F2 *Advanced Financial Reporting* you looked at the dividend valuation model to calculate the cost of equity. In this section we will revisit this topic as you will need to apply this to business valuations in Chapter 11.

4.1 The cost of ordinary share capital

New funds from equity shareholders are obtained either from **new issues of shares** or from **retained earnings**. Both of these sources of funds have a cost.

(a) Shareholders will **not** be prepared to **provide funds** for a **new issue** of **shares** unless the return on their investment is sufficiently attractive.

(b) Retained earnings also have a cost. This is an **opportunity cost**, the dividend forgone by shareholders.

Equity is a **high-risk investment** as ordinary shareholders are the last to be paid in a liquidation. Equity is therefore the **most expensive** form of finance.

4.2 The dividend valuation model

KEY TERMS

Cum dividend or CUM DIV means the purchaser of shares is entitled to receive the next dividend payment.

Ex-dividend or EX DIV means that the purchaser of shares is not entitled to receive the next dividend payment.

If we begin by ignoring share issue costs, the cost of equity, both for new issues and retained earnings, could be estimated by means of a **dividend valuation model**, on the assumption that the market value of shares is directly related to expected future dividends on the shares.

If the future dividend per share is expected to be **constant** in amount, then the **ex-dividend** share price will be calculated by the formula:

$$P_0 = \frac{d}{(1+k_e)} + \frac{d}{(1+k_e)^2} + \frac{d}{(1+k_e)^3} + ... = \frac{d}{k_e} \text{, so } k_e = \frac{d}{P_0}$$

Where k_e is the shareholders' cost of capital

d is the annual dividend per share, starting at year 1 and then continuing annually in perpetuity.

P_0 is the ex-dividend share price (the price of a share where the share's new owner is **not** entitled to the dividend that is soon to be paid).

> Cost of ordinary (equity) share capital, paying an annual dividend d in perpetuity, and having a current ex div price P_0:
>
> $$k_e = \frac{d}{P_0}$$

We shall look at the dividend valuation model again in Chapter 11, in the context of valuation of shares.

Example: Dividend valuation model

Cygnus has a dividend cover ratio of 4.0 times and expects zero growth in dividends. The company has one million £1 ordinary shares in issue and the market capitalisation (value) of the company is £50 million. After-tax profits for next year are expected to be £20 million.

What is the expected rate of return from the ordinary shares?

Solution

Total dividends $= \dfrac{\text{£20 million}}{4} = \text{£5 million}$

$k_e = \dfrac{\text{£5 million}}{\text{£50 million}} = 10\%$

4.3 The dividend growth model

Shareholders will normally expect dividends to increase year by year and not to remain constant in perpetuity. The **fundamental theory of share values** states that the market price of a share is the present value of the discounted future cash flows of revenues from the share, so the market value given an expected constant annual growth in dividends would be:

$$P_0 = \frac{d_0(1+g)}{(1+k_e)} + \frac{d_0(1+g)^2}{(1+k_e)^2} + \dots$$

Where P_0 is the current market price (ex div)
  d_0 is the current net dividend
  k_e is the shareholders' cost of capital
  g is the expected annual growth in dividend payments

and both k_e and g are expressed as proportions.

It is often convenient to assume a constant expected dividend growth rate in perpetuity. The formula above then simplifies to:

$$P_0 = \frac{d_0(1+g)}{(k_e - g)}$$

Re-arranging this, we get a formula for the ordinary shareholders' cost of capital.

EXAM

Cost of ordinary (equity) share capital, having a current ex div price, P_0, having just paid a dividend, d_0, with the dividend growing in perpetuity by a constant g% per annum:

$$k_e = \frac{d_0(1+g)}{P_0} + g \text{ or } k_e = \frac{d_1}{P_0} + g$$

Where d_1 is the dividend in year 1, so that:

$d_1 = d_0(1+g)$

Question 8.3

Cost of equity

Learning outcome: C(2)(a)

A share has a current market value of 96p, and the last dividend was 12p. If the expected annual growth rate of dividends is 4%, calculate the cost of equity capital.

4.4 Estimating the growth rate

There are two methods for estimating the growth rate that you need to be familiar with.

4.4.1 Historic growth

Firstly, the future growth rate can be predicted from an **analysis of the growth in dividends** over the past few years.

Year	Dividends €	Earnings €
20X1	150,000	400,000
20X2	192,000	510,000
20X3	206,000	550,000
20X4	245,000	650,000
20X5	262,350	700,000

Dividends have risen from €150,000 in 20X1 to €262,350 in 20X5. The increase represents four years' growth. (Check that you can see that there are four years' growth, and not five years' growth, in the table.) The average growth rate, g, may be calculated as follows. Assume the current market price is €3.35.

$$\text{Dividend in 20X1} \times (1+g)^4 = \text{Dividend in 20X5}$$

$$(1+g)^4 = \frac{\text{Dividend in 20X5}}{\text{Dividend in 20X1}}$$

$$= \frac{€262,350}{€150,000}$$

$$= 1.749$$

$$1+g = \sqrt[4]{1.749} = 1.15$$

$$g = 0.15, \text{ ie } 15\%$$

The growth rate over the last four years is assumed to be expected by shareholders into the indefinite future, so the cost of equity, k_e, is:

$$\frac{d_0(1+g)}{P_0} + g = \frac{0.26235(1.15)}{3.35} + 0.15 = 0.24, \text{ ie } 24\%$$

Alternatively, the historic growth formula can be written as:

$$g = \sqrt[n]{\frac{\text{dividend in year x}}{\text{dividend in year x-n}}} - 1$$

Where   n is the number of years' growth
          year x is the final year's dividend

Question 8.4	Growth rate

Learning outcome: C(2)(a)

The following figures have been extracted from the accounts of Mezzo:

Year	Dividends €	Earnings €
20X1	100,000	350,000
20X2	125,000	400,000
20X3	125,000	370,000
20X4	160,000	450,000
20X5	200,000	550,000

You have been asked to calculate the cost of equity for the company. What growth rate would you use in the calculations?

4.4.2 Current reinvestment level

Alternatively, the growth rate can be estimated using the **current reinvestment level** (Gordon's growth approximation).

Retained profits will earn a certain rate of return and so growth will come from the yield on the retained funds. The rate of growth in dividends is expressed as:

EXAM

g = bR

where   b is proportion of profits retained for reinvestment
         g is the annual growth rate in dividends
         R is yield on new investments (this is often taken to be the accounting rate of return)

So, if a company retains 65% of its earnings for capital investment projects it has identified, and these projects are expected to have an average return of 8%:

g = bR = 65% × 8% = 5.2%

4.5 Non-constant growth

The dividend model can be adapted to value dividends that are forecast to grow at more than one growth rate. This approach normally assumes that dividend growth is forecast to go through **two phases**:

Phase 1 (eg next 2 years)	**Phase 2 (eg year 3 onwards)**
Growth is forecast at an unusually high (or low) rate	Growth returns to a constant rate
Use an NPV approach to calculate the PV of the dividends for the finite time period (ie, PV of dividends for T_1 and T_2)	Use the formula to assess the NPV of the constant growth phase, however the time periods need to be adapted eg, $$P_0 = \frac{d_1}{K_e - g} \quad \text{is adapted to} \quad P_2 = \frac{d_3}{K_e - g}$$ Then the value given by this formula needs to be discounted back to a present value (here using the discount rate for T_2).

Example: Dividend valuation model – non constant growth

It is 1 January 20X1, ABC Co paid a dividend last year of $100,000. Dividends are expected to grow by 5% per year for the next two years, and then by 3% per year thereafter. The cost of equity of ABC Co is 9%.

Calculate the value of ABC Co, to the nearest $000.

Solution

Phase 1

Time	1	2
	$	$
Dividend (5% growth)	105,000	110,250
Discount factor @9%	0.917	0.842
Present value at 1/1/X1	96,285	92,831

Total present value = $189,116, so **$189,000** to the nearest $000.

Phase 2

From time 3 the growth rate is 3%

$$P_0 = \frac{d_1}{K_e - g} \quad \text{is adapted to} \quad P_2 = \frac{d_3}{K_e - g}$$

$$P_2 = \frac{110,250 \times 1.03}{0.09 - 0.03} = \$1,893,000 \text{ (to the nearest \$000)}$$

Then discounting at a T2 discount factor of 0.842:

$$P_0 = \frac{110,250 \times 1.03}{0.09 - 0.03} = 1,893,000 \times 0.842 = \$1,594,000 \text{ (to the nearest \$000)}$$

Total of phase 1 and phase 2 = 189,000 + 1,594,000 = **$1,783,000**

4.6 Cost of preference shares

For preference shares the future cash flows are the dividend payments in perpetuity so that:

$$k_{pref} = \frac{d}{P_0}$$

Where P_0 is the current market price of preference share capital after payment of the current dividend
         d   is the dividend received
         k_{pref} is the cost of preference share capital

Exam skills

Don't forget that tax relief is **not given** for preference share dividends.

When calculating the weighted average cost of capital (see Chapter 9), the cost of preferred shares is a separate component and should not be combined with the cost of debt or the cost of equity.

Section summary

- The **dividend valuation model** can be used to estimate a cost of equity, on the assumption that the market value of shares is directly related to the expected future dividends on the shares.

- The **dividend growth rate** can be calculated using historic growth or current.

5 The Capital Asset Pricing Model (CAPM)

Introduction

We now look at the other method of calculating the cost of equity, which uses the **capital asset pricing model (CAPM)**. This model incorporates **risk**. In Chapters 11 and 12, we will use the cost of equity as a discount rate in company valuations using discounted cash flow (DCF) analysis.

5.1 Systematic risk and unsystematic risk

Whenever an investor invests in some shares, or a company invests in a new project, there will be some **risk** involved. The actual return on the investment might be better or worse than that hoped for. To some extent, risk is unavoidable (unless the investor settles for risk-free securities such as gilts).

Provided that the investor **diversifies** his investments in a suitably wide **portfolio**, the investments which perform well and those which perform badly should tend to cancel each other out, and much risk can be diversified away. In the same way, a company which invests in a number of projects will find that some do well and some do badly, but taking the whole portfolio of investments, average returns should turn out much as expected.

Risks that can be diversified away are referred to as **unsystematic risk**. But there is another sort of risk too. Some investments are by their very nature more risky than others. This has nothing to do with chance variations up or down in actual returns compared with what an investor should expect. This **inherent risk** – the **systematic risk** or **market risk** – **cannot be diversified away**.

KEY TERMS

MARKET or SYSTEMATIC RISK is risk that cannot be diversified away. NON-SYSTEMATIC or UNSYSTEMATIC RISK applies to a single investment or class of investments, and can be reduced or eliminated by diversification.   *(CIMA Official Terminology)*

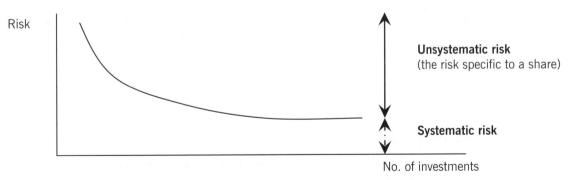

In return for accepting systematic risk, a risk-averse investor will expect to earn a return which is **higher** than the return on a risk-free investment.

The amount of systematic risk in an investment varies between different types of investment.

5.2 Systematic risk and unsystematic risk: implications for investments

The implications of systematic risk and unsystematic risk are as follows:

(a) If an investor wants to **avoid risk** altogether, they must **invest entirely** in **risk-free securities.**

(b) If an investor **holds shares in just a few companies**, there will be **some unsystematic risk** as well as systematic risk in the portfolio, because they will not have spread his risk enough to diversify away the unsystematic risk. To eliminate unsystematic risk, they must build up a well diversified portfolio of investments.

(c) If an investor holds a **balanced portfolio** of all the stocks and shares on the stock market, they will incur systematic risk which is exactly equal to the average systematic risk in the stock market as a whole.

(d) **Shares in individual companies** will have **different systematic risk characteristics** to this market average. Some shares will be less risky and some will be more risky than the stock market average. Similarly, some investments will be more risky and some will be less risky than a company's 'average' investments.

5.3 The beta factor

The capital asset pricing model is mainly concerned with how systematic risk is measured, and how systematic risk affects required returns and share prices. **Systematic risk** is measured using **beta factors**.

KEY TERM

BETA FACTOR is the measure of the systematic risk of a security relative to the market portfolio. If a share price were to rise or fall at double the market rate, it would have a beta factor of 2.0. Conversely, if the share price moved at half the market rate, the beta factor would be 0.5.   *(CIMA Official Terminology)*

Increasing risk

→

Beta < 1	**Beta = 1**	**Beta > 1**
Share < average risk	**Share = average risk**	**Share > average risk**

CASE STUDY

The following are examples of beta factors of well-known companies. Note the differences in betas between companies within the same sector and the differences in betas across sectors.

Company	*Sector*	*Beta factor*
Easyjet	Airlines	0.60
Pfizer	Pharmaceuticals	0.90
Volkswagen	Auto and truck manufacturers	1.57
Honda	Auto and truck manufacturers	1.29

(Source: reuters.com, 4 October 2017)

5.4 Risk and returns

CAPM theory includes the following propositions:

(a) Investors in shares require a **return** in **excess of the risk-free rate**, to compensate them for systematic risk.

(b) Investors should **not require** a **premium** for **unsystematic risk**, because this can be diversified away by holding a wide portfolio of investments.

(c) Because systematic risk varies between companies, investors will require a **higher return** from shares in those companies where the systematic risk is bigger.

The same propositions can be applied to capital investments by companies:

(a)   Companies will want a **return on a project** to **exceed** the **risk-free rate**, to compensate them for systematic risk.

(b)   **Unsystematic risk** can be **diversified away**, and so a premium for unsystematic risk should not be required.

(c)   Companies should want a **bigger return** on projects where **systematic risk is greater**.

A major **assumption in CAPM** is that there is a linear relationship between the return obtained from an individual security and the average return from all securities in the market.

5.5 Example: CAPM (1)

The following information is available about the performance of an individual company's shares and the stock market as a whole.

	Individual company	*Stock market as a whole*
Price at start of period	105.0	480.0
Price at end of period	110.0	490.0
Dividend during period	7.6	39.2

The expected return on the company's shares R_i and the expected return on the 'market portfolio' of shares R_m may be calculated as:

$$\frac{\text{Capital gain (or loss)} + \text{dividend}}{\text{Price at start of period}}$$

$$R_i = \frac{(110 - 105) + 7.6}{105} = 0.12 \qquad R_m = \frac{(490 - 480) + 39.2}{480} = 0.1025$$

A statistical analysis of 'historic' returns from a security and from the 'average' market may suggest that a **linear relationship** can be assumed to exist between them. A series of comparative figures could be prepared (month by month) of the return from a company's shares and the average return of the market as a whole. The results could be drawn on a scattergraph and a 'line of best fit' drawn (using linear regression techniques) as shown in the diagram below.

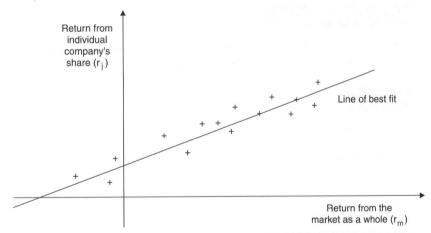

This analysis would show three things:

(a)   The return from the security and the return from the market as a whole will tend to **rise or fall together**.

(b)   The return from the security may be higher or lower than the market return. This is because the **systematic risk** of the individual security differs from that of the market as a whole.

(c)   The scattergraph may not give a good line of best fit, unless a large number of data items are plotted, because actual returns are affected by **unsystematic risk** as well as by systematic risk.

Note that returns can be negative. A share price fall represents a capital loss, which is a negative return.

The conclusion from this analysis is that individual securities will be either more or less risky than the market average in a fairly predictable way. The measure of this relationship between market returns and an individual security's returns, reflecting differences in systematic risk characteristics, can be developed into a beta factor for the individual security.

5.6 The market risk premium

KEY TERM

MARKET RISK PREMIUM is the difference between the expected rate of return on a market portfolio and the risk-free rate of return over the same period.   *(CIMA Official Terminology)*

The market risk premium **(R_m – R_f)** represents the excess of market returns over those associated with investing in risk-free assets.

The CAPM makes use of the principle that **returns on shares** in the **market as a whole** are expected to be higher than the returns on risk-free investments. The difference between market returns and risk-free returns is called an **excess return**. For example, if the return on British Government bonds is 9% and market returns are 13%, the excess return on the market's shares as a whole is 4%.

The difference between the risk-free return and the expected return on an individual security can be measured as the **excess return for the market as a whole multiplied by the security's beta factor**.

5.7 The CAPM formula

The capital asset pricing model is a statement of the principles explained above. It can be stated as follows:

EXAM

$$k_e = R_f + (R_m – R_f)\,\beta$$

Where k_e is the cost of equity capital

           R_f is the risk-free rate of return

           R_m is the return from the market as a whole

           β is the beta factor of the individual security

Example: CAPM (1)

Shares in Louie and Dewie have a beta of 0.9. The expected returns to the market are 10% and the risk-free rate of return is 4%. What is the cost of equity capital for Louie and Dewie?

Solution

k_e = $R_f + (R_m – R_f)\,\beta$

    = $4 + ((10 – 4) \times 0.9)$

    = 9.4%

Example: CAPM (2)

Investors have an expected rate of return of 8% from ordinary shares in Algol, which have a beta of 1.2. The expected returns to the market are 7%.

What will be the expected rate of return from ordinary shares in Rigel, which have a beta of 1.8?

Solution

Algol: $k_e = R_f + (R_m - R_f)\beta$

$8 = R_f + (7 - R_f) \times 1.2$

$8 = R_f + 8.4 - 1.2R_f$

$0.2R_f = 0.4$

$R_f = 2$

Rigel: $k_e = 2 + (7 - 2)1.8$

$= 11\%$

Question 8.5   Returns

Learning outcome: C(2)(a)

The risk-free rate of return is 7%. The average market return is 11%.

(a)   What will be the return expected from a share whose beta factor is 0.9?

(b)   What would be the share's expected value if it is expected to earn an annual dividend of 5.3c, with no capital growth?

5.7.1 Alpha values

The **alpha value** can be seen as a measure of how wrong the CAPM is.

Alpha values:

(a)   Reflect only temporary, abnormal returns, if CAPM is a realistic model

(b)   Can be positive or negative

(c)   Over time, will tend towards zero for any individual share, and for a well-diversified portfolio taken as a whole will be 0

(d)   May exist due to the inaccuracies and limitations of the CAPM

If the **alpha value** is **positive**, investors who don't hold shares will be tempted to buy them (to take advantage of the abnormal return), and investors who do hold shares will want to hold on to them so share prices will rise. If the **alpha value** is **negative**, investors won't want to buy them, and current holders will want to sell them, so share prices will fall.

5.7.2 Example: Alpha values

ABC plc's shares have a beta value of 1.2 and an alpha value of +2%. The market return is 10% and the risk-free rate of return is 6%.

Required return 6% + (10% - 6%) × 1.2 = 10.8%

Current return = expected return ± alpha value = 10.8% + 2% = 12.8%

5.8 Problems with applying the CAPM in practice

(a)   The need to **determine** the **excess return** $(R_m - R_f)$; expected, rather than historical, returns should be used, although historical returns are often used in practice

(b)   The need to **determine** the **risk-free rate**; a risk-free investment might be a government security, however, interest rates vary with the term of the lending.

(c)   **Errors** in the **statistical analysis used** to calculate beta values; betas may also **change over** time

(d)   The CAPM is also **unable to forecast accurately returns** for companies with **low price/earnings** ratios and to take account of seasonal 'month-of-the-year' effects and 'day-of-the-week' effects that appear to influence returns on shares.

Question 8.6

Beta factor

Learning outcome: C(2)(a)

(a)   What does beta measure, and what do betas of 0.5, 1 and 1.5 mean?
(b)   What factors determine the level of beta which a company may have?

Section summary

- The **capital asset pricing model** can be used to calculate a cost of equity and incorporates **risk**.

- The CAPM is based on a comparison of the **systematic risk** of **individual investments** with the risks of **all shares** in the **market**.

- The **beta factor** measures a share's volatility in terms of market risk.

- Problems of CAPM include **unrealistic assumptions** and the **required estimates being difficult to make**.

Chapter Summary

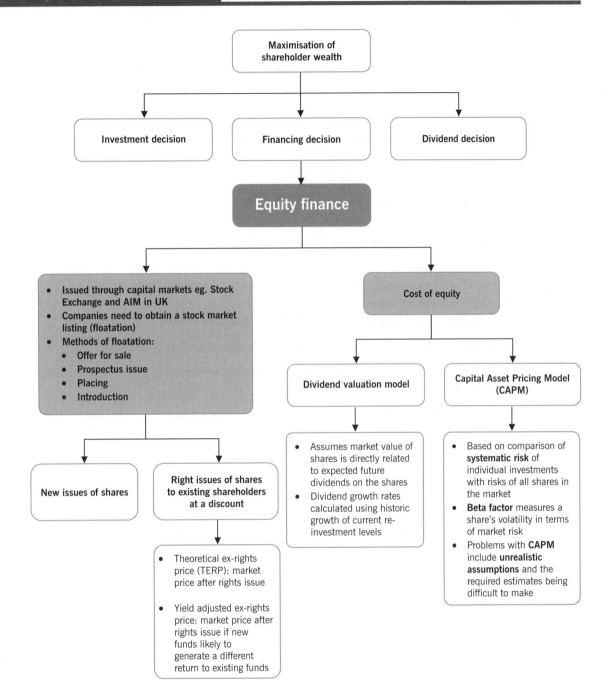

Quick Quiz

1   Identify four reasons why a company may seek a stock market listing.

2   A company's shares have a nominal value of £1 and a market value of £3. In a rights issue, one new share would be issued for every three shares at a price of £2.60. What is the theoretical ex-rights price?

3   The risk-free rate of return is 8%, average market return is 14% and a share's beta factor is 0.5. What is the cost of equity?

4   Which of the following is least likely to be a reason for seeking a stock market flotation?

   A   Improving the existing owners' control over the business
   B   Access to a wider pool of finance
   C   Enhancement of the company's image
   D   Transfer of capital to other uses

5   Which of the following is not true of a rights issue by a listed company?

   A   Rights issues do not require a prospectus
   B   The rights issues price can be at a discount to market price
   C   If shareholders do not take up the rights, the rights lapse
   D   Relative voting rights are unaffected if shareholders exercise their rights

6   Which theory of share price behaviour does the following statement describe?

   'The analysis of external and internal influences upon the operations of a company with a view to assisting in investment decisions.'

   A   Technical analysis
   B   Random walk theory
   C   Fundamental analysis theory
   D   Chartism

Answers to Quick Quiz

1   Four of the following five:

  • Access to a wider pool of finance
  • Improved marketability of shares
  • Transfer of capital to other uses (eg founder members liquidating holdings)
  • Enhancement of company image
  • Making growth by acquisition possible

2   ((£3 × 3) + £2.60) ÷ 4 = £2.90

3   k_e = 8 + ((14 − 8) × 0.5) = 11%

4   A   Flotation is likely to involve a significant loss of control to a wider circle of investors.

5   C   Shareholders have the option of renouncing the rights and selling them on the market.

6   C   Fundamental analysis theory.

Answers to Questions

8.1 Effects of rights issue

(a)

	$
Current market value of 5 existing shares (× $2.10)	10.50
Rights issue price of one new share	1.80
Theoretical value of 6 shares	12.30

  (i)   Theoretical ex-rights price = $12.30/6 shares = $2.05 per share.

  (ii)   The value of the rights for each new share is $2.05 − $1.80 = $0.25. The value of the rights for each existing share is therefore $0.25/5 shares = $0.05 per share.

(b)   (i)   Rights issue

	Million
Number of shares in issue ($50 million/$0.25 per share)	200
New shares in rights issue (1 for 5)	40
Total number of shares after the issue	240

Current earnings = $40 million less 30% tax = $28 million
Current EPS = $28 million/200 million shares = $0.14
Current P/E ratio = 2.1/0.14 = 15 times

	$m
Profit before taxation (+ 25%)	50
Taxation at 30%	(15)
Profit after tax (earnings)	35

Earnings per share = $35 million/240 million shares = $0.146
Assumed P/E ratio (no change) = 15
Assumed share price in one year's time: $0.146 × 15 = $2.19

8.2 Rights issue

Value of the portfolio for a shareholder with 3 shares before the rights issue

	£
3 shares @ £4.00	12.00
1 share @ £3.20	3.20
$\overline{4}$	$\overline{15.20}$

So the value per share after the rights issue (or TERP) is 15.20/4 = £3.80.

Alternative solution

The theoretical ex-rights price $= \dfrac{1}{3+1} ((3 \times £4) + £3.20)) = £3.80$ per share

	£
Theoretical ex-rights price	3.80
Price per new share	3.20
Value of rights per new share	$\overline{0.60}$

The value of the rights attached to each existing share is $\dfrac{£0.60}{3} = £0.20$.

We will assume that a shareholder is able to sell his rights for £0.20 per existing share held.

(a)   If the shareholder **sells all his rights**:

	£
Sale value of rights (900 × £0.20)	180
Market value of his 900 shares, ex rights (× £3.80)	3,420
Total wealth	$\overline{3,600}$
Total value of 900 shares cum rights (× £4)	£3,600

The shareholder would neither gain nor lose wealth. He would not be required to provide any additional funds to the company, but his shareholding as a proportion of the total equity of the company will be lower.

(b)   If the shareholder **exercises half of the rights** (buys 450/3 = 150 shares at £3.20) and sells the other half:

	£
Sale value of rights (450 × £0.20)	90
Market value of his 1,050 shares, ex rights (× £3.80)	3,990
	$\overline{4,080}$
Total value of 900 shares cum rights (× £4)	3,600
Additional investment (150 × £3.20)	480
	$\overline{4,080}$

The shareholder would neither gain nor lose wealth, although he will have increased his investment in the company by £480.

(c)   If the shareholder **does nothing**, but all other shareholders either exercise their rights or sell them, he would lose wealth as follows.

	£
Market value of 900 shares cum rights (× £4)	3,600
Market value of 900 shares ex rights (× £3.80)	3,420
Loss in wealth	$\overline{180}$

It follows that the shareholder, to protect his existing investment, should either **exercise his rights** or **sell them** to another investor. If he does not exercise his rights, the new securities he was entitled to subscribe for might be sold for his benefit by the company, and this would protect him from losing wealth.

8.3 Cost of equity

$$\text{Cost of equity capital} = \frac{12(1 + 0.04)}{96} + 0.04$$

$$= 0.13 + 0.04$$
$$= 0.17$$
$$= 17\%$$

8.4 Growth rate

Let 'g' = rate of growth in dividends.

$$\text{Dividend in 20X1} \times (1 + g)^4 = \text{Dividend in 20X5}$$
$$(1 + g)^4 = \text{Dividend in 20X5} \div \text{Dividend in 20X1}$$
$$(1 + g)^4 = 200,000 \div 100,000$$
$$(1 + g)^4 = 2.0$$
$$1 + g = \sqrt[4]{2}$$
$$1 + g = 1.19$$
$$g = 19\%$$

8.5 Returns

(a) $7\% + ((11\% - 7\%) \times 0.9) = 10.6\%$

(b) $\dfrac{5.3c}{10.6\%} = 50c$

8.6 Beta factor

(a) **Beta measures** the systematic risk of a risky investment such as a share in a company. The total risk of the share can be subdivided into two parts, known as **systematic (or market) risk** and **unsystematic (or unique) risk**. The systematic risk depends on the sensitivity of the return of the share to general economic and market factors such as periods of boom and recession. The capital asset pricing model shows how the return which investors expect from shares should depend only on systematic risk, not on unsystematic risk, which can be eliminated by holding a well diversified portfolio.

Beta is calibrated such that the average risk of stock market investments has a **beta of 1**. Thus shares with betas of 0.5 or 1.5 would have half or 1½ times the average sensitivity to market variations respectively.

This is reflected by higher volatility of share prices for shares with a beta of 1.5 than for those with a beta of 0.5. For example, a 10% increase in general stock market prices would be expected to be reflected as a 5% increase for a share with a beta of 0.5 and a 15% increase for a share with a beta of 1.5, with a similar effect for price reductions.

(b) The beta of a company will be the **weighted average** of the beta of its shares and the beta of its debt. The beta of debt is very low, but not zero, because corporate debt bears default risk, which in turn is dependent on the volatility of the company's cash flows.

Factors determining the beta of a company's equity shares include:

(i) **Sensitivity** of the company's **cash flows** to economic factors, as stated above. For example sales of new cars are more sensitive than sales of basic foods and necessities.

(ii) The company's **operating gearing**. A high level of fixed costs in the company's cost structure will cause high variations in operating profit compared with variations in sales.

(iii)   The company's **financial gearing**. High borrowing and interest costs will cause high variations in equity earnings compared with variations in operating profit, increasing the equity beta as equity returns become more variable in relation to the market as a whole. This effect will be countered by the low beta of debt when computing the weighted average beta of the whole company.

Now try the questions from the Practice Question Bank	Question	Level
	Section A: 8.1 – 8.5	Practice
	Section B: 4	Practice

CAPITAL STRUCTURE

This chapter looks at the key decision of capital structure, ie the proportion of debt and equity finance a company should use. We look at the impact of capital structure on **key ratios** of interest to investors.

We revisit the calculation of the **weighted average cost of capital** from earlier studies and look at theories that attempt to explain the effect that changing capital structure has on the cost of capital and market value of a company.

The chapter ends by looking at how group companies often maximise their capital structure to reduce taxation.

9

Topic list	learning outcomes	syllabus references	ability required
1 The capital structure decision	B(1)(a)	B(1)(a)(i),(iii)	evaluation
2 Effect of capital structure on ratios	B(1)(a)	B(1)(a)(iii)	evaluation
3 Theories of capital structure	B(1)(a)	B(1)(a)(i),(ii) C(2)(a)(ix)	evaluation
4 Capital structure of group companies	B(1)(a)	B(1)(a)(iv)	evaluation

Chapter Overview

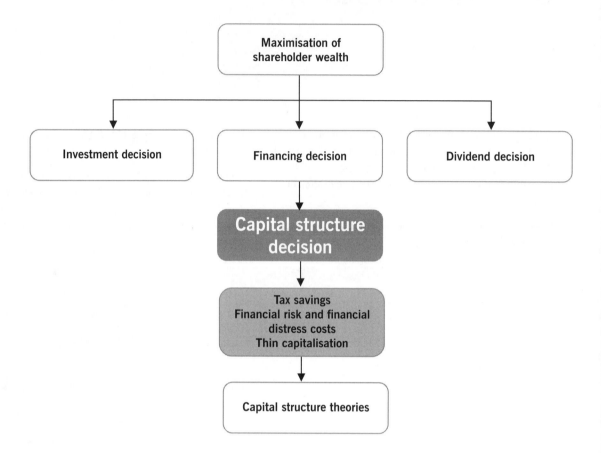

1 The capital structure decision

Introduction

We have previously looked at the sources and costs of debt and equity finance. We now need to look at what **proportion of debt and equity** an entity should use. Debt finance can create valuable **tax savings** which can reduce the cost of capital and increase shareholder value. However, too much debt increases **financial risk**.

1.1 Capital structure

KEY TERM

CAPITAL STRUCTURE refers to the way in which an organisation is financed, by a combination of long-term capital (ordinary shares and reserves, preferred shares, bonds, bank loans, convertible bonds and so on) and short-term liabilities, such as a bank overdraft and trade payables. The mix of finance can be measured by **gearing** ratios.

The assets of a business must be financed somehow. When a business is growing, the additional assets must be financed by additional capital. As part of this decision it is necessary to consider the duration of the financing and remember the concept covered earlier that long-term assets should be financed by long-term funds.

1.2 The advantages of using debt finance

(a) Debt is a **cheaper form of finance** than shares because, unlike preferred shares, debt interest is tax deductible in most tax regimes.

(b) Debt should be **more attractive** to investors because it will be **secured** against the assets of the company.

(c) **Debt holders** rank above **shareholders** in the event of a liquidation.

(d) **Issue costs** should be **lower** for debt than for shares.

(e) There is **no immediate change** in the existing structure of control, although this will change over time as conversion rights are exercised.

(f) There is **no immediate dilution** in earnings and dividends per share.

(g) Lenders do not participate in high profits compared with shares.

(h) Debt acts as a **discipline on management** as careful management of working capital and cash flow is needed.

1.3 Disadvantages of debt

(a) **Interest** has to be paid on debt no matter what the company's profits are. A particular disadvantage is that the company may find itself locked into long-term debt at unfavourable rates of interest. By contrast, the company is not legally obliged to pay dividends.

(b) If the business struggles to pay the interest on debt, **direct financial distress costs** may be incurred in the form of higher debt payments and costs of managing the liquidation process.

(c) **Indirect financial distress costs** can include a loss of sales, higher costs from suppliers or sale of inventory at below market value.

(d) **Agency costs** occur when managers may be reluctant to invest if gearing levels are already high.

(e) Money has to be made available for **redemption** or **repayment** of debt.

(f)   Heavy borrowing **increases the financial risks** for ordinary shareholders who may demand a **higher rate of return** because an increased interest burden increases the risks that dividends will not be paid.

(g)   There might be restrictions on a company's power to borrow. The **company's constitution** may limit borrowing. These borrowing limits cannot be altered except with the approval of the shareholders at a general meeting of the company. **Restrictive covenants attached to existing debt** may **limit borrowing** by specifying a maximum gearing level. These limits can only be overcome by redeeming the debt. Restrictive covenants also require the borrower to satisfy certain criteria such as minimum interest coverage.

(h)   Debt is not necessarily always **available** to all companies. Small companies traditionally struggle to raise long-term debt finance and during a recession debt finance is less readily available than in a period of economic growth.

1.4 Company circumstances

One determinant of the suitability of the gearing mix is the stability of the company. It may seem obvious, but it is worth stressing that debt financing will be more appropriate when:

*   The company is in a **healthy competitive position**
*   **Cash flows** and **earnings** are stable
*   The **bulk of the company's assets** are **tangible**
*   The **liquidity** and **cash flow position** is **strong**
*   The **debt-equity ratio** is low
*   **Share prices** are **low**
*   **Profit margins** are **reasonable**

Life cycle issues are therefore important. Young, growing companies tend to have **unpredictable and unstable cash flows** so debt finance is less appropriate than for mature companies.

CASE STUDY

Manchester United has €200million more net debt than any other football club in Europe, new research from Uefa has shown.

The European Club Football Landscape report shows the amount of money the Old Trafford club owes has now grown to €536m (£464m).

While debt levels across the continent have decreased each year for the past five years – something Uefa puts down to its financial fair play regulations – United's has grown by 25 per cent in the past year alone.

The amount of debt accrued by United since the Glazer family bought the club in 2005 has been a source of great anger among the club's fans.

Nevertheless, it's important to look at these figures in context. As the Uefa report highlights, the level of debt should be viewed alongside revenue and long-term assets – an area of notable strength for United.

(Source: Independent, 12 January 2017)

Section summary

Debt finance can create valuable tax savings which can **reduce the cost of capital** and **increase shareholder value.** However, too much debt increases **financial risk** and incurs **financial distress costs.**

2 Effect of capital structure on ratios

Introduction

This section links to forecasting and analysis that we covered in Chapter 2. If an entity changes its capital structure, it will impact on a number of key ratios such as gearing, interest cover and EPS.

2.1 Gearing

In Chapter 2, we revised gearing briefly. You should remember that the financial risk of a company's capital structure can be measured by a **gearing ratio**, a **debt ratio** or **debt/equity ratio** and by the **interest cover**. A gearing ratio should not be given without stating how it has been defined.

Exam skills

You need to be able to explain and calculate the level of financial gearing using alternative measures. The question may specify how gearing should be calculated eg debt to total value of entity using market values.

Financial gearing measures the relationship between shareholders' capital plus reserves, and either prior charge capital or borrowings, or both.

Commonly used measures of financial gearing are based on the statement of financial position values of the fixed interest and equity capital. They include:

$$\frac{\text{Prior charge capital}}{\text{Equity capital (including reserves)}} \quad \text{and} \quad \frac{\text{Prior charge capital}}{\text{Total capital employed *}}$$

* Either including or excluding minority interests, deferred tax and deferred income.

With the first definition above, a company is low geared if the gearing ratio is less than 100%, highly geared if the ratio is over 100% and neutrally geared if it is exactly 100%. With the second definition, a company is neutrally geared if the ratio is 50%, low geared below that, and highly geared above that.

Question 9.1	Gearing

Learning outcome: C(2)(a)

From the following statement of financial position, compute the company's financial gearing ratio.

	$'000	$'000	$'000
Non-current assets			12,400
Current assets		1,000	
Payables: amounts falling due within one year			
Loans	120		
Bank overdraft	260		
Trade payables	430		
Bills of exchange	70		
		880	
Net current assets			120
Total assets less current liabilities			12,520
Payables: amounts falling due after more than one year			
Bonds		4,700	
Bank loans		500	
			(5,200)
Provisions for liabilities and charges: deferred taxation			(300)
Deferred income			(250)
Total net assets			6,770

	$'000	$'000	$'000
Capital and reserves			
			$'000
Called up share capital			
Ordinary shares			1,500
Preferred shares			500
			2,000
Share premium account			760
Revaluation reserve			1,200
Accumulated profits			2,810
Total share capital and reserves			6,770

2.1.1 Gearing ratios based on market values

An alternative method of calculating a gearing ratio is one based on **market values**:

$$\frac{\text{Market value of debt (including preference shares)}}{\text{Market value of equity} + \text{Market value of debt}}$$

The advantage of this method is that potential investors in a company are able to judge the further debt capacity of the company more clearly by **reference** to **market values** than they could by looking at statement of financial position values.

The disadvantage of a gearing ratio based on market values is that it **disregards** the **value** of the company's **assets**, which might be used to secure further loans. A gearing ratio based on statement of financial position values arguably gives a better indication of the **security for lenders** of fixed interest capital.

2.1.2 Changing financial gearing

Financial gearing is an attempt to quantify the **degree of risk** involved in holding equity shares in a company, both in terms of the company's ability to remain in business and in terms of expected ordinary dividends from the company.

The more geared the company is, the **greater the risk** that little (if anything) will be available to distribute by way of dividend to the ordinary shareholders. The more geared the company, the greater the percentage change in profit available for ordinary shareholders for any given percentage change in profit before interest and tax.

This means that there will be greater **volatility** of amounts available for ordinary shareholders, and presumably therefore greater volatility in dividends paid to those shareholders, where a company is highly geared. That is the risk. You may do extremely well or extremely badly without a particularly large movement in the profit from operations of the company.

Gearing ultimately measures the company's ability to **remain in business**. A highly geared company has a large amount of interest to pay annually. If those borrowings are 'secured' in any way then the holders of the debt are perfectly entitled to force the company to realise assets to pay their interest if funds are not available from other sources. Clearly, the more highly geared a company, the more likely this is to occur if and when profits fall.

2.1.3 Operating gearing

Financial risk, as we have seen, can be measured by financial gearing. **Business risk** refers to the risk of making only low profits, or even losses, due to the nature of the business that the company is involved in. One way of measuring business risk is by calculating a company's **operating gearing** or 'operational gearing'.

$$\text{Operating gearing or leverage} = \frac{\text{Contribution}}{\text{Profit before interest and tax (PBIT)}}$$

Contribution is sales minus variable cost of sales.

The significance of operating gearing is as follows.

(a)   **If contribution is high but PBIT is low**, fixed costs will be high, and only just covered by contribution. Business risk, as measured by operating gearing, will be high.

(b)   **If contribution is not much bigger than PBIT**, fixed costs will be low, and fairly easily covered. Business risk, as measured by operating gearing, will be low.

2.2 Interest cover

Like gearing, **interest cover** is a measure of financial risk which is designed to show the risks in terms of profit rather than in terms of capital values.

$$\textbf{Interest cover} = \frac{\text{Profit before interest and tax}}{\text{Interest payable}}$$

As a general guide, an interest cover of **less than three times** is considered low, indicating that profitability is too low given the gearing of the company.

Example: Effect of a change in capital structure on ratios

You need to be able to demonstrate the **impact of changing capital structures on investor ratios.** The following example illustrates how such a question could be set out.

A summarised statement of financial position of Rufus is as follows.

	£m
Assets less current liabilities	150
Debt capital	(70)
	80
Share capital (20 million shares of £1)	20
Reserves	60
	80

The company's profits in the year just ended are as follows.

	£m
Profit from operations	21.0
Interest	6.0
Profit before tax	15.0
Taxation at 30%	4.5
Profit after tax (earnings)	10.5
Dividends	6.5
Retained profits	4.0

The company is now considering an investment of £25 million. This will add £5 million each year to profits before interest and tax.

(a)   There are two ways of financing this investment. One would be to borrow £25 million at a cost of 8% per annum in interest. The other would be to raise the money by means of a 1 for 4 rights issue.

(b)   Whichever financing method is used, the company will increase dividends per share next year from 32.5p to 35p.

(c)   The company does not intend to allow its gearing level, measured as debt finance as a proportion of equity capital plus debt finance, to exceed 55% as at the end of any financial year. In addition, the company will not accept any dilution in earnings per share.

Assume that the rate of taxation will remain at 30% and that debt interest costs will be £6 million plus the interest cost of any new debt capital.

Required

(a) Produce a profit forecast for next year, assuming that the new project is undertaken and is financed (i) by debt capital or (ii) by a rights issue.

(b) Calculate the earnings per share next year, with each financing method.

(c) Calculate the effect on gearing as at the end of next year, with each financing method.

(d) Explain whether either or both methods of funding would be acceptable.

Solution

Current earnings per share are £10.5 million/20 million shares = 52.5 pence.

If the project is financed by £25 million of debt at 8%, interest charges will rise by £2 million. If the project is financed by a 1 for 4 rights issue, there will be 25 million shares in issue.

	Finance with debt £m	*Finance with rights issue* £m
Profit before interest and tax (+ 5.0)	26.00	26.00
Interest	8.00	6.00
	18.00	20.00
Taxation (30%)	5.40	6.00
Profit after tax	12.60	14.00
Dividends (35p per share)	7.00	8.75
Retained profits	5.60	5.25
Earnings (profits after tax)	£12.6 m	£14.0 m
Number of shares	20 million	25 million
Earnings per share	63 p	56 p

The projected statement of financial position as at the end of the year will be:

	Finance with debt £m	*Finance with rights issue* £m
Assets less current liabilities	180.6	180.25
(150 + new capital 25 + retained profits)		
Debt capital	(95.0)	(70.00)
	85.6	110.25
Share capital	20.0	25.00
Reserves	65.6	* 85.25
	85.6	110.25

* The rights issue raises £25 million, of which £5 million is represented in the statement of financial position by share capital and the remaining £20 million by share premium. The reserves are therefore the current amount (£60 million) plus the share premium of £20 million plus accumulated profits of £5.25 million.

	Finance with debt	*Finance with rights issue*
Debt capital	95.0	70.0
Debt capital plus equity finance	(95.0 + 85.6)	(70.0 + 110.25)
Gearing	53%	39%

Either financing method would be acceptable, since the company's requirements for no dilution in EPS would be met with a rights issue as well as by borrowing, and the company's requirement for the gearing level to remain below 55% is (just) met even if the company were to borrow the money.

> **Section summary**
>
> - **Financial gearing** measures the relationship between **shareholders' funds** and **prior charge capital**.
>
> - **Operating gearing** measures the relationship between **contribution** and **profit before interest and tax**.
>
> - If a company can generate returns on capital in excess of the interest payable on debt, financial gearing will **raise the EPS**. Gearing will, however, also increase **the variability of returns** for shareholders and increase the chance of **corporate failure**.

3 Theories of capital structure

Introduction

There are two main theories which attempt to explain the effect of changes in capital structure on cost of capital and therefore the market value of a company. These are the **traditional theory** and the **net operating income approach** (Modigliani and Miller).

3.1 Weighted Average Cost of Capital (WACC)

The calculation of WACC is covered in F2 *Advanced Financial Reporting*. Before we look at how changes in capital structure affect WACC, let's recap the definition and formula for WACC.

KEY TERM

WEIGHTED AVERAGE COST OF CAPITAL is the average cost of the company's finance (equity, debentures, bank loans) weighted according to the proportion each element bears to the total pool of capital. Weighting is usually based on market valuations, current yields and costs after tax.

(CIMA Official Terminology)

A general formula for the weighted average cost of capital (or k_0) is as follows.

EXAM

$$WACC = k_e \left[\frac{V_E}{V_E + V_D} \right] + k_d (1 - t) \left[\frac{V_D}{V_E + V_D} \right]$$

Where k_e is the cost of equity
            k_d is the cost of debt
            V_E is the market value of issued shares (market capitalisation)
            V_D is the market value of debt

Preference shares can be added in if necessary.

The use of WACC as a discount rate for company valuation using discounted cash flow (DCF) analysis is covered in Chapters 11 and 12.

3.2 The traditional view of WACC

The **traditional view** is as follows:

(a)   As the **level of gearing increases**, the **cost of debt** remains **unchanged** up to a certain level of gearing. Beyond this level, the cost of debt will increase as interest cover falls, the amount of assets available for security falls and the risk of bankruptcy increases.

(b)   The **cost of equity** rises as the level of **gearing increases** and **financial risk increases**.

(c) The **weighted average cost of capital** does **not remain constant**, but rather falls initially as the proportion of debt capital increases, and then begins to increase as the rising cost of equity (and possibly of debt) becomes more significant.

(d) The **optimum level of gearing** is where the **company's weighted average cost of capital is minimised**.

The traditional view about the cost of capital is illustrated in the following figure. It shows that the weighted average cost of capital will be minimised at a particular level of gearing P.

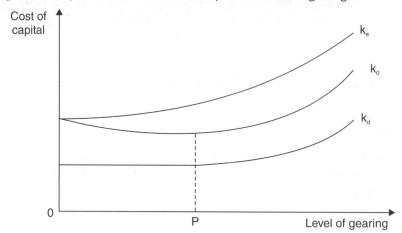

Where k_e is the cost of equity in the geared company
k_d is the cost of debt
k_0 is the weighted average cost of capital

The traditional view is that the weighted average cost of capital, when plotted against the level of gearing, is saucer shaped. The optimum capital structure is where the weighted average cost of capital is lowest, at point P.

3.3 The net operating income (Modigliani-Miller (MM)) view of WACC

The net operating income approach takes a different view of the effect of gearing on WACC. In their 1958 theory, Modigliani and Miller (MM) proposed that the total market value of a company, in the absence of tax, will be determined only by two factors:

- The **total earnings** of the company
- The **level of operating (business) risk** attached to those earnings

The total market value would be computed by discounting the total earnings at a rate that is appropriate to the level of operating risk. This rate would represent the WACC of the company.

Thus Modigliani and Miller concluded that **the capital structure of a company would have no effect on its overall value or WACC**.

3.3.1 Assumptions of net operating income approach

Modigliani and Miller made various assumptions in arriving at this conclusion, including:

(a) A **perfect capital market** exists, in which investors have the same information, upon which they act rationally, to arrive at the same expectations about future earnings and risks.

(b) There are no **tax or transaction costs**.

(c) **Debt is risk-free** and freely available at the same cost to investors and companies alike.

Modigliani and Miller justified their approach by the use of **arbitrage**.

KEY TERM

ARBITRAGE is the simultaneous purchase and sale of a security in different markets, with the aim of making a risk-free profit through the exploitation of any price difference between the markets.

(CIMA Official Terminology)

Arbitrage can be used to show that once all opportunities for profit have been exploited, the market values of two companies with the same earnings in equivalent business risk classes will have moved to an equal value.

If Modigliani and Miller's theory holds, it implies:

(a)   The **cost of debt remains unchanged** as the level of gearing increases.

(b)   The **cost of equity rises** in such a way as to keep the **weighted average cost of capital constant**.

This would be represented on a graph as shown below.

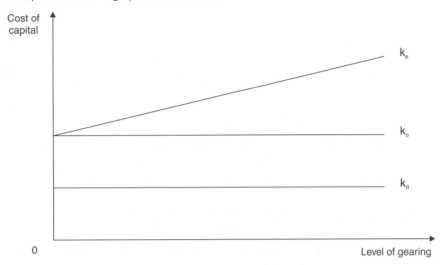

3.4 Modigliani-Miller theory adjusted for taxation

Having argued that debt has no benefit in the absence of taxation, MM then went on to demonstrate that debt can be beneficial where tax relief applies.

Allowing for **taxation reduces the cost of debt capital** by multiplying it by a factor $(1 - t)$ where t is the rate of tax (assuming the debt to be irredeemable).

MM modified their theory to admit that tax relief on interest payments does make debt capital cheaper to a company, and therefore **reduces the weighted average cost of capital** where a company has debt in its capital structure. They claimed that the weighted average cost of capital will continue to fall, up to gearing of 100%.

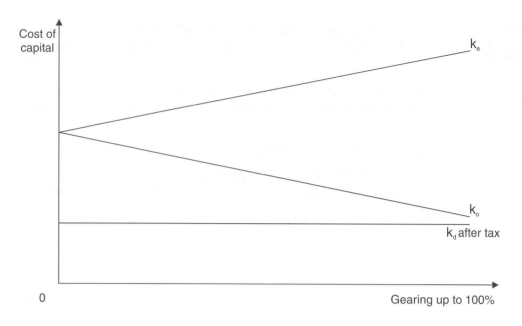

3.5 Formulae and MM theory

MM developed the following formula as part of their with-taxation theory:

$$V_g = V_u + TB$$

Where V_g = value of debt plus equity in geared company

V_u = value of equity in an equivalent ungeared company

TB = tax shield on debt (T is the corporate tax rate and B is the market value of the geared company's debt)

This formula shows that the greater the value of debt, the greater the value of the company and so supports the idea that a company should be geared as highly as possible to maximise its value.

A further formula arising from the MM theory is:

$$k_{eg} = k_{eu} + (k_{eu} - k_d)\frac{V_d}{V_e}(1 - T)$$

Where k_{eg} is the cost of equity in a geared company

k_{eu} is the cost of equity in an ungeared company

V_d, V_e are the market values of debt and equity respectively

k_d is the cost of debt pre-tax

T is the corporate tax rate

This formula shows that the cost of equity will increase when the relative value of debt to equity increases.

MM also came up with an adjusted cost of capital formula as follows

$$k_{adj} = k_{eu}(1 - tL)$$

Where k_{adj} is the weighted average cost of capital in a geared company

k_{eu} is the cost of equity in an ungeared company

t is the corporate tax rate

L is the gearing ratio measured by debt/(debt + equity)

This formula shows that WACC is reduced when gearing increases ie when more debt is taken on.

3.6 Weaknesses in MM theory

MM theory has been criticised as follows.

(a)   MM theory assumes that **capital markets are perfect**. For example, a company will always be able to raise finance to fund worthwhile projects. This ignores the danger that higher gearing can lead to **financial distress costs** and **agency problems** (see Section 1.3).

(b)   **Transaction costs** will restrict the arbitrage process.

(c)   Investors are **assumed to act rationally** which may not be the case in practice.

3.7 Capital structure in the real world

In the real world some of the theoretical assumptions in MM theory **do not hold**. The most unrealistic are that perfect capital markets exist and that debt is risk free. Almost every borrower would agree that there is **greater risk** at very high levels of gearing and lenders will feel the same. This risk is that the borrower will not be able to service its interest payments and the company may become **insolvent**.

In reality there are a number of factors that can influence the capital structure.

3.7.1 Debt capacity

Debt capacity refers to the maximum amount of debt that a company can support or obtain. A company will have a greater capacity to borrow if it has a number of assets that can be offered as security on the debt.

A company can only increase its borrowing if there are lenders willing to **provide finance**. This may not necessarily always be easy depending on the **financial position** of the company and the state of the **economy**.

3.7.2 Debt covenants

Existing debt may have covenants attached, which require certain **targets** to be met by the borrower and therefore **reduce the flexibility** of management. Existing covenants may **prevent** or limit opportunities for further borrowing. Examples of financial covenants include target interest cover ratios or cash flow/earnings target levels. Breaching covenants may trigger an early repayment of the debt or other penalties.

3.7.3 Increasing debt costs

MM theory assumes that the cost of debt is unchanged at all levels of gearing. In reality as a borrower takes on greater levels of debt, and is perceived to be **riskier**, the lender's required rate of return is likely to **increase**.

3.7.4 Tax exhaustion

The benefit of tax relief on debt is only available while the borrower is making a taxable profit. If gearing is high enough, there will be a point where the interest payments will reduce taxable profit to zero and any further debt will not benefit from tax relief. This is known as **tax exhaustion**.

However as the borrower would be making a loss, this would also be likely to cause debt covenants to be breached, which may create more important problems for the company.

3.8 Capital structure conclusions

The practical implications of these capital structure theories can be generalised as follows.

Level of gearing

Low   High

     ← ————————————————————————————————— →

Young company	Mature company
Volatile cash flows	Stable cash flows
Tax benefits are likely to be exceeded by financial distress costs	Tax benefits are likely to be greater than financial distress costs

Exam skills

You may need to be able to discuss whether the choice of capital structure for an entity is likely to affect its overall value.

Section summary

- The **traditional theory of cost of capital** suggests that WACC is influenced by gearing; **Modigliani and Miller** disagree.

- Under the **traditional theory of cost of capital**, the cost declines initially and then rises as gearing increases. The **optimal capital structure** will be the point at which WACC is lowest.

- Modigliani and Miller stated that, in the absence of tax, a company's **capital structure** would have **no impact** upon its WACC.

- Modigliani and Miller went on to demonstrate that debt can be beneficial where **tax relief** applies and a company should use as much debt finance as possible.

4   Capital structure of group companies

Introduction

In many multinational groups of companies, the debt to equity profile is structured to reduce tax in order to increase shareholder wealth.

4.1 Structuring the debt/equity profile of group companies

In multinational groups of companies, parent companies can choose the mixture of debt and equity to finance subsidiaries. Since interest payments on debt are tax deductible and dividend payments are not, it would be more tax efficient for a company to have higher levels of debt than equity. However, companies on their own are unlikely to have high levels of debt to equity as this would be too risky for investors and lenders. Companies within a group, however, can have higher levels of debt to equity by borrowing from other group companies.

4.2 Thin capitalisation

In Chapter 2, we briefly looked at thin capitalisation. A company that has a significantly higher level of debt compared to equity than it could achieve on its own is described as **thinly capitalised.**

Thin capitalisation can be tax efficient for both the lender and the borrower. The borrowing company within the group pays interest to the lending company. This allows the borrowing company to reduce its taxable profits by the amount of interest paid. The lending company receives interest income from the borrowing company. However if the lending company is incorporated in a country with a low tax rate, or in a country which does not tax interest income, it pays relatively low or zero tax on this income. By structuring the financing and interest arrangements carefully, a multinational group can therefore influence the profit it reports and the tax it pays.

4.3 Tax avoidance rules

To counteract companies exploiting thin capitalisation to reduce tax, some countries have introduced tax legislation to place limits on the amount of interest that can be deducted from taxable profits, for example:

Arms length limits

The maximum amount of debt on which interest is tax deductible is limited to the amount that an independent arm's length lender would provide to a company.

Ratio limits

The maximum amount of debt on which interest is tax deductible is limited to a set ratio such as the ratio of debt to equity. For example, in Australia, the maximum ratio of debt to equity is 60:40 for general entities.

Earnings stripping approach

Some countries adopt a ratio approach which focuses on the amount of interest paid in relation to some other variable eg the amount of interest to operating profit. Germany for example, caps deductible interest at 30% of EBITDA.

Section summary

Thin capitalisation describes companies that have a significantly higher proportion of debt finance to equity finance.

Thin capitalisation occurs in many **group companies**, since it is easier to obtain debt finance from other group companies than third party lenders.

Thin capitalisation is used as a technique for **tax avoidance**, since interest payments on debt finance can be deducted from taxable profits in most countries.

Certain tax authorities have **anti-avoidance legislation** that places limits on the amount of interest that can be tax deductible.

Chapter Summary

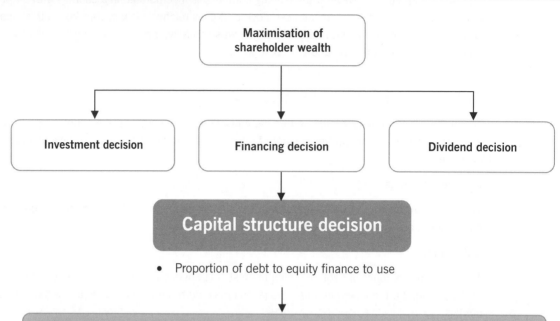

Maximisation of shareholder wealth

Investment decision

Financing decision

Dividend decision

Capital structure decision

- Proportion of debt to equity finance to use

- Debt finance can create valuable tax savings that can drive down cost of capital and increase shareholder value
- However too much debt increases financial risk and incurs financial distress costs
- Capital structures of group companies often have high levels of debt compared to equity for tax savings – they are thinly capitalised

Weighted average cost of capital (WACC)

- Average cost of finance (equity, debentures, bank loans)
- Weighted according to the proportion each element bears to the total pool of capital

Capital structure theories
Traditional theory:

- WACC falls initially as the proportion of debt capital increases, and then begins to increase as the rising cost of equity (and possibly of debt) becomes more significant
- Optimal capital structure at point where WACC lowest

Modigliani and Miller (MM) theory:
- Ignoring tax, capital structure has no impact on WACC
- MM went onto to demonstrate that debt can be beneficial where tax relief applies and a company should use as much debt as possible

Quick Quiz

1   **Fill in the blanks:**

$$\ldots\ldots\ldots\ldots\ldots\ldots\ldots\ldots\ldots \text{ gearing} = \frac{\text{Prior charge capital}}{\text{Total capital employed}}$$

$$\ldots\ldots\ldots\ldots\ldots\ldots\ldots\ldots\ldots \text{ gearing} = \frac{\text{Contribution}}{\text{Profit before interest and tax}}$$

2   Identify the variables k_e, k_d, V_E and V_D in the following weighted average cost of capital formula.

$$\text{WACC} = k_e \left[\frac{V_E}{V_E + V_D} \right] + k_d \, (1 - t) \left[\frac{V_D}{V_E + V_D} \right]$$

3   When calculating the weighted average cost of capital, which of the following is the preferred method of weighting?

   A   Book values of debt and equity
   B   Average levels of the market values of debt and equity (ignoring reserves) over five years
   C   Current market values of debt and equity (ignoring reserves)
   D   Current market values of debt and equity (plus reserves)

4   According to the traditional view of WACC, what happens to WACC as gearing increases?

5   What is thin capitalisation?

Answers to Quick Quiz

1. Financial gearing $= \dfrac{\text{Prior charge capital}}{\text{Total capital employed}}$

   Operating gearing $= \dfrac{\text{Contribution}}{\text{Profit before interest and tax}}$

2. k_e is the cost of equity

   k_d is the cost of debt

   V_E is the market value of equity in the firm

   V_D is the market value of debt in the firm

3. C   Current market values of debt and equity (ignoring reserves)

4. As gearing increases, WACC declines initially (as the additional cheap debt outweighs the increase in the cost of equity arising from the extra gearing risk), until there is an optimal capital structure. Beyond this point, WACC then rises as the increase in the cost of equity more than outweighs the benefit of additional cheap debt.

5. Thin capitalisation describes a company that has a significantly higher proportion of debt to equity in its capital structure, than it could normally achieve on its own. Thinly capitalised companies are often referred to as highly geared.

Answers to Questions

9.1 Gearing

	$'000
Prior charge capital	
Preferred shares	500
Bonds	4,700
Long-term bank loans	500
Prior charge capital, ignoring short-term debt	5,700
Short-term loans	120
Overdraft	260
Prior charge capital, including short-term interest bearing debt	6,080

Either figure, $6,080,000 or $5,700,000, could be used. If gearing is calculated with capital employed in the denominator, and capital employed is non-current assets plus net current assets, it would be better to exclude short-term interest bearing debt from prior charge capital. This is because short-term debt is set off against current assets in arriving at the figure for net current assets.

Equity = 1,500 + 760 + 1,200 + 2,810 = $6,270,000

The gearing ratio can be calculated in any of the following ways.

(a) $\dfrac{\text{Prior charge capital}}{\text{Equity}} \times 100\% = \dfrac{6,080}{6,270} \times 100\% = 97.0\%$

(b) $\dfrac{\text{Prior charge capital}}{\text{Equity plus prior charge capital}} \times 100\% = \dfrac{6,080}{(6,080+6,270)} \times 100\% = 49.2\%$

(c) $\dfrac{\text{Prior charge capital}}{\text{Total capital employed}} \times 100\% = \dfrac{5,700}{12,520} \times 100\% = 45.5\%$

Now try the questions from the Practice Question Bank

Question
Section A: 9.1 – 9.2

Level
Practice

CORPORATE FINANCE

STRATEGIC IMPLICATIONS OF ACQUISITIONS

In this chapter, we are concerned with the issues of acquisitions, mergers and acquisitions (takeovers) from the point of view of financial management and financial strategy.

We look at topics such as the reasons for mergers and acquisitions, their advantages and disadvantages, the synergies they produce and the impact on stakeholders.

In Chapter 13, we apply company valuation techniques from Chapter 11 to merger and acquisition scenarios, and look at what happens after a takeover.

Topic list	learning outcomes	syllabus references	ability required
1 Mergers and takeovers (acquisitions)	C(1)(a)	C(1)(a)(ii),(iii),(v)	evaluation
2 The conduct of a takeover	C(1)(a), C(3)(a)	C(1)(a)(ii), C(3)(a)(iv)	evaluation
3 Regulation of takeovers	C(1)(a)	C(1)(a)(vi)	evaluation
4 Impact of mergers and takeovers on stakeholders	C(1)(a)	C(1)(a)(i)	evaluation

Chapter Overview

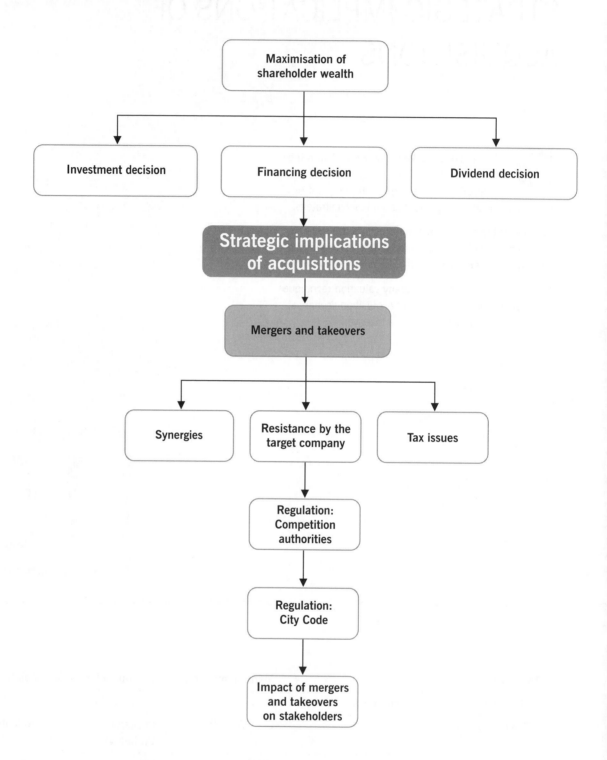

1 Mergers and takeovers (acquisitions)

Introduction

In this section we explain what is meant by the terms mergers, takeovers and acquisitions and the reasons why they happen.

1.1 Definition of mergers and takeovers

KEY TERMS

TAKEOVER: the **acquisition** by a company of a controlling interest in the voting share capital of another company, usually achieved by the purchase of a majority of the voting shares.

(CIMA Official Terminology)

REVERSE TAKEOVER: when the smaller company takes over the larger one, so that the predator company has to increase its equity by over 100% to complete the takeover.

MERGER: a business combination that results in the creation of a new reporting entity formed from the combining parties, in which the shareholders of the combining entities come together in a partnership for the mutual sharing of the risks and benefits of the combined entity, and in which no party to the combination in substance obtains control over any other, or is otherwise seen to be dominant, whether by virtue of the proportion of its shareholders' rights in the combined entity, the influence of its directors or otherwise.   *(FRS 6) (CIMA Official Terminology)*

HORIZONTAL INTEGRATION is characterised by a firm adding new products to its existing market, or new markets to its existing products.

VERTICAL INTEGRATION, or vertical diversification, occurs when a company becomes either its own supplier of raw materials or components (ie **backward** vertical integration) or its own distributor or sales agent (ie **forward** vertical integration).

CONCENTRIC DIVERSIFICATION occurs when a company seeks to add new products that have technological and/or marketing synergies with the existing product line. These products will normally appeal to new classes of customer.

CONGLOMERATE DIVERSIFICATION consists of making entirely new products for new classes of customers. These new products have no relationship to the company's current technology, products or markets.

The distinction between mergers and takeovers (acquisitions) is not always clear, for example when a large company 'merges' with another smaller company. The methods used for mergers are often the same as the methods used to make takeovers. In practice, the number of genuine mergers is small relative to the number of takeovers. In the business world, the terms mergers, acquisitions and takeovers are used interchangeably.

Exam skills

Business amalgamations (mergers and takeovers) are likely to be a key topic for exam questions in *Financial Strategy* and the integrated case study. There is a significant amount of overlap with Paper E3 *Strategic Management*.

Mergers or acquisitions should be undertaken to make profits **in the long term** as well as in the short term.

(a)   **Acquisitions** may provide a means of entering a market at a **lower cost** than would be incurred if the company tried to develop its own resources, or a means of acquiring the business of a competitor. Acquisitions or mergers which might reduce or eliminate competition in a market may be prohibited by competition authorities.

(b)   **Mergers** have tended to be more common in industries with a history of little growth and low returns. Highly profitable companies tend to seek acquisitions rather than mergers.

1.2 Reasons for mergers and takeovers

The main reasons why one company may wish to acquire the shares or the business of another may be categorised as follows.

Operating economies	For example, elimination of duplicate facilities
Management acquisition	Acquisition of competent and go-ahead team to compensate for lack of internal management abilities
Diversification	Securing long-term future by spreading risk through diversification
Asset backing	Company with high earnings: assets ratios reducing risk through acquiring company with substantial assets
Quality of earnings	Reducing risk by acquiring company with less risky earnings
Finance and liquidity	Improve liquidity and ability to raise finance through acquisition of more stable company
Growth	Cheaper way of growing than internal expansion
Tax factors	Tax-efficient way of transferring cash out of corporate sector; in some jurisdictions, means of utilising tax losses by setting them against profits of acquired companies
Defensive merger	Stop competitors obtaining advantage
Strategic opportunities	Acquiring a company that provides a strategic fit (see below)
Asset stripping	Acquiring an undervalued company in order to sell off the assets to make a profit
Big Data access	Big data refers to a collection of data sets too large and complex to analyse using traditional database management tools. A technology company may want to acquire a company for the data it holds on users which can be of great value to that company

1.3 Big data

KEY TERM

BIG DATA has been defined by Gartner (a leading IT research firm) as 'high-volume, high-velocity and high-variety information assets that demand cost-effective, innovative forms of information processing for enhanced insight and decision making'.

Big data has been described as data that requires a lot of computer power to analyse – a rule of thumb is that if you can analyse a set of data on your home computer, it is not big data.

As mentioned in the previous section, access to another company's big data can be a key reason for wanting to acquire that company.

1.3.1 Big data concerns

Privacy: While big data can be a valuable 'asset' to company, there are certain risks associated with it. In addition to being beneficial for companies and customers, big data also has the potential to harm individuals, if it gets into the wrong hands. A key question is who should control our data. Big data is borderless, but cultural attitudes towards privacy are very different across the world. Concerns about whether or not governments are also gathering big data about individuals, including their own citizens, raises questions about the balance between the benefits and the infringement of rights.

Security: Companies using big data should ensure that they are not infringing the security of other organisations and their customers.

This also relates to people who are unaware of the security risks posed by their own actions, such as people who post their location on social media, revealing that they are on holiday, and are then targeted by robbers.

Intellectual property: This may include the ownership of material posted on social media and how it can be used.

Big data is also covered earlier studies

CASE STUDY

In 2013, Facebook acquired the photo-sharing app company Instagram for $1billion. Although Instagram was not profitable, it had 30 million worldwide users before the acquisition. Acquiring the data of Instagram users is valuable to Facebook. For example it could allow Facebook to track the movements of users who upload a photo on a mobile device, and place targeted advertisements to the user.

1.4 Advantages of mergers as an expansion strategy

As an expansion strategy mergers are thought to provide a quicker way of acquiring productive capacity and **intangible assets** and accessing **overseas markets**. There are four main advantages and these are summarised below:

Speed

The acquisition of another company is a quicker way of implementing a business plan, as the company acquires another organisation that is already in operation. An acquisition also allows a company to reach a certain optimal level of production much quicker than through organic growth. Acquisition as a strategy for expansion is particularly suitable for management with rather short time horizons.

Lower cost

An acquisition may be a cheaper way of acquiring productive capacity than through organic growth. An acquisition can take place for instance through an exchange of shares which does not have an impact on the financial resources of the firm.

Acquisition of intangible assets

A firm, through an acquisition, will acquire not only tangible assets but also intangible assets, such as brand recognition, reputation, customer loyalty and intellectual property which are more difficult to achieve with organic growth.

Access to overseas markets

When a company wants to expand its operations in an overseas market, acquiring a local firm may be the only option of breaking into the overseas market.

1.5 Disadvantages of mergers as an expansion strategy

An expansion strategy through acquisition is associated with exposure to a higher level of **business and financial risk.** The risks associated with expansion through acquisitions are:

Exposure to business risk

Acquisitions normally represent large investments by the bidding company and account for a large proportion of their financial resources. If the acquired company does not perform as well as it was envisaged, then the effect on the acquiring firm may be catastrophic.

Exposure to financial risk

During the acquisition process, the acquiring firm may have less than complete information on the target company, and aspects may exist that have been kept hidden from outsiders.

Acquisition premium

When a company acquires another company, it normally pays a premium over its present market value. This premium is normally justified by the management of the bidding company as necessary for the benefits that will accrue from the acquisition. However, too large a premium may render the acquisition unprofitable.

Managerial competence

When a firm is acquired, which is large relative to the acquiring firm, the management of the acquiring firm may not have the experience or ability to deal with operations on the new larger scale, even if the acquired company retains its own management.

Integration problems

Most acquisitions are beset with problems of integration as each company has its own culture, history and ways of operation.

1.6 A strategic approach to takeovers

A strategic approach to takeovers would imply that acquisitions are only made after a full analysis of the underlying strengths of the acquirer company, and identification of candidates' **'strategic fit' with its existing activities**. Possible strategic reasons for a takeover are matched with suggested ways of achieving the aim in the following list from a publication of 3i (Investors in Industry), which specialises in offering advice on takeovers.

Strategic opportunities	
Where you are	How to get to where you want to be
Growing steadily but in a mature market with limited growth prospects	Acquire a company in a younger market with a higher growth rate.
Marketing an incomplete product range, or having the potential to sell other products or services to your existing customers	Acquire a company with a complementary product range.
Operating at maximum productive capacity	Acquire a company making similar products operating substantially below capacity.
Underutilising management resources	Acquire a company into which your talents can extend.
Needing more control of suppliers or customers	Acquire a company which is, or gives access to, a significant customer or supplier.
Lacking key clients in a targeted sector	Acquire a company with the right customer profile.
Preparing for flotation but needing to improve your statement of financial position	Acquire a suitable company which will enhance earnings per share.
Needing to increase market share	Acquire an important competitor.
Needing to widen your capability	Acquire a company with the key talents and/or technology.

1.7 Synergies

KEY TERM

SYNERGY is where the present value of the combined enterprise is greater than the sum of the net present value of the individual firms.

When two or more companies join together, there should be a 'synergistic' effect. Synergy can be described as the **2 + 2 = 5** effect, whereby a group after a takeover achieves combined results that reflect a better rate of return than was being achieved by the same resources used in two separate operations before the takeover.

The three main types of synergy to be gained from acquisitions or mergers are **revenue**, **cost** and **financial** synergies.

The existence of synergies has been presented as one of the two main explanations that may increase shareholder value in an acquisition. Indeed the identification, quantification and announcement of these synergies are an essential part of the process as shareholders of the companies need to be persuaded to back the merger.

1.7.1 Revenue synergy

Revenue synergy exists when the acquisition of the target company will result in **higher revenues** for the acquiring company, **higher return on equity** or a **longer period of growth**. Revenue synergies arise from:

(a) Increased market power
(b) Marketing synergies
(c) Strategic synergies

Revenue synergies are more difficult to quantify relative to **financial** and **cost synergies**. When companies merge, cost synergies are relatively easy to assess pre-deal and to implement post-deal. But revenue synergies are more difficult. It is hard to be sure how customers will react to the new organisation (in financial services mergers, massive customer defection is quite common), whether customers will actually buy the new, expanded 'total systems capabilities', and how much of the company's declared cost savings they will demand in price concessions (this is common in automotive supplier mergers and acquisitions where the customers have huge purchasing power over the suppliers). Nevertheless, revenue synergies must be identified and delivered. The stock markets will be content with cost synergies for the first year after the deal, but thereafter they will want to see growth. Customer relationship management and product technology management are the two core business processes that will enable the delivery of revenue.

1.7.2 Cost synergy

A **cost synergy** results primarily from the existence of **economies of scale**. As the level of operation increases, the marginal cost falls and this will be manifested in greater operating margins for the combined entity. The resulting **costs** from **economies of scale** are normally estimated to be substantial.

1.7.3 Sources of financial synergy

Diversification

Acquiring another firm as a way of reducing risk cannot create wealth for two publicly traded firms, with diversified stockholders, but it could create wealth for private firms or closely held publicly traded firms. A takeover, motivated only by diversification considerations, has no effect on the combined value of the two firms involved in the takeover. The value of the combined firms will always be the sum of the values of the independent firms. In the case of private firms or closely held firms, where the owners may not be diversified personally, there might be a potential value gain from diversification.

Cash slack

When a firm with significant excess cash acquires a firm with great projects but insufficient capital, the combination can create value. Managers may reject profitable investment opportunities if they have to raise new capital to finance them. It may therefore make sense for a company with excess cash and no investment opportunities to take over a cash-poor firm with good investment opportunities, or *vice versa*. The additional value of combining these two firms lies in the present value of the projects that would not have been taken if they had stayed apart, but can now be taken because of the availability of cash.

Tax benefits

The tax paid by two firms combined together may be lower than the taxes paid by them as individual firms. If one of the firms has tax deductions that it cannot use because it is losing money, while the other firm has income on which it pays significant taxes, the combining of the two firms can lead to tax benefits that can be shared by the two firms. Furthermore, many cross-border acquisitions are driven by tax considerations (see also Section 1.8 below).

Debt capacity

By combining two firms, each of which has little or no capacity to carry debt, it is possible to create a firm that may have the capacity to borrow money and create value. Diversification will lead to an increase in debt capacity and an increase in the value of the firm. This has to be weighed against the immediate transfer of wealth that occurs to existing bondholders in both firms from the stockholders. When two firms in different businesses merge, the combined firm will have less variable earnings, and may be able to borrow more (have a higher debt ratio) than the individual firms.

CASE STUDY

Britain's biggest retailer Tesco agreed a surprise 3.7 billion pound ($4.6 billion) takeover of food supplier Booker, increasing its exposure to the fast growing catering sector.

Tesco will gain exposure to the 120,000 independent retailers, 107,000 small businesses and 450,000 caterers Booker serves. Booker clients include chains such as Wagamama, Carluccio's, Byron, as well as celebrity chef Rick Stein.

Booker owns about 200 cash and carry warehouses in the UK and supplies the Budgens, Londis and Family Shopper grocery chains, which are run as franchise operations.

Tesco and Booker said the deal would lead to synergies of at least 200 million pounds within three years, from procurement, distribution and central functions, and would boost earnings per share in the second full year of the deal.

Implementation costs would be about 145 million pounds.

However, analysts said the deal could face close regulatory scrutiny, particularly because of its impact on customers at smaller convenience stores and food industry suppliers.

(Source: Reuters, January 27 2017)

1.8 Factors in a takeover decision

Several factors will need to be considered before deciding to try to take over a target business. These include the following:

Price factors

(a)   What would the **cost** of acquisition be?

(b)   Would the acquisition be **worth** the price?

(c)   Alternatively, factors (a) and (b) above could be expressed in terms of:

What is the **highest price** that it would be worth paying to acquire the business?

The value of a business could be assessed in terms of:

(i)   Its earnings

(ii)   Its assets

(iii)   Its prospects for sales and earnings growth

(iv)   How it would contribute to the strategy of the 'predator' company

The valuation of companies was covered in Chapter 9 of this Study Text.

Other factors

(d)   Would the takeover be regarded as **desirable** by the predator company's shareholders and (in the case of quoted companies) the stock market in general?

(e)   Are the owners of the target company **amenable** to a takeover bid? Or would they be likely to adopt defensive tactics to resist a bid?

(f)   What form would the **purchase consideration take?** An acquisition is accomplished by buying the shares of a target company. The purchase consideration might be cash, but the purchasing company might issue new shares (or loan stock) and exchange them for shares in the company taken over. If purchase is by means of a share exchange, the former shareholders in the company taken over will acquire an interest in the new, enlarged company.

(g)   How would the takeover be **reflected in the published accounts** of the predator company?

(h)   Would there be any **other potential problems** arising from the proposed takeover, such as future dividend policy and service contracts for key personnel?

1.9 Taxation issues

As we have seen in Chapter 2, taxation issues play an important role in the strategy of a company. Acquisitions can often be motivated by tax reasons, especially in cases where the target company is based in a lower tax regime.

1.9.1 Tax losses

In some countries, it is possible for an acquiring company to offset past losses of an acquired subsidiary against the present profits of the parent company. However, in certain countries (eg the UK), there are stricter tax rules that prevent this.

1.9.2 Cross-border tax benefits

In Chapters 2 and 6, we saw how multinationals can reduce their tax bill by exploiting differences in taxation rates between group companies (eg through the use of **transfer pricing** and **thin capitalisation**).

Therefore, low tax rates can be a key reason for acquiring an overseas company. For example, a company could merge with an overseas company and re-incorporate in a low tax regime, such as Ireland. This is known as **tax inversion.** However some countries, such as the US, have introduced rules to prevent companies exploiting this (see Case Study below).

KEY TERMS

TAX INVERSION: A transaction used by a company whereby it becomes a subsidiary of a new parent company in another country for the purpose of falling under beneficial tax laws. Typically they are used by US companies to move to lower tax domiciles, in Europe in particular.

CASE STUDY

Tax inversion

In 2014, US pharmaceutical firm Pfizer made a hostile takeover bid for UK pharmaceutical firm AstraZeneca. If the bid had been successful, Pfizer planned to shift its tax domicile to the UK, which had a lower tax rate than the US and would therefore reduce its overall tax bill. The bid was rejected by AstraZeneca shareholders.

Following a spate of similar tax inversion-driven mergers by US firms, the US government introduced rules to clamp down on such mergers in Autumn 2014. The new rules make it more difficult for US companies to meet the criteria for a tax inversion merger, and also make it harder for companies who have inverted their tax domicile to move cash between countries without paying US taxes.

1.9.3 Withholding tax

The impact of withholding tax on certain types of income from an overseas branch will have to be carefully assessed, although the impact of this is reduced if a double taxation agreement between the two countries is in place.

1.10 Acquisition by venture capital or private equity

Acquisitions are often made or supported by private equity (PE) or venture capital (VC) investors. These sources of finance were discussed in Chapter 8.

The main differences between these types of investor are as follows:

	Venture capital	Private equity
Nature of investment	VC investors tend to invest in many companies, expecting some to fail, but a small number to make huge returns to compensate for the companies that fail	PE investors tend to invest large amounts in a small number of companies.
Type of target companies	VCs tend to invest in young companies especially start-ups	PEs tend to invest in mature, established companies.
Typical shareholding	Less than 50%	100%

Question 10.1   Reasons for mergers and takeovers

Learning outcome: B(1)(b)

Gasco, a public limited company with a market value of around £7 billion, is a major supplier of gas to both business and domestic customers. The company also provides maintenance contracts for gas and central heating customers using the well-known brand name Gas For All. Customers can call emergency lines for assistance for any gas-related incident, such as a suspected leak. Gasco employs its own highly trained workforce to deal with all such situations quickly and effectively. The company also operates a major new credit card, which has been extensively marketed and which gives users concessions, such as reductions in their gas bills.

Gasco has recently bid £1.1bn for CarCare, a long established mutual organisation (ie it is owned by its members) that is the country's leading motoring organisation. CarCare is financed primarily by an annual subscription from its 4.4 million members. In addition the organisation obtains income from a range of other activities such as a high profile car insurance brokerage, a travel agency and assistance with all types of travel arrangements. Its main service to members is the provision of a roadside breakdown service, which is now an extremely competitive market with many other companies involved. Although many of its competitors use local garages to deal with breakdowns, CarCare uses its own road patrols.

CarCare members have to approve the takeover, which once completed provided them each with a windfall of around £300 each.

Gasco intend to preserve the CarCare name which is extremely well known by consumers.

Required

Discuss the possible reasons why GasCo is seeking to buy CarCare.

Section summary

- **Takeovers** often target companies that are good **strategic fits** with the acquiring companies, often to acquire a new product range or to develop a presence in a new market.

- **Mergers** have been more common in industries with low growth and returns.

2 The conduct of a takeover

Introduction

In this section we look at what can happen when a takeover is announced. The target company may resist the takeover and we discuss possible defensive tactics.

2.1 Will the bidding company's shareholders approve of a takeover?

When a company is planning a takeover bid for another company, its board of directors should give some thought to **how its own shareholders might react** to the bid. A company does not have to ask its shareholders for their approval of every takeover.

(a) When a large takeover is planned by a listed company involving **the issue of a substantial number of new shares by the predator company** (to pay for the takeover), Stock Exchange rules may require the company to obtain the formal approval of its shareholders to the takeover bid at a general meeting (probably an extraordinary general meeting, called specifically to approve the takeover bid).

(b) If shareholders, and the stock market in general, think the takeover is not a good one the **market value of the company's shares is likely to fall**. The company's directors have a responsibility to protect their shareholders' interests, and are accountable to them at the annual general meeting of the company.

A takeover bid might seem **unattractive** to shareholders of the bidding company because:

(a) It might **reduce the EPS** of their company.

(b) The **target company** is in a risky industry, or is in danger of going into liquidation.

(c) It might **reduce the net asset backing** per share of the company, because the target company will probably be bought at a price which is well in excess of its net asset value.

2.2 Will a takeover bid be resisted by the target company?

Quite often, a takeover bid will be resisted. Resistance comes from the target company's board of directors, who adopt defensive tactics, and ultimately the target company's shareholders, who can refuse to sell their shares to the bidding company.

Resistance can be overcome by offering a higher price.

(a) In cases where an **unquoted** company is the target company, if resistance to a takeover cannot be overcome, the takeover will not take place, and negotiations would simply break down.

(b)   Where the target company is a **quoted company**, the situation is different. The target company will have many shareholders, some of whom will want to accept the offer for their shares, and some of whom will not. In addition, the target company's board of directors might resist a takeover even though their shareholders might want to accept the offer.

Because there are likely to be major **differences of opinion** about whether to accept a takeover bid or not, companies in most jurisdictions are subject to formal rules for the conduct of takeover bids. These and other regulatory issues are covered later in the chapter.

2.3 Contesting an offer

The directors of a target company must **act in the interests of their shareholders, employees and creditors**. They may decide to contest an offer on several grounds.

(a)   The offer may be **unacceptable** because the **terms are poor**. Rejection of the offer may lead to an improved bid.

(b)   The merger or takeover may have **no obvious advantage**.

(c)   **Employees** may be **strongly opposed** to the bid.

(d)   The **founder members of the business** may oppose the bid, and appeal to the loyalty of other shareholders.

When a company receives a takeover bid which the board of directors considers unwelcome, the directors must act quickly to fight off the bid.

2.4 Defensive tactics

The steps that might be taken to **thwart a bid** or **make it seem less attractive** include:

(a)   **Revaluing assets** or **issuing a forecast of attractive future profits and dividends** to persuade shareholders that to sell their shares would be unwise, that the offer price is too low, and that it would be better for them to retain their shares.

(b)   **Lobbying** to have the offer referred to the competition authorities.

(c)   Launching an **advertising campaign** against the takeover bid (one technique is to attack the accounts of the predator company).

(d)   Finding a '**white knight**', a company which will make a welcome takeover bid.

(e)   Making a **counter bid** for the predator company (this can only be done if the companies are of reasonably similar size).

(f)   Arranging a **management buyout.**

(g)   Introducing a '**shark repellent**', which is a tactic designed to repel a hostile takeover, eg changing the company's constitution to require a large majority to approve the takeover.

(h)   Introducing a '**poison pill**', which is a form of shark repellent designed to make a company's shares less attractive to the acquirer (see below).

CASE STUDY

Swiss pharmaceutical company Roche launched a hostile takeover bid for US diagnostics company Illumina in early 2012. Illumina adopted defensive tactics and announced that it would adopt a 'poison pill' to protect its shareholders. This meant that Illumina shareholders can buy new shares if any bidder acquires 15 per cent of the company's shares. This move protects the company by making Illumina more expensive to acquire. As a result of defensive tactics Roche let its offer expire in April 2012.

2.5 Costs of contested takeover bids

Takeover bids, when contested, can be very expensive, involving:

- Costs of professional services, eg merchant bank and public relations agency
- Advertising costs
- Underwriting costs
- Interest costs
- Possible capital loss on buying and selling the target company's shares

2.6 Gaining the consent of the target company shareholders

A takeover bid will only succeed if the predator company can persuade enough shareholders in the target company to sell their shares. Shareholders will only do this if they **are dissatisfied with the performance** of their company and its shares, or they are **attracted by a high offer** and the chance to make a good capital gain.

Section summary

A takeover may be **resisted** by the target company, if its directors believe that the terms are poor or there are no obvious advantages. Possible **defensive tactics** include issuing a forecast of attractive future profits, lobbying or finding a white knight (a company that would make a welcome takeover bid).

3 Regulation of takeovers

Introduction

During an acquisition a company must be careful to comply with regulations and legislation. This section looks at the types of regulation to be aware of.

3.1 Takeover regulation

The UK Panel on Takeovers and Mergers (**Takeover panel**) was formed in 1968 to regulate the conduct of parties in a takeover situation. It issued and administers the **City Code** which provides a framework for the conduct of takeovers and is designed to ensure that shareholders are treated fairly during the bid process.

As a result of the **EU Takeover Directive (2004)**, the Code has a statutory basis and any listed company that does not comply may have its membership of the London Stock Exchange suspended.

3.1.1 The City Code: general principles

The City Code is divided into six general principles and detailed rules which must be observed by persons involved in a merger or takeover transaction. The general principles include the following.

(1)   'All holders of the securities of an offeree company of the same class must be afforded equivalent treatment.' In other words, a company making a takeover bid cannot offer one set of purchase terms to some shareholders in the target company, and a different set of terms to other shareholders holding shares of the same class in that company.

(2)   'The holders of the securities of an offeree company must have sufficient time and information to enable them to reach a properly informed decision on the bid.'

(3)   'The board of an offeree company must act in the interests of the company as a whole and must not deny the holders of securities the opportunity to decide on the merits of the bid.'

(4)   'False markets must not be created in the securities of the offeree company, of the offeror company, or of any other company concerned by the bid.' This is to avoid artificial price movement and to ensure the market is not distorted.

(5)   'An offeror must only announce a bid after ensuring that he/she can fulfil in full any cash consideration and after taking reasonable measures to secure the implementation of any other type of consideration.'

(6)   'An offeree company must not be hindered in the conduct of its affairs for longer than is reasonable by a bid for its securities.'

3.1.2 The City Code: rules

In addition to its general principles, the City Code also contains a number of detailed rules, which are intended to govern the conduct of the parties in a takeover bid. These rules relate to matters such as:

(a)   How the approach to the target company should be made by the predator company
(b)   The announcement of a takeover bid
(c)   The obligation of the target company board to seek independent advice (eg from a merchant bank)
(d)   Conduct during the offer
(e)   A time barrier to rebidding if an offer fails

Exam skills

The details of this code do not need to be memorised but you do need to be aware of its existence and purpose.

3.2 Competition legislation

Takeovers and mergers may be investigated by **competition authorities** to ensure that one company cannot **dominate** a market.

In the UK this is the responsibility of the Competition and Markets Authority (CMA) (formerly the OFT/ Competition Commission). Within the EU, the European Commission can review mergers that create turnover concentrations with a 'Community dimension'.

CASE STUDY

In March 2012, an acquisition of BMI (a loss-making subsidiary of German airline Lufthansa) by IAG (owner of British Airways and Iberia) was given the go-ahead by the EU Competition Commission despite the dominant position that this would give IAG in the airline industry, particularly out of London Heathrow airport.

The decision was approved because IAG agreed to relinquish up to 14 take-off and landing slots that BMI held.

In contrast, in March 2009 the UK's Competition Commission reported on the dominant position of BAA (now known as Heathrow Airport Holdings) and ownership of airports in the UK.

The Commission observed that BAA had dominance of the market in the south-east of England and in the Scottish lowlands.

BAA was ordered to sell Gatwick, Stansted and Edinburgh or Glasgow airports by the Commission.

BAA sold Gatwick to a private equity firm for £1.5 billion in 2009 before the Commission issued its ruling and in late 2011 decided to sell Edinburgh rather than Glasgow. Edinburgh airport was sold, to the same private equity firm as Gatwick, in 2012 for £807 million.

The sale of Stansted (to Manchester Airports Group) for £1.5 billion was completed in February 2013.

Section summary

Directors of companies of any size must treat all shareholders **fairly** and give them **sufficient information** about the takeover. Larger mergers will be of interest to the **competition authorities**.

4 Impact of mergers and takeovers on stakeholders

Introduction

We need to consider the effect of mergers and takeovers on stakeholders other than shareholders.

4.1 To what extent do the stakeholders in a merger or takeover benefit from it?

The following comments are based upon extensive empirical research.

(a) **Acquiring company shareholders**

At least half of mergers studied have shown a decline in profitability compared with industry averages. Returns to equity can often be poor relative to the market in the early years, particularly for equity-financed bids and first- time players. Costs of mergers frequently outweigh the gains.

(b) **Target company shareholders**

In the majority of cases, it is the target shareholders who benefit most from a takeover. Bidding companies invariable have to offer a significant premium over the market price prevailing prior to the bid in order to achieve the purchase.

(c) **Acquiring company management**

The management of the newly enlarged organisation will often enjoy increased status and influence, as well as increased salary and benefits.

(d) **Target company management**

While some key personnel may be kept on for some time after the takeover, a significant number of managers will find themselves out of a job. However, a 'golden handshake' and the prospect of equally remunerative employment elsewhere may lessen the blow of this somewhat.

(e) **Other employees**

Commonly the economy of scale cost savings anticipated in a merger will be largely achieved by the loss of jobs, as duplicated service operations are eliminated and loss-making divisions closed down. However, in some instances, the increased competitive strength of the newly enlarged enterprise can lead to expansion of operations and the need for an increased workforce.

(f) **Financial institutions**

These are perhaps the outright winners. The more complex the deal, the longer the battle, and the more legal and financial problems encountered, the greater their fee income, regardless of the end result.

Question 10.2

Learning outcome: B(1)(b)

Required

Using the information provided in Question 10.1 above, discuss how the various stakeholders of CarCare might react to the takeover.

Section summary

Don't forget that **managers**, **employees** and **financial institutions** are key stakeholders in mergers as well as shareholders.

Chapter Summary

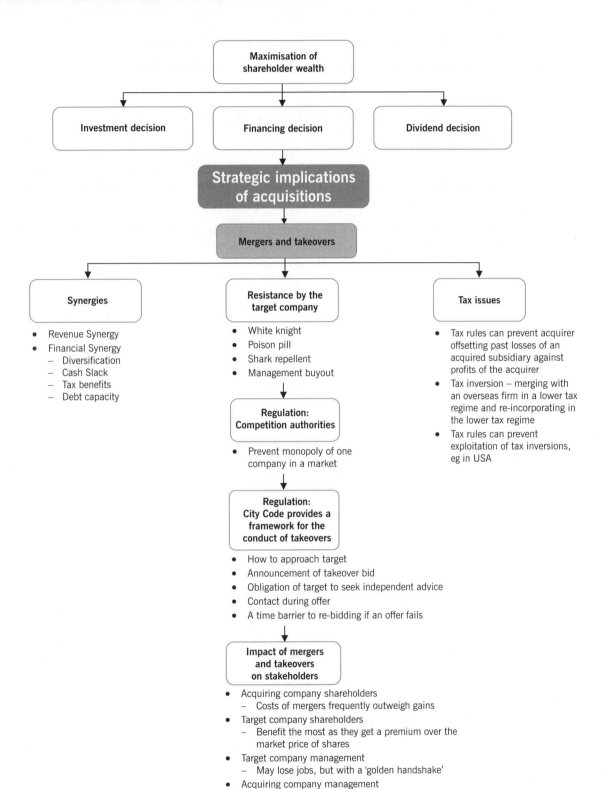

Quick Quiz

1   What are the sources of financial synergy?

2   What are the main advantages of mergers as an expansion strategy?

3   What are the main disadvantages of mergers as an expansion strategy?

4   What is meant by a 'white knight'?

5   What is a 'poison pill' in the context of takeovers and mergers?

6   **Fill in the blank:**

.... is 'the acquisition by a company of a controlling interest in the voting share capital of another company, usually achieved by the purchase of a majority of the voting shares.' (CIMA Official Terminology)

7   A smaller company takes over a larger one, so that the smaller company must increase its voting equity by over 100% to complete the takeover. What is this process called?

Answers to Quick Quiz

1   Diversification and reduction in volatility

    Cash slack

    Tax benefits

    Debt capacity

2   Speed of growth

    Lower cost

    Acquisition of intangible assets

    Access to overseas markets

3   Exposure to business risk

    Exposure to financial risk

    Acquisition premium

    Managerial incompetence

4   A company which will make a welcome takeover bid

5   An anti-takeover device

6   A takeover

7   A reverse takeover

Answers to Questions

10.1 Reasons for mergers and takeovers

There is frequently a mix of good and bad reasons behind a takeover bid. Among the good reasons, the most significant is the possibility of creating **synergy,** which means that the value of cash flows from the combined business is higher than the value of cash flows from the two individual businesses. Although CarCare and Gasco are in different market sectors, there are a number of areas which may generate synergy.

(i)   **Elimination of duplicated resources**. The most obvious areas are the marketing systems, the call centre systems and local offices and training facilities for mobile repair and emergency staff. Head office overheads may also be reduced.

(ii)   **Cross-selling**. Opportunities exist to cross-sell products to customers on the other company's database.

(iii)   **Building a critical mass** for non-core business. This might apply to the financial services areas of both businesses. The credit card and insurance businesses may gain from a combined brand name.

(iv)   **Reduction in the risk of the company's cash flow profile**. CarCare receives membership subscriptions in advance, whereas Gasco's customers will pay mainly in arrears. The combined cash flows will be perceived as less risky by shareholders and lenders.

(v)   The takeover of CarCare will **abolish its mutual status** and will allow equity funds for expansion to be raised more easily, by share issues made by the parent company, reducing the cost of capital.

Among the many possible bad reasons for takeover are:

(i)   The directors of Gasco **seeking the prestige** of a larger company
(ii)   Diversification with no real strategic objective
(iii) Gasco using up surplus cash, again with no strategic objective

10.2 Stakeholder impact of takeovers

Stakeholders

The major stakeholders of CarCare are its members, who are both owners and customers, its directors and employees, and its creditors. Competitors will also be highly interested in the takeover.

Members

The members will have **mixed reactions.** The replacement of mutual status with marketable equity shares or cash will give them an immediate '**windfall**' **gain,** which many will welcome. However, the cost of this is **lost influence** on the future direction of CarCare. As customers, many may fear a reduction in the quality of service, particularly in the light of increased competition in the market and the fact that Gasco has to demonstrate that it is making a **return on its investment**. Others may disagree, on the basis that Gasco will be able to raise money for expansion, modernisation and improvements more easily than CarCare could as a mutual organisation.

CarCare's directors have a duty to ensure that they act in the **best interest** of **members.** However they will also be concerned about their own positions after the takeover and will wish to seek suitable positions in the new company's management structure. Some may fear loss of their jobs.

Employees

Employees will have **mixed reactions** depending on whether they are likely to be presented with additional opportunities or loss of status or redundancy. There is likely to be some **rationalisation** of the workforce except for those with highly specific skills, and for those who remain there may also be the threat of relocation. Employees will be seeking answers to these questions before the takeover happens, but are unlikely to receive comprehensive answers.

Creditors

Creditors, including bankers, will probably be **happy** with the **merger** provided that Gasco has no financial problems.

Competitors

Some competitors will fear that they will **lose market share** if the takeover enables new finance for expansion, improvement and marketing of CarCare. Others will be more optimistic, believing that CarCare will become less sensitive to the needs of customers.

Now try the questions from the Practice Question Bank	**Question** Section A: 10.1 – 10.3	**Level** Practice

INTRODUCTION TO VALUATION TECHNIQUES

In the next two chapters of the Study Text we shall be concentrating on **methods of calculating the valuations** of organisations of different types. We shall cover the **main methods of valuation** in this chapter, and demonstrate how **market efficiency** and **changing capital structure** affect valuation. The most important use of valuation techniques is in a merger or acquisition situation; this is covered in Chapter 13.

Since valuation is examined frequently, the next two chapters are two of the most important in this Text. You need to be able to use a range of measures to calculate the value of a whole entity, and also to discuss why they show different values and which measure is the most useful.

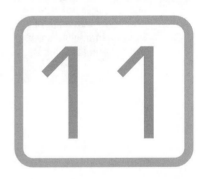

Topic list	learning outcomes	syllabus references	ability required
1 Reasons for valuations	C(2)(b)	C(2)(b)(i)(ii)	evaluation
2 Asset valuation bases	C(2)(a),(b)	C(2)(a)(i), C(2)(b)(i),(ii)	evaluation
3 Earnings valuation bases	C(2)(a),(b)	C(2)(a)(iv) C(2)(b)(i),(ii)	evaluation
4 Dividend valuation bases	C(2)(a),(b)	C(2)(a)(v) C(2)(b)(i),(ii)	evaluation
5 Cash flow valuation methods	C(2)(a)	C(2)(a)(vi),(ix) C(2)(b)(i),(ii)	evaluation
6 The efficient market hypothesis	C(2)(a)	C(2)(a)(x)	evaluation
7 Intangible assets and intellectual capital	C(2)(a)	C(2)(a)(ii)	evaluation

Chapter Overview

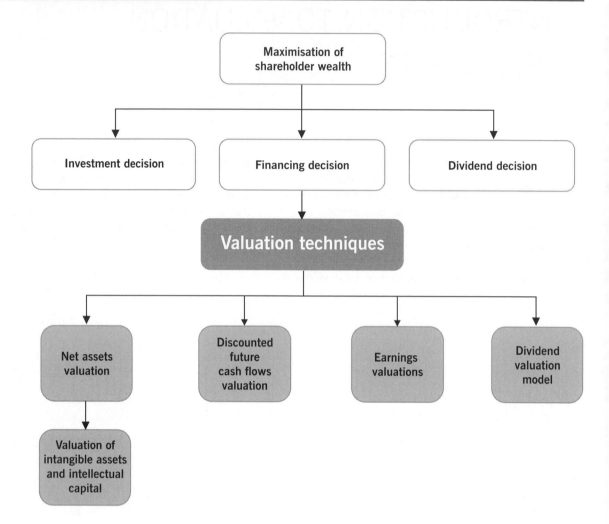

1 Reasons for valuations

Introduction

There are a number of different ways of putting a value on an entity. Valuation is a key part of the investment decision as it is very important not to pay too much for an acquisition.

1.1 When valuations are required

Given quoted share prices on the Stock Exchange, why devise techniques for estimating the value of a share? A share valuation will be necessary:

(a) For **quoted companies**, when there is a takeover bid and the offer price is an estimated 'fair value' in excess of the current market price of the shares.

(b) For **unquoted** companies, when:

    (i) The company wishes to 'go public' and must fix an issue price for its shares

    (ii) There is a scheme of merger

    (iii) Shares are sold

    (iv) Shares need to be valued for the purposes of taxation

    (v) Shares are pledged as collateral for a loan

(c) For **subsidiary companies**, when the group's holding company is negotiating the sale of the subsidiary to a management buyout team or to an external buyer

(d) For **any company**, where a shareholder wishes to dispose of their holding; some of the valuation methods we describe will be most appropriate if a large or controlling interest is being sold, however even a small shareholding may be a significant disposal if the purchasers can increase their holding to a controlling interest as a result of the acquisition

(e) For **any company**, when the company is being broken up in a liquidation situation or the company needs to obtain additional finance, or refinance current debt

1.2 Stakeholder concerns

Exam skills

Remember that valuation should never be a purely mechanical exercise. When evaluating how realistic your valuation methods are, you should bear in mind the impact of stakeholders on the valuation process.

1.2.1 Legal issues

In a number of situations, stakeholders will be given important **legal rights.** As we saw in Chapter 10, in **merger and acquisition situations** shareholders have rights to be treated fairly by the directors of the companies that are joining together. Governments may also be interested if the merger leads to an organisation that is considered to be too large or dominant in its markets.

Insolvency legislation will give creditor stakeholders prior rights to receive the proceeds of dissolution, and may give them rights to object to arrangements designed to avoid insolvency.

1.2.2 Other situations

In certain circumstances the **attitude of stakeholders** other than shareholders will significantly influence valuation. A good example is a **takeover situation** where the acquiring company is paying for the skills and expertise of its target's employees. If **key employees** are unhappy with the takeover, and decide to leave, then the valuation of the target will be impaired.

1.3 General factors affecting valuation

As well as the calculations, buyers and sellers will also take into account the **industry situation**, the **fixed and human assets** of the company, and a number of factors relating to **shareholdings**:

- The **size** of shareholding to be acquired
- The **distribution** of other shareholdings
- The **rights** related to the shares
- Any **restrictions** on transfers

Exam skills

In an exam situation as well as in practice, it is unlikely that one method would be used in isolation. Several valuations might be made, each using a different technique or different assumptions. The valuations could then be compared, and a final price reached as a compromise between the different values. Remember that some methods may be more appropriate for valuing a small parcel of shares, others for valuing a whole company.

1.4 Valuation of quoted or unquoted company?

1.4.1 Quoted companies

A **quoted (listed) company** will have a **current stock market value** also known as its market capitalisation. Where small holdings of shares are being traded, this is the relevant price for the transaction.

However, if one company is looking to purchase another by buying shares, this value will **not give a suitable price** because the current shareholders will not have any extra incentive to sell their holdings at the current market price.

As a result a premium to the existing market price is normally offered. Therefore, in an exam question the current stock market price should be used as a **base figure** for calculations to give a suitable price.

1.4.2 Unquoted companies

Since an unquoted company has no stock market price, determining a valuation may be more difficult. There is likely to be **less available information** to help a potential purchaser assess the value of the company. Typically this process will involve using a similar quoted company (proxy company).

The techniques we are now going to cover produce a **range of values** which can be summarised as follows:

Maximum value ↑ Value the cash flows or earnings under new ownership

Value the dividends under the existing management

Minimum value ↓ Value the assets

Section summary

There is no one correct business valuation. It makes sense to use several methods of valuation, and to compare the values they produce.

2 Asset valuation bases

Introduction

We start by looking at the lowest valuation of a business. The asset basis can be used to provide a minimum value which can be useful if a business is difficult to sell.

2.1 The net assets method of share valuation

Using this method of valuation, the value of a share in a particular class is equal to the **net tangible assets,** divided by the **number of shares. Intangible assets** (including goodwill) should be **excluded,** unless they have a market value (for example patents and copyrights, which could be sold). The valuation of intangible assets in general, and intellectual capital in particular, is discussed at the end of this chapter.

Example: Net assets method of share valuation

The summary statement of financial position of Cactus is as follows.

	$	$	$
Non-current assets			
Land and buildings		160,000	
Plant and machinery		100,000	
Motor vehicles		20,000	
			280,000
Current assets			
Inventory		80,000	
Receivables		60,000	
Short-term investments		15,000	
Cash		5,000	
			160,000
Total assets			**440,000**
Equity			
Ordinary shares of $1		80,000	
Reserves		140,000	
			220,000
4.9% preference shares of $1			50,000
Total equity			270,000
Current liabilities			
Payables		60,000	
Taxation		20,000	
Proposed ordinary dividend		20,000	
			100,000
12% bonds			70,000
Total liabilities			170,000
Total equity and liabilities			**440,000**

What is the value of an ordinary share using the net assets basis of valuation?

Solution

If the figures given for asset values are not questioned, the valuation would be as follows:

	$	$
Total value of assets	440,000	
Less liabilities	(170,000)	
Total value of assets less liabilities		270,000
Less: preference shares		(50,000)
Net asset value of equity		220,000
Number of ordinary shares		80,000
Value per share		$2.75

2.2 Choice of valuation bases

The difficulty in an asset valuation method is establishing the **asset values** to use. Values ought to be realistic. The figure attached to an individual asset may vary considerably depending on whether it is valued on a **going concern** or a **break-up** basis.

Possibilities include:

- **Historical basis** – unlikely to give a realistic value as it is dependent upon the business's depreciation and amortisation policy

- **Replacement basis** – if the assets are to be used on an ongoing basis

- **Realisable basis** – if the assets are to be sold, or the business as a whole broken up. This won't be relevant if a minority shareholder is selling his stake, as the assets will continue in the business's use.

The following list should give you some idea of the factors that must be considered.

(a)   Do the assets need **professional valuation?** If so, how much will this cost?

(b)   Have the **liabilities** been accurately quantified, for example deferred taxation? Are there any contingent liabilities? Will any balancing tax charges arise on disposal?

(c)   How have the **current assets** been valued? Are all receivables collectable? Is all inventory realisable? Can all the assets be physically located and brought into a saleable condition? This may be difficult in certain circumstances where the assets are situated abroad.

(d)   Can any **hidden liabilities** be accurately assessed? Would there be redundancy payments and closure costs?

(e)   Is there an **available market** in which the assets can be realised (on a break-up basis)? If so, do the balance sheet values truly reflect these break-up values?

(f)   Are there any **prior charges** on the assets?

(g)   Does the business have a regular **revaluation and replacement** policy? What are the bases of the valuation? As a broad rule, valuations will be more useful the better they estimate the **future cash flows** that are derived from the asset.

(h)   Are there factors that might indicate that the **going concern valuation** of the business **as a whole** is **significantly higher** than the valuation of the individual assets?

(i)   What shareholdings are being sold? If a minority interest is being disposed of, realisable value is of limited relevance as the assets will not be sold.

2.3 Use of net asset basis

The net assets basis of valuation might be used in the following circumstances.

(a) As a **'floor value'** for a business that is up for sale – shareholders will be reluctant to sell for less than the NAV. However, if the sale is essential for cash flow purposes or to realign with corporate strategy, even the asset value may not be realised.

(b) **As a measure of the 'security' in a share value**. The **asset backing** for shares provides a measure of the **possible loss** if the company fails to make the expected earnings or dividend payments. Valuable tangible assets may be a good reason for acquiring a company, especially freehold property which might be expected to increase in value over time.

(c) **As a measure of comparison in a scheme of merger**

A **merger** is essentially a business combination of two or more companies, of which none obtains control over any other.

For example, if company A, which has a low asset backing, is planning a merger with company B, which has a high asset backing, the shareholders of B might consider that their shares' value ought to reflect this. It might therefore be agreed that a something should be added to the value of the company B shares to allow for this difference in asset backing.

For these reasons, it is always advisable to calculate the **net assets per share**.

Section summary

The **net assets valuation** method can be used as one of many valuation methods, or to provide a lower limit for the value of a company. By itself it is unlikely to produce the most realistic value.

3 Earnings valuation bases

Introduction

The highest business valuation is usually calculated by valuing the earnings under new ownership. This method uses the P/E ratio which shows the stock market's view of the growth prospects of a company.

3.1 The P/E ratio (earnings) method of valuation

This is a common method of valuing a **controlling interest** in a company, where the owner can decide on **dividend** and **retentions policy**. The P/E ratio relates earnings per share to a share's value.

Since P/E ratio $= \dfrac{\text{Market value}}{\text{EPS}}$, then market value per share = EPS × P/E ratio.

Remember that earnings per share (EPS) $= \dfrac{\text{Profit / loss attributable to ordinary shareholders}}{\text{Weighted average number of ordinary shares}}$

The P/E ratio produces an **earnings-based** valuation of shares by deciding a suitable P/E ratio and multiplying this by the EPS for the shares which are being valued.

Market valuation or capitalisation = P/E ratio × Earnings per share

The EPS could be a historical EPS or a prospective future EPS. For a given EPS figure, a higher P/E ratio will result in a higher price.

3.2 Significance of high P/E ratio

A high P/E ratio may indicate:

(a) **Expectations that the EPS will grow rapidly**

A **high price is being paid for future profit prospects**. Many small but successful and fast-growing companies are valued on the stock market on a high P/E ratio. Some stocks (for example those of some internet companies in the late 1990s) have reached high valuations before making any profits at all, on the strength of expected future earnings.

(b) **Security of earnings**

A well-established, low-risk company would be valued on a higher P/E ratio than a similar company whose earnings are subject to greater uncertainty.

(c) **Status**

If a quoted company (the predator) made a share-for-share takeover bid for an unquoted company (the target), it would normally expect its own shares to be valued on a **higher P/E ratio** than the target company's shares. This is because a quoted company ought to be a **lower-risk** company; but in addition, there is an advantage in having shares which are quoted on a stock market: the shares can be **readily sold**. The P/E ratio of an unquoted company's shares might be around 50% to 60% of the P/E ratio of a similar public company with a full Stock Exchange listing.

3.2.1 Problems with using P/E ratios

However using the price-earnings ratios of quoted companies to value unquoted companies may be problematic.

(a) Finding a quoted company with a **similar range of activities** may be difficult. Quoted companies are often **diversified**.

(b) A **single year's P/E ratio** may not be a good basis, if earnings are volatile, or the quoted company's share price is at an abnormal level, due for example to the expectation of a takeover bid.

(c) If a P/E ratio trend is used, then **historical data** will be being used to value how the unquoted company will do in the future.

(d) The quoted company may have a **different capital structure** to the unquoted company.

CASE STUDY

Some sample P/E ratios taken from the Financial Times on 20 June 2014:

Market indices

FTSE 100	14.14
FTSE all-share	14.87

Industry sector averages (main market)

Chemicals	18.46
Food producers	12.65
General retailers	17.09
Health care equipment and services	28.43
Mobile telecommunications	3.01
Software and computer services	25.33

Example: Earnings method of valuation

Spider is considering the takeover of an unquoted company, Fly. Spider's shares are quoted on the Stock Exchange at a price of £3.20 and since the most recent published EPS of the company is 20p, the company's P/E ratio is 16. Fly is a company with 100,000 shares and current earnings of £50,000, 50p per share. How might Spider decide on an offer price?

Solution

The decision about the offer price is likely to be preceded by the estimation of a 'reasonable' P/E ratio in the light of the particular circumstances.

(a)   If Fly is in the **same industry** as Spider, its P/E ratio ought to be lower, because of its lower status as an unquoted company.

(b)   If Fly is in a **different industry**, a suitable P/E ratio might be based on the P/E ratio that is typical for quoted companies in that industry.

(c)   If Fly is thought to be **growing fast**, so that its EPS will rise rapidly in the years to come, the P/E ratio that should be used for the share valuation will be higher than if only small EPS growth is expected.

(d)   If the acquisition of Fly would **contribute substantially to Spider's own profitability and growth**, or to any other strategic objective that Spider has, then Spider should be willing to offer a higher P/E ratio valuation, in order to secure acceptance of the offer by Fly's shareholders.

Of course, the P/E ratio on which Spider bases its offer will probably be lower than the P/E ratio that Fly's shareholders think their shares ought to be valued on. Some haggling over the price might be necessary.

Spider might decide that Fly's shares ought to be valued on a P/E ratio of 60% × 16 = 9.6, that is, at 9.6 × 50p = £4.80 each.

Fly's shareholders might reject this offer, and suggest a valuation based on a P/E ratio of, say, 12.5, that is, 12.5 × 50p = £6.25.

Spider's management might then come back with a revised offer, say valuation on a P/E ratio of 10.5, that is, 10.5 × 50p = £5.25.

The haggling will go on until the negotiations either break down or succeed in arriving at an agreed price.

3.3 Guidelines for a P/E ratio-based valuation

When a company is thinking of acquiring an **unquoted** company in a takeover, the final offer price will be agreed by **negotiation**, but a list of some of the factors affecting the valuer's choice of P/E ratio is given below:

(a)   General **economic** and **financial** conditions

(b)   The type of **industry** and the prospects of that industry. Use of current P/E ratios may give an unrealistically low valuation if these ratios are being affected by a lack of confidence throughout the industry.

(c)   The **size** of the undertaking and its **status** within its industry. If an unquoted company's earnings are growing annually and are currently around £300,000 or so, then it could probably get a quote in its own right on the Alternative Investment Market, and a higher P/E ratio should therefore be used when valuing its shares.

(d)   **Marketability**. The market in shares that do not have a Stock Exchange quotation is always a restricted one and a higher yield is therefore required.

(e)   The **diversity** of shareholdings and the **financial status** of any principal shareholders

(f)   The **reliability** of profit estimates and the past profit record. Use of profits and P/E ratios over time may give a more reliable valuation, especially if they are being compared with industry levels over that time.

(g)   **Asset backing** and **liquidity**

(h)   The **nature of the assets**, for example whether some of the non-current assets are of a highly specialised nature, and so have only a small break-up value

(i)   **Gearing**. A relatively high gearing ratio will generally mean greater financial risk for ordinary shareholders and call for a higher rate of return on equity.

(j)   The extent to which the business is dependent on the **technical skills** of one or more individuals

(k)   The predator may need to be particularly careful when valuing an unlisted company of using a P/E ratio of a **'similar' listed company**. The predator should obtain reasonable evidence that the listed company does have the same risk and growth characteristics, and has similar policies on significant areas such as directors' remuneration.

Exam skills

For examination purposes, you should normally **take a figure around one-half to two-thirds** of the industry average when valuing an unquoted company.

3.3.1 Use of predator's P/E ratios

A predator company may sometimes use their higher P/E ratio to value a target company. This use of a higher P/E ratio is known as **bootstrapping.** This assumes that the predator **can improve the target's business**, which may be a dangerous assumption to make. The predator's intentions will also be important; the choice of P/E ratio may depend on whether the predator envisages demerging some of the target's operations, or retaining them all. It may be better to use an adjusted industry P/E ratio, or some other method.

3.3.2 Use of forecast earnings

When one company is thinking about taking over another, it should look at the target company's **forecast earnings**, not just its historical results.

Forecasts of **earnings growth** should only be used if:

(a)   There are good reasons to believe that earnings growth will be achieved

(b)   A reasonable estimate of growth can be made

(c)   Forecasts supplied by the target company's directors are made in good faith and using reasonable assumptions and fair accounting policies

Question 11.1 | Earnings valuation

Learning outcome: C(2)(a)

Flycatcher wishes to make a takeover bid for the shares of an unquoted company, Mayfly. The earnings of Mayfly over the past five years have been as follows.

20X0	$50,000	20X3	$71,000
20X1	$72,000	20X4	$75,000
20X2	$68,000		

The average P/E ratio of quoted companies in the industry in which Mayfly operates is 10. Quoted companies which are similar in many respects to Mayfly are:

(a) Bumblebee, which has a P/E ratio of 15, but is a company with very good growth prospects

(b) Wasp, which has had a poor profit record for several years, and has a P/E ratio of 7

What would be a suitable range of valuations for the shares of Mayfly?

3.4 The earnings yield valuation method

$$\text{Earnings yield (EY)} = \frac{\text{EPS}}{\text{Market price per share}} \times 100\%$$

This method is effectively a variation on the P/E method (the EY being the reciprocal of the P/E ratio), using an appropriate earnings yield effectively as a discount rate to value the earnings:

$$\text{Market value} = \frac{\text{Earnings}}{\text{EY}}$$

Exactly the same guidelines apply to this method as for the P/E method. Note that where **high growth** is envisaged, **the EY will be low,** as current earnings will be low relative to a market price that has built-in future earnings growth. A stable earnings yield may suggest a company with low risk characteristics.

Section summary

- **P/E ratios** are used when a large block of shares, or a whole business, is being valued. This method can be problematic when quoted companies' P/E ratios are used to value unquoted companies.

- Other earnings methods include the **earnings yield** valuation method.

4 Dividend valuation bases

Introduction

We looked at the dividend valuation model to calculate the cost of equity in F2 *Advanced Financial Reporting* and in Chapter 8. The dividend valuation method involves the present value of the future dividends. It will produce a mid-range valuation that is generally more relevant to small shareholdings rather than the whole company.

4.1 Using the dividend valuation model

The dividend valuation model is based on the theory that an equilibrium price for any share (or bond) on a stock market is:

- The **future expected stream of income** from the security
- **Discounted** at a suitable **cost of capital**

Equilibrium market price is thus a **present value** of a **future expected income stream**. The annual income stream for a share is the expected dividend every year in perpetuity.

Using the **dividend growth model** we have:

EXAM

$$P_0 = \frac{d_0(1+g)}{(k_e - g)} \text{ or } P_0 = \frac{d_1}{(k_e - g)}$$

Where
d_0 = Current year's dividend
g = Growth rate in earnings and dividends
k_e = Shareholders' required rate of return
$d_0(1 + g)$ = Expected dividend in one year's time (d_1)
P_0 = Market value excluding any dividend currently payable (ex div)

KEY TERMS

Cum dividend or CUM DIV means the purchaser of shares is entitled to receive the next dividend payment which is due shortly.

Ex dividend or EX DIV means that the purchaser of shares is not entitled to receive the next dividend payment, which is due shortly.

Question 11.2	DVM

Learning outcome: C(2)(a)

Target paid a dividend of $250,000 this year. The current return to shareholders of quoted companies in the same industry as Target is 12%, although it is expected that an additional risk premium of 2% will be applicable to Target, being a smaller and unquoted company. Compute the expected valuation of Target, if:

(a) The current level of dividend is expected to continue into the foreseeable future.
(b) The dividend is expected to grow at a rate of 4% pa into the foreseeable future.
(c) The dividend is expected to grow at a 3% rate for three years and 2% afterwards.

4.2 Assumptions of dividend models

The dividend models are underpinned by a number of assumptions that you should bear in mind.

(a) Investors act **rationally** and **homogenously** and have **perfect information** available. The model fails to take into account the **different expectations** or shareholders, nor how much they are motivated by dividends vs future capital appreciation on their shares.

(b) The d_0 figure used does **not vary significantly** from the **trend or risk of dividends**. If d_0 does appear to be a rogue figure, it may be better to use an adjusted trend figure, calculated on the basis of the past few years' dividends.

(c) The **estimates** of future dividends and prices used, and also the cost of capital are **reasonable**. As with other methods, it may be difficult to make a confident estimate of the cost of capital. Dividend estimates may be made from historical trends that may not be a good guide for a future if for example there is a takeover, or derived from uncertain forecasts about future earnings, which assumes that there are **enough profitable projects** in the future to **maintain dividend levels**.

(d) Investors' attitudes to receiving different cash flows at different times can be modelled using **discounted cash flow arithmetic.**

(e) Directors use dividends to **signal** the strength of the company's position (however companies that pay zero dividends do not have zero share values).

(f) Dividends either show **no growth** or **constant growth**. If the growth rate is calculated using g=bR, then the model assumes that b and R are constant

(g) **Other influences** on share prices are **ignored**.

(h) The company's **earnings** will **increase** sufficiently to maintain dividend growth levels.

(i) The **discount rate** used exceeds the **dividend growth rate**.

(j) **Tax and issue expenses** are ignored.

4.3 Disadvantages of the simple dividend growth model

- It is difficult to estimate future dividend growth
- It is inaccurate to assume that growth will be constant
- It creates zero values for zero dividend companies
- It creates negative values for high growth companies, if $g > K_e$

Section summary

The dividend valuation model is based on the present value of the future dividends being generated by the **existing** management. It is generally more relevant for **small shareholdings**.

5 Cash flow valuation methods

Introduction

The discounted cash flow method calculates the present value of the future cash flows that will be generated by the (new or current) management.

5.1 The discounted future cash flows method of share valuation

This method of share valuation may be appropriate when one company intends to buy the assets of another company and to make further investments in order to **improve cash flows** in the future.

Example: Discounted future cash flows method of share valuation

Diversification wishes to make a bid for Tadpole, an all-equity financed company. Tadpole makes after-tax profits of $40,000 a year. Diversification believes that if further money is spent on additional investments, the after-tax cash flows (ignoring the purchase consideration) could be as follows:

Year	Cash flow (net of tax) $
0	(100,000)
1	(80,000)
2	60,000
3	100,000
4	150,000
5	150,000

The cost of capital of Diversification is 15% and the company expects all its investments to pay back, in discounted terms, within five years. What is the maximum price that the company should be willing to pay for the shares of Tadpole?

Solution

The maximum price is one which would make the return from the total investment exactly 15% over five years, so that the NPV at 15% would be 0.

Year	Cash flows ignoring purchase consideration $	Discount factor (from tables) @ 15%	Present value $
0	(100,000)	1.000	(100,000)
1	(80,000)	0.870	(69,600)
2	60,000	0.756	45,360
3	100,000	0.658	65,800
4	150,000	0.572	85,800
5	150,000	0.497	74,550
Maximum purchase price			101,910

5.2 Calculation of appropriate discount rate

It can be difficult to calculate the cost of capital to use as a discount rate for cash flow valuation. In the above example, Diversification used its own cost of capital to discount the cash flows of Tadpole. There are a number of reasons why this may not be appropriate.

(a) The **business risk** of the new investment may not match that of the investing company. If Tadpole is in a completely different line of business from Diversification, its cash flows are likely to be subject to differing degrees of risk, and this should be taken into account when valuing them.

(b) The **method of finance** of the new investment may not match the current debt/equity mix of the investing company, which may have an effect on the cost of capital to be used.

If you are not given the cost of capital to use in an exam, you will be expected to calculate an appropriate cost of capital. The cost of capital should reflect the risk of the cash flows.

We will look at specific choices of the discount rate in Chapter 12.

5.3 Calculation of free cash flow (FCF)

Free cash flow is the amount of cash that is available for distribution to investors after having covered all of an entity's required investment in working capital and non-current assets required to sustain its operations.

There are many ways to define free cash flow. CIMA F3 questions will use the following terms:

Free cash flow and free cash flow to equity

- These terms both refer to sustainable cash flow attributable to **equity investors**.

Cash flow to equity and cash flow attributable to equity investors

- These terms refer to cash generated by the company after tax, reinvestment needs and debt-related cash flows.

Cash flow to all investors and cash flow attributable to all investors

- These terms refer to cash generated by the company after tax and reinvestment needs but **before** debt-related cash flows.

In the exam you may need calculate these cash flows from profit data, the approach you will need to use is shown in the following table.

Cash flow to all investors	Cash flow to equity
The cash available for payment to investors (shareholders and debt holders)	The cash available for payment to shareholders (also called dividend capacity)
PBIT	PBIT
less	**less**
tax (excluding tax relief on interest)	interest, tax and any debt repayment.
plus	**plus**
depreciation	depreciation, any capital raised from new debt issues.
adjust for	**adjust for**
cash items such as capex/disposal of non-current assets; changes in working capital.	cash items such as capex/disposal of non-current assets; changes in working capital.

5.3.1 Matching cash flows to an appropriate cost of capital

It is important to match the cash flow used in the valuation exercise to **an appropriate cost of capital.**

Cash flows **attributable to equity investors** should be discounted at the **cost of equity.** This will provide a valuation of the equity (the ordinary shares) of the company.

However, cash flows **attributable to all investors** should be discounted at the **weighted average cost of capital.** This will provide a valuation of the entity to its **investors**, in other words the value of the company's equity **plus** the value of the company's debt. If you know a company's entity value, you can obtain the equity value by **deducting** the value of debt.

An exam question may specify which method to use, however you may need to judge which appropriate needs to be employed. For example, if you only have information about cash flows attributable to equity, you should calculate equity value using a **cost of equity**.

These approaches are summarised in the following table.

Cash flow to all investors(FCF)	Cash flow to equity
The cash available for payment to investors (shareholders and debt holders)	The cash available for payment to shareholders
Approach 1	**Approach 2**
(1) Identify the **cash flows to all investors** of the target company **(before interest)**	(1) Identify the **cash flows to equity** of the target company **(after interest)**
(2) Discount at **WACC**	(2) Discount at the cost of equity, **Ke**
(3) NPV of the entity	(3) NPV of the equity
(4) **Subtract the value of debt from Step 3 to obtain the value of the equity**	

5.4 Drawbacks of cash flow methods

Cash flow methods of valuation can be used to place a **maximum value** on an entity and incorporate the **time value of** money.

However, whichever method is used, cash flow methods suffer from the following general drawbacks.

(a)   As we have seen above, selection of an **appropriate cost of capital** may prove difficult.

(b)   **Estimating future cash flows**, particularly of companies that are being acquired, may be **very difficult**.

(c)   Cash flows are most appropriate for valuing **controlling interests**, which might have a significant influence on whether expected cash flows are attained.

5.5 Summary of valuation techniques

MAXIMUM VALUE (under new management)

- NPV

    –   Includes expected synergies
    –   Discount free cash flows at target's WACC

- P/E method

    –   Adjust P/E
    –   P/E × EPS

FAIR VALUE (under existing method)

- Dividend valuation – use target's growth rate, most suitable for valuing a minority holding.

MINIMUM VALUE

- Assets basis – most appropriate for a capital intensive business.

Section summary

Discounted future cash flows valuation may be used to value a company.

Free cash flows are a development of the DCF method.

Question 11.3

Business valuation

Learning outcomes: C(2)(a),(b)

Profed provides a tuition service to professional students. This includes courses of lectures provided on their own premises and provision of study material for home study. Most of the lecturers are qualified professionals with many years' experience in both their profession and tuition. Study materials are written and word processed in-house, but sent out to an external printer.

The business was started fifteen years ago, and now employs around 40 full-time lecturers, 10 authors and 20 support staff. Freelance lecturers and authors are employed from time to time in times of peak demand.

The shareholders of Profed mainly comprise the original founders of the business who would now like to realise their investment. In order to arrive at an estimate of what they believe the business is worth, they have identified a long-established quoted company, City Tutors, who have a similar business, although they also publish texts for external sale to universities, colleges etc.

Summary financial statistics for the two companies for the most recent financial year are as follows:

	Profed	City Tutors
Issued shares (million)	4	10
Net asset values (£m)	7.2	15
Earnings per share (pence)	35	20
Dividend per share (pence)	20	18
Debt to equity ratio	1:7	1:65
Share price (pence)		362
Expected rate of growth in earnings/dividends	9% p.a.	7.5% p.a.

Notes

1   The net assets of Profed are the net book values of tangible non-current assets plus net working capital. However:

  • A recent valuation of the buildings was £1.5 million above book value.

  • Inventory includes past editions of text books which have a realisable value of £100,000 below their cost.

  • Due to a dispute with one of their clients, an additional allowance for bad debts of £750,000 would be prudent.

2   Growth rates should be assumed to be constant per annum; Profed's earnings growth rate estimate was provided by the marketing manager, based on expected growth in sales adjusted by normal profit margins. City Tutors' growth rates were gleaned from press reports.

3   Profed uses a discount rate of 15% to appraise its investments, and has done for many years.

Required

(a)   Compute a range of valuations for the business of Profed, using the information available and stating any assumptions made.

(b)   Comment upon the strengths and weaknesses of the methods you used in (a) and their suitability for valuing Profed.

Exam skills

In a business valuation question, there is no one 'correct' answer. You need to be able to present a well reasoned report that takes into account a number of different viewpoints while making reasonable assumptions

---

As well as assessing valuation issues in the integrated case study, you may also have to consider whether a premium should be paid to secure a particularly desirable acquisition.

6 The efficient market hypothesis

Introduction

Quoted companies are already valued by their share prices on stock markets. In this section we look at the efficient market hypothesis, which proposes that markets are efficient, so a company's share price reflects all current information and is therefore a reliable indication of its true value.

6.1 The definition of efficiency

KEY TERM

EFFICIENT MARKET HYPOTHESIS is the hypothesis that the stock market responds immediately to all available information, with the effect that an individual investor cannot, in the long run, expect to obtain greater than average returns from a diversified portfolio of shares.   *(CIMA Official Terminology)*

Different types of efficiency can be distinguished in the context of the operation of financial markets.

(a)   **Allocative efficiency**

If financial markets allow funds to be directed towards firms which make the most productive use of them, then there is **allocative efficiency** in these markets.

(b)   **Operational efficiency**

Transaction costs are incurred by **participants** in financial markets, for example commissions on share transactions, margins between interest rates for lending and for borrowing, and loan arrangement fees. Financial markets have **operational efficiency** if transaction costs are kept as low as possible. Transaction costs are kept low where there is open competition between brokers and other market participants.

(c)   **Informational processing efficiency**

The **information processing efficiency** of a stock market means the ability of a stock market to price stocks and shares fairly and quickly. An efficient market in this sense is one in which the market prices of all securities reflect all the available information.

6.2 Features of efficient markets

It has been argued that the UK and US stock markets are **efficient** capital markets; that is, markets in which:

(a)   The prices of securities bought and sold **reflect all the relevant information** which is available to the buyers and sellers. In other words, share prices change quickly to reflect all new information about future prospects.

(b)   No **individual dominates** the market.

(c)   **Transaction costs** of buying and selling are not so high as to discourage trading significantly.

(d)   Investors are **rational.**

(e)   There are low, or no, costs of **acquiring information.**

6.3 Impact of efficiency on share prices

If the stock market is efficient, share prices should vary in a **rational** way.

(a)   If a company makes an investment with a **positive net present value**, shareholders will get to know about it and the market price of its shares will rise in anticipation of future dividend increases.

(b)   If a company makes a **bad investment** shareholders will find out and so the **price** of its **shares will fall**.

(c)   If interest rates rise, **shareholders will want a higher return** from their investments, so market prices will fall.

6.4 Varying degrees of efficiency

There are three degrees or 'forms' of **efficiency**: **weak form**, **semi-strong form** and **strong form**.

6.4.1 Weak form efficiency

Under the weak form hypothesis of market efficiency, share prices reflect all available information about **past** changes in the share price.

Since new information arrives unexpectedly, changes in share prices should occur in a **random fashion.** If it is correct, then using technical analysis to study past share price movements will not give anyone an advantage, because the information they use to predict share prices is already reflected in the share price.

6.4.2 Semi-strong form efficiency

If a stock market displays semi-strong efficiency, current share prices reflect:

*   All relevant information about past price movements and their implications
*   All knowledge which is available publicly

This means that individuals cannot 'beat the market' by reading the newspapers or annual reports, since the information contained in these will be reflected in the share price.

Tests to prove semi-strong efficiency have concentrated on the speed and accuracy of stock market response to information and on the ability of the market to **anticipate share price changes** before new information is formally announced. For example, if two companies plan a merger, share prices of the two companies will inevitably change once the merger plans are formally announced. The market would show semi-strong efficiency, however, if it were able to anticipate such an announcement, so that share prices of the companies concerned would change in advance of the merger plans being confirmed.

Research in both the UK and the US has suggested that market prices anticipate mergers several months before they are formally announced, and the conclusion drawn is that the stock markets in these countries **do** exhibit semi-strong efficiency.

6.4.3 Strong form efficiency

If a stock market displays a strong form of efficiency, share prices reflect **all** information whether publicly available or not.

*   From past price changes
*   From public knowledge or anticipation
*   From specialists' or experts' insider knowledge (eg investment managers)

6.5 Implications of efficient market hypothesis for the financial manager

If the markets are quite strongly efficient, the main consequence for financial managers will be that they simply need to **concentrate** on **maximising the net present value** of the **company's investments** in order to maximise the wealth of shareholders. Managers need not worry, for example, about the effect on share prices of financial results in the published accounts because investors will make **allowances** for **low profits** or **dividends** in the current year if higher profits or dividends are expected in the future.

If the market is strongly efficient, there is little point in financial managers attempting strategies that will attempt to mislead the markets.

(a)   There is no point for example in trying to identify a correct date when **shares** should be **issued**, since share prices will always reflect the true worth of the company.

(b)   The market will identify any attempts to **window dress the accounts** and put an optimistic spin on the figures.

(c)   The market will decide what **level of return** it requires for the risk involved in making an investment in the company. It is pointless for the company to try to change the market's view by issuing different types of capital instruments.

Similarly if the company is looking to expand, the directors will be wasting their time if they seek as **takeover targets** companies whose shares are undervalued, since the market will fairly value all companies' shares.

Only if the market is semi-strongly efficient, and the financial managers possess **inside information** that would significantly alter the price of the company's shares if released to the market, could they perhaps gain an advantage. However attempts to take account of this inside information may breach insider dealing laws.

The different characteristics of a semi-strong form and a strong form efficient market thus affect the **timing** of share price movements, in cases where the relevant information becomes available to the market eventually. The difference between the two forms of market efficiency concerns **when** the share prices change, not by how much prices eventually change.

6.6 Impact of market efficiency

6.6.1 Availability of information

The different methods we have discussed above are built upon different levels of efficiency. Broadly speaking, methods based on **historical or current position** require the market to have a **lower** degree of efficiency than methods that are based on **future cash flows** or **dividend flows**.

As most studies suggest that stock markets are **semi-strong efficient**, share prices are based on analysis of all **known information**. Directors therefore need to take the correct investment, financing and risk management decisions and make this information public.

6.6.2 Mergers and takeovers

Market efficiency is particularly important when companies are considering making an offer for another company. If the market is semi-strong efficient, the target's shares will be valued at a **fair price**; hence any premium offered on those shares has to be justified in terms of post-acquisition gains or savings.

However if the market is **very efficient**, arguably it will anticipate that a merger will take place and these gains will be realised. There is some evidence from the major stock exchanges that mergers are anticipated some months in advance. The more this happens, and the more likely benefits from anticipated mergers are factored into the share price, the less a premium is likely to be value for money for an acquirer.

Exam skills

Bear the efficient market hypothesis in mind when considering how a company's value might be affected by the financing or investment decisions it takes. Knowledge of **what** and **when** information will be incorporated into a quoted share price is likely to influence how and when information regarding financial management decisions is made public.

In particular, since current share prices can be crucial to the success or otherwise of takeover **bids and new share issues**, it will be important to be aware of how the market is likely to react to varying levels of information released. The market may not react predictably, nor in a way a business wants it to, if it does not have full information.

Section summary

The theory behind share price movements can be explained by the three forms of the **efficient market hypothesis**.

- **Weak form efficiency** implies that prices reflect all relevant information about past price movements and their implications.

- **Semi-strong form efficiency** implies that prices reflect past price movements and publicly available knowledge.

- **Strong form efficiency** implies that prices reflect past price movements, publicly available knowledge and inside knowledge.

7   Intangible assets and intellectual capital

Introduction

The valuation of intangible assets and intellectual capital is particularly difficult. This section looks at the various types of intangible assets that a business may benefit from and how they might be valued.

7.1 Valuation of intangibles

The asset based valuation method discussed earlier specifically excluded most intangible assets from the computation. This rendered this method unsuitable for the valuation of most established businesses, particularly those in the **service industry**.

7.1.1 Intangible assets and goodwill

KEY TERMS

INTANGIBLE ASSETS are identifiable non-monetary assets without physical substance which must be controlled by the entity as the result of past events and from which the entity expects a flow of future economic benefits.

GOODWILL (acquired) is future economic benefits arising from assets that are not capable of being individually identified and separately recognised.   *(CIMA Official Terminology)*

The above definition of intangible assets distinguishes:

(a)   Intangible assets from tangible assets, by the phrase 'do not have physical substance'

(b)   Intangible assets from goodwill, by the word 'identifiable' (an identifiable asset is legally defined as one that can be disposed of separately without disposing of a business of the entity)

The strict accounting distinctions do not need to concern us here. We are interested in any element of business that may have some value.

Certain intangible assets can be recorded at their **historical cost**. Examples include patents and trademarks being recorded at **registration value** and franchises being recorded at **contract cost**. However over time these historical values may become poor reflections of the assets' value in use or of their market value.

7.1.2 Intellectual capital

KEY TERM

INTELLECTUAL CAPITAL is knowledge which can be used to create value. Intellectual capital includes:

(a)   Human resources: the collective skills, experience and knowledge of employees

(b)   Intellectual assets: knowledge which is defined and codified such as a drawing, computer program or collection of data

(c)   Intellectual property: intellectual assets which can be legally protected, such as patents and copyrights   *(CIMA Official Terminology)*

As the demand for **knowledge-based products** grows with the changing structure of the global economy, knowledge plays an expanding role in achieving competitive advantage. **Employees** may therefore be extremely valuable to a business, and they should be included in a full assets-based valuation.

The principles of valuation discussed below should be taken as applying to all assets, resources or property that are defined as intangible assets or intellectual capital, which will include:

*   Patents, trademarks and copyrights
*   Franchises and licensing agreements
*   Research and development
*   Brands
*   Technology, management and consulting processes
*   Know-how, education, vocational qualification
*   Customer loyalty
*   Distribution channels
*   Management philosophy

7.2 Measurement of intangible assets of an enterprise

The **expanding intellectual capital** of firms accentuates the need for methods of valuation for comparative purposes, for example when an acquisition or buy-out is being considered.

There are a number of methods of estimating the value of intangible assets, including:

*   Market-to-book values
*   Calculated intangible value

7.2.1 Market-to-book values

This method represents the value of a firm's intellectual capital as **the difference between the book value of tangible assets and the market value of the firm**. For example, if a company's market value is $8 million and its book value is $5 million, the $3 million difference is taken to represent the value of the firm's intangible (or intellectual) assets.

Although obviously **simple**, this method's simplicity merely serves to indicate that it fails to take account of **real world complexities.** There may be imperfections in the market valuation, and book values are subject to accounting standards which reflect historic cost and amortisation policies rather than true market values of tangible non-current assets.

In addition, the accounting valuation does not attempt to value a company as a whole, but rather as a **sum of separate asset values** computed under particular accounting conventions. The market, on the other hand, values the entire company as a **going concern**, following its defined strategy.

7.2.2 Calculated intangible values

NCI Research has developed the method of **calculated intangible value (CIV)** for calculating the fair market value of a firm's intangible assets. CIV calculates an 'excess return' on tangible assets. This figure is then used in determining the **proportion of return** attributable to intangible assets.

A step-by-step approach would be as follows:

 Calculate average pre-tax earnings and average year end tangible asset values over a time period.

 Divide earnings by average assets to get the return on assets.

 Multiply the industry average return on assets percentage by the entity's average tangible asset values. Subtract this from the entity's pre-tax earnings to calculate the excess return.

 Subtract tax from the excess return to give the after-tax premium attributable to intangible assets.

 Calculate the NPV of the premium by dividing it by the entity's cost of capital.

While this seemingly straightforward approach, using readily available information, seems attractive, it does have two problems.

(a) It uses **average industry ROA** as a basis for computing excess returns, which may be **distorted by** extreme values.

(b) The choice of **discount rate** to apply to the excess returns to value the intangible asset needs to be made with care. To ensure comparability between companies and industries, some sort of **average cost of capital** should perhaps be applied. This again has the potential problems of **distortion.**

7.3 Valuation of individual intangible assets

7.3.1 Relief from royalties method

This method involves trying to determine:

(a) The value obtainable from licensing out the right to exploit the intangible asset to a third party, or

(b) The royalties that the owner of the intangible asset is relieved from paying through being the owner rather than the licensee

A **notional royalty rate** is estimated as a percentage of revenue expected to be generated by the intangible asset. The estimated royalty stream can then be **capitalised**, for example by discounting at a risk-free market rate, to find an estimated market value.

This relatively simple valuation method is easiest to apply if the intangible asset is already subject to licensing agreements. If they are not, the valuer might reach an appropriate figure from other comparable licensing arrangements.

7.3.2 Premium profits method

The premium profits method is often used for **brands**. It bases the valuation on capitalisation of the **extra profits generated** by the brand or other intangible asset in excess of profits made by businesses lacking the intangible asset or brand.

The premium profits specifically attributable to the brand or other intangible asset may be estimated (for example) by comparing the price of branded products and unbranded products. The estimated premium profits can then be capitalised by discounting at a risk-adjusted market rate.

7.3.3 Capitalisation of earnings method

With the capitalised earnings method, the **maintainable earnings accruing to the intangible asset** are estimated. An **earnings multiple** is then applied to the earnings, taking account of expected risks and rewards, including the prospects for future earnings growth and the risks involved. This method of valuation is often used to value **publishing titles**.

7.3.4 Comparison with market transactions method

This method looks at **actual market transactions** in similar intangible assets. A multiple of revenue or earnings from the intangible asset might then be derived from a similar market transaction.

A problem with this method is that many **intangible assets are unique** and it may therefore be difficult to identify 'similar' market transactions, although this might be done by examining acquisitions and disposals of businesses that include similar intangible assets.

The method might be used alongside other valuation methods, to provide a comparison.

Section summary

The valuation of **intangible assets** and **intellectual capital** presents special problems. Various methods can be used to value them including the relief from royalties, premium profits and capitalisation of earnings methods.

Chapter Summary

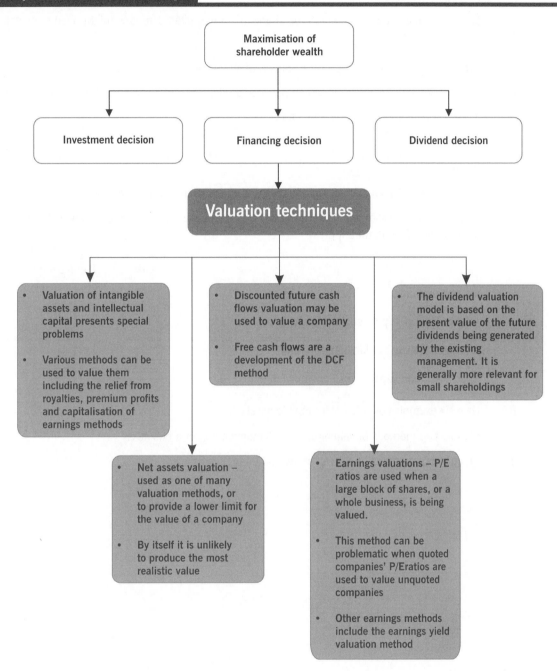

Maximisation of shareholder wealth

Investment decision

Financing decision

Dividend decision

Valuation techniques

- Valuation of intangible assets and intellectual capital presents special problems
- Various methods can be used to value them including the relief from royalties, premium profits and capitalisation of earnings methods

- Discounted future cash flows valuation may be used to value a company
- Free cash flows are a development of the DCF method

- The dividend valuation model is based on the present value of the future dividends being generated by the existing management. It is generally more relevant for small shareholdings

- Net assets valuation – used as one of many valuation methods, or to provide a lower limit for the value of a company
- By itself it is unlikely to produce the most realistic value

- Earnings valuations – P/E ratios are used when a large block of shares, or a whole business, is being valued.
- This method can be problematic when quoted companies' P/Eratios are used to value unquoted companies
- Other earnings methods include the earnings yield valuation method

Quick Quiz

1   Give four circumstances in which the shares of an unquoted company might need to be valued.

2   How is the P/E ratio related to EPS?

3   What is meant by 'multiples' in the context of share valuation?

4   Suggest two circumstances in which net assets might be used as a basis for valuation of a company.

5   There is one correct value for a business.

     True   ☐

     False   ☐

6   What is meant by 'efficiency', in the context of the efficient market hypothesis?

7   The different 'forms' of the efficient market hypothesis state that share prices reflect **which** types of information? Tick all that apply.

	Form of EMH		
	Weak	*Semi-strong*	*Strong*
No information	☐	☐	☐
All information in past share price records	☐	☐	☐
All other publicly available information	☐	☐	☐
Specialists' and experts' 'insider' knowledge	☐	☐	☐

8   Give six examples of types of intangible assets.

9   Identify two methods of valuing the intellectual capital of a business.

10   Identify four methods of valuing individual intangible assets.

Answers to Quick Quiz

1   (a)   Setting an issue price if the company is floating its shares
    (b)   When shares are sold
    (c)   For tax purposes
    (d)   When shares are pledged as collateral for a loan

2   P/E ratio = Share price/EPS

3   The P/E ratio: the multiple of earnings at which a company's shares are traded

4   (a)   As a measure of asset backing
    (b)   For comparison, in a scheme of merger

5   False. In a business valuation, there is no one correct answer. A range of valuations should be calculated.

6   Efficiency in processing information in the pricing of stocks and shares

7

	Form of EMH		
	Weak	Semi-strong	Strong
No information	☐	☐	☐
All information in past share price records	☑	☑	☑
All other publicly available information	☐	☑	☑
Specialists' and experts' 'insider' knowledge	☐	☐	☑

8   Patents; trademarks; brands; copyrights; franchises; research and development

9   Market-to-book values; calculated intangible value

10   Relief from royalties; premium profits; capitalisation of earnings; comparison with market transactions

 # Answers to Questions

11.1 Earnings valuation

(a)   **Earnings.** Average earnings over the last five years have been $67,200, and over the last four years $71,500. There might appear to be some growth prospects, but estimates of future earnings are uncertain.

A low estimate of earnings in 20X5 would be, perhaps, $71,500.

A high estimate of earnings might be $75,000 or more. This solution will use the most recent earnings figure of $75,000 as the high estimate.

(b)   **P/E ratio.** A P/E ratio of 15 (Bumblebee's) would be much too high for Mayfly, because the growth of Mayfly's earnings is not as certain, and Mayfly is an unquoted company.

On the other hand, Mayfly's expectations of earnings are probably better than those of Wasp. A suitable P/E ratio might be based on the industry's average, 10; but since Mayfly is an unquoted company and therefore more risky, a lower P/E ratio might be more appropriate: perhaps 60% to 70% of 10 = 6 or 7, or conceivably even as low as 50% of 10 = 5.

The valuation of Mayfly's shares might therefore range between:

High P/E ratio and high earnings: $7 \times \$75,000 = \$525,000$ and

Low P/E ratio and low earnings: $5 \times \$71,500 = \$357,500$

11.2 DVM

$k_e = 12\% + 2\% = 14\%$ (0.14) $d_0 = \$250,000$ g (in (b)) = 4% or 0.04

(a) $P_0 = \dfrac{d_0}{k_e} = \dfrac{\$250,000}{0.14} = \$1,785,714$

(b) $P_0 = \dfrac{d_0(1+g)}{k_e - g} = \dfrac{\$250,000\,(1.04)}{0.14 - 0.04} = \$2,600,000$

(c)

	Time 1	Time 2	Time 4	Time 4 onwards
Dividend ($'000)	258	266	274	279
Annuity to infinity $(1/k_e - g)$				8.333
Present value at year 3				2,325
Discount factor @ 14%	0.877	0.769	0.675	0.675
Present value	226	205	185	1,569
Total	**$2,185,000**			

11.3 Business valuation

(a)   The information provided allows us to value Profed on three bases: net assets, P/E ratio and dividend valuation.

All three will be computed, even though their validity may be questioned in part (b) of the answer.

Assets based

	£'000
Net assets at book value	7,200
Add: increased valuation of buildings	1,500
Less: decreased value of inventory and receivables	(850)
Net asset value of equity	7,850
Value per share	£1.96

P/E ratio

	Profed	City Tutors
Issued shares (million)	4	10
Share price (pence)		362
Market value (£m)		36.2
Earnings per shares (pence)	35	20
P/E ratio (share price ÷ EPS)		18.1

The P/E for a similar quoted company is 18.1. This will take account of factors such as marketability of shares, status of company, growth potential that will differ from those for Profed. Profed's growth rate has been estimated as higher than that of City Tutors, possibly because it is a younger, developing company, although the basis for the estimate may be questionable.

All other things being equal, the P/E ratio for an unquoted company should be taken as between one-half to two-thirds of that of an equivalent quoted company. Being generous, in view of the possible higher growth prospects of Profed, we might estimate an appropriate P/E ratio of around 12, assuming Profed is to remain a private company.

This will value Profed at 12 × £0.35 = £4.20 per share, a total valuation of £16.8m.

Dividend valuation model

The dividend valuation method gives the share price as

$$\frac{\text{Next year's dividend}}{\text{Cost of equity - growth rate}}$$

which assumes dividends being paid into perpetuity, and growth at a constant rate.

For Profed, next year's dividend = £0.20 × 1.09 = £0.218 per share

While we are given a discount rate of 15% as being traditionally used by the directors of Profed for investment appraisal, there appears to be no rational basis for this. We can instead use the information for City Courses to estimate a cost of equity for Profed. This is assuming the business risks to be similar, and ignoring the small difference in their gearing ratio.

Again, from the DVM, cost of equity = $\frac{\text{next year's dividend}}{\text{market price}}$ + growth rate

For City Tutors, cost of equity = $\frac{£0.18 \times 1.075}{£3.62} + 0.075 = 12.84\%$

Using, say, 13% as a cost of equity for Profed:

Share price = $\frac{£0.218}{0.13 - 0.09}$ = £5.45

valuing the whole of the share capital at £21.8 million

Range for valuation

The three methods used have thus come up with a range of value of Profed as follows:

	Value per share £	Total valuation £m
Net assets	1.96	7.9
P/E ratio	4.20	16.8
Dividend valuation	5.45	21.8

(b)   **Comment on relative merits of the methods used, and their suitability**

Asset based valuation

Valuing a company on the **basis of its asset values** alone is rarely appropriate if it is to be sold on a going concern basis. Exceptions would include property investment companies and investment trusts, the market values of the assets of which will bear a close relationship to their earning capacities.

Profed is typical of a lot of service companies, a large part of whose value lies in the **skill, knowledge and reputation of its personnel**. This is not reflected in the net asset values, and renders this method quite inappropriate. A potential purchaser of Profed will generally value its intangible assets such as knowledge, expertise, customer/supplier relationships, brands etc more highly than those that can be measured in accounting terms.

Knowledge of the net asset value (NAV) of a company will, however, be important as a **floor value** for a company in financial difficulties or subject to a takeover bid. Shareholders will be reluctant to sell for less than the net asset value even if future prospects are poor.

P/E ratio valuation

The P/E ratio measures the **multiple of the current year's earnings** that is reflected in the **market price** of a share. It is thus a method that reflects the earnings potential of a company from a market point of view. Provided the marketing is efficient, it is likely to give the most meaningful basis for valuation.

One of the first things to say is that the market price of a share at any point in time is determined by supply and demand forces prevalent during small transactions, and will be dependent upon a lot of factors in addition to a realistic appraisal of future prospects. A downturn in the market, economies and political changes can all affect the day-to-day price of a share, and thus its prevailing P/E ratio. It is not known whether the share price given for City Tutors was taken on one particular day, or was some sort of average over a period. The latter would perhaps give a sounder basis from which to compute an applicable P/E ratio.

Even if the P/E ratio of City Tutors can be taken to be **indicative of its true worth**, using it as a basis to value a smaller, unquoted company in the same industry can be problematic.

The status and marketability of shares in a quoted company have tangible effects on value but these are difficult to measure.

The P/E ratio will also be affected by **growth prospects** – the higher the growth expected, the higher the ratio. The growth rate incorporated by the shareholders of City Tutors is probably based on a more rational approach than that used by Profed.

If the growth prospects of Profed, as would be perceived by the market, did not coincide with those of **Profed management** it is difficult to see how the P/E ratio should be adjusted for relative levels of growth.

In the valuation in (a) a crude adjustment has been made to City Tutors' P/E ratio to arrive at a ratio to use to value Profed's earnings. This can result in a very inaccurate result if account has not been taken of all the differences involved.

Dividend based valuation

The dividend valuation model (DVM) is a **cash flow based approach**, which valued the dividends that the shareholders expect to receive from the company by discounting them at their required rate of return. It is perhaps more appropriate for valuing a minority shareholding where the holder has no influence over the level of dividends to be paid than for valuing a whole company, where the total cash flows will be of greater relevance.

The practical problems with the dividend valuation model lie mainly in its **assumptions**. Even accepting that the required 'perfect capital market' assumptions may be satisfied to some extent, in reality, the formula used in (a) assumes constant growth rates and constant required rates of return in perpetuity.

Determination of an **appropriate cost of equity** is particularly difficult for a unquoted company, and the use of an 'equivalent' quoted company's data carries the same drawbacks as discussed above. Similar problems arise in estimating future growth rates, and the results from the model are highly sensitive to changes in both these inputs.

It is also highly dependent upon the **current year's dividend** being a representative base from which to start.

The dividend valuation model valuation provided in (a) results in a higher valuation than that under the P/E ratio approach. Reasons for this may be:

- The **share price** for City Courses may be currently **depressed below its normal level**, resulting in an inappropriately low P/E ratio.

- The **adjustment** to get to an **appropriate P/E ratio** for Profed may have been too harsh, particularly in light of its apparently better growth prospects.

- The **cost of equity** used in the dividend valuation model was that of City Courses. The validity of this will largely depend upon the relative levels of risk of the two companies. Although they both operate the same type of business, the fact that City Courses sells its material externally means it is perhaps less reliant on a fixed customer base.

- Even if business risks and gearing risk may be thought to be comparable, a prospective buyer of Profed may consider investment in a **younger, unquoted company** to carry **greater personal risk**. His required return may thus be higher than that envisaged in the dividend valuation model, reducing the valuation.

	Question	Level
Now try the questions from the Practice Question Bank	Section A: 11.1 – 11.7	Practice
	Section B: 6, 7, 10	Practice

ADVANCED VALUATION TECHNIQUES

This chapter follows on from Chapter 11, where we looked at the different methods of valuing a business. In this chapter, we look at issues with valuations such as the choice of an appropriate discount rate for valuing a company, including using the cost of capital of a comparative company with similar business risk and capital structure.

We also look at gearing and ungeared betas of comparative companies to derive the cost of capital, in situations where the comparative company has a different capital structure.

We also look at the impact of changes in capital structure on business valuations, and how to value unquoted companies using geared and ungeared betas.

Topic list	learning outcomes	syllabus references	ability required
1 Valuation issues	C(2)(a)	C(2)(a)(vi),(xii)	evaluation
2 Choice of appropriate discount rate	C(2)(a)	C(2)(a)(viii),(xi)	evaluation
3 Valuation and change in capital structure	B(1)(a),C(2)(a)(b)	B(1)(a)(i),(ii)	evaluation
		C(2)(a)(viii),(b)(ii)	

Chapter Overview

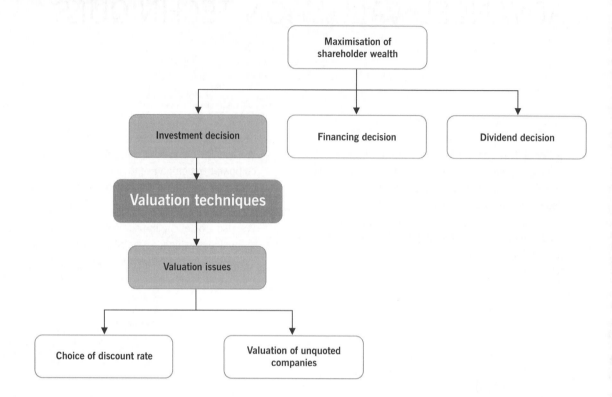

1   Valuation issues

Introduction

In this section we look at some issues involved in valuations.

1.1 Cash flow valuation complications

A cash flow valuation may involve the following complications:

- Foreign currency and taxation
- Sensitivity analysis
- Grants
- Cost of capital (see next section)

1.1.1 Foreign currency and taxation issues

Using the **cash flow method** of valuation, the **post-tax** cash flows of a potential target will be discounted to calculate the NPV of the acquisition target.

In cross-border acquisitions the cash flows may need to be adjusted to reflect the impact of **withholding tax** and **double taxation** agreements.

Withholding tax	This is a local tax on remittances paid to an overseas investor – normally applied to interest and dividend payments.
Double taxation agreement (DTA)	Tax will be payable on profits made in an overseas subsidiary but any tax already paid overseas, including withholding tax, will be deductible if a DTA is in place.

The present value of the cash flows expected from an **overseas acquisition** will also be affected by expectations of future changes in the exchange rate. If, for example, the **overseas currency** is forecast to **devalue** then this will **reduce the value** of the cash flows being generated.

1.1.2 Sensitivity analysis

As with any investment appraisal, the conclusion from a cash flow valuation needs to be treated with caution because it is based on several assumptions. Sensitivity analysis identifies the percentage change in the assumption that is required to change the NPV to zero, ie given the proposed acquisition price, what would have to happen for the NPV to fall to zero.

1.2 Impact of government grants on entity valuations

Government incentives such as capital or revenue grants will have an impact on the valuation of an entity.

Capital grants are often available in many countries to provide assistance with the cost of assets such as plant and machinery.

International accounting standard IAS 20 *Accounting for Government Grants and Disclosure of Government Assistance* requires grants to be credited to the statement of financial position and then recognised as income on the same basis as the related expenditure on the asset, ie depreciation. The initial method of recognition in the statement of financial position can either be to deduct the grant from the carrying value of the asset, or to credit the grant to deferred income.

Therefore in a net assets valuation, consideration should be given to the value of the asset to use, eg whether to use the **replacement cost** or **realisable value** of the asset, rather than the reduced **carrying value** of the asset. Furthermore, consideration should be given to any potential liability to pay back the grant in the event that the conditions of the grant are not complied with.

Revenue grants are often available to assist with the costs of revenue expenditure, ie running costs. Revenue grants are recognised as income on the same basis as the expenditure to which they relate is incurred. This can either be in 'other income' or deducted from the related expenditure. This should be taken into account in the figures used in earnings valuations.

Section summary

- Cash flows of overseas target companies for acquisition will be affected by forecast changes in **currency rates**.

- **Withholding tax** may affect cash flows of overseas target companies, if a double taxation agreement is not in place.

- **Sensitivity analysis** should be used to assess changes in assumptions made in cash flow valuations.

- **Capital grants** may affect the value of assets to use in a net assets valuation.

- **Revenue grants** may affect the value of earnings to use in an earnings valuation.

2 Choice of appropriate discount rate

Introduction

As we have seen in Chapter 11, the selection of an appropriate cost of capital may prove difficult. The cost of capital used should match the business risk. In this section we look at the different types of discount rate to use in different situations.

2.1 Cost of equity

As we have seen in Chapter 8, the cost of equity can be calculated using the **capital asset pricing model (CAPM),** or the **dividend valuation model**.

The cost of equity is appropriate to use as a discount rate to discount cash flows **after** tax and interest, to obtain the value of equity in a company.

2.2 Weighted average cost of capital (WACC)

We looked at calculating WACC in Chapter 9. WACC is appropriate to use as a discount rate to discount cash flows after tax but **before** interest since these represent the cash flows available to all the providers of finance. The value of equity is then determined by subtracting the value of debt.

2.3 Using a cost of capital of a comparative company

In some valuations it is difficult to calculate a cost of capital (eg when valuing an unquoted company) due to lack of information. Therefore it may be appropriate to use a proxy cost of capital of a comparative quoted company. However, the comparative company should have a similar **business risk** (ie similar industry) and **financial risk** (ie similar gearing) to the unquoted company. Otherwise, it may be more appropriate to use a **risk-adjusted** cost of capital, discussed in the next section.

2.4 Risk-adjusted WACC (using CAPM and MM theory)

MM theory can be used to calculate the cost of capital in situations where an investment has a differing **business risk** and a differing **financial risk** from the existing business.

In these situations, a **risk-adjusted cost of capital** should be used. This is also known as a **project-specific cost of capital** as it can be used in investment appraisal for investments with differing business and financial risks from the existing business.

This can also be used as an appropriate cost of capital for a specific **division** of a company if this has differing risks, and also as a method of estimating the cost of capital for valuing an **unquoted company** (see Section 3 below).

The risk-adjusted WACC can be calculated by **degearing and regearing betas**. There are two approaches to this, but both have the same end result, as we will see in the section below, 'Using the geared and ungeared beta formula to calculate WACC'.

2.4.1 Beta values and the effect of gearing

If a company is geared and its **financial risk is therefore higher** than the risk of an all-equity company, then the beta value of the geared company's equity will be higher than the beta value of a similar ungeared company's equity.

2.4.2 Geared betas and ungeared betas

The connection between MM theory and the CAPM means that it is possible to establish a mathematical relationship between the beta value of an ungeared company and the beta value of a similar, but geared, company. The beta value of a geared company will be higher than the beta value of a company identical in every respect except that it is ungeared and therefore all equity financed. This is because of the extra financial risk caused by using debt finance. The mathematical relationship between the 'ungeared' (or asset) and 'geared' betas is as follows:

$$\beta_u = \beta_g \frac{V_E}{V_E + V_D(1-t)} + \beta_d \frac{V_D(1-t)}{V_E + V_D(1-t)}$$

Where β_u is the beta factor of an ungeared company: the ungeared beta
            β_g is the beta factor of equity in a similar, but geared company: the geared beta
            β_d is the beta factor of debt in the geared company
            V_D is the market value of the debt capital in the geared company
            V_E is the market value of the equity capital in the geared company
            t   is the rate of corporate tax

Debt is often assumed to be risk-free and its beta (β_d) is then taken as zero, in which case the formula above reduces to the following form.

$$\beta_u = \beta_g \times \frac{V_E}{V_E + V_D(1-t)} \quad \text{or, without tax,} \quad \beta_u = \beta_g \times \frac{V_E}{V_E + V_D}$$

2.4.3 Using the geared and ungeared beta formula to calculate WACC

If a company plans to acquire a company or invest in a project which involves diversification into a new line of business, the investment will involve a different level of **business risk** from that applying to the company's existing business. A discount rate should be calculated which is specific to the new line of business, and which takes account of both the business risk of the new line of business and the company's own gearing level.

There are **two methods** which can be used to calculate a risk-adjusted cost of capital both of which start by calculating an ungeared beta.

2.4.4 Approach 1

 STEP 1 Find a company's equity beta in the area the business is moving into and strip out the effect of gearing to create an ungeared beta. The ungeared beta reflects the business risk of the company only.

$$\beta_u = \beta_g \frac{V_E}{V_E + V_D(1 - t)}$$

 STEP 2 Use the ungeared beta to calculate the ungeared k_e using the CAPM formula

 STEP 3 Use this ungeared k_e to calculate the WACC using the MM formula

EXAM

$k_{adj} = k_{eu}(1 - tL)$

Where k_{adj} is the weighted average cost of capital of a geared company

k_{eu} is the cost of equity and the WACC of a similar ungeared company

t is the tax saving due to interest payments expressed as a decimal, usually equal to the tax rate

L is equivalent to $\dfrac{V_D}{V_D + V_E}$

Example: Approach 1

A company's debt: equity ratio, by market values, is 2:5. The corporate debt, which is assumed to be risk-free, yields 11% before tax. The beta value of the company's equity is currently 1.1. The average returns on stock market equity are 16%.

The company is now proposing to invest in a project which would involve diversification into a new industry, and the following information is available about this industry.

(a) Average equity beta = 1.59
(b) Average debt: equity ratio in the industry = 1:2 (by market value)

The rate of corporation tax is 30%. What would be a suitable cost of capital to apply to the project?

Solution

 STEP 1 Find a company's equity beta in the area the business is moving into and strip out the effect of gearing to create an ungeared beta.

The beta value for the industry is 1.59.

$$\beta_u = 1.59 \left(\frac{2}{2 + (1(1 - 0.30))} \right) = 1.18$$

 STEP 2 Use the ungeared beta to calculate the ungeared k_{eu}

$k_{eu} = 11\% + ((16 - 11) \times 1.18) = 16.9\%$

Use this ungeared k_{eu} to calculate the WACC using the MM formula

$$k_{adj} = k_{eu}(1 - tL)$$

The project will presumably be financed in a gearing ratio of 2:5 debt to equity, and so

$$L = \frac{2}{2+5}$$

$$k_{adj} = 16.9\% \times (1 - (0.3 \times 2/7) = 15.45\%$$

2.4.5 Approach 2

Find a company's equity beta in the area the business is moving into and strip out the effect of gearing to create an ungeared beta. The ungeared beta reflects the business risk of the company only.

$$\beta_u = \beta_g \frac{V_E}{V_E + V_D(1-t)}$$

Regear the beta using the company's gearing using the formula

$$\beta_g = \beta_u + (\beta_u - \beta_d)^* \frac{V_D(1-t)}{V_E}$$

and calculate the k_e geared, using the CAPM formula.

Note: the regeared beta now reflects both business risk and financial risk.

*As mentioned above, a company's debt is often assumed to be risk-free, in which case β_d = 0.

Use this k_e geared to calculate the WACC using the formula below.

EXAM

$$WACC = k_e \left[\frac{V_E}{V_E + V_D}\right] + k_d (1-t) \left[\frac{V_D}{V_E + V_D}\right]$$

Example: Approach 2

Using the information from the example above, the second approach can be used as follows:

$$\beta_u = 1.59 \left(\frac{2}{2+(1(1-0.30))}\right) = 1.18$$

Regear the beta to reflect the company's own gearing level of 2:5.

$$\beta_g = 1.18 + 1.18 \times [(2 \times 0.70)/5] = 1.51$$

This is a project-specific beta for the firm's equity capital, and so using the CAPM, we can estimate the project-specific cost of equity as:

$$k_{eg} = 11\% + (16\% - 11\%) \, 1.51 = 18.55\%$$

The project will presumably be financed in a gearing ratio of 2:5 debt to equity, and so the project-specific cost of capital ought to be:

$[^5/_7 \times 18.55\%] + [^2/_7 \times 70\% \times 11\%] = 15.45\%$

Exam alert

You will need to be able to ungear and regear a beta in order to calculate a value for a company.

Question 12.1	Geared and ungeared betas (1)

Learning outcome: C(2)(a)

Two companies are identical in every respect except for their capital structure. XY has a debt to equity ratio of 1:3, and its equity has a beta value of 1.20. PQ has a debt to equity ratio of 2:3. Corporation tax is at 30%. Estimate a beta value for PQ's equity.

Question 12.2	Geared and ungeared betas (2)

Learning outcome: C(2)(a)

Backwoods is a major international company with its head office in the UK, wanting to raise £150 million to establish a new production plant in the eastern region of Germany. Backwoods evaluates its investments using NPV, but is not sure what cost of capital to use in the discounting process for this project evaluation.

The company is also proposing to increase its equity finance in the near future for UK expansion, resulting overall in little change in the company's market-weighted capital gearing.

The summarised financial data for the company before the expansion are shown below.

Statement of profit or loss for the year ended 31 December 20X1

	£m
Revenue	1,984
Gross profit	432
Profit after tax	81
Dividends	37
Retained earnings	44

Statement of financial position as at 31 December 20X1

	£m
Non-current assets	846
Working capital	350
Total assets	1,196

	£m
Shareholders' funds	
Issued ordinary shares of £0.50 each nominal value	225
Reserves	761
Total equity	986
Medium-term and long- term loans	210
Total equity and liabilities	1,196

Medium-term and long-term loans include £75m 14% fixed rate bonds due to mature in five years' time and redeemable at par. The current market price of these bonds is £120.00 and they have a cost of debt of 9%. Other medium and long-term loans are floating rate UK bank loans at LIBOR plus 1%, with a cost of debt of 7%.

The rate of tax on company profits is 30%. The company's ordinary shares are currently trading at 376 pence.

The equity beta of Backwoods is estimated to be 1.18. The systematic risk of debt may be assumed to be zero. The risk-free rate is 7.75% and market return is 14.5%.

The estimated equity beta of the main German competitor in the same industry as the new proposed plant in the eastern region of Germany is 1.5, and the competitor's capital gearing is 35% equity and 65% debt by book values, and 60% equity and 40% debt by market values.

Required

Estimate the cost of capital that the company should use as the discount rate for its proposed investment in eastern Germany. State clearly any assumptions that you make.

Section summary

- The **cost of equity** can be calculated using the **Capital Asset Pricing Model (CAPM)**, or the **dividend valuation model**.

- The cost of equity is appropriate to use as a discount rate to discount cash flows after tax and interest, to obtain the value of equity in a company.

- **Weighted average cost of capital (WACC)** is appropriate to use as a discount rate to discount cash flows after tax but before interest since these represent the earnings available to all the providers of finance. The value of equity is then determined by subtracting the value of debt.

- Where a target company is a private company, its cost of capital cannot be calculated from market value. Therefore, the cost of capital of a **comparative company** to the target company can be used as a benchmark in estimating the target's cost of capital. This assumes the comparative company has similar business and financial risks.

- If the comparative company has differing levels of business and financial risks, a **risk-adjusted cost of capital** should be used. There are two approaches to this but both have the same end result.

  The first approach involves the following steps:

  – **Ungear** (strip out the effect of debt) the **comparative company's beta** (to provide an approximate measure of the business risk of the target).

  – Calculate the **ungeared cost of equity** using the CAPM formula.

  – Calculate the **geared cost of capital** using the **ungeared cost of equity** and the gearing ratio for the target, in the Modigliani and Miller formula for WACC.

  The second approach involves the following steps:

  – **Ungear** (strip out the effect of debt) the **comparative company's beta**.

  – **Regear the beta** using the target company's gearing.

  – Calculate the **geared cost of equity** using the CAPM formula.

  – Calculate the **cost of capital** using the **geared cost of equity** in the standard formula for WACC.

Exam skills

When choosing an appropriate cost of capital to use as a discount rate, you should consider the scenario in the question, eg valuing a division, entire entity, quoted company or unquoted company.

3 Valuation and change in capital structure

Introduction

In this section we look at the impact of the change in capital structure on business valuations. We have looked at capital structure earlier in the Study Text.

3.1 Net operating income approach

We saw earlier in this text that Modigliani and Miller stated in their basic theory that the level of gearing would not affect the value of shares in a taxless world. However, if taxation was introduced, the weighted average cost of capital will continue to fall as gearing increased.

You will remember that Modigliani and Miller argued that since WACC falls as gearing rises, and the value of a company should rise as its WACC falls, **the value of a geared company (V_g) will always be greater than its ungeared counterpart (V_u)**, but only by the amount of the debt-associated tax saving of the geared company, assuming a permanent change in gearing.

EXAM

$$V_g = V_u + TB_c.$$

The additional amount of value in the geared company, TB_c is known as the value of the **'tax shield'** on debt.

However, the positive tax effects of debt finance will be exhausted where there is insufficient tax liability to use the tax relief which is available. This is known as **tax shield exhaustion**.

Example: MM with taxes

Notnil and Newbegin are companies in the same industry. They have the same business risk and operating characteristics, but Notnil is a geared company whereas Newbegin is all equity financed. Notnil earns three times as much profit before interest as Newbegin. Both companies pursue a policy of paying out all their earnings each year as dividends.

The market value of each company is currently as follows.

		Notnil $m		Newbegin $m
Equity	(10m shares)	36	(20m shares)	15
Debt	($12m of 12% bonds)	14		
		50		15

The annual profit before interest of Notnil is $3,000,000 and that of Newbegin is $1,000,000. The rate of tax is 30%. It is thought that the current market value per ordinary share in Newbegin is at the equilibrium level, and that the market value of Notnil's debt capital is also at its equilibrium level. There is some doubt, however, about whether the value of Notnil's shares is at its equilibrium level.

Apply the MM formula to establish the equilibrium price of Notnil's shares.

Solution

$V_g = V_u + TB_c$

V_u = the market value of an equivalent ungeared company. Equivalence is in both size and risk of earnings. Since Notnil earnings (before interest) are three times the size of Newbegin's, V_u is three times the value of Newbegin's equity:

$3 \times \$15,000,000 = \$45,000,000.$

$TB_c = \$14,000,000 \times 30\% = \$4,200,000$

$V_g = \$45,000,000 + \$4,200,000 = \$49,200,000.$

Since the market value of debt in Notnil is $14,000,000, it follows that the market value of Notnil's equity should be $49,200,000 – $14,000,000 = $35,200,000.

$$\text{Value per share} = \frac{\$35,200,000}{10,000,000} = \$3.52 \text{ per share}$$

Since the current share price is $3.60 per share, MM would argue that the shares in Notnil are currently over-valued by the market, by $800,000 in total or 8c per share. MM argue that this discrepancy would be rapidly removed by the process of arbitrage until the equity value of Notnil was as predicted by their model.

Question 12.3	WACC and MM theory

Learning outcome: C(2)(a)

CD and YZ are identical in every respect except for their gearing. The market value of each company is as follows.

	CD $m		YZ $m
Equity (5m shares)	?	(8m shares)	24
Debt ($20m of 5% bonds)	10		
	?		24

According to MM theory, what is the value of CD shares, given a corporation tax rate of 30%?

3.2 Valuation of an unquoted company

There is a problem with valuing unquoted companies using earnings or dividends bases, as a cost of equity (k_e) is needed. There are two methods of calculating a cost of equity, the CAPM and the dividend model, but both are difficult to apply to an unquoted company.

To deal with this problem, we can use the beta of a quoted company to help to calculate k_e. We looked at **gearing and ungearing betas** in Section 2 above in the context of a risk-adjusted cost of capital. We can use a very similar approach to calculate a geared cost of equity and then the value of a company as follows:.

STEP 1 Find the equity beta of a similar quoted company and strip out the effect of gearing to create an ungeared beta.

$$\beta_u = \beta_g \frac{V_E}{V_E + V_D(1 - t)}$$

 STEP 2 Regear the beta using the company's gearing using the formula

$$\beta_g = \beta_u + (\beta_u - \beta_d) \frac{V_D(1 - t)}{V_E}$$ and calculate the k_e geared using the CAPM formula.

 STEP 3 Use this k_e geared to calculate the value of the company using the formula

$$P_0 = \frac{d_0(1 + g)}{k_e - g} .$$

 ## Section summary

- **Modigliani and Miller** state that in a world with taxes, market value should continue to rise as gearing rises, because tax benefits arise from interest paid.

- It can be difficult to **value unquoted companies** as obtaining a **cost of equity** is difficult. The **beta of a quoted company** can be used to calculate the cost of equity.

Chapter Summary

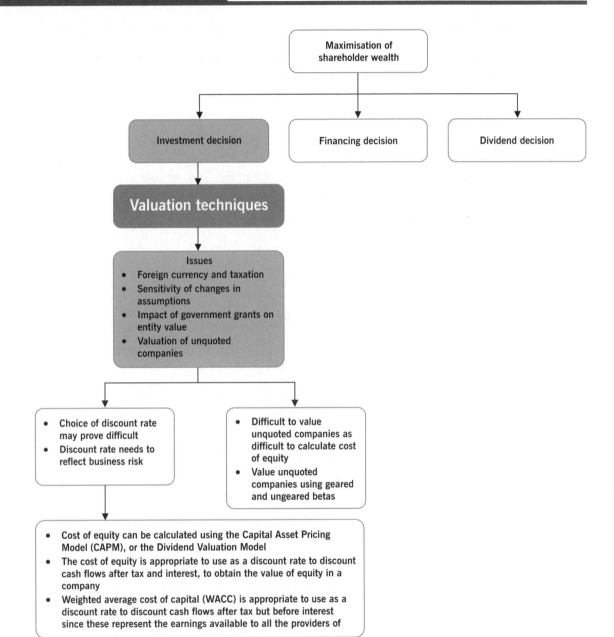

Maximisation of shareholder wealth

Investment decision

Financing decision

Dividend decision

Valuation techniques

Issues
- Foreign currency and taxation
- Sensitivity of changes in assumptions
- Impact of government grants on entity value
- Valuation of unquoted companies

- Choice of discount rate may prove difficult
- Discount rate needs to reflect business risk

- Difficult to value unquoted companies as difficult to calculate cost of equity
- Value unquoted companies using geared and ungeared betas

- Cost of equity can be calculated using the Capital Asset Pricing Model (CAPM), or the Dividend Valuation Model
- The cost of equity is appropriate to use as a discount rate to discount cash flows after tax and interest, to obtain the value of equity in a company
- Weighted average cost of capital (WACC) is appropriate to use as a discount rate to discount cash flows after tax but before interest since these represent the earnings available to all the providers of

- The cost of capital of a comparative company to the target company can be used as a benchmark in calculating the cost of capital.
- However if the comparative company has a different level of systematic risk, a risk-adjusted cost of capital should be used
- This can also be used as an appropriate cost of capital for a specific division of a company if this has a different level of risk

Quick Quiz

1   What factors should be considered in the valuation of cash flows of an overseas target?

2   The traditional view of gearing states that market value should be maximised at the optimum capital structure, where cost of capital is **maximised**.

True ☐

False ☐

3   **Fill in the blank:**

The positive tax effects of debt finance will be exhausted where there is insufficient tax liability to use the tax relief which is available. This is known as ....

4   Ungearing and regearing betas is a method used for calculating the cost of equity of an unquoted company.

True ☐

False ☐

5   What three steps are involved in calculating a risk-adjusted cost of capital?

Answers to Quick Quiz

1   Withholding tax; changes in currency rates.

2   False. It is where the cost of capital in minimised.

3   Tax shield exhaustion.

4   True.

5   Either:

 Find a company's equity beta in the area the business is moving into and strip out the effect of gearing to create an ungeared beta.

$$\beta_u = \beta_g \frac{V_E}{V_E + V_D(1-t)}$$

 Use the ungeared beta to calculate the ungeared k_e.

 Use this ungeared k_e to calculate the WACC using the MM formula.

$k_{adj} = k_{eu}(1-tL)$

Or:

 Find a company's equity beta in the area the business is moving into and strip out the effect of gearing to create an ungeared beta.

$$\beta_u = \beta_g \frac{V_E}{V_E + V_D(1-t)}$$

 Regear the beta using the company's gearing using the formula

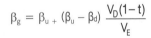

$$\beta_g = \beta_u + (\beta_u - \beta_d)\frac{V_D(1-t)}{V_E}$$

and calculate the k_e geared.

 Use this k_e geared to calculate the WACC.

Answers to Questions

12.1 Geared and ungeared betas (1)

Estimate an ungeared beta from XY data.

$$\beta_u = 1.20 \left(\frac{3}{3+(1(1-0.30))} \right) = 0.973$$

Estimate a geared beta for PQ using this ungeared beta.

$$\beta_g = 0.973 \left(\frac{3+(2(1-0.30))}{3} \right) = 1.427$$

12.2 Geared and ungeared betas (2)

The discount rate that should be used is the weighted average cost of capital (WACC), with weightings based on market values. The cost of capital should take into account the systematic risk of the new investment, and therefore it will not be appropriate to use the company's existing equity beta. Instead, the estimated equity beta of the main German competitor in the same industry as the new proposed plant will be ungeared, and then the capital structure of Backwoods applied to find the WACC to be used for the discount rate.

Since the systematic risk of debt can be assumed to be zero, the German equity beta can be 'ungeared' using the following expression:

$$\beta_u = \beta_g \frac{V_E}{V_E + V_D(1-t)}$$

Where:

β_u	=	asset beta
β_g	=	equity beta
V_E	=	proportion of equity in capital structure
V_D	=	proportion of debt in capital structure
t	=	tax rate

For the German company:

$$\beta_u \quad = 1.5 \left(\frac{60}{60+40\,(1-0.30)} \right) = 1.023$$

The next step is to calculate the debt and equity of Backwoods based on market values.

		£m
Equity	450m shares at 376p	1,692.0
Debt: bank loans	(210 – 75)	135.0
Debt: bonds	(75 million × 1.20)	90.0
Total debt		225.0
Total market value		1,917.0

The beta can now be re-geared

$$\beta_g = 1.023 + 1.023 \times [(225 \times 0.7)/1,692] = 1.118$$

This can now be substituted into the capital asset pricing model (CAPM) to find the cost of equity.

$$k_e = R_f + [R_m - R_f]\beta$$

Where: k_e = cost of equity
            R_f = risk free rate of return
            R_m = market rate of return
            k_e = 7.75% + (14.5% − 7.75%) × 1.118 = 15.30%

The WACC can now be calculated:

$$\left(15.3 \times \frac{1,692}{1,917}\right) + \left(7 \times \frac{135}{1,917}\right) + \left(9 \times \frac{90}{1,917}\right) = 14.4\%$$

Note. You have been given both costs of debt. In the exam you may well be asked to calculate the cost of debt.

12.3 WACC and MM theory

Value of CD in total $V_g = V_u + TB_c$ where V_u is the value of YZ.

V_g = $24,000,000 + $10,000,000 × 30% = $27,000,000.

CD's equity is valued at $27,000,000 − debt of $10,000,000 = $17,000,000, or $3.40 per share.

Now try the questions from the Practice Question Bank	Question	Level
	Section A: 12.1 – 12.3	Practice

POST ACQUISITION ISSUES

 In this final chapter, we look at the post acquisition issues from the perspective of the acquirer and from the target company, and why some acquisitions fail.

We look at the value of a company before and after acquisition and the different forms of payment for acquisition.

We end the chapter by looking at the different types of exit strategies an acquirer may take.

Topic list	learning outcomes	syllabus references	ability required
1 Payment methods	C(3)(a),(b)	C(3)(a)(i)(ii)(iii),(b)(i)	evaluation
2 Valuation of mergers and takeovers	C(3)(b)	C(3)(b)(i)	evaluation
3 Post-acquisition integration	C(3)(b)	C(3)(b)(ii)	evaluation
4 Exit strategies	C(3)(b)	C(3)(b)(iii)	evaluation

Chapter Overview

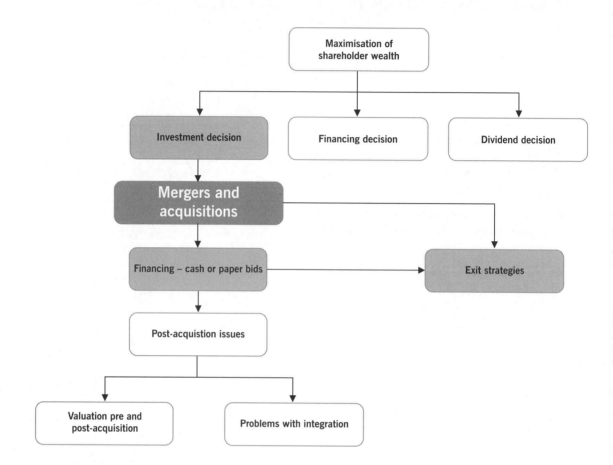

1   Payment methods

Introduction

In this section we look at how an acquisition can be financed and discuss the factors that will influence the choice of method of payment.

1.1 Methods of payment

The terms of a takeover will involve a purchase of the shares of the target company for **cash** or for **'paper'** (shares, or possibly bonds). A purchase of a target company's shares with shares of the predator company is referred to as a **share exchange**.

1.2 Cash purchases

If the purchase consideration is in **cash**, the shareholders of the target company will simply be bought out. For example, suppose that there are two companies:

	Big	Small
Net assets (book value)	$1,500,000	$200,000
Number of shares	100,000	10,000
Earnings	$2,000,000	$40,000

Big negotiates a takeover of Small for $400,000 in cash.

As a result, Big will end up with:

(a)   Net assets (book value) of:

$1,500,000 + $200,000 – $400,000 cash = $1,300,000

(b)   100,000 shares (no change)

(c)   Expected earnings of $2,040,000, minus the loss of interest (net of tax) which would have been obtained from the investment of the $400,000 in cash which was given up to acquire Small

1.3 Financing cash offers

A cash offer can be financed from:

(a)   **Cash retained from earnings**. This is a common way when the firm to be acquired is small compared to the acquiring firm, but not very common if the target firm is large relative to the acquiring firm. A company may occasionally divest some of its own assets to accumulate cash prior to bidding for another company.

(b)   **The proceeds of a debt issue**. That is, the company may raise money by issuing bonds. This is not an approach that is normally taken, because the act of issuing bonds will alert the markets to the intentions of the company to bid for another company and it may lead investors to buy the shares of potential targets, raising their prices.

(c)   **A loan facility from a bank**. This can be done as a short-term funding strategy, until the bid is accepted and then the company is free to make a bond issue.

(d)   **Mezzanine finance**. This may be the only route for companies that do not have access to the bond markets in order to issue bonds.

Exam skills

You may be asked in the exam about the consequences of using different finance sources to support a cash offer. In the integrated case study, you may be expected to evaluate whether a cash bid or a paper bid is more appropriate.

1.4 Purchases by share exchange

One company can acquire another company by **issuing shares** to pay for the acquisition. The new shares might be issued:

(a) **In exchange for shares in the target company**. Thus, if A acquires B, A might issue shares which it gives to B's shareholders in exchange for their shares. The B shareholders therefore become new shareholders of A. This is a takeover for a 'paper' consideration. Paper offers will often be accompanied by a **cash alternative.**

(b) **To raise cash on the stock market**. This will then be used to buy the target company's shares. To the target company shareholders, this is a cash bid.

Sometimes, a company might acquire another in a share exchange, but the shares are then **sold immediately** on a stock market to raise cash for the seller.

Whatever the detailed arrangements of a takeover with paper, the end result will be an **increase in the issued share capital of the predator company**.

Example: Share consideration (1)

Arcturus has agreed to acquire all the ordinary shares in Mira and has also agreed a share-for-share exchange as the form of consideration. The following information is available:

	Arcturus £m	Mira £m
Operating profit	100	20
Net profit before taxation	80	14
Net profit after taxation	60	10
Share capital – £0.50 ordinary shares	£20m	£5m
Price/earnings ratio	10	12

The agreed share price for Mira will result in its shareholders receiving a premium of 25% on the current share price.

How many new shares must Arcturus issue to purchase the shares in Mira?

Solution

Market value Arcturus (10 × £60m) = £600m

Value per share (£600m/40m) = £15 per share

Market value Mira (12 × £10m) = £120m

Value of bid (£120m × 1.25) = £150m

Number of shares issued (£150m/£15) = 10 million shares

Example: Share consideration (2)

Demeter wishes to take over Semele. The following information relates to the two companies:

	Number of ordinary shares in issue	Market price per ordinary share
Demeter	20 million	£10.00
Semele	6 million	£3.00

The market price of each company's shares is regarded as an accurate reflection of their intrinsic value.

The takeover is expected to lead to research and development savings after taxation that have a present value of £12 million. The bid offer consists of one share in Demeter for every three shares held in Semele, plus £1.00 in cash for every three shares held in Semele.

By how much would the wealth of a shareholder who owns 3,000 shares in Semele increase if the takeover was successful?

Solution

Number of shares to be issued	=	6m × $\frac{1}{3}$ = 2 million
Total number of shares in issue after takeover	=	20m + 2m = 22 million
Cash payment	=	£2 million
Value of combined company after takeover	=	£200m + 18m + 12m – 2m
	=	£228 million
Value of 1,000 shares after takeover	=	£228m × 1,000 ÷ 22,000,000 = £10,364

	£
Share value	10,364
Cash	1,000
	11,364
Value of 3,000 shares before take over (3,000 × £3)	9,000
	2,364

Example: Share consideration (3)

X and Y are both listed companies.

	X plc	Y plc
Profit before tax for the year just ended	£4m	£3.5m
Profit after tax for the year just ended	£2.75m	£2.4m
Number of shares	10m	5m
P/E ratio (current)	12	10

X has made an offer to acquire all the share capital of Y. The offer price is 5 new shares in X for every 3 shares in Y.

What is the premium in % in the price offered to the shareholders of Y?

Solution

EPS, X = (£2.75 million/10 million shares) = £0.275

Share price, X = £0.275 × 12 = £3.30

EPS, Y = (£2.4 million/5 million shares) = £0.48

Share price, Y = £0.48 × 10 = £4.80

Offer = 5 shares in X, value 5 × £3.30, £16.50, for 3 shares in Y.

Current market value of 3 shares in Y = 3 × £4.80 = £14.40.

The premium in the offer price is therefore (£16.50 – £14.40) ÷ £14.40 = 14.6%.

1.5 Use of bonds

Alternative forms of paper consideration, including debentures, loan notes and preference shares, are not so commonly used, due to:

- Difficulties in **establishing a rate of return** that is attractive to target shareholders
- The **effects on the gearing levels** of the acquiring company
- The **change in the structure of the target shareholders'** portfolios
- The **securities being potentially less marketable** and lacking voting rights

Issuing **convertible bonds** will overcome some of these drawbacks, by offering the target shareholders the option of partaking in the future profits of the company if they wish.

Example: Loan consideration

Trim offers to buy 100% of the equity shares of Slim from its three owners. The purchase price will be £7 million, made up of 1.5 million new shares of Trim and £2 million in 10% bonds. The annual profits before tax of Slim have been £1 million for each of the past three years, after making suitable adjustments for directors' salaries and differences in accounting policies, and this level of profits is expected to continue after the takeover by Trim.

Trim has announced its intention of paying a dividend of £0.12 per share next year.

Assuming no synergy as the result of the acquisition, by how much will the earnings of Trim be expected to increase next year, when the profits of Slim are taken into account? Company tax is 30%.

Solution

	£'000	£'000
Slim profit before tax		1,000
Less: tax (30%)		300
		700
Interest on bonds	200	
Less: tax reduction	60	
Net increase in interest		140
Increase in profit after tax for Trim		560

1.6 The choice between a cash offer and a paper offer

The choice between cash and paper offers (or a combination of both) will depend on how the different methods are viewed by the company and its existing shareholders, and on the attitudes of the shareholders of the target company. The **factors** that the directors of the bidding company must consider include the following.

Company and its existing shareholders	
Dilution of EPS	Fall in EPS attributable to existing shareholders may occur if purchase consideration is in equity shares.

Company and its existing shareholders	
Cost to the company	Use of bonds to back a cash offer will attract tax relief on interest and have lower cost than equity. Convertible bonds can have lower interest.
Gearing	A highly geared company may not be able to issue further bonds to obtain cash for cash offer.
Control	Control could change considerably if large number of new shares is issued.
Authorised share capital increase	This may be required if consideration is in form of shares, and will involve calling a general meeting to pass the necessary resolution.
Borrowing limits increase	General meeting resolution is also required if borrowing limits have to change.
Taxation	If consideration is cash, many investors may suffer immediate liability to tax on capital gain.
Income	If consideration is not cash, arrangement must mean existing income is maintained, or be compensated by suitable capital gain or reasonable growth expectations.
Future investments	Shareholders who want to retain stake in target business may prefer shares.
Share price	If consideration is shares, recipients will want to be sure that the shares retain their values.

CASE STUDY

In January 2010, UK confectionery company Cadbury finally capitulated to a hostile takeover bid by Kraft, the US company that manufactures such well-known products as Kraft cheese slices and Toblerone. The £11.6 billion takeover – which valued Cadbury's shares at £8.50 per share (including a special dividend of 10p) – was financed partly by cash and partly by shares. Kraft sold its North American frozen pizza business to Nestle for $3.7 billion and used the proceeds to help fund the cash element of the bid. Of the £8.50 per share, £5 was paid in cash and the remainder in shares, with Cadbury shareholders receiving 0.1874 Kraft shares for every one Cadbury share.

1.7 Earn-out arrangements

The purchase consideration may not all be paid at the time of acquisition. Part of it may be deferred, payable upon the target company reaching certain performance targets.

KEY TERM

An EARN-OUT ARRANGEMENT is a procedure whereby owners/managers selling an entity receive a portion of their consideration linked to the financial performance of the business during a specific period after the sale. The arrangement gives a measure of security to the new owners, who pass some of the financial risk associated with the purchase of a new enterprise to the sellers.   *(CIMA Official Terminology)*

For example, the consideration may be structured as follows:

(a)   An initial amount payable at the time of acquisition

(b)   A guaranteed minimum amount of deferred consideration, payable in, say, three years time

(c)   An additional amount of deferred consideration, payable if a specified target performance is achieved over the next three years

The total of the **initial and guaranteed deferred consideration** amounts may be based upon an **assets-based approach to valuation**, or on an **earnings basis**, using, for example, the average level of expected profits over a given future period.

The **additional amount of deferred consideration** might be payable if the acquired company's **average profits or revenues** over the next three years exceeds a certain amount.

This method would only be appropriate if the acquired company was to be **run independently** of the **buyer's company**, at least for the period upon which the contingent consideration is based. If the acquired business were to be immediately integrated within the buyer's, it would be difficult to identify separately the relevant sales or profits.

Under these types of arrangement, then, the **overall valuation** of the business will have a **variable element**. The buyer will need to estimate the minimum, maximum and expected total amounts they may have to pay, with corresponding probabilities relating to the likelihood of the business reaching the specified targets. In particular, they will have to ensure that they could, if necessary, afford to pay the maximum amount, regardless of how unlikely that is to arise.

1.8 Mezzanine finance and takeover bids

When the purchase consideration in a takeover bid is cash, the cash must be obtained somehow by the bidding company, in order to pay for the shares that it buys. Occasionally, the company will have sufficient cash in hand to pay for the target company's shares. More frequently, the cash will have to be raised, possibly from existing shareholders, by means of **a rights issue** or, more probably, by **borrowing from** banks or other financial institutions.

When cash for a takeover is raised by borrowing, the loans would normally be **medium-term** and **secured**.

However, there have been many takeover bids, with a **cash purchase option** for the target company's shareholders, where the bidding company has arranged loans that:

(a)   Are short to medium-term

(b)   Are unsecured (that is, 'junior' debt, low in the priority list for repayment in the event of liquidation of the borrower)

(c)   Because they are unsecured, attract a much higher rate of interest than secured debt (typically 4% or 5% above LIBOR)

(d)   Often, give the lender the option to exchange the loan for shares after the takeover

This type of borrowing is called **mezzanine finance** (because it lies between equity and debt financing) – a form of finance which is also often used in **management buyouts** (which are discussed later in this chapter).

1.9 Leveraged buyouts

A leveraged buyout (LBO) is a takeover of a company by an investor (often private equity) using significant debt. Typically the debt used to fund the takeover is secured on the assets of the target company. The cashflow generated by the target company is then used to service and repay the debt. The target company would normally need to have low existing debt, stable cashflows and good asset backing.

This approach allows a private equity investor to acquire a large company with minimal cash or risk, since they are borrowing against the acquired company's assets and earnings. A range of different debt is usually used and any short-term debt instruments may need refinancing soon after the deal. The overall aim is to improve the running of the target over a 3–5 year period, generate additional profits, repay the debt and sell the company for a profit. However, if the company is not resold or floated before any longer term LBO debt becomes due then it will need to be refinanced.

LBOs were very common in the mid 2000s as a result of low interest rates. As a result of the global financial crisis, a significant amount of LBO debt has needed refinancing between 2012 and 2014 and this is expected to continue. The increasing regulatory requirements on banks may reduce the availability of debt for refinancing and result in the need for restructuring or even insolvency.

1.10 Managing the refinancing of the target's debt

Many debt agreements carry a change of control clause which means that when a company completes an acquisition it may well have to refinance the target company's debt. The acquiring company will need to ensure that it has factored this into its financial planning.

This may require a short-term line of credit to act as a bridging loan while refinancing is being arranged.

Exam alert

In the exam, you could well get a situation where the cash vs shares decision is finely balanced, and financing the cash offer may be the critical issue.

Section summary

Payment can be in the form of **cash**, a **share exchange** or **convertible bonds**. The choice will depend on available cash, desired levels of gearing, shareholders' taxation position and changes in control.

2 Valuation of mergers and takeovers

Introduction

Shareholders of both of the companies involved in a merger or acquisition will be very aware of the effect on share prices and earnings per share. In this section we look at various examples illustrating what can happen.

2.1 The market values of the companies' shares during a takeover bid

Share prices can be very important during a takeover bid. Suppose that Velvet decides to make a takeover bid for the shares of Noggin. Noggin shares are currently quoted on the market at £2 each. Velvet shares are quoted at £4.50 and Velvet offers one of its shares for every two shares in Noggin, thus making an offer at current market values worth £2.25 per share in Noggin. This is only the value of the bid so long as Velvet's shares remain valued at £4.50. If their value falls, the bid will become less attractive.

Companies that make takeover bids with a **share exchange offer** are thus always concerned that the market value of their shares **should not fall** during the takeover negotiations, before the target company's shareholders have decided whether to accept the bid.

If the market price of the target company's shares rises above the offer price during the course of a takeover bid, the bid price will seem too low, and the takeover is then likely to fail, with shareholders in the target company refusing to sell their shares to the bidder.

2.2 EPS before and after a takeover

If one company acquires another by issuing shares, its EPS will go up or down according to the P/E ratio at which the target company has been bought.

(a)   If the **target company's shares** are bought at a **higher P/E ratio** than the predator company's shares, the **predator company's shareholders** will suffer a **fall in EPS**.

(b)   If the **target company's shares** are **valued at a lower P/E ratio**, the **predator company's shareholders** will benefit from a **rise in EPS**.

Example: mergers and takeovers (1)

Giant takes over Tiddler by offering two shares in Giant for one share in Tiddler. Details about each company are as follows:

	Giant	Tiddler
Number of shares	2,800,000	100,000
Market value per share	£4	–
Annual earnings	£560,000	£50,000
EPS	20p	50p
P/E ratio	20	

By offering two shares in Giant worth £4 each for one share in Tiddler, the valuation placed on each Tiddler share is £8, and with Tiddler's EPS of 50p, this implies that Tiddler would be acquired on a P/E ratio of 16. This is lower than the P/E ratio of Giant, which is 20.

If the acquisition produces no synergy, and there is no growth in the earnings of either Giant or its new subsidiary Tiddler, then the EPS of Giant would still be higher than before, because Tiddler was bought on a lower P/E ratio. The combined group's results would be as follows.

	Giant group
Number of shares (2,800,000 + 200,000)	3,000,000
Annual earnings (560,000 + 50,000)	610,000
EPS	20.33p

If the P/E ratio is still 20, the market value per share would be £4.07, which is 7p more than the pre-takeover price.

The process of buying a company with a higher P/E in order to boost your own P/E is known as **bootstrapping**. Whether the stock market is fooled by this process is debatable. The P/E ratio is likely to fall after the takeover in the absence of synergistic or other gains.

Example: mergers and takeovers (2)

Redwood agrees to acquire the shares of Hawthorn in a share exchange arrangement. The agreed P/E ratio for Hawthorn's shares is 15.

	Redwood	Hawthorn
Number of shares	3,000,000	100,000
Market price per share	£2	–
Earnings	£600,000	£120,000
P/E ratio	10	

The EPS of Hawthorn is £1.20, and so the agreed price per share will be £1.20 × 15 = £18. In a share exchange agreement, Redwood would have to issue nine new shares (valued at £2 each) to acquire each share in Hawthorn, and so a total of 900,000 new shares must be issued to complete the takeover.

After the takeover, the enlarged company would have 3,900,000 shares in issue and, assuming no earnings growth, total earnings of £720,000. This would give an EPS of:

$$\frac{£720,000}{3,900,000} = 18.5p$$

The pre-takeover EPS of Redwood was 20p, and so the EPS would fall. This is because Hawthorne has been bought on a higher P/E ratio (15 compared with Redwood's 10).

2.3 Buying companies on a higher P/E ratio, but with profit growth

Buying companies on a higher P/E ratio will result in a fall in EPS unless there is **profit growth** to offset this fall. For example, suppose that Starving acquires Bigmeal, by offering two shares in Starving for three shares in Bigmeal. Details of each company are as follows:

	Starving	Bigmeal
Number of shares	5,000,000	3,000,000
Value per share	£6	£4
Annual earnings		
Current	£2,000,000	£600,000
Next year	£2,200,000	£950,000
EPS	40p	20p
P/E ratio	15	20

Starving is acquiring Bigmeal on a higher P/E ratio, and it is only the profit growth in the acquired subsidiary that gives the enlarged Starving group its growth in EPS.

	Starving group
Number of shares (5,000,000 + 2,000,000)	7,000,000
Earnings	
If no profit growth (2,000,000 + 600,000) £2,600,000	EPS would have been 37.24p
With profit growth (2,200,000 + 950,000) £3,150,000	EPS will be 45p

If an acquisition strategy involves buying companies on a higher P/E ratio, it is therefore essential for continuing EPS growth that the acquired companies offer prospects of strong profit growth.

2.4 Further points to consider: net assets per share and the quality of earnings

You might think that dilution of earnings must be avoided at all cost. However, there are three cases where a dilution of earnings might be accepted on an acquisition if there were other advantages to be gained.

(a) **Earnings growth** may hide the dilution in EPS as above.

(b) A company might be willing to accept earnings dilution if the **quality of the acquired company's earnings** is superior to that of the acquiring company.

(c) A trading company with high earnings, but with few assets, may want to increase its assets base by acquiring a company which is strong in assets but weak in earnings so that assets and earnings get more into line with each other. In this case, **dilution in earnings is compensated for by an increase in net asset backing.**

Example: mergers and takeovers (3)

Intangible has an issued capital of 2,000,000 £1 ordinary shares. Net assets (excluding goodwill) are £2,500,000 and annual earnings average £1,500,000. The company is valued by the stock market on a P/E ratio of 8. Tangible has an issued capital of 1,000,000 ordinary shares. Net assets (excluding goodwill) are £3,500,000 and annual earnings average £400,000. The shareholders of Tangible accept an all-equity offer from Intangible valuing each share in Tangible at £4.

Calculate Intangible's earnings and assets per share before and after the acquisition of Tangible.

Solution

(a) Before the acquisition of Tangible, the position is as follows:

$$\text{Earnings per share (EPS)} = \frac{£1,500,000}{2,000,000} = 75\text{p}$$

$$\text{Assets per share (APS)} = \frac{£2,500,000}{2,000,000} = £1.25$$

(b) Tangible's EPS figure is 40p (£400,000 ÷ 1,000,000), and the company is being bought on a multiple of 10 at £4 per share. As the takeover consideration is being satisfied by shares, Intangible's earnings will be diluted because Intangible is valuing Tangible on a higher multiple of earnings than itself. Intangible will have to issue 666,667 shares valued at £6 each (earnings of 75p per share at a multiple of 8) to satisfy the £4,000,000 consideration. The results for Intangible will be as follows:

$$\text{EPS} = \frac{£1,900,000}{2,666,667} = 71.25\text{p (3.75p lower than the previous 75p)}$$

$$\text{APS} = \frac{£6,000,000}{2,666,667} = £2.25 \text{ (£1 higher than the previous £1.25)}$$

If Intangible is still valued on the stock market on a P/E ratio of 8, the share price should fall by approximately 30p (8 × 3.75p, the fall in EPS) but because the asset backing has been increased substantially the company will probably now be valued on a higher P/E ratio than 8.

The shareholders in Tangible would receive 666,667 shares in Intangible in exchange for their current 1,000,000 shares; that is, two shares in Intangible for every three shares currently held.

(a) *Earnings*

	£
Three shares in Tangible earn (3 × 40p)	1.200
Two shares in Intangible will earn (2 × 71.25p)	1.425
Increase in earnings, per three shares held in Tangible	0.225

(b) *Assets*

	£
Three shares in Tangible have an asset backing of (3 × £3.5)	10.50
Two shares in Intangible will have an asset backing of (2 × £2.25)	4.50
Loss in asset backing, per three shares held in Tangible	6.00

The shareholders in Tangible would be trading asset backing for an increase in earnings.

2.5 Valuation using post-merger dividends or cash flows

An alternative method to using the P/E ratios, is to consider the dividends or cash flows of the merged company. Reliable **cash flow estimates** should take into account the effects of the merger such as economies of scale and greater combined power.

2.5.1 Dividend method

The steps are as follows:

- Estimate the **initial dividends** of the **combined company** and the **dividend growth rate.**

- Estimate the **new cost of capital**; if the cost of the two old companies differs significantly, some sort of weighted average method will be required.

- Calculate the **value of the combined company** using the dividend valuation model.

- Compare the **value of the combined company** with the **pre-merger value** of the acquirer. The excess is the value of the target.

In practice, the level of dividends and dividend cover expected by shareholders in both companies may create difficulties before the merger or takeover is agreed.

2.5.2 Cash flow method

The steps here are as follows:

- Estimate the **cash flows of the combined company**, including the acquired's, the acquirer's and the additional cash flows arising from the beneficial effects of the merger.

- Estimate the **new cost of capital** as above.

- Calculate the **net present value** of the combined cash flows.

- Compare the **value of the combined cash flows** with the acquirer's cash flows if no merger took place. The excess is the value of the target.

| Question 13.1 | Bid terms |

Learning outcomes: C(3)(a),(b)

Themis is a fast-growing business which operates a chain of motels situated in motorway service stations throughout the UK. The company is committed to an aggressive strategy of expansion through acquisition and has recently made a bid for the shares of Arethusa that operates a chain of restaurants also situated in motorway service stations throughout the UK. Themis has offered 1 share for every 3 shares held in Arethusa. The following financial data concerning each company is available.

STATEMENTS OF COMPREHENSIVE INCOME FOR THE YEAR ENDED 31 MAY 20X9

	Themis	Arethusa
	£m	£m
Revenue	564	242
Profit from operations	181	41
Finance costs	9	2
Net profit before taxation	172	39
Taxation	45	11
Net profit after taxation	127	28
Dividends	16	24
Accumulated profits	111	4

STATEMENT OF FINANCIAL POSITION AS AT 31 MAY 20X9

	Themis	Arethusa
	£m	£m
Non-current assets	261	117
Net current assets	82	45
	343	162
Less: payables due beyond one year	62	6
	281	156
Capital and reserves		
Ordinary share capital	150	50
Accumulated profits	131	106
	281	156

The ordinary share capital of Themis consists of £0.50 shares and the ordinary share capital of Arethusa consists of £1 shares. The Board of Directors of Themis believes there is a strong synergy between the two businesses which will lead to an increase in after-tax profits of £15m per year following acquisition.

Share prices for each company in recent years have been as follows:

Year ended 31 May	20X6	20X7	20X8	20X9 (ie present)
	£	£	£	£
Themis	3.50	4.80	6.90	9.30
Arethusa	2.40	3.20	3.40	2.90

A shareholder in Arethusa has expressed concern over the bid. He points out that, following acquisition, the annual dividends are likely to be lower as Themis normally pays small dividends. As the shareholder relies on dividend income to cover his living expenses, he is concerned that he will be worse off following acquisition of Arethusa. He also believes that the price offered for the shares of Arethusa is too low.

Required

(a)   Calculate:

   (i)   The total value of the proposed bid

   (ii)   The earnings per share of Themis following the successful takeover of Arethusa

   (iii)   The share price of Themis following the takeover, assuming the price-earnings ratio of the company is maintained and the synergy achieved

(b)   Discuss the bid from the viewpoint of the shareholders of Arethusa and include in your discussion the shareholder's concerns mentioned above.

Question 13.2   Post-merger valuation

Learning outcomes: C(3)(a),(b)

Nyasa is committed to increasing its earnings per share through a policy of acquisition. The company has acquired several businesses in the past five years and is now considering the acquisition of Turkana. Financial information relating to Nyasa and Turkana is as follows:

ABBREVIATED STATEMENTS OF CONSOLIDATED INCOME FOR THE YEAR ENDED 30 APRIL 20X1

	Nyasa	Turkana
	£m	£m
Revenue	120.4	80.9
Profit from operations	15.8	8.4
Finance costs	9.5	3.8
Profit before taxation	6.3	4.6
Taxation	2.1	1.6
Profit after taxation	4.2	3.0

STATEMENTS OF FINANCIAL POSITION AS AT 30 APRIL 20X1

	Nyasa	Turkana
	£m	£m
Non-current assets	50.5	28.6
Net current assets	12.4	8.2
	62.9	36.8
Less Payables due beyond one year	4.6	3.1
	58.3	33.7
Capital and reserves		
£1 Ordinary shares	40.0	12.0
Reserves	18.3	21.7
	58.3	33.7
Price/earnings ratio prior to bid	18	14

Nyasa has offered the shareholders of Turkana four shares in Nyasa for every three shares held. After-tax savings in overheads of £1.5m per annum are expected from the acquisition of Turkana.

Required

(a)   Calculate:

      (i)   The total value of the proposed bid

      (ii)   The earnings per share for Nyasa following the successful takeover of Turkana

      (iii)   The share price of Nyasa following the takeover, assuming that the price/earnings ratio is maintained and the savings achieved

(b)   Calculate the effect of the proposed acquisition from the perspective of a shareholder who holds 3,000 ordinary shares in:

      (i)   Nyasa
      (ii)   Turkana

Comment on your results.

Section summary

Shareholders of both the companies involved in a merger will be sensitive to the effect of the merger on **share prices** and **earnings per share**.

3 Post-acquisition integration

Introduction

Many takeovers fail to achieve their full potential because of lack of attention paid to what happens after the takeover. In this section we look at what problems occur and how they can be addressed.

3.1 Problems of integration

Failures of takeovers often result from **inadequate integration** of the companies after the takeover has taken place. There is a tendency for senior management to devote their energies to the next acquisition rather than to the newly acquired firm. The particular approach adopted will depend upon the **culture** of the organisation as well as the **nature** of the company acquired and **how it fits** into the amalgamated organisation (eg horizontally, vertically, or as part of a diversified conglomerate).

3.2 Drucker's Golden Rules

P F Drucker has suggested Five Golden Rules for the process of post-acquisition integration.

Rule 1	Within a year, the acquiring company should put top **M**anagement with relevant skills in place.
Rule 2	The acquiring company must ensure it can **A**dd value to the target (that is, ensure targets are set, communicated to customers and synergies are realised).
Rule 3	The acquiring company must show **R**espect to the products, management and track record of the target.
Rule 4	Ensure there is a **C**ommon core of unity (for example take actions to ensure systems are compatible).
Rule 5	Strategies should be developed for **H**olding on to existing staff (for example, loyalty bonuses).

Remember the mnemonic '**MARCH**'.

3.3 Jones's Integration Sequence

C S Jones has proposed a five-step integration sequence.

Decide on and communicate initial reporting relationships

This will reduce uncertainty. The issue of whether to impose relationships at the beginning, although these may be subject to change, or to wait for the organisation structure to become more established (see Step 5 below) needs to be addressed.

Achieve rapid control of key factors

This will require access to the right accurate information. Control of information channels needs to be gained without dampening motivation. Note that it may have been poor financial controls which led to the demise of the acquired company.

Resource audit

Both physical and human assets are examined in order to get a clear picture. This includes examining the roles of each of the main stakeholders (staff, customers and suppliers) and evaluating the products sold.

Redefine corporate objectives and develop strategic plans

These should harmonise with those of the acquirer company as appropriate, depending on the degree of autonomy managers are to have to develop their own systems of management control.

Revise the organisational structure

Successful post-acquisition integration requires careful management of the human factor to avoid loss of motivation. Employees in the acquired company will want to know how they and their company are to fit into the structure and strategy of the amalgamated enterprise. Morale can, hopefully, be preserved by **reducing uncertainty** and by providing appropriate performance incentives, staff benefits and career prospects. If redundancies are felt to be necessary, voluntary redundancies should be offered first.

3.4 Service contracts for key personnel

When the target company employs certain key personnel, on whom the success of the company has been based, the predator company might want to ensure that these key people do not leave as soon as the takeover occurs.

To do this, it might be necessary to insist as a condition of the offer that the key people should agree to sign **service contracts**, tying them to the company for a certain time (perhaps three years). Service contracts would have to be attractive to the employees concerned, perhaps through offering a high salary or other benefits such as share options in the predator company. Where key personnel are shareholders, they might be bound not to sell shares for a period.

3.5 Merging systems

The degree to which the information, control and reporting systems of the two companies involved in a takeover are merged will depend to some extent upon the **degree of integration** envisaged. There are two extremes of integration:

(a) **Complete absorption of the target firm**, where the cultures, operational procedures and organisational structures of the two firms are to be fused together. This approach is most suitable where significant cost reductions are expected to be achieved through economies of scale, and combining marketing and distribution effort to enhance revenues.

(b) **The preservation approach**, where the target company is to become an independent subsidiary of the holding company. This would be most beneficial for the merger of companies with very different products, markets and cultures.

In the circumstances of a complete absorption, the two companies will become one, and thus a **common operational system** must be developed. The acquiring company's management should not immediately impose their own systems upon the target company's operations, assuming them to be superior. This is likely to **alienate** acquired employees.

It is probably best to **use the system already in place** in the acquired company, initially supplemented by requests for additional reports felt to be immediately necessary for adequate information and control flows between the two management bodies. As the integration process proceeds, the best aspects of each of the companies' systems will be identified and a **common system developed.**

Where the two companies are to operate independently, it is likely that some changes will be needed to financial control procedures to get the two group companies in line. Essentially, however, the target company's management may **continue with their own cultures, operations and systems.**

Exam alert

Any post-merger value enhancing strategies must be relevant to the entities involved.

3.6 Failure of mergers and takeovers

The aim of any takeover will be to **generate value for the acquiring shareholders.** Where this does not happen, there may be a number of reasons, including **a strategic plan that fails to produce the benefits expected,** or **over-optimism** about future market conditions, operating synergies and the amount of time and money required to make the merger work.

A third recurring reason for failure is **poor integration management**, in particular:

(a)   **Inflexibility.** This can happen in the application of integration plans drawn up prior to the event. Once the takeover has happened, management must be prepared to adapt plans in the light of changed circumstances or inaccurate prior information.

(b)   **Poor man management.** Lack of communication of goals and future prospects of employees, and failure to recognise and deal with the uncertainty and anxiety invariably felt by them.

Section summary

Many takeovers fail to achieve their full potential because of lack of attention paid to **post-acquisition integration**. A clear programme should be in place, designed to redefine objectives and strategy, and take appropriate care of the human element.

4   Exit strategies

Introduction

An **exit strategy** is a way to terminate ownership of a company or the operation of part of the company. You need to be able to discuss the types of exit strategy that are available and their implications.

4.1 Divestment

KEY TERM

A DIVESTMENT is disposal of part of its activities by an entity.   *(CIMA Official Terminology)*

Mergers and takeovers are not inevitably good strategy for a business. In some circumstances, strategies of internal growth, no growth or even some form of divestment might be preferable.

Businesses must though have regard for the impact on:

- The **performance** of the company

- **Workforce morale** and performance

- **Stock market reaction** (the market dislikes uncertainty so must be given as much information as soon as possible)

4.2 Demergers

A **demerger** is the opposite of a merger. It is the **splitting up of a corporate body into two or more separate and independent bodies.** For example, the ABC Group might demerge by splitting into two independently operating companies, AB and C. Existing shareholders are given a stake in each of the new separate companies.

Demerging, in its strictest sense, stops short of selling out, but is an attempt to ensure that share prices reflect the true value of the underlying operations. In large diversified conglomerates, so many different businesses are combined into one organisation that it becomes difficult for analysts to understand them fully.

In addition, a management running ten businesses instead of two could be seen to lose some focus.

The potential disadvantages with demergers are as follows:

(a)   **Economies of scale may be lost**, where the demerged parts of the business had operations in common to which economies of scale applied.

(b)   The smaller companies which result from the demerger will have **lower revenue, profits and status** than the group before the demerger.

(c)   There may be **higher overhead costs** as a percentage of **revenue**, resulting from (b).

(d)   The ability to **raise extra finance**, especially debt finance, to support new investments and expansion may be **reduced**.

(e)   **Vulnerability** to takeover may be **increased**.

CASE STUDY

In March 2010, Liberty International, the UK real estate company, confirmed the demerger of its central London properties from its regional shopping centres. Two new companies – Capital Shopping Centres and Capital & Counties – are expected to be listed on the London Stock Exchange as early as summer 2010.

David Fischel, Liberty's chief executive, commented:

'The Capital & Counties business … [is] a very different business to the shopping centre business … The demerger will enable Capital Shopping Centres and Capital & Counties to achieve greater value for shareholders over time than the current Liberty International would as one combined business.'

(Source: Financial Times, 9 March 2010)

4.3 Sell-offs

A **sell-off** is a form of **divestment** involving the sale of part of a company to a third party, usually another company. Generally, cash will be received in exchange.

A company may carry out a sell-off for one of the following reasons:

(a)   As **part of its strategic planning** it has decided to restructure, concentrating management effort on particular parts of the business. Control problems may be reduced if peripheral activities are sold off.

(b) It **wishes to sell off a part of its business** which makes losses, and so to improve the company's future reported consolidated profit performance. This may be in the form of a management buyout (MBO) – see below.

(c) In order to **protect the rest of the business from takeover**, it may choose to sell a part of the business which is particularly attractive to a buyer.

(d) The company may be **short of cash**.

(e) A subsidiary with **high risk** in its operating cash flows could be **sold**, so as to reduce the business risk of the group as a whole.

(f) A **subsidiary** could be **sold at a profit**. Some companies have specialised in taking over large groups of companies, and then selling off parts of the newly acquired groups, so that the proceeds of sales more than pay for the original takeovers.

A sell-off may, however, **disrupt** the rest of the organisation, especially if key players within the organisation disappear as a result.

4.4 Liquidations

The extreme form of a sell-off is where the entire business is sold off in a **liquidation**. In a voluntary dissolution, the shareholders might decide to close the whole business, sell off all the assets and distribute net funds raised to shareholders.

CASE STUDY

Woolworths, the UK high street chain, went into administration in November 2008 with debts of £385m. The administrator, Deloitte, sold off the assets (including inventory and fixtures and fittings) at discount prices.

4.5 Spin-offs

In a **spin-off**, a new company is created whose shares are owned by the shareholders of the original company which is making the distribution of assets. There is no change in the ownership of assets, as the shareholders own the same proportion of shares in the new company as they did in the old company. Assets of the part of the business to be separated off are transferred into the new company, which will usually have different management from the old company. In more complex cases, a spin-off may involve the original company being split into a number of separate companies.

For a number of possible reasons such as those set out below, a spin-off appears generally to meet with favour from stock market investors.

(a) The change may make a **merger or takeover** of some part of the business **easier** in the future, or may protect parts of the business from predators.

(b) There may be **improved efficiency** and **more streamlined management** within the new structure.

(c) It may be **easier** to **see the value of the separated parts** of the business now that they are no longer hidden within a conglomerate.

(d) The **requirements** of **regulatory agencies** might be **met more easily** within the new structure, for example if the agency is able to exercise price control over a particular part of the business which was previously hidden within the conglomerate structure.

(e) After the spin-off, shareholders have the **opportunity to adjust the proportions** of their **holdings** between the different companies created.

CASE STUDY

In April 2012 Chesapeake Energy, the second largest US natural gas producer, filed details of its plan to spin off its oilfield services division via an IPO with an estimated value of $862.5m. This is part of a plan to bolster Chesapeake's finances and to reduce its debt levels.

4.6 Going private

A public company **'goes private'** when a **small group of individuals**, possibly including existing shareholders and/or managers and with or without support from a financial institution, **buys all of the company's shares.** This form of restructuring is relatively common in the US and may involve the shares in the company ceasing to be listed on a stock exchange.

Advantages in going private could include the following:

(a)   The costs of meeting listing requirements can be saved.

(b)   The company is protected from volatility in share prices which financial problems may create.

(c)   The company will be less vulnerable to hostile takeover bids.

(d)   Management can concentrate on the long-term needs of the business rather than the short-term expectations of shareholders.

(e)   Shareholders are likely to be closer to management in a private company, reducing costs arising from the separation of ownership and control (the 'agency problem').

CASE STUDY

The *San Francisco Business Times* reported that several companies were considering going private, particularly young companies with shares under pressure in public markets. Tighter scrutiny of public company finances, together with new federal disclosure laws, had added to the cost of financing through public equity markets. Going private would allow greater flexibility to restructure operations, and a potential increase in value for those companies whose cash at bank or non-current assets were worth far more than the depressed stock market value.

4.7 Management buyouts (MBOs)

KEY TERM

A MANAGEMENT BUYOUT is the purchase of a business from its existing owners by members of the management team, generally in association with a financing institution.   *(CIMA Official Terminology)*

A **management buyout** is the purchase of all or part of a business from its owners by its managers. For example, the directors of a subsidiary company in a group might buy the company from the holding company, with the intention of running it as proprietors of a separate business entity.

(a)   **To the managers,** the buyout would be a method of setting up in business for themselves.

(b)   **To the group**, the buyout would be a method of **divestment**, selling off the subsidiary as a going concern.

A large organisation's board of directors may agree to a management buyout of a subsidiary for any of a number of different reasons:

(a)   The **subsidiary** may be **peripheral** to the group's mainstream activities, and no longer fit in with the group's overall strategy.

(b)   The group may wish to **sell off a loss-making subsidiary**, and a management team may think that it can restore the subsidiary's fortunes.

(c)   The parent company may need to **raise cash quickly**.

(d)   The subsidiary may be part of a **group that has just been taken over** and the new parent company may wish to sell off parts of the group it has just acquired.

(e)   The **best offer price** might come from a **small management group** wanting to arrange a buyout.

(f)   When a group has taken the decision to sell a subsidiary, it will probably **get better co-operation** from the management and employees of the subsidiary if the sale is a management buyout.

A private company's shareholders might agree to sell out to a management team because they need cash, they want to retire, or the business is not profitable enough for them.

4.7.1 The parties to a buyout

There are usually three parties to a management buyout:

(a)   A **management team** wanting to make a buyout; this team ought to have the skills and ability to convince financial backers that it is worth supporting

(b)   **Directors** of a group of companies

(c)   **Financial backers** of the buyout team, who will usually want an equity stake in the bought-out business, because of the **venture capital risk** they are taking (often, several financial backers provide the venture capital for a single buyout)

4.7.2 The role of the venture capitalist

Venture capitalists are far more inclined to fund MBOs, management buy-ins (MBI) and corporate expansion projects than the more risky and relatively costly early stage investments such as start-ups. The minimum investment considered will normally be around £100,000, with average investment of £1 million–£2 million.

While the return required on venture capital for the high-risk, early stage investments may be as high as 80%, where the funding is for a well-established business with sound management, it is more commonly around the 25%–30% mark. This may be achieved by the successful investments, of course there will be many more that fail, and the overall returns on venture capital funds averages out at around 10%–15%.

For MBOs and MBIs the venture capitalist will not necessarily provide the majority of the finance. A £50 million buyout may be funded by, say, £15 million venture capital, £20 million debt finance and £15 million mezzanine debt.

Venture capital funds may require:

- A 20%–30% shareholding
- Special rights to appoint a number of directors
- The company to seek their prior approval for new issues or acquisitions

Venture capitalists generally like to have a predetermined **target exit date,** the point at which they can recoup some or all of their investment in an MBO. At the outset, they will wish to establish various **exit routes**, the possibilities including:

- The sale of shares following a **flotation** on a recognised stock exchange
- The **sale** of the company to another firm
- The **repurchase** of the venture capitalist's shares by the company or its owners
- The sales of the venture capitalist's shares to an **institution** such as an investment trust

4.7.3 The appraisal of proposed buyouts

Management-owned companies seem to achieve better performance probably because of:

- A **favourable buyout price** having been **achieved**
- **Personal motivation and determination**
- **Quicker decision making** and so **more flexibility**
- **Keener decisions** and action on pricing and debt collection
- **Savings in overheads**, eg in contributions to a large head office

However, many management buyouts, once they occur, begin with some redundancies to cut running costs.

An institutional investor (such as a venture capitalist) should evaluate a buyout before deciding whether or not to finance. Aspects of any buyout that ought to be checked are as follows:

(a)   Does the management team have the **full range of management skills** that are needed (for example a technical expert and a finance director)? Does it have the right blend of experience? Does it have the commitment?

(b)   Why is the **company for sale**? The possible reasons for buyouts have already been listed. If the reason is that the parent company wants to get rid of a loss-making subsidiary, what evidence is there to suggest that the company can be made profitable after a buyout?

(c)   What are the **projected profits and cash flows of the business**? The prospective returns must justify the risks involved.

(d)   What is **being bought**? The buyout team might be buying the shares of the company, or only selected assets of the company. Are the assets that are being acquired sufficient for the task? Will more assets have to be bought? When will the existing assets need replacing? How much extra finance would be needed for these asset purchases? Can the company be operated profitably?

(e)   What is **the price**? Is the price right or is it too high?

(f)   What **financial contribution** can be made by members of the management team themselves?

(g)   What are the **exit routes** and when might they be taken?

4.7.4 Problems with buyouts

A common problem with management buyouts is that the managers have little or no experience in **financial management** or **financial accounting**. Managers will also be required to take tough decisions. A good way of approaching the problem is **scenario analysis** addressing the effect of taking a major decision in isolation. However, the results may be painful, including the ditching of long established products.

Other problems are:

(a)   Tax and legal complications

(b)   Difficulties in deciding on a fair price to be paid

(c)   Convincing employees of the need to change working practices or to accept redundancy

(d)   Inadequate resources to finance the maintenance and replacement of tangible non-current assets

(e)   The maintenance of employees' employment or pension rights

(f)   Accepting the board representation requirement that many sources of funds will insist upon

(g)   The loss of key employees if the company moves geographically, or wage rates are decreased too far, or employment conditions are unacceptable in other ways

(h)   Maintaining continuity of relationships with suppliers and customers

(i)   Lack of time to make decisions

4.7.5 Conflicts of interest

In a management buyout there is a potential conflict of interest as management are part of the buyout group of the company. Since they will have internal knowledge of the company, they could use this to their advantage to the lowest price, whereas it would be in the interest of the company to be sold for the highest price or not to be sold at all.

 The issues discussed in this chapter may be very important when you come to take the integrated case study. You may be asked to consider various options including mergers, strategic alliances (and doing nothing)

Section summary

- A **demerger** is the splitting up of corporate bodies into two or more separate bodies, to ensure share prices reflect the true value of underlying operations.

- A **sell-off** is the sale of part of a company to a third party, generally for cash.

- A **spin-off** is the creation of a new company, where the shareholders of the original company own the shares.

- A company **goes private** when a small group of individuals buys all the company's shares. Going private may **decrease costs** and make the company **less vulnerable** to hostile takeover bids.

- A **management buyout** is the purchase of all or part of the business by its managers. Management buyouts can be the best way of maintaining links with a subsidiary, and can ensure the co-operation of management. The main complication with **management buyouts** is obtaining the consent of all parties involved. Venture capital may be an important source of financial backing.

- Management buyouts present a potential conflict of interest between the interests of management and the interests of the company.

Chapter Summary

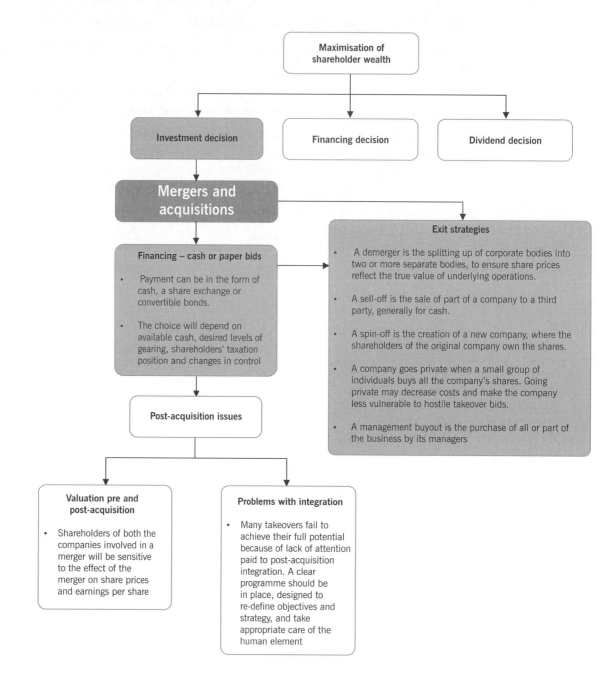

Maximisation of shareholder wealth

Investment decision

Financing decision

Dividend decision

Mergers and acquisitions

Financing – cash or paper bids

- Payment can be in the form of cash, a share exchange or convertible bonds.

- The choice will depend on available cash, desired levels of gearing, shareholders' taxation position and changes in control

Post-acquisition issues

Exit strategies

- A demerger is the splitting up of corporate bodies into two or more separate bodies, to ensure share prices reflect the true value of underlying operations.

- A sell-off is the sale of part of a company to a third party, generally for cash.

- A spin-off is the creation of a new company, where the shareholders of the original company own the shares.

- A company goes private when a small group of individuals buys all the company's shares. Going private may decrease costs and make the company less vulnerable to hostile takeover bids.

- A management buyout is the purchase of all or part of the business by its managers

Valuation pre and post-acquisition

- Shareholders of both the companies involved in a merger will be sensitive to the effect of the merger on share prices and earnings per share

Problems with integration

- Many takeovers fail to achieve their full potential because of lack of attention paid to post-acquisition integration. A clear programme should be in place, designed to re-define objectives and strategy, and take appropriate care of the human element

Quick Quiz

1   What is the name of the arrangement where part of the purchase consideration is only paid when the target company reaches certain performance targets?

2   What are Drucker's Five Golden Rules for post-acquisition integration?

3   If the target company's shares are valued at a lower P/E ratio, the predator company's shareholders will suffer a fall in EPS.

True ☐

False ☐

4   Why might management-owned companies achieve improved performance?

5   What are the main exit routes for a venture capitalist?

Answers to Quick Quiz

1   An earn-out arrangement

2   (1)   Common sense of unity shared by acquirer and acquiree

     (2)   Acquirer should ask 'what can we offer them'?

     (3)   Acquirer should treat products, markets and customers of acquired company with respect

     (4)   Acquiring company should provide top management with relevant skills for managing acquired company within one year

     (5)   Cross-company promotions of staff within one year

3   False. The predator company's shareholders will benefit from a rise in earnings per share.

4   (a)   Personal motivation and determination
     (b)   Quicker and more flexible decision making
     (c)   Keener decisions, eg on pricing
     (d)   Overhead savings

5   •   The sale of shares following a **flotation** on a recognised stock exchange
     •   The **sale** of the company to another firm
     •   The **repurchase** of the venture capitalist's shares by the company or its owners
     •   The sales of the venture capitalist's shares to an **institution** such as an investment trust

Answers to Questions

13.1 Bid terms

(a)   (i)   *Number of shares in Arethusa: 50 million*

            Themis shares issued to acquire Arethusa (1 for 3): 50 million/3 = 16,666,667

            Value of the bid, at £9.30 per Themis share = 16,666,667 × £9.30 = £155 million.

       (ii)

	£m
After-tax profits:	
Themis	127
Arethusa	28
Increase due to synergy	15
Earnings of combined group	170

Number of Themis shares in issue	
Prior to takeover (150 m × £1/50p)	300,000,000
Issued to finance takeover	16,666,667
	316,666,667

            EPS after the takeover = £170 million/316,666,667 shares = 53.7p per share, say 54p per share.

       (iii)   EPS of Themis before the takeover = £127 million/300 million share = 42.3p

            P/E ratio of Themis before the takeover = £9.30/£0.423 = 21.99, say 22.

            Share price of Themis after the takeover = 54p × 22 = £11.88.

(b)   Arethusa shareholders are being offered shares in Themis, currently valued at £9.30 each, in exchange for every three shares they hold in Arethusa, currently valued at (3 × £2.90) £8.70. The offer price represents a **premium** to the current market price of Arethusa shares of just £0.60 per £8.70 of shares, which is about 5%. This **bid premium** seems very low.

The **current share price of Themis** is £9.30, having risen from £6.90 last year. The possibility that the share price will remain at this level (a P/E ratio of 22), or might even rise after the takeover, should be questioned. A fall in the Themis share price of about 5% or more (to less than £8.70) would mean that Arethusa shareholders would suffer a loss by agreeing to the takeover offer.

In contrast, the **current EPS of Arethusa** is (£28 million/50 million shares) 56p and the P/E ratio is therefore just 5.2 (£2.90/56p). There is a very **large difference** between the **P/E ratios** at which the two companies are currently valued, adding weight to the concern that either Themis shares are currently overvalued or Arethusa shares are undervalued by the market.

On the other hand, Arethusa shareholders might take the view that shares in Themis are likely to **rise still further** in value after the takeover. Accepting the offer from Themis would therefore enable them to make a further capital gain after the takeover has occurred.

Arethusa shareholders might want to invest in a company with a **high dividend payout policy**, and so would not want to hold on to their Themis shares after a takeover. If so, they should sell their Themis shares and invest in a different company. Concerns about dividend policy should not affect the response of Arethusa shareholders to the takeover offer.

13.2 Post-merger valuation

(a)   *Workings*

$$\text{Nyasa current EPS} = \frac{\text{Total earnings}}{\text{Number of shares}} = \frac{£4.2\,\text{million}}{40\,\text{million}} = 10.5\text{p}$$

P/E ratio = 18

Current market price of Nyasa shares = 18 × 10.5p = 189p.

$$\text{Turkana current EPS} = \frac{£3.0\,\text{million}}{12\,\text{million shares}} = 25\text{p}$$

P/E ratio = 14

Current price of Turkana shares = 14 × 25p = 350p.

(i)   The bid price is 4 Nyasa shares for every 3 Turkana shares.

This values 3 Turkana shares at (4 × 189p) = 756p.

Bid value per Turkana share = 756p/3 = 252p per share.

The total value of the proposed bid, given 12 million Turkana shares:

12 million × 252p = £30.24 million.

The bid, if successful, would result in the issue of (12 million × 4/3) 16 million new Nyasa shares.

(ii)   Total earnings after takeover

	£m
Nyasa earnings	4.2
Turkana earnings	3.0
Savings from the acquisition	1.5
	8.7

Number of shares (40 million + 16 million)   56m

EPS following the takeover: £8.7 million/56 million = £0.155, ie 15.5p.

(iii)   Share price of Nyasa after the takeover, assuming a P/E ratio of 18:

15.5p × 18 = £2.79

(b)   **Holder of 3,000 shares in Nyasa**

	£
Value of shares before the takeover (× £1.89)	5,670
Value of shares after the takeover (× £2.79)	8,370
Increase in value of investment	2,700

Holder of 3,000 shares in Turkana

	£
Value of 3,000 shares before the takeover (3,000 × £3.50)	10,500
Value of shares after the takeover (4,000 × £2.79)	11,160
Increase in value of investment	660

The takeover would **increase the total value** of the **equity shares** of the companies, on the assumption that a P/E ratio of 18 can be maintained. There are two reasons for this increase in value:

(i)   The earnings of Turkana will be re-rated from a P/E of 14 to a P/E of 18.

(ii)   There will be savings of £1.5 million, adding (× 18) £27 million to equity values.

Under the terms of the current bid, Nyasa shareholders would enjoy an **increase in the value of their investment** by (£2,700/£5,670) almost 50%. Turkana shareholders would also expect some increase in the value of their investment but only by (£660/£10,500) about 6%. Most of the increase in the equity valuation arising from the acquisition would therefore be enjoyed by the Nyasa shareholders.

The estimated increase in the equity valuation is dependent on the assumption of savings of £1.5 million and the assumption that a **P/E ratio of 18** will be **maintained**. If these assumptions turn out to be over-optimistic, the value of Nyasa shares after the takeover will be lower than £2.79, and there would be a serious risk that the value of the investment of Turkana shareholders would fall as a result of the takeover.

The offer from Nyasa is therefore too low, and the directors of Turkana would recommend rejection of the bid on these grounds.

Now try the questions from the Practice Question Bank	**Question**	**Level**
	Section A: 13.1 – 13.3	Practice
	Section B: 8, 9, 10	Practice

APPENDIX 1:
DISCOUNTED CASH FLOW

This appendix is designed to refresh your memory of discounted cash flow techniques. It is essential that you are comfortable with these techniques as they are used in numerous parts of the syllabus. Work through the content and questions carefully to ensure you can do the necessary calculations and are familiar with the terminology used.

1 Discounted cash flow

Discounted cash flow, or **DCF** for short, is an investment appraisal technique which takes into account both the timings of cash flows and also total profitability over a project's life.

Two important points about DCF are as follows.

(a) DCF looks at the **cash flows** of a project, not the accounting profits. Cash flows are considered because they show the costs and benefits of a project when they actually occur and ignore notional costs such as depreciation.

(b) The **timing** of cash flows is taken into account by **discounting them**. The effect of discounting is to give a bigger value per $1 for cash flows that occur earlier: $1 earned after one year will be worth more than $1 earned after two years, which in turn will be worth more than $1 earned after five years, and so on.

1.1 Compounding

Suppose that a company has $10,000 to invest, and wants to earn a return of 10% (compound interest) on its investments. This means that if the $10,000 could be invested at 10%, the value of the investment with interest would build up as follows.

(a) After 1 year $10,000 \times (1.10) = $11,000

(b) After 2 years $10,000 \times (1.10)^2 = $12,100

(c) After 3 years $10,000 \times (1.10)^3 = $13,310 and so on

This is **compounding**. The formula for the future value of an investment plus accumulated interest after n time periods is:

$$FV = PV (1 + r)^n$$

Where   FV   is the future value of the investment with interest

              PV   is the initial or 'present' value of the investment

              r   is the compound rate of return per time period, expressed as a proportion (so 10% = 0.10, 5% = 0.05 and so on)

              n   is the number of time periods

1.2 Discounting

Discounting starts with the future value, and converts a future value to a present value. For example, if a company expects to earn a (compound) rate of return of 10% on its investments, how much would it need to invest now to have the following investments?

(a) $11,000 after 1 year
(b) $12,100 after 2 years
(c) $13,310 after 3 years

The answer is $10,000 in each case, and we can calculate it by discounting. The discounting formula to calculate the present value of a future sum of money at the end of n time periods is:

$$PV = FV \frac{1}{(1+r)^n}$$

(a) After 1 year, $11,000 \times \dfrac{1}{1.10} = \$10,000$

(b) After 2 years, $12,100 \times \dfrac{1}{1.10^2} = \$10,000$

(c) After 3 years, $13,310 \times \dfrac{1}{1.10^3} = \$10,000$

Discounting can be applied to both money receivable and also to money payable at a future date. By discounting all payments and receipts from a capital investment to a present value, they can be compared on a common basis at a value which takes account of when the various cash flows will take place.

1.3 Present value tables

Present value tables are provided in your exam (and in Appendix 2 of this study text), and give the present value factor or **discount factor** for given values of n and r. They can only be used for whole numbers up to 20% and are rounded so lose some accuracy, but they simplify and speed up your calculations.

Look up the discount factor in the table and multiply the value of the cash flow by the discount factor.

(a) Calculate the present value of $60,000 at year 6, if a return of 15% per annum is obtainable.
(b) Calculate the present value of $100,000 at year 5, if a return of 6% per annum is obtainable.

Solution

(a) Present value = 60,000 × 0.432 = $25,920
(b) Present value = 100,000 × 0.747 = $74,700

1.4 Annuity tables

To calculate the present value of a constant annual cash flow, or annuity, we can multiply the annual cash flows by the sum of the discount factors for the relevant years. These total factors are known as **cumulative present value factors** or **annuity factors**. As with 'present value factors of $1 in year n', there are tables for annuity factors, which are shown in Appendix 2 of this text. For example, the cumulative present value factor of $1 per annum for five years at 11% per annum is in the column for 11% and the year 5 row, and is 3.696.

(a) What is the present value of $1,000 in contribution earned each year from years 1–10, when the required return on investment is 11%?

(b) What is the present value of $2,000 costs incurred each year from years 3–6 when the cost of capital is 5%?

Solution

(a) $1,000 × 5.889 = $5,889

(b)

PV of $1 per annum for years 1–6 at 5%	5.076
Less PV of $1 per annum for years 1–2 at 5%	1.859
PV of $1 per annum for years 3–6	3.217

PV = $2,000 × 3.217 = $6,434

1.5 Annual cash flows in perpetuity

You need to know how to calculate the cumulative present value of $1 per annum for every year in perpetuity (that is, forever).

When the cost of capital is r, the cumulative PV of $1 per annum in perpetuity is **$1/r**.

For example, the PV of $1 per annum in perpetuity at a discount rate of 10% would be $1/0.10 = $10.

Similarly, the PV of $1 per annum in perpetuity at a discount rate of 15% would be $1/0.15 = $6.67 and at a discount rate of 20% it would be $1/0.20 = $5.

2 The net present value method

The NPV method compares the **present value** of all the **cash inflows** from an investment with the **present value** of all the **cash outflows** from an investment. The NPV is thus calculated as the PV of **cash inflows** minus the PV of **cash outflows**.

NPV	
NPV positive	Return from investment's cash inflows in excess of cost of capital ⇒ undertake project
NPV negative	Return from investment's cash inflows below cost of capital ⇒ don't undertake project
NPV 0	Return from investment's cash inflows same as cost of capital

2.1 Example: NPV

A company is considering a capital investment, where the estimated cash flows are as follows.

Year	Cash flow $
0 (ie now)	(100,000)
1	60,000
2	80,000
3	40,000
4	30,000

The company's cost of capital is 15%. You are required to calculate the NPV of the project and to assess whether it should be undertaken.

Solution

Year	Cash flow $	Discount factor @ 15%	Present value $
0	(100,000)	1.000	(100,000)
1	60,000	0.870	52,200
2	80,000	0.756	60,480
3	40,000	0.658	26,320
4	30,000	0.572	17,160
		NPV =	56,160

Note. The discount factor for any cash flow 'now' (year 0) is always = 1, regardless of what the cost of capital is. The PV of cash inflows exceeds the PV of cash outflows by $56,160, which means that the project will earn a DCF yield in excess of 15%. It should therefore be undertaken.

2.2 Timing of cash flows: conventions used in DCF

Discounted cash flow applies discounting arithmetic to the relevant costs and benefits of an investment project. Discounting, which reduces the value of future cash flows to a present value equivalent, is clearly concerned with the timing of the cash flows. As a general rule, the following guidelines may be applied.

(a) A cash outlay to be incurred at the beginning of an investment project (**'now'**) occurs in **year 0**. The present value of $1 now, in year 0, is $1 regardless of the value of r.

(b) A cash outlay, saving or inflow which occurs **during the course of a time period** (say, one year) is assumed to occur all at once **at the end of the time period** (at the end of the year). Receipts of $10,000 during year 1 are therefore taken to occur at the end of year 1.

(c) A cash outlay or receipt which occurs **at the beginning of a time period** (say at the beginning of one year) is taken to occur **at the end of the previous year**. Therefore a cash outlay of $5,000 at the beginning of year 2 is taken to occur at the end of year 1.

3 The internal rate of return method

The **internal rate of return (IRR)** method is to calculate the **exact DCF rate of return** which the project is expected to achieve, in other words the rate at which the **NPV is zero**. If the expected rate of return (the IRR or DCF yield) **exceeds** a **target rate** of return, the project would be worth undertaking (ignoring risk and uncertainty factors).

To calculate the IRR.

 Calculate the net present value using a 10% discount rate

 Calculate the NPV using a second discount rate

    (a) If the NPV is **positive**, use a second rate that is **greater** than the first rate
    (b) If the NPV is **negative**, use a second rate that is **less** than the first rate

 Use the two NPV values to **estimate the IRR**. The formula to apply is as follows:

$$IRR \approx a + \left(\left(\frac{NPV_a}{NPV_a - NPV_b} \right)(b-a) \right)\%$$

Where   a   =   the lower of the two rates of return used
          b   =   the higher of the two rates of return used
      NPV_a =   the NPV obtained using rate a
      NPV_b =   the NPV obtained using rate b

3.1 Example: the IRR method

A company is trying to decide whether to buy a machine for $80,000 which will save costs of $20,000 per annum for 5 years and which will have a resale value of $10,000 at the end of year 5. If it is the company's policy to undertake projects only if they are expected to yield a DCF return of 10% or more, ascertain whether this project should be undertaken.

Solution

 STEP 1 Calculate the first NPV, using the company's cost of capital of 10%

Year	Cash flow $	PV factor 10%	PV of cash flow $
0	(80,000)	1.000	(80,000)
1–5	20,000	3.791	75,820
5	10,000	0.621	6,210
		NPV =	2,030

This is positive, which means that the IRR is more than 10%.

STEP 2 Calculate the second NPV, using a rate that is **greater** than the first rate, as the first rate gave a positive answer.

Suppose we try 12%.

Year	Cash flow $	PV factor 12%	PV of cash flow $
0	(80,000)	1.000	(80,000)
1–5	20,000	3.605	72,100
5	10,000	0.567	5,670
		NPV =	(2,230)

This is fairly close to zero and **negative**. The IRR is therefore greater than 10% (positive NPV of $2,030) but less than 12% (negative NPV of $2,230).

 STEP 3 Use the two NPV values to estimate the IRR.

The interpolation method assumes that the NPV rises in linear fashion between the two NPVs close to 0. The IRR is therefore assumed to be on a straight line between NPV = $2,030 at 10% and NPV = –$2,230 at 12%.

Using the formula

$$IRR \approx a + \left(\left(\frac{NPV_a}{NPV_a - NPV_b}\right)(b-a)\right)\%$$

$$IRR \approx 10 + \left[\frac{2,030}{2,030 + 2,230} \times (12-10)\right]\% = 10.95\%, \text{ say } 11\%$$

If it is company policy to undertake investments which are expected to yield 10% or more, this project would be undertaken.

APPENDIX 2: MATHEMATICAL TABLES AND EXAM FORMULAE

Please check the CIMA website for the latest information on what information will be provided in the exams.

PRESENT VALUE TABLE

Present value of 1.00 unit of currency ie $(1+r)^{-n}$ where r = interest rate, n = number of periods until payment or receipt.

Periods (n)	\multicolumn{10}{c}{Interest rates (r)}
	1%	2%	3%	4%	5%	6%	7%	8%	9%	10%
1	0.990	0.980	0.971	0.962	0.952	0.943	0.935	0.926	0.917	0.909
2	0.980	0.961	0.943	0.925	0.907	0.890	0.873	0.857	0.842	0.826
3	0.971	0.942	0.915	0.889	0.864	0.840	0.816	0.794	0.772	0.751
4	0.961	0.924	0.888	0.855	0.823	0.792	0.763	0.735	0.708	0.683
5	0.951	0.906	0.863	0.822	0.784	0.747	0.713	0.681	0.650	0.621
6	0.942	0.888	0.837	0.790	0.746	0.705	0.666	0.630	0.596	0.564
7	0.933	0.871	0.813	0.760	0.711	0.665	0.623	0.583	0.547	0.513
8	0.923	0.853	0.789	0.731	0.677	0.627	0.582	0.540	0.502	0.467
9	0.914	0.837	0.766	0.703	0.645	0.592	0.544	0.500	0.460	0.424
10	0.905	0.820	0.744	0.676	0.614	0.558	0.508	0.463	0.422	0.386
11	0.896	0.804	0.722	0.650	0.585	0.527	0.475	0.429	0.388	0.350
12	0.887	0.788	0.701	0.625	0.557	0.497	0.444	0.397	0.356	0.319
13	0.879	0.773	0.681	0.601	0.530	0.469	0.415	0.368	0.326	0.290
14	0.870	0.758	0.661	0.577	0.505	0.442	0.388	0.340	0.299	0.263
15	0.861	0.743	0.642	0.555	0.481	0.417	0.362	0.315	0.275	0.239
16	0.853	0.728	0.623	0.534	0.458	0.394	0.339	0.292	0.252	0.218
17	0.844	0.714	0.605	0.513	0.436	0.371	0.317	0.270	0.231	0.198
18	0.836	0.700	0.587	0.494	0.416	0.350	0.296	0.250	0.212	0.180
19	0.828	0.686	0.570	0.475	0.396	0.331	0.277	0.232	0.194	0.164
20	0.820	0.673	0.554	0.456	0.377	0.312	0.258	0.215	0.178	0.149

Periods (n)	\multicolumn{10}{c}{Interest rates (r)}
	11%	12%	13%	14%	15%	16%	17%	18%	19%	20%
1	0.901	0.893	0.885	0.877	0.870	0.862	0.855	0.847	0.840	0.833
2	0.812	0.797	0.783	0.769	0.756	0.743	0.731	0.718	0.706	0.694
3	0.731	0.712	0.693	0.675	0.658	0.641	0.624	0.609	0.593	0.579
4	0.659	0.636	0.613	0.592	0.572	0.552	0.534	0.516	0.499	0.482
5	0.593	0.567	0.543	0.519	0.497	0.476	0.456	0.437	0.419	0.402
6	0.535	0.507	0.480	0.456	0.432	0.410	0.390	0.370	0.352	0.335
7	0.482	0.452	0.425	0.400	0.376	0.354	0.333	0.314	0.296	0.279
8	0.434	0.404	0.376	0.351	0.327	0.305	0.285	0.266	0.249	0.233
9	0.391	0.361	0.333	0.308	0.284	0.263	0.243	0.225	0.209	0.194
10	0.352	0.322	0.295	0.270	0.247	0.227	0.208	0.191	0.176	0.162
11	0.317	0.287	0.261	0.237	0.215	0.195	0.178	0.162	0.148	0.135
12	0.286	0.257	0.231	0.208	0.187	0.168	0.152	0.137	0.124	0.112
13	0.258	0.229	0.204	0.182	0.163	0.145	0.130	0.116	0.104	0.093
14	0.232	0.205	0.181	0.160	0.141	0.125	0.111	0.099	0.088	0.078
15	0.209	0.183	0.160	0.140	0.123	0.108	0.095	0.084	0.074	0.065
16	0.188	0.163	0.141	0.123	0.107	0.093	0.081	0.071	0.062	0.054
17	0.170	0.146	0.125	0.108	0.093	0.080	0.069	0.060	0.052	0.045
18	0.153	0.130	0.111	0.095	0.081	0.069	0.059	0.051	0.044	0.038
19	0.138	0.116	0.098	0.083	0.070	0.060	0.051	0.043	0.037	0.031
20	0.124	0.104	0.087	0.073	0.061	0.051	0.043	0.037	0.031	0.026

CUMULATIVE PRESENT VALUE TABLE

This table shows the present value of 1.00 unit of currency per annum, receivable or payable at the end

of each year for *n* years $\dfrac{1-(1+r)^{-n}}{r}$

Periods (n)	Interest rates (r)									
	1%	2%	3%	4%	5%	6%	7%	8%	9%	10%
1	0.990	0.980	0.971	0.962	0.952	0.943	0.935	0.926	0.917	0.909
2	1.970	1.942	1.913	1.886	1.859	1.833	1.808	1.783	1.759	1.736
3	2.941	2.884	2.829	2.775	2.723	2.673	2.624	2.577	2.531	2.487
4	3.902	3.808	3.717	3.630	3.546	3.465	3.387	3.312	3.240	3.170
5	4.853	4.713	4.580	4.452	4.329	4.212	4.100	3.993	3.890	3.791
6	5.795	5.601	5.417	5.242	5.076	4.917	4.767	4.623	4.486	4.355
7	6.728	6.472	6.230	6.002	5.786	5.582	5.389	5.206	5.033	4.868
8	7.652	7.325	7.020	6.733	6.463	6.210	5.971	5.747	5.535	5.335
9	8.566	8.162	7.786	7.435	7.108	6.802	6.515	6.247	5.995	5.759
10	9.471	8.983	8.530	8.111	7.722	7.360	7.024	6.710	6.418	6.145
11	10.368	9.787	9.253	8.760	8.306	7.887	7.499	7.139	6.805	6.495
12	11.255	10.575	9.954	9.385	8.863	8.384	7.943	7.536	7.161	6.814
13	12.134	11.348	10.635	9.986	9.394	8.853	8.358	7.904	7.487	7.103
14	13.004	12.106	11.296	10.563	9.899	9.295	8.745	8.244	7.786	7.367
15	13.865	12.849	11.938	11.118	10.380	9.712	9.108	8.559	8.061	7.606
16	14.718	13.578	12.561	11.652	10.838	10.106	9.447	8.851	8.313	7.824
17	15.562	14.292	13.166	12.166	11.274	10.477	9.763	9.122	8.544	8.022
18	16.398	14.992	13.754	12.659	11.690	10.828	10.059	9.372	8.756	8.201
19	17.226	15.679	14.324	13.134	12.085	11.158	10.336	9.604	8.950	8.365
20	18.046	16.351	14.878	13.590	12.462	11.470	10.594	9.818	9.129	8.514

Periods (n)	Interest rates (r)									
	11%	12%	13%	14%	15%	16%	17%	18%	19%	20%
1	0.901	0.893	0.885	0.877	0.870	0.862	0.855	0.847	0.840	0.833
2	1.713	1.690	1.668	1.647	1.626	1.605	1.585	1.566	1.547	1.528
3	2.444	2.402	2.361	2.322	2.283	2.246	2.210	2.174	2.140	2.106
4	3.102	3.037	2.974	2.914	2.855	2.798	2.743	2.690	2.639	2.589
5	3.696	3.605	3.517	3.433	3.352	3.274	3.199	3.127	3.058	2.991
6	4.231	4.111	3.998	3.889	3.784	3.685	3.589	3.498	3.410	3.326
7	4.712	4.564	4.423	4.288	4.160	4.039	3.922	3.812	3.706	3.605
8	5.146	4.968	4.799	4.639	4.487	4.344	4.207	4.078	3.954	3.837
9	5.537	5.328	5.132	4.946	4.772	4.607	4.451	4.303	4.163	4.031
10	5.889	5.650	5.426	5.216	5.019	4.833	4.659	4.494	4.339	4.192
11	6.207	5.938	5.687	5.453	5.234	5.029	4.836	4.656	4.486	4.327
12	6.492	6.194	5.918	5.660	5.421	5.197	4.988	4.793	4.611	4.439
13	6.750	6.424	6.122	5.842	5.583	5.342	5.118	4.910	4.715	4.533
14	6.982	6.628	6.302	6.002	5.724	5.468	5.229	5.008	4.802	4.611
15	7.191	6.811	6.462	6.142	5.847	5.575	5.324	5.092	4.876	4.675
16	7.379	6.974	6.604	6.265	5.954	5.668	5.405	5.162	4.938	4.730
17	7.549	7.120	6.729	6.373	6.047	5.749	5.475	5.222	4.990	4.775
18	7.702	7.250	6.840	6.467	6.128	5.818	5.534	5.273	5.033	4.812
19	7.839	7.366	6.938	6.550	6.198	5.877	5.584	5.316	5.070	4.843
20	7.963	7.469	7.025	6.623	6.259	5.929	5.628	5.353	5.101	4.870

FORMULAE

DVM

$$P_0 = \frac{d_1}{k_e - g}$$

$$k_e = \frac{d_1}{P_0} + g$$

$$g = r \times b$$

CAPM

$$k = R_f + [R_m - R_f]\beta$$

$$\beta_{eu} = \beta_{eg}\left[\frac{V_E}{V_E + V_D[1-t]}\right] + \beta_d\left[\frac{V_D[1-t]}{V_E + V_D[1-t]}\right]$$

$$\beta_{eg} = \beta_{eu} + [\beta_{eu} - \beta_d]\left[\frac{V_D[1-t]}{V_E}\right]$$

WACC

$$WACC = k_{eg}\left[\frac{V_E}{V_E + V_D}\right] + k_d[1-t]\left[\frac{V_D}{V_E + V_D}\right]$$

FX, interest rates & inflation

$$F_0 = S_0 \times \frac{[1 + r\,var]}{[1 + r\,base]}$$

$$S_1 = S_0 \times \frac{[1 + r\,var]}{[1 + r\,base]}$$

$$(1 + r_{nominal}) = (1 + r_{real}) \times (1 + inflation)$$

MM

$$V_g = V_u + TB$$

$$k_{eg} = k_{eu} + [k_{eu} - k_d]\left[\frac{V_D[1-t]}{V_E}\right]$$

$$WACC = k_{eu}\left[1 - \left[\frac{V_D t}{V_E + V_D}\right]\right]$$

TERP

$$\text{TERP} = \frac{1}{N+1}[(N \times \text{cum rights price}) + \text{issue price}]$$

$$\text{Yield-adjusted TERP} = \frac{1}{N+1}[(N \times \text{cum rights price}) + \text{issue price} \times (Y_{new}/Y_{old})]$$

PRACTICE QUESTION AND ANSWER BANK

Section A

The following questions are multi-choice. These are designed to give you practice in answering questions in this format which are part of the current objective test (OT) style exam for this paper.

Chapter 1

Learning outcome: A1(a)

1   What should be the main objective of the managers of a profit-making company?

    A   Maximise shareholder wealth

    B   Maximise their own rewards

    C   Reduce the negative impact on the environment

    D   Create more jobs

Learning outcome: A1(a)

2   You have been asked to classify the following stakeholders of an organisation as internal, connected or external:

- Employees
- Management
- Shareholders
- Customers
- Pressure groups
- Banks

Which of the following is the correct classification?

    A   Internal stakeholders: shareholders, management; Connected stakeholders: employees, customers, banks; External stakeholders: pressure groups

    B   Internal stakeholders: employees, management; Connected stakeholders: shareholders, customers, banks; External stakeholders: pressure groups

    C   Internal stakeholders: pressure groups; Connected stakeholders: employees, management; External stakeholders: shareholders, customers, banks

    D   Internal stakeholders: employees, customers; Connected stakeholders: shareholders, management, pressure groups; External stakeholders: banks

Learning outcome: A1(a)

3   In the context of managing performance in 'not for profit' organisations, which of the following definitions is incorrect?

    A   Value for money means providing a service in a way which is economical, efficient and effective.

    B   Economy means doing things cheaply: not spending $2 when the same thing can be bought for $1.

    C   Efficiency means doing things quickly: minimising the amount of time that is spent on a given activity.

    D   Effectiveness means doing the right things: spending funds so as to achieve the organisation's objectives.

Learning outcome: A1(a)

4   Which of the following are examples of 'social and relationship' non-financial performance measures?

I   Volume of customer complaints

II   Employee turnover

III   Employee morale

IV   Customer satisfaction

V   Carbon emissions

A   I, II, III and V

B   I, II, III and IV

C   I and III

D   I and IV

Learning outcome: A1(b)

5   The figures shown below are an extract from the accounts of R Ltd for the year ended 31 December 20X5. Capital employed is $1.5m.

	$
Revenue	1,000,000
Less cost of sales	(400,000)
Gross profit	600,000
Expenses	(300,000)
	300,000
Interest	(50,000)
Profit for the year	250,000
Dividends	(50,000)
Retained profit	200,000

Two of R's financial objectives for the year ended 31 December 20X5 were as follows.

I   Asset turnover of 0.5 or more

II   Return on capital employed of 18% or more

Evaluate which of these objectives have been achieved.

A   I only

B   II only

C   I and II

D   Neither achieved

Chapter 2

Learning outcome: A1(b)

1   B Co achieved an operating profit margin of 21% in the year to 31 March 20X1. Revenue was $3.3 million.

The company was financed by 2 million 50c ordinary shares, 500,000 $1 preference shares and $1 million of long-term debt. Reserves stood at $600,000.

What was the ROCE for the period?

A   21.00%

B   22.35%

C   33.00%

D   69.30%

Learning outcome: A1(b)

2   What measure is used to assess the relationship between the market value of a company's shares and the earnings from those shares?

A   EBITDA

B   P/E ratio

C   EPS

D   Share price

Learning outcome: A1(b)

3   The nominal rate of interest is 11%. The expected annual rate of inflation is 5%. What is the real rate of interest?

A   5.7%

B   6%

C   16%

D   16.55%

Chapter 3

Learning outcome: A1(c)

1   Which of the following is **not** a category of capital in the International Integrated Reporting Council's International Framework?

A   Natural capital

B   Human capital

C   Organisational capital

D   Social and relationship capital

Learning outcome: A2(c)

2   What is the purpose of hedging?

A   To reduce costs only

B   To make a profit by accepting risk

C   To reduce or eliminate exposure to risk

D   To protect profits made from undertaking a risky position

Learning outcome: A2(c)

3   Which of the following statements is not true?

A   For a fair value hedge, the gain or loss resulting from remeasuring the hedging instrument at fair value is recognised directly in equity through the statement of changes in equity.

B   For a fair value hedge, the gain or loss on the hedged item attributable to the hedged risk should adjust the carrying amount of the hedged item and be recognised in the statement of profit or loss.

C   For a cash flow hedge, the portion of the gain or loss on the hedging instrument that is determined to be an effective hedge shall be recognised directly in equity through the statement of changes in equity.

D   For a cash flow hedge, the ineffective portion of the gain or loss on the hedging instrument should be recognised in profit or loss.

Learning outcome: A1(c)

4   Which of the following is **not** a general standard disclosure in the GRI guidelines for sustainability reporting?

A   Strategy and analysis

B   Organisational profile

C   Identified material aspects and boundaries

D   Disclosures on management approach

Learning outcome: A1(c)

5   Which of the following are examples of intellectual capital in the International Integrated Reporting Council's (IIRC) Integrated Reporting Framework?

I   Shared norms and common values and behaviours

II   Tacit knowledge

III   Ability to understand, develop and implement an organisation's strategy

IV   Intangibles associated with the brand and reputation that an organisation has developed

V   Alignment with and support for an organisation's governance framework, risk management approach and ethical values

A   I, II, III and IV

B   II and IV

C   II only

D   I, II, III and V

Chapter 4

Learning outcome: B2(b)

1 Which of the following statements is true?

Dividend policy will be influenced by:

(i) The need to remain profitable

(ii) The company's liquidity position

(iii) The need to repay debt in the near future

(iv) Any dividend restraints that might be imposed by debt covenants in loan agreements

A None of the above

B All of the above

C I only

D III only

Learning outcome: B2(b)

2 'Dividend payments come out of leftover equity only after investment opportunities have been exhausted.' This describes what type of dividend policy?

A Constant growth

B Constant percentage of annual earnings

C Special dividend

D Residual dividend

Learning outcome: B2(b)

3 Modigliani and Miller's irrelevance theory of dividend policy proposes that in a tax-free world:

A Shareholders are indifferent between dividends and capital gains

B Dividend policy affects the market value of a company

C A company should only pay dividends after exhausting all investment opportunities

D Shareholders will prefer a current dividend to a future capital gain

Learning outcome: B2(b)

4 The following statements about dividends and dividend policy were made at a recent board meeting by three different directors:

Director I: According to the residual theory of dividend policy, once we have invested in or retained sufficient profits for future positive net present value opportunities, we should pay out the remaining profit as dividends.

Director II: That may cause our dividends to vary year on year. I thought companies generally try to smooth out dividend payments by adjusting gradually to changes in earnings, so as to avoid sending out confusing signals to investors.

Director III: We can avoid paying out cash by declaring a scrip dividend. Our existing shareholders will be given new shares in the business at no extra cost to themselves.

Which combination of the directors' statements is true?

A   I and II only

B   I and III only

C   II and III only

D   I, II and III

Learning outcome: B2(b)

5   Which of the following arguments support the relevance of dividend policy?

    I   Informational content of dividends

    II   Investor's preference for current income

    III   Differing tax rates for dividends and capital gains

    A   I and II only

    B   I and III only

    C   II and III only

    D   I, II and III

Chapter 5

Learning outcome: B1(b)

1   A 'eurobond' (international bond) is:

    A   Any government security issued by an EU member state

    B   Any security issued by the European Commission

    C   Any security issued to provide funds for the European Monetary System

    D   A bond traded in one country but denominated in the currency of another country

Learning outcome: B1(b)

2   Bonds that are issued by a company at a large discount to their eventual redemption value, but on which no interest is paid until redemption, are called:

    A   Deep discount bonds

    B   Zero coupon bonds

    C   Equity bonds

    D   Floating rate bonds

Learning outcome: B1(b)

3   Which of the following statements is **not** true?

    A   Companies can obtain long-term debt finance by issuing debt securities through capital markets.

    B   In the UK, the main capital markets are the Stock Exchange and the Alternative Investment Market.

    C   Any company can issue debt securities through capital markets.

    D   Companies do not have to go through capital markets to issue debt securities.

Learning outcome: B1(b)

4   A stock market acts as both a primary and a secondary market for securities. Which of the following characterises the role of stock markets as secondary markets?

    A   They enable companies to raise new capital.

    B   They enable investors to sell their investments.

    C   They permit takeovers by means of share exchange.

    D   Owners of a company coming to the market for the first time can realise the value of some of their investment in the flotation.

Learning outcome: B1(b)

5   Which of the following statements describes convertible debt?

    A   A liability that gives the holder the right to convert into another instrument, normally ordinary shares, at a pre-determined price or rate and time.

    B   A right given by a company to an investor, allowing them to subscribe for new shares at a fixed, pre-determined price.

    C   Bonds issued at a discount to their redemption value, but no interest is paid on them.

    D   Bonds offered at a large discount on the face value of the debt so that a significant proportion of the return to the investor comes by way of a capital gain on redemption rather than through interest payment.

Chapter 6

Learning outcome: B1(b)

1   Under the terms of a swap arrangement, Louie has paid interest at 10%, Dewie at LIBOR + 1%.

    The parties have swapped floating rate interest at LIBOR + 1%. What amount of fixed rate interest do they need to swap for Louie to end up paying net interest of LIBOR – 0.5%?

    A   10%

    B   11.5%

    C   9.5%

    D   11%

Learning outcome: B1(b)

2   Which of the following is **not** an advantage of interest rate swaps?

    A   Swaps can be reversed if necessary.

    B   Transaction costs are low, particularly if an intermediary is not used.

    C   If a company takes on a fixed-rate swap, it can benefit from favourable movements in interest rates.

    D   Swaps are relatively easy to arrange.

Learning outcome: B1(b)

3   Which of the following best describes refinancing risk?

    A   Risk that a lender will demand early repayment of debt

    B   Risk that a company cannot repay or refinance existing debts

    C   Risk that interest rates will rise

    D   Risk that a company will face liquidity problems

Learning outcome: B1(b)

4   To what does interest rate risk relate?

    A   The sensitivity of profits and cash flow to fluctuations in the interest rate

    B   The fact that a company has chosen to borrow at a fixed rather than a variable rate

    C   The difference between short-term interest rates prevailing in two money markets at any given time

    D   The fact that the foreign currency exchange rate between two countries will reflect the difference in their interest rates

Chapter 7

Learning outcome: B1(b)

1   Alpha Ltd has the choice of buying an asset for £50,000; the asset has a 5-year life and no residual value, 25% straight line capital allowances are available (with the first claim in 1 years' time). Alternatively, Alpha could lease the assets for 5 years at a cost of £12,000 p.a. payable in advance. Corporation tax is 28% payable with no delay.

    The company has a post-tax cost of debt of 6%.

    The net (cost)/benefit of leasing) is:

    A   (£706)

    B   £1,478

    C   £13,606

    D   £11,422

Learning outcome: B1(b)

2   Cemstone has decided to acquire a new grinding machine. It cannot afford to purchase the machine outright, and has therefore arranged to pay for it in regular instalments using a finance house. What type of arrangement is this?

    A   Finance lease

    B   Operating lease

    C   Lender credit

    D   Vendor credit

Learning outcome: B1(b)

3   Which of the following is not true of operating leases?

    A   The lessor purchases equipment from the manufacturer and leases it to the lessee.

    B   The lessor retains ownership of the equipment.

    C   The lessee is responsible for the upkeep, servicing and maintenance of the asset.

    D   The period of the lease if fairly short, less than the expected economic life of the asset.

Learning outcome: B1(b)

4   A way to determine whether debt or lease financing would be preferable for a machine is to:

     A   Compare the interest paid under each alternative

     B   Compare the payback periods for each alternative

     C   Compare the net present values of the cash flows under each alternative, using the after-tax cost of borrowing as the discount rate

     D   Compare the net present values of the cash flows under each alternative, using the weighted average cost of capital as the discount rate

Learning outcome: B1(b)

5   Company X has decided to install a new milling machine. The machine costs $20,000 and it would have a useful life of five years with a trade-in value of $4 000 at the end of the fifth year. A decision has now to be taken on the method of financing the project.

Option 1

The company could purchase the machine for cash, using bank loan facilities at an after tax cost of borrowing of 9%.

Option 2

The company could lease the machine under an agreement which would entail payment of $4,800 at the end of each year for the next five years.

The rate of tax is 30%. If the machine is purchased, the company will be able to claim a tax depreciation allowance of 100% in year 1. Tax is payable with a year's delay. Assume that the lease payments are fully tax-allowable.

Which would be the cheapest option?

     A   Option 1

     B   Option 2

Chapter 8

Learning outcome: B1(c)

1   Which of the following is least likely to be a reason for seeking a stock market flotation?

     A   Transfer of capital to other uses

     B   Access to a wider pool of finance

     C   Enhancement of the company's image

     D   Improving the existing owners' control over the business

Learning outcome: B1(c)

2   Which of the following is **not** true of a rights issue by a listed company?

     A   Rights issues do not require a prospectus.

     B   If shareholders do not take up the rights, the rights lapse.

     C   The rights issue price is at a discount to market price.

     D   Relative voting rights are unaffected if shareholders exercise their rights.

Learning outcome: B1(c)

3 A company whose shares currently sell at £7.50 each plans to make a rights issue of one share at £6.00 for every four existing shares.

What is the theoretical ex-rights price of the shares after the issue?

A £7.50

B £7.20

C £6.75

D £6.30

Learning outcome: C2(a)

4 The following two statements concern the propositions which underpin the capital asset pricing model (CAPM).

I Investors in shares require a return in excess of the risk-free rate to compensate for systematic risk.

II Investors will require higher returns from shares in companies where the level of systematic risk is higher.

Which one of the following combinations (True/False) is correct?

Statement	I	II
A	True	True
B	True	False
C	False	True
D	False	False

5 A portfolio consisting entirely of risk-free securities will have a beta factor of:

A -1

B 0

C +1

D none of the above

Chapter 9

Learning outcome: B1(a)

1   A company plans to raise $10m via a one for five rights issue. Half the capital raised will be used to redeem long-term debt currently quoted at par and the remainder will be used to finance a project with an NPV of $1m. The company pays corporation tax at 50%. What will be the change in total value of the company as a result of the above actions, if Modigliani and Miller theories on tax hold?

    A $3.5m

    B $5.0m

    C $6.0m

    D $11.0m

Learning outcome: B1(a)

2   A firm has a weighted cost of capital of 15% and a ratio of debt value to total value of 1:4. The rate of corporation tax is 35%. Ignore any impact of personal taxes.

    If the firm increases the proportion of debt to one third of the total value of the firm, what is the new cost of capital?

    A   11.75%

    B   13.25%

    C   14.52%

    D   14.56%

Chapter 10

Learning outcome: C1(a)

1   Which of the following statements regarding mergers and acquisitions are true?

    (i)   A reverse takeover is when the smaller company takes over the larger one, so that the predator company has to increase its equity by over 100% to complete the takeover.

    (ii)   The three main types of synergy to be gained from mergers or acquisitions are revenue, cost and financial synergies.

    (iii)   One reason a company may wish to acquire another company is to gain access to large data sets of the target company such as customers'/users' information (big data).

    (iv)   Mergers can be a cheaper method of growth than expanding internally.

    A   All of the above

    B   None of the above

    C   (i) only

    D   (iv) only

Learning outcome: C1(a)

2   Which of the following methods of reducing tax in group companies is known as tax inversion?

   A   A transaction used by a company whereby it becomes a subsidiary of a new parent company in another country for the purpose of falling under beneficial tax laws

   B   The setting of prices of charges for goods and services traded between group companies

   C   A parent company funding a subsidiary company with a significantly higher level of debt compared to equity that it could achieve on its own

   D   An acquiring company offsetting past losses of an acquired subsidiary against the present profits of the parent company

Learning outcome: C1(a)

3   Which of the following defence strategies describes a tactic to make the target's shares less attractive to the acquirer?

   A   Poison pill

   B   Management buyout

   C   White knight

   D   Counter bid

Chapter 11

Learning outcome: C2(a)

Data for questions 1–3

The directors of Mace plc are considering the acquisition of Dickson Ltd, a much smaller company making annual profits before tax of £200,000 (constant). The current rate of tax is 28%. Dickson Ltd's balance sheet is as follows:

	£	£
Non-current assets (net book value)		800,000
Inventory	504,000	
Receivables (less provision of 1% for doubtful debts)	396,000	
Bank balances		20,000
		920,000
Bank overdraft		50,000
Trade payables		490,000
		(540,000)
		1,180,000
Share capital and reserves		1,180,000

The estimated values of Dickson Ltd's assets are as follows:

	Replacement cost £	Net realisable value £
Non-current assets	850,000	600,000
Inventory	540,000	580,000

It is generally agreed that 2% of total debtors will be uncollectable.

Mace has a P/E ratio of 15. Dickson's cost of equity is 10%, and pays out 90% of its earnings as a dividend.

1   What is minimum bid that Mace plc should make for Dickson Ltd?

    A   £1,048,080

    B   £1,032,000

    C   £1,052,000

    D   £1,582,000

2   If Mace plc and Dickson Ltd are in the same industry, what is the maximum price that Mace should pay for Dickson?

    A   £3,000,000

    B   £2,160,000

    C   £840,000

    D   £1,052,000

3   Dickson Ltd, on the basis of its dividends, is worth:

    A   £1,800,000

    B   £1,440,000

    C   £1,296,000

    D   £1,052,000

Learning outcome: C2(a)

4   ProWall and Cleaverfield are listed companies in the same industry. Their P/E ratios and share prices are shown below.

	P/E ratio	Current share price ex div
ProWall	10	$6.00
Cleaverfield	16	$4.80

Which of the following statements will best explain the higher P/E ratio of Cleaverfield?

    A   Cleaverfield is a much larger company than ProWall.

    B   Cleaverfield has higher EPS growth prospects than ProWall.

    C   Cleaverfield is regarded as a higher risk investment than ProWall.

    D   Cleaverfield retains a higher proportion of its annual post-tax profits than ProWall.

Learning outcome: C2(a)

5   Which of the following statements about the efficient markets hypothesis are correct?

Statement

1   The weak form of the hypothesis implies that it is impossible for an investor to earn superior returns by looking at patterns in share price changes.

2   The semi-strong form of the hypothesis implies that it is impossible for an investor to earn superior returns by studying company reports and accounts, newspaper and investment journals etc.

3   The strong form of the hypothesis implies that since security prices reflect all available information, there is no way that most investors can achieve consistently superior returns.

A   Statements 1 and 2 only are correct.

B   Statements 1 and 3 only are correct.

C   Statements 2 and 3 only are correct.

D   Statements 1, 2 and 3 are all correct.

Learning outcome: C2(a)

6   Chancer plc is considering the acquisition of Risky plc. Risky plc is estimated to have cash flows to all investors of £1,200,000 in the next year, growing at a rate of 4% p.a. for the foreseeable future. Risky has debt with a book value of £10m and a market value of £12m.

Chancer has a weighted average cost of capital of 10% and a cost of equity of 12%.

What is the value of Risky using the cash flow basis?

A   £10m

B   £20m

C   £8m

D   £15m

Learning outcome: C2(a)

7   On 29 September Jones, a company listed on the Stock Exchange, made a confidential offer to buy all the shares in Taylor Co, at a price in excess of their current market value. At a private meeting held the same day, the directors of Taylor Co agreed to accept the offer and made a public announcement of this decision two months later on 29 November.

What would you expect to see happen to Taylor Co's share price on 29 November, under the semi-strong and strong forms of market efficiency?

Share price reaction

	Semi-strong form	Strong form
A	Increase	Increase
B	Increase	No effect
C	No effect	Increase
D	No effect	No effect

Chapter 12

Learning outcome: C2(a)

1   Blogs Co is going to obtain a stock market listing and a valuation therefore needs to be calculated for the company.

Blogs' debt to equity ratio is 2:5, its annual earnings this year were $600,000 and it regularly pays 50% of earnings as dividends, with 5% growth expected each year.

A quoted company in the same industry as Blogs has a debt to equity ratio of 1:2 and a beta of 1.62.

The risk-free return is 4%, the market return is 9% and tax is at 30%.

The valuation of Blogs Co is:

A $4,251,387

B $6,343,245

C $4,701,493

D $3,893,624

Learning outcome: C2(a)

2   An all-equity company has a market value of $90 million. The company plans to raise $10m by issuing debentures. These will be invested in a project with a NPV of $1.5m and with the same business risk as the company. What will be the new value of the company, if corporation tax is 35% and the Modigliani and Miller model holds?

A $100.0m

B $101.5m

C $103.5m

D $105.0m

Learning outcome: C2(a)

3   EW plc is considering acquiring Pet Stop Ltd, an unquoted company in the pet accessory market. A similar quoted company in this market, Gould plc, has a beta factor of 1.20 and a debt to equity ratio of 1:4.

Pet stop has a debt to equity ratio of 1:3. The rate of corporate tax is 28%, the risk-free return is 4% and the market return is 8%. Assume that the debt beta is zero.

Which of the following is the correct weighted average cost of capital to be used as a discount rate for the valuation of Pet Stop Ltd?

A   7.8%

B   7.5%

C   7.3%

D   7.6%

Chapter 13

Learning outcome: C3(b)

1   Sheridan plc and Norwen plc are planning a merger. Shareholders in Norwen would accept 2 shares in Sheridan for every share they hold. The current position is:

	Sheridan plc	*Norwen plc*
Number of shares	20 million	6 million
Annual Earnings	£5 million	£2.2 million
P/E ratio	8	12

As a result of the merger, annual earnings of the enlarged company would be 10% higher than the sum of earnings of each company before the merger. The expected post-merger P/E ratio is 11.

By how much would the shareholders in Norwen plc gain from the merger?

A   £2.97 million

B   £3.30 million

C   £4.02 million

D   £6.27 million

Learning outcome: C3(b)

2   Use the details from question 1 – what is the maximum paper bid that Sheridan plc could offer without damaging the wealth of its own shareholders.

A   3 shares in Sheridan plc to 1 share in Norwen plc

B   4 shares in Sheridan plc to 1 share in Norwen plc

C   1 share in Sheridan plc to 4 shares in Norwen plc

D   No change in the current bid

Learning outcome: C3(b)

3   Which of the following are rules in Drucker's Golden Rules of post-acquisition integration?

(i)   Within a year, the acquiring company should put top Management with relevant skills in place.

(ii)   The acquiring company must ensure it can Add value to the target (that is, ensure targets are set, communicated to customers and synergies are realised).

(iii) The acquiring company must show Respect to the products, management and track record of the target.

(iv)   Ensure there is a Common core of unity (for example take actions to ensure systems are compatible).

(v)   Strategies should be developed for Holding onto existing staff (for example, loyalty bonuses).

A   (i), (ii) and (iii) only

B   (iii), (iv) and (v) only

C   All of the above

D   None of the above

Section B

The following questions are based on exam questions from the previous syllabus. Although they are not indicative of the current format of exam questions (OT and ICS), they contain content relevant to the current syllabus and provide excellent practice in learning this content.

1   Earnings per share   45 mins

Learning outcome: A1(a)

(a)   'Financial managers need only concentrate on meeting the needs of shareholders by maximising earnings per share – no other group matters.'

Discuss.   **(10 marks)**

(b)   Many decisions in financial management are taken in a framework of conflicting stakeholder viewpoints. Identify the stakeholders and some of the financial management issues involved in the following situations.

    (i)   A private company converting into a public company

    (ii)   A highly geared company, such as Eurotunnel, attempting to restructure its capital finance

    (iii)   A large conglomerate 'spinning off' its numerous divisions by selling them, or setting them up as separate companies (eg Hanson)

    (iv)   Japanese car-makers, such as Nissan and Honda, building new car plants in other countries
           (15 marks)

           (Total = 25 marks)

2   Subsidiaries   36 mins

Learning outcome: A1(b)

Your company has two subsidiaries, X and Y, both providing computer services, notably software development and implementation. The UK market for such services is said to be growing at about 20% a year. The business is seasonal, peaking between September and March.

You have available the comparative data shown in the Appendix to this question below. The holding company's policy is to leave the financing and management of subsidiaries entirely to the subsidiaries' directors.

Required

In the light of this information, compare and contrast the performance of the two subsidiaries.

It may be assumed that the difference in size of the two companies does not invalidate a comparison of the ratios provided.

Appendix

Data in this Appendix should be accepted as correct. Any apparent internal inconsistencies are due to rounding of the figures.

	X	Y
Revenue in most recent year (€'000)		
Home	2,856	6,080
Export	2,080	1,084
Total	4,936	7,164
Index of revenue 20X9		
(20X6 = 100)		
Home	190%	235%
Export	220%	150%
Total	200%	220%
Operating profit 20X9 (€'000)	840	720
Operating capital employed 20X9 (€'000)	625	1,895

Ratio analysis

		X 20X9	X 20X8	X 20X7	Y 20X9	Y 20X8	Y 20X7
Return on operating capital employed	%	134	142	47	38	40	52
Operating profit: Sales	%	17	16	6	10	8	5
Sales: Operating capital employed	×	8	9	8	4	5	10
Percentages to sales value:							
Cost of sales	%	65	67	71	49	49	51
Selling and distribution costs	%	12	11	15	15	16	19
Administration expenses	%	6	6	8	26	27	25
Number of employees		123	127	88	123	114	91
Sales per employee	€'000	40	37	31	58	52	47
Average remuneration per employee	€'000	13	13	12	16	4	13
Tangible non-current assets turnover rate	×	20	21	14	9	11	14
Additions, at cost	%	57	47	58	303	9	124
Percentage depreciated	%	45	36	20	41	60	72
Product development costs carried forward as a percentage of revenue	%	0	0	0	10	8	6
Receivables: Sales	%	18	18	22	61	41	39
Inventory: Sales	%	0	1	0	2	2	1
Cash: Sales	%	7	9	2	1	1	0
Trade payables: Sales	%	2	2	3	32	21	24
Trade payables: Receivables	%	11	14	15	53	50	62
Current ratio (:1)		1.5	1.3	1.2	1.1	1.1	0.9
Liquid ratio (:1)		1.5	1.3	1.2	1.0	1.0	0.9
Liquid ratio excluding bank overdraft		0	0	0	1.4	1.5	1.2
Total debt : Total assets	%	61	71	109	75	72	84

3 Cuando

36 mins

Learning outcome: B2(b)

Cuando is an online retailer of books, CDs and DVDs. The company was set up five years ago by a wealthy entrepreneur, David Nile, and has now grown to the point where the board of directors has decided that a listing should be sought on the local stock exchange. David Nile owns 80% of the ordinary shares and has agreed to sell all of these as part of the public offering.

Recently, the board of directors began to debate the future dividend policy of the company, assuming that the stock exchange listing would be successful. However, there was a clear divergence of views. The Chairman felt that the current dividend policy was unacceptable and needed to be changed. He argued that the company had been investing heavily in its distribution methods and in advertising in the early

years and that dividend policy had not been a pressing issue. However, the proposed listing must now lead to a reconsideration of the importance of dividends. The Chief Operating Officer, on the other hand, felt that the Chairman's concerns were unfounded as the pattern of dividends had no effect on shareholder wealth.

Information concerning the company since it was first set up is as follows:

Year ended 30 November	Net profits after taxation £'000s	Ordinary dividends £'000s	Ordinary shares in issue 000s
20X0	650	320	800
20X1	520	150	1,000
20X2	760	480	1,000
20X3	1,240	600	1,500
20X4	1,450	540	1,500

Required

(a) Evaluate the views expressed by the Chief Operating Officer and by the Chairman. **(10 marks)**

(b) Analyse the dividend policy that has been pursued to date and discuss whether a change would be in the interests of shareholders. **(6 marks)**

(c) Discuss the key points that should be taken into account when establishing an appropriate dividend policy for the company. **(4 marks)**

(Total = 20 marks)

4 PG

30 mins

Learning outcomes: B1(c), C2(a)

PG has a paid-up ordinary share capital of £4,500,000 represented by 6 million shares of 75p each. It has no loan capital. Earnings after tax in the most recent year were £3,600,000. The P/E ratio of the company is 15.

The company is planning to make a large new investment which will cost £10,500,000, and is considering raising the necessary finance through a rights issue at 800p.

Required

(i) Calculate the current market price of PG's ordinary shares.

(ii) Calculate the theoretical ex-rights price, and state what factors in practice might invalidate your calculation.

(iii) Briefly explain what is meant by a deep-discounted rights issue, identifying the main reasons why a company might raise finance by this method.

5 Ducey

30 mins

Learning outcome: B1(b)

Ducey has decided to acquire some new plant and machinery and is now considering whether to buy or to lease it. The machinery in question has a useful life of four years and is expected to have no residual value at the end of that time. It would cost £176,000 to buy which would be financed by borrowing. Alternatively it could be leased for four years at an annual rental of £55,000 payable annually in advance.

The tax rate is 30%. If purchased the machine would attract tax-allowable depreciation of 25% (reducing balance basis) per annum. A balancing allowance or charge would be made on disposal. If leased, the rental would be allowed fully against tax. Tax is paid (and allowances received) one year in arrears.

The before-tax cost of borrowing to Ducey is estimated to be 19%.

Required

(a)   Advise Ducey whether to buy or to lease the machine on the assumption that the company has sufficient taxable profits to fully absorb all tax allowances rising from the buy or lease decision.

(b)   Advise Ducey whether to buy or to lease the machine on the basis that the company is in a permanent non-tax paying position.

(c)   Describe briefly any other factors which the company should take into account when making the lease or buy decision.

6   Bases of valuation   45 mins

Learning outcomes: C2(a),(b)

The directors of Carmen plc, a large conglomerate, are considering the acquisition of the entire share capital of Manon Ltd, which manufactures a range of engineering machinery. Neither company has any long-term debt capital. The directors of Carmen plc believe that if Manon is taken over, the business risk of Carmen will not be affected.

The accounting reference date of Manon is 31 July. Its statement of financial position as on 31 July 20X4 is expected to be as follows:

		£	£
Non-current assets (net of depreciation)			651,600
Current assets:	Inventory and work in progress	515,900	
	Receivables	745,000	
	Bank balances	158,100	
			1,419,000
			2,070,600
Current liabilities:	Payables	753,600	
	Bank overdraft	862,900	
			1,616,500
Capital and reserves:	Issued ordinary shares of £1 each		50,000
	Distributable reserves		404,100
			2,070,600

Manon's summarised financial record for the five years to 31 July 20X4 is as follows:

Year ended 31 July	20X0	20X1	20X2	20X3	20X4 (estimated)
	£	£	£	£	£
Profit before non-recurring items	30,400	69,000	49,400	48,200	53,200
Non-recurring items	2,900	(2,200)	(6,100)	(9,800)	(1,000)
Profit after non-recurring items	33,300	66,800	43,300	38,400	52,200
Less: dividends	20,500	22,600	25,000	25,000	25,000
Added to reserves	12,800	44,200	18,300	13,400	27,200

The following additional information is available:

(a)   There have been no changes in the issued share capital of Manon during the past five years.

(b)   The estimated values of Manon's non-current assets and inventory and work in progress as on 31 July 20X4 are as follows:

	Replacement cost	Realisable value
	£	£
Non-current assets	725,000	450,000
Inventory and work in progress	550,000	570,000

(c)   It is expected that 2% of Manon's receivables at 31 July 20X4 will be uncollectable.

(d) The cost of capital of Carmen plc is 9%. The directors of Manon Ltd estimate that the shareholders of Manon require a minimum return of 12% per annum from their investment in the company.

(e) The current P/E ratio of Carmen plc is 12. Quoted companies with business activities and profitability similar to those of Manon have P/E ratios of approximately 10, although these companies tend to be much larger than Manon.

Required

(a) Estimate the value of the total equity of Manon Ltd as on 31 July 20X4 using each of the following bases.

    (i)   Statement of financial position value

    (ii)   Replacement cost of the assets

    (iii) Realisable value of the assets

    (iv) The dividend valuation model

    (v)   The P/E ratio model   **(13 marks)**

(b) Explain the role and limitations of each of the above five valuation bases in the process by which a price might be agreed for the purchase by Carmen plc of the total equity capital of Manon Ltd.

    (7 marks)

(c) State and justify briefly the approximate range within which the purchase price is likely to be agreed.   **(5 marks)**

Ignore taxation.   **(Total = 25 marks)**

7 Perseus   45 mins

Learning outcomes: C2(a),(b)

Perseus is a wholly-owned subsidiary of Minos. Although the subsidiary has provided satisfactory levels of performance, Minos is considering the sale of the subsidiary to another conglomerate. Minos is experiencing trading problems in other parts of its operations and needs to sell Perseus in order to raise much-needed finance. The most recent statement of financial position of Perseus is as follows:

Statement of financial position as at 30 November 20X2

	$m	$m	$m
Non-current assets			
Freehold land and buildings at cost		58.5	
Less: Accumulated depreciation		10.2	
			48.3
Fixtures and fittings at cost		8.6	
Less: Accumulated depreciation		2.9	
			5.7
Motor vehicles at cost		3.2	
Less: Accumulated depreciation		1.4	
			1.8
			55.8
Current assets			
Inventory at cost	49.5		
Trade receivables	23.4		
Cash at bank	21.5		
		94.4	

	$m	$m	$m
Less: Payables: amounts falling due within one year			
Trade payables	25.9		
Tax	5.4		
		31.3	63.1
Bonds			118.9
Less: payables: amounts falling due after one year			49.0
			69.9
Capital and reserves			
Ordinary $0.50 shares			25.0
Accumulated profits			44.9
			69.9

Extracts from the statement of consolidated income for the year ended 30 November 20X2 are as follows:

	$m
Net profit after taxation	10.7
Dividend proposed and paid	3.3

The following details were taken from a financial newspaper concerning the shares of Tityus, a similar business operating in the same industry that is listed on the Stock Exchange.

20X1 – 20X2

High	Low	Stock	Price	± or	Dividend (net)	Cover (times)	Yield (gross %)	P/E (times)
640c	580c	Tityus	615c	+ 5c	12.0c	2.5	2.2	20.5

An independent valuer has recently estimated the current realisable value of the company's assets as follows:

	$m
Freehold land and buildings	104.2
Fixtures and fittings	3.5
Motor vehicles	0.4
Inventory	58.0

The statement of financial position values of the remaining assets were considered to reflect their net realisable values.

Tax on dividends is at the lower rate of income tax of 10%.

Required

(a) Calculate the value per share of Perseus using the following valuation methods:

    (i)   Net assets (liquidation) basis
    (ii)   Dividend yield basis
    (iii) Price/earnings ratio basis

(b) Briefly evaluate the strengths and weaknesses of each of the share valuation methods set out in (a) above.

8 Olivine   **36 mins**

Learning outcome: C3(b)

Olivine is a holiday tour operator that is committed to a policy of expansion. The company has enjoyed record growth in recent years and is now seeking to acquire other companies in order to maintain its growth momentum. It has recently taken an interest in Halite, a charter airline business, as the Board of Directors of Olivine believes that there is a good strategic fit between the two companies. Both companies have the same level of risk. Abbreviated financial statements relating to each company are set out below:

ABBREVIATED STATEMENT OF CONSOLIDATED INCOME FOR THE YEAR ENDED 30 November 20X3

	Olivine £m	Halite £m
Sales	182.6	75.2
Operating profit	43.6	21.4
Interest charges	12.3	10.2
Net profit before taxation	31.3	11.2
Company tax	6.3	1.6
Net profit after taxation	25.0	9.6
Dividends	6.0	4.0
Accumulated profits for the year	19.0	5.6

Summarised statements of financial position as at 30 November 20X3

	Olivine £m	Halite £m
Non-current assets	135.4	127.2
Net current assets	65.2	3.2
	200.6	130.4
Payables due after more than one year	120.5	104.8
	80.1	25.6
Capital and reserves		
£0.50 ordinary shares	20.0	8.0
Retained profit	60.1	17.6
	80.1	25.6
Price/earnings ratio before the bid	20	15

The Board of Directors of Olivine is considering making an offer to the shareholders of Halite of five shares in Olivine for every four shares held. It is believed that a rationalisation of administrative functions arising from the merger would reap after-tax benefits of £2.4m.

Required

(a)   Calculate:

    (i)   The total value of the proposed offer

    (ii)   The earnings per share of Olivine following the successful acquisition of Halite

    (iii)   The share price of Olivine following acquisition, assuming that the benefits of the acquisition are achieved and that the price/earnings ratio declines by 5%   **(10 marks)**

(b)   Calculate the effect of the proposed takeover on the wealth of the shareholders of each company.
(5 marks)

(c)   Discuss your results in (a) and (b) above and state what recommendations, if any, you would make to the directors of Olivine.   **(5 marks)**

(Total = 20 marks)

9 K and H

45 mins

Learning outcome: C3(b)

K wishes to acquire H. The directors of K are trying to justify the acquisition to the shareholders of both companies on the grounds that it will increase the wealth of all shareholders. The supporting financial evidence produced by K's directors is summarised below.

	K £'000	H £'000
Operating profit	12,400	5,800
Less interest payable	4,431	2,200
Profit before tax	7,969	3,600
Less taxation	2,789	1,260
Earnings available to ordinary shareholders	5,180	2,340
Earnings per share (pre-acquisition)	14.80 pence	29.25 pence
Market price per share (pre-acquisition)	222 pence	322 pence
Estimated market price (post-acquisition)	240 pence	
Estimated equivalent value of one old H share (post-acquisition)		360 pence

Payment is to be made with K ordinary shares, at an exchange ratio of 3 K shares for every 2 H shares.

Required

(a) Demonstrate how the directors of K produced their estimates of post-acquisition value and, if you do not agree with these estimates, produce revised estimates of post-acquisition values. All calculations must be shown. State clearly any assumptions that you make.

(10 marks)

(b) If the acquisition is contested by H, using K's estimate of its post-acquisition market price calculate the maximum price that K could offer without reducing the wealth of its existing shareholders.

(3 marks)

(c) The board of directors of H later informally indicate that they are prepared to recommend to their shareholders a 2 for 1 share offer.

Further information regarding the effect of the acquisition on K is given below:

(i) The acquisition will result in an increase in the total pre-acquisition after tax operating cash flows of £2,750,000 a year indefinitely.

(ii) Rationalisation will allow machinery with a realisable value of £7,200,000 to be disposed of at the end of the next year.

(iii) Redundancy payments will total £3,500,000 immediately and £8,400,000 at the end of the next year.

(iv) K's cost of capital is estimated to be 14% a year.

All values are after any appropriate taxation. Assume that the pre-acquisition market values of K and H shares have not changed.

Recommend, using your own estimates of post-acquisition values, whether K should be prepared to make a 2 for 1 offer for the shares of H. **(6 marks)**

(d) Disregarding the information in (c) above and assuming no increase in the total post-acquisition earnings, evaluate whether this acquisition is likely to have any effect on the value of debt of K.

(6 marks)

(Total = 25 marks)

10 Premoco

90 mins

Learning outcomes: C2(a),(b), C3(a),(b)

Background information

It is currently November 20X7. Premoco operates in oil and related industries. Its shares are quoted on the London Stock Exchange. In its retailing operations the company has concentrated on providing high-quality service and facilities at its service stations rather than competing solely on the price of petrol. Approximately 75% of its revenue and 60% of its profits are from sales of petrol, the remainder coming from other services (car wash and retail sales from its convenience stores which are available at each service station).

The company has been highly profitable in the past as a result of astute buying of petroleum products on the open market. The company does not enter into supplier agreements with the major oil companies except on very short-term deals. However, profit margins are now under increasing pressure as a result of intensifying competition and the cost of complying with environmental legislation.

Future strategy

The Managing Director of the company, David Wong, is assessing three possible acquisitions which would help the company increase the percentage of its non-petroleum revenue and profits.

Option 1. Nafco owns fifteen service stations in the south of England. These sites are of poor image, the company having, in the past, aimed at selling petrol at the lowest possible prices and providing little in the way of other services. However, the sites are in good locations and therefore suitable for renovation and development. The institutional investors in Nafco are known to be dissatisfied with the company's recent performance and can be expected to support a bid if the terms are right. Nafco's service stations are too small for the major oil companies to want to operate, so Premoco foresees little competition from alternative buyers. One of Premoco's suppliers of petroleum products has indicated it might be willing to provide development finance for up to 50% of the acquisition cost at only 5% interest per annum, repayable over ten years. However, this would involve Premoco entering into a long-term supply agreement for all fifteen sites.

Option 2. Oiltrans specialises in oil distribution from the depots owned by the major oil companies to their retail outlets. Its shares have been quoted on the stock market for the past two years. It operates a fleet of oil tankers, some owned and some leased. Premoco has used Oiltrans' services in the past and knows it has an up-to-date and well-managed fleet. However, a bid for Oiltrans would almost certainly be regarded as hostile and, as 40% of the shares are owned by the directors and their families, a successful bid is far from assured.

Option 3. Carsals owns six car showrooms in prestige locations, all of which operate the franchise of a major motor manufacturer. It is a long-established family-owned business which is not listed on a stock market. The managing director and major shareholder is planning to retire shortly and his children have shown no interest in taking over the business. He has therefore approached David Wong, whom he has known for some years, asking if Premoco would be interested in buying Carsals.

Premoco's financial advisers have produced estimates of the expected NPV and the first full-year post-merger earnings of Premoco with each of the three acquisition options. These are as follows:

	Estimated post-merger earnings in first full year following merger	*Estimated NPV of combined organisation*
	£m	£m
Premoco plus Nafco	32	512
Premoco plus Oiltrans	35	595
Premoco plus Carsals	23	368

Financial statistics and other information on Premoco and the three possible acquisitions are shown below.

Extracts from Premoco's statement of financial position at 30 June 20X7

	£m	£m
Non-current assets (NBV)		140.00
Current assets:		
Inventory and receivables	120.00	
Bank and cash	80.00	
		200.00
		340.00
Ordinary £1 share capital: (authorised £30 million)		
Issued		20.00
Reserves		180.00
Secured loan stock 8% redeemable in 8 years time		50.00
Current liabilities		90.00
		340.00

Summary financial statistics

	Premoco	Nafco	Oiltrans	Carsals
Last year end	30.6.X7	30.6.X7	30.6.X7	31.3.X7
Shares in issue (millions)	20	10	12	0.5
Earnings per share (pence)	103	75	85	160
Dividend per share (pence)	31	55	42	112
Share price (pence)	1,648	675	1,530	N/a
Net asset value (£ million)	250	60	65	6
Debt ratio (outstanding debt as % of total market value)	13.0	30.0	15.0	0
Forecast annual growth rate %	11	5	14	9
Beta coefficient	1.2	0.9	1.3	1.25

(1) The forecast growth rates have been provided by Premoco's financial advisers. They are based on publicly available information and assume all companies continue to operate independently and that dividend policies, capital structure and risk characteristics remain unchanged.

(2) The beta shown for Carsals is the equity beta of a larger, quoted company in a similar line of business. This company has a gearing ratio (debt : debt + equity) of 20%. Assume a debt beta of zero.

You should ignore any taxation issues throughout this question.

Required

(a) Calculate, for Premoco and, where relevant, for the three acquisition options before the merger:

   (i) The current market value and P/E ratio

   (ii) The cost of equity using the CAPM

   (iii) The prospective market value using the constant growth dividend valuation model assuming the return on the market is 12% and the return on the risk-free asset is 6%. **(10 marks)**

(b) You now have up to three values for each company as an independent entity. These are the current market value and the value using the dividend valuation model (as you have calculated for part (a)), and asset value (given in the scenario).

   Discuss the usefulness and limitations of each of these methods of company valuation to Premoco in its acquisition decision. **(12 marks)**

(c) Assume you are working as one of Premoco's financial advisers. Write a report to David Wong, the Managing Director, which discusses the following issues for each acquisition option:

   (i) The price to be offered to the target company's shareholders; you should recommend a range of terms within which Premoco should be prepared to negotiate

   (ii) Whether cash or a share exchange would be the most appropriate method of financing the bid

(iii)   The business implications (effect on existing operation, growth prospects, risk etc)

You should recognise that there is no single correct solution to the issues raised in this part of the case. The exercise is to assess and analyse the information available (state any assumptions you make), and then use your judgement to offer credible advice.   **(28 marks)**

(Total = 50 marks)

Section A

Chapter 1

1 A Maximise shareholder wealth

2 B Internal stakeholders: employees, management; Connected stakeholders: shareholders, customers, banks; External stakeholders: pressure groups

3 C Efficiency means doing things well: getting the best use out of what money is spent on.

4 D Employee turnover and employee morale are examples of 'human' non-financial performance measures. Carbon emissions is an example of a 'natural' non-financial performance measure.

5 A The asset turnover ratio is calculated as revenue divided by capital employed:

Asset turnover = Revenue/Capital employed = $1m/$1.5m = 0.67

Return on capital employed = PBIT/Capital employed = $0.25m/$1.5m = 16.7%

Chapter 2

1 B This can be calculated by using the formula ROCE = Operating profit margin × asset turnover. Operating profit margin is given as 21%.

Revenue		$3.3 million
Capital employed:	Ordinary share capital (2 million × 50c)	$1 million
	Preference share capital (0.5 million × $1)	$0.5 million
	Reserves	$0.6 million
	Debt	$1 million
		$3.1 million

Note that capital employed can either be expressed in terms of net assets or, as in this case, in terms of the financing of those assets.

Asset turnover = Revenue/capital employed

= $3.3 million/$3.1 million

= 1.0645

ROCE: 21% × 1.0645 = 22.35%

2 B The relationship between the market value of a company's shares and the earnings from them is measured using the price earnings (P/E) ratio: market price/earnings per share.

3 A 1 + real rate of interest = (1 + nominal rate of interest)/(1 + rate of inflation)

1 + real rate of interest = 1.11/1.05

= 1.057

Real interest rate is 1 − 1.057 = 5.7%.

Chapter 3

1 C Organisational capital is not a category of capital in the Integrated Reporting Framework.

2 C Hedging, sometimes called exposure management, is a form of risk management used by companies to offset a variety of market risks.

3 A For a fair value hedge, the gain or loss resulting from remeasuring the hedging instrument at fair value is recognised in the statement of profit or loss.

4   D   Disclosures on management approach are a specific standard disclosure.

5   C   'Tacit knowledge' is an example of intellectual capital in the Integrated Reporting Framework.

Although 'Intangibles associated with the brand and reputation that an organisation has developed' may appear to be part of intellectual capital, it is categorised as social and relationship capital in the IIRC's Integrated Reporting Framework.

Chapter 4

1   B   All statements are correct.

2   D   Residual dividend

3   A   Shareholders are indifferent between dividends and capital gains.

4   D   All statements are correct.

5   D   Modigliani-Miller's dividend irrelevance theory states that the value of a company is determined solely by the 'earning power' of its assets and investments, rather than its dividend policy. However, statements I, II and III all support the view that dividend policy can have an impact. Information available to shareholders is imperfect, and they may not be aware of the future investment plans and expected profits of their company, thus some investors do use the dividend as an indicator of the company's success. Shareholders will tend to prefer a current dividend to future capital gains (or deferred dividends) because the future is more uncertain. Also differing rates of taxation on dividends and capital gains can create a preference for a high dividend or high earnings retention.

Chapter 5

1   D   A bond traded in one country but denominated in the currency of another country

2   B   Zero coupon bonds are rare. Floating rate bonds, which are bonds on which the interest rate is altered periodically to bring it into line with current market rates of interest, become more attractive to both borrowers and lenders when market interest rates are volatile.

3   C   Companies need to obtain a stock exchange listing to trade on capital markets.

4   B   The primary market is for companies bringing shares to the market or issuing new shares to raise fresh capital. The existence of a secondary market for their shares makes takeovers by listed companies possible; however, the primary function of a secondary market is for the trading of shares already in issue.

5   A   Convertible debt is a liability that gives the holder the right to convert into another instrument, normally ordinary shares, at a pre-determined price or rate and time.

     B   Describes a warrant; C describes a zero coupon bond; D describes a deep discount bond.

Chapter 6

1 B Fixed interest swapped – Louie interest paid – Floating rate interest swapped = – (LIBOR – 0.5%)

Fixed interest swapped – 10% – (LIBOR + 1%) = – (LIBOR – 0.5%)

Fixed interest swapped = 10% + (LIBOR + 1%) – (LIBOR – 0.5%) = 11.5%

2 C If a company takes on a fixed rate swap, it won't be able to take advantage of favourable movements in interest rates.

3 B Refinancing risk is the risk that a company cannot repay or refinance existing debts.

4 A Interest rate risk is the risk of higher or lower profits or losses than expected, as a result of uncertainty about future movements in an interest rate, or the general level of interest rates.

Chapter 7

1 A

Evaluation of the benefit of leasing

Time	0	1–4	
Save outlay	50,000		
Lose tax saved on capital allowances		(3,500)	– workings £50,000 × 0.25 × 0.28
Cost of lease	(12,000)	(12,000)	
Tax savings	3,360	3,360	
Net	41,360	(12,140)	
d.f. at 6%	1.000		
PV	41,360	(42,066)	

NPV = (£706)

2 D This is also known as hire purchase.

3 C The lessor is responsible for the upkeep, servicing, maintenance of the asset in a finance lease not an operating lease

4 C The decision whether to lease or borrow money to buy the machine is a financing decision.

Leasing is another form of debt finance and so the two forms of debt finance can be compared by discounting the relevant cash flows at an after-tax cost of borrowing.

5 A The cheapest option would be to purchase the machine (option 1).

The present value (PV) of purchase costs

Year	Item	Cash flow $	Discount factor 9%	PV $
0	Equipment cost	(20,000)	1.000	(20,000)
5	Trade-in value	4,000	0.650	2,600
2	Tax savings, from allowances 30% x $20,000	6,000	0.842	5,052
6	Balancing charge 30% x $4,000	(1,200)	0.596	(715)
NPV of purchase				(13,063)

The PV of leasing costs

Year	Lease payment $	Savings in tax (30%) $	Discount factor 9%	PV $
1–5	(4,800) p.a.		3.890	(18,672)
2–6		1,440 p.a.	3.569 (W)	5,139
NPV of leasing				(13,533)

Workings

6 year cumulative present value factor 9%	4.486
1 year present value factor 9%	(0.917)
	3.569

Tutorial note

This question is more detailed than a typical 2 mark OT question, but is given here to show possible elements that could be contained in an OT question on the lease or buy decision.

Chapter 8

1   D   Flotation is likely to involve a significant loss of control to a wider circle of investors.

2   B   Shareholders have the option of renouncing the rights and selling them on the market.

3   B

4 × 7.50	=	30.00
1 × 6.00	=	6.00
		36.00 ÷ 5 = £7.20

4   A   The capital asset pricing model assumes investors are already well diversified and therefore unconcerned with unsystematic risk. It is concerned with how systematic risk affects required returns and share prices. Investors in shares require a return in excess of the risk-free rate, to compensate them for systematic risk. The higher the systematic risk, the higher the return required.

5   B   Beta factor is the measure of the systematic risk of a security relative to the risk of the market portfolio. A beta of 0 equates to a risk-free investment with returns that do not fluctuate despite fluctuations in the market.

Chapter 9

1   A

	$million	
Increase of	10.0	– new equity
Decrease of	(5.0)	– debt reduced
Effect of gearing change (0.5 × 5)	(2.5)	
Increased NPV	1.0	
	3.5	

2   C   WACC of an equivalent ungeared company calculated using:

$$k_{adj} = k_{eu}(1 - tL)$$

Where k_{adj} is the weighted average cost of capital in a geared company
k_{eu} is the cost of equity in an ungeared company
t is the corporate tax rate
L is the gearing ratio measured by debt/(debt + equity)

$$15\% = K_{eu} \times (1 - (0.35 \times \tfrac{1}{4}))$$

$$\therefore K_{eu} = \frac{15\%}{0.9125} = 16.438\%$$

Using the formula again:

$$k_{adj} = 16.438\% \times (1 - (0.35 \times \tfrac{1}{3}))$$

$$= 14.52\%$$

Chapter 10

1   A   All statements are true.

2   A   A transaction used by a company whereby it becomes a subsidiary of a new parent company in another country for the purpose of falling under beneficial tax laws is known as tax inversion.

B describes transfer pricing. A company in a higher tax rate country can charge, say, management fees or royalties a group company in a lower tax country, at unrealistically high prices This shifts profits from the high tax rate country to low tax rate country, and lowers the tax bill.

C describes thin capitalisation. Companies that are thinly capitalised have significantly high debt on which tax relief can be claimed, however many some countries have tax rules to limit this.

D describes a method of reducing tax by offsetting losses of other group companies; however some countries have tax rules to prevent this.

3   A   A poison pill is a tactic whereby a company tries to make its shares less attractive to the acquirer.

A management buyout is the purchase of all or part of a business from its owners by its managers.

A white knight is a company which will make a welcome takeover bid.

A counter bid can be made for the predator company, but this can only be done if the companies are of a reasonably similar size.

Chapter 11

1   C

	£
Non-current assets	600,000
Inventory	580,000
Receivables, 98% of £396,000 × (100 ÷ 99)	392,000
Bank balances	20,000
Bank overdraft and trade payables	(540,000)
	1,052,000

2   B   P/E × earnings = 15 × (£200,000 × (1 – tax of 28%)) = 15 × £144,000 = £2,160,000

This is approximately what Dickson will be worth under Mace's ownership – so a higher price cannot be justified on the information provided. In reality a discount might be applied to reflect the fact that Dickson is a limited company.

3   C   £144,000 × 0.9 = £129,600 dividend

P_0 = £129,600/ 0.1 = £1,296,000 (since g is zero, P_0 = D_1 / K_e))

4   B   A higher P/E ratio for listed companies is generally attributable to a lower perceived risk (the opposite of answer C) or higher EPS and dividend growth prospects (answer B).

The size of company (answer A) is not particularly related to P/E ratio for listed companies, because smaller listed companies will often have a higher P/E because of better growth prospects.

High profit retention (answer D) may or may not lead to high EPS growth, depending on available investment opportunities.

5   D   All three statements are correct, and you need to understand them in order to appreciate the efficient markets hypothesis.

Statement 1. The weak-form hypothesis states that share prices efficiently reflect all the information that has been made available and that is therefore contained in the record of past share prices. Since the current share price reflects all that is known about past share price changes, it is impossible to predict future price changes from the same information. Share price changes can only occur (randomly up or down) when new information becomes available.

Statement 2. The semi-strong form hypothesis states that share prices efficiently reflect all the information available from past share prices and other published information. Since all this information rapidly and accurately affects share prices when it becomes available, individual investors cannot study the same information to 'beat the market' and earn higher returns – except by luck or 'inside information'.

Statement 3. The strong form hypothesis states that share prices efficiently reflect all information that can be obtained through the most thorough fundamental analysis of companies and the economy. All share prices are fair, and so investors cannot earn consistently superior returns – except by luck.

6   C   Free cash flows = £1.2m (this is before interest)
Discount at WACC 10% NPV = £1.2m / (0.1 – g) = £20m
then subtract debt £12m = £8m.

7   B   Under the semi-strong form of market efficiency, the share price will increase when information is made publicly available. Under the strong form of market efficiency, the information will already have been reflected in the share price.

Chapter 12

1   C

$$\beta_u = 1.62 \left[\frac{2}{2 + 1(1 - 0.3)} \right] = 1.2$$

$$\beta_g = 1.2 + 1.2 \left[\frac{(2(1 - 0.3))}{5} \right] = 1.54$$

$$k_e = 4\% + (9\% - 4\%)1.54 = 11.7\%$$

$$d_0 = 50\% \times 600,000 = 300,000$$

$$g = 5\%$$

$$P_0 = \frac{300,000(1 + 0.05)}{0.117 - 0.05} = \$4,701,493$$

2   D   MVu   = 90m + 10m + 1.5

= 101.5m

MV$_g$ = MV$_u$ + Dt

∴ MV$_g$ = 101.5m + (0.35 × 10)

= 105m

3   B

$$\beta_u = \beta_g \left[\frac{V_E}{V_E + V_D(1-t)} \right] + \beta_D \left[\frac{V_D}{V_E + V_D(1-t)} \right]$$

$$= 1.20 \left[\frac{4}{4 + 1(1 - 0.28)} \right] + 0$$

$$= 1.017$$

$$\beta_g = \beta_u + (\beta_u - \beta_d) \frac{V_D(1-t)}{V_E}$$

$$= 1.017 + 1.017 \left[\frac{1 \times 0.72}{3} \right] = 1.26$$

K$_e$ = 4 + (8 – 4)1.26 = 9.04%

Given that the beta of debt is zero we will assume that the K$_d$ is the risk free rate of 4%.

$$\text{WACC} = k_e \left[\frac{V_E}{V_E + V_D} \right] + k_d (1 - t) \left[\frac{V_D}{V_E + V_D} \right]$$

$$\text{WACC} = 9.04 \frac{3}{4} + 4(1 - 0.28) \frac{1}{4}$$

= 7.5%

If you have calculated the answer to be 7.8%, you have ignored the tax relief on debt finance in the WACC calculation. The other incorrect answers can be obtained if you have forgotten to adjust the equity beta.

Chapter 13

1   D

Post-merger combined earnings	= £7.92 million
Value of combination (£7.92m × 11)	= £87.12 million
Value per share (87.12/32)	= £2.7225
Value of shares held by Norwen plc shareholders	= £32.67 million (£2.7225 × 12m shares)
Value of Norwen plc pre-merger (2.2 m × 12)	= £26.40 million
Gain	= £6.27 million

2   B

Post-merger combined earnings	= £7.92 million
Value of combination	= £87.12 million
Value per Sheridan share today (5/20 eps × p/e 8)	= £2.00
Max no. shares in issue (87.12/2)	= 43.56 million
Current shares in Sheridan	= 20 million
Maximum number of <u>new</u> shares	= 23.56 million Sheridan plc shares for 6m Norwen plc shares ie 4 shares in Sheridan for 1 Norwen plc share is the maximum bid

3   C

Section B

1 Earnings per share

> **Top tips**. You would not get a complete question on stakeholders, but might well need to bring them into discussions about the consequences of a merger or the results of an investment. You could take a less even-handed approach than we have in (a) provided you justified your arguments and gave some attention to opposing arguments. However if you take a fairly extreme position, you have to discuss the problems of doing so. On the one hand will government wish to intervene to prevent anti-social behaviour; on the other hand how do you measure success in fulfilling the requirements of stakeholders? What happens if those requirements conflict?
>
> In (b) note how the interests of stakeholders who are **not directly involved** in decisions may be affected. Note also the potential **conflicts** – a sell-off may benefit shareholders but not employees. Instead of trying to avoid damaging stakeholder interests, a more practical solution may be to **compensate** them for damage incurred. Alternatively the damage may spur them to action – for example competitors damaged by a new car plant.

(a) **Profit maximisation**

One of the principles of the market economy is that if the owners of businesses attempt to achieve **maximum profitability** and **earnings** this will help to increase the wealth of society. As a result, it is usually assumed that a proper objective for private sector organisations is profit maximisation. This view is substantially correct. In general, the market economy has outperformed planned economies in most places in the world. Two key objectives of financial managers must therefore be the **effective management** of shareholders' funds and the provision of financial information which will help to increase shareholder wealth.

Problems with profit maximisation

However, profit-seeking organisations can also cause problems for society. For example, **monopolists** are able to earn large returns which are disproportionate to the benefits they bring to society. The **costs of pollution** fall on society rather than on the company which is causing it. A company may increase profitability by making some of its workforce redundant but the costs of unemployed people fall on society through the social security system.

The question that then follows is: 'should individual companies be concerned with these market imperfections?'

Government's role

There are two opposing viewpoints. On the one hand it can be argued that companies should only be concerned with **maximisation of shareholders' wealth**. It is the role of government to pick up the problems of market imperfections (eg by breaking up monopolies, by fining polluters and by paying social security benefits).

Stakeholder interests

An alternative viewpoint is that a company is a coalition of **different stakeholder** groups: shareholders, lenders, managers, employees, customers, suppliers, government and society as a whole. The objectives of all these groups, which are often in conflict, need to be considered by company managers when making decisions. From this viewpoint, financial managers cannot be content with meeting the needs of shareholders only.

Consideration of stakeholders

The truth is somewhere in between. The overriding objective of companies is to create **long-term wealth for shareholders**. However this can only be done if we consider the likely behaviour of other stakeholders. For example, if we create extra short-term profits by cutting employee benefits or delaying payments to creditors there are likely to be **repercussions** which reduce longer term shareholder wealth. Or if we fail to motivate managers and employees adequately, the costs of the resulting inefficiencies will ultimately be borne by shareholders.

Conclusion

In summary, the financial manager is concerned with managing the company's funds on behalf of shareholders, and producing information which shows the likely effect of management decisions on shareholder wealth. However management decisions will be made after also considering other stakeholder groups and a good financial manager will be aware that financial information is only one input to the final decision.

> **Top tips.** Only three of the situations need be addressed in your answer.

(b)   (i)   **A private company converting into a public company**

When a private company converts into a public company, some of the existing shareholder/managers will sell their shares to outside investors. In addition, new shares may be issued. The **dilution of ownership** might cause loss of control by the existing management.

The stakeholders involved in potential conflicts are as follows:

1   **Existing shareholder/managers**

They will want to sell some of their shareholding at as high a price as possible. This may motivate them to overstate their company's prospects. Those shareholder/ managers who wish to retire from the business may be in conflict with those who wish to stay in control – the latter may oppose the conversion into a public company.

2   **New outside shareholders**

Most of these will hold **minority stakes** in the company and will receive their rewards as **dividends only**. This may put them in conflict with the existing shareholder/ managers who receive rewards as salaries as well as dividends. On conversion to a public company there should be clear policies on dividends and directors' remuneration.

3   **Employees, including managers who are not shareholders**

Part of the reason for the success of the company will be the efforts made by employees. They may feel that they should benefit when the company goes public. One way of organising this is to create **employee share options** or other bonus schemes.

(ii)   **A highly geared company attempting to restructure its capital finance**

The major conflict here is between **shareholders** and **lenders**. If a company is very highly geared, the shareholders may be tempted to take very high risks. If the gamble fails, they have limited liability and can only lose the value of their shares. If they are lucky, they may make returns many times the value of their shares. The problem is that the shareholders are effectively gambling with money provided by lenders, but those lenders will get no extra return to compensate for the risk.

Removal of risk

In restructuring the company, something must be done either to shift risk away from the lenders or to reward the lenders for taking a risk.

Risk can be **shifted away** from lenders by taking **security** on previously unsecured loans or by **writing restrictive covenants** into loan agreements (eg the company agrees to set a ceiling to dividend payouts until gearing is reduced, and to confine its business to agreed activities).

Lenders can be **compensated** for taking risks by either negotiating increased interest rates or by the issue of 'sweeteners' with the loans, such as share warrants or the issue of convertible loan stock.

Other stakeholders

Other stakeholders who will be interested in the arrangements include **trade creditors** (who will be interested that loan creditors do not improve their position at the expense of themselves) and **managers**, who are likely to be more risk averse than shareholders if their livelihood depends on the company's continuing existence.

(iii) **A large conglomerate spinning off its divisions**

Large conglomerates may sometimes have a market capitalisation which is less than the total realisable value of the subsidiaries. This is referred to as **'conglomerate discount'**. It arises because more synergy could be found by the combination of the group's businesses with competitors than by running a diversified group where there is no obvious benefit from remaining together.

For many years, Hanson Trust was the exception to this situation, but subsequently it decided to break up the group.

The stakeholders involved in potential conflicts are as follows:

1   **Shareholders**

They will see the chance of immediate gains in share price if subsidiaries are sold.

2   **Subsidiary company directors and employees**

They may either gain opportunities (eg if their company becomes independent) or suffer the threat of job loss (eg if their company is sold to a competitor).

(iv) **Japanese car makers building new car plants in other countries**

The stakeholders involved in potential conflicts are as follows:

1   **The shareholders and management of the Japanese company**

They will be able to gain from the combination of advanced technology with a cheaper workforce.

2   **Local employees and managers engaged by the Japanese company**

They will gain enhanced skills and better work prospects.

3   **The government of the local country, representing the tax payers**

The **reduction in unemployment** will ease the taxpayers' burden and increase the government's popularity (provided that subsidies offered by the government do not outweigh the benefits!)

4   **Shareholders, managers and employees of local car making firms**

These will be in conflict with the other stakeholders above as existing manufacturers lose market share.

5   **Employees of car plants based in Japan**

These are likely to lose work if car making is relocated to lower wage areas. They will need to compete on the basis of higher efficiency.

2   Subsidiaries

> **Top tips.** The very important point that current appearances might be deceptive is made first. The answer brings out other points you may need to consider when undertaking a financial analysis:
>
> - Distortions built into various ratios, for example the effects of recent investments in assets
> - Problems making comparisons, for example different classifications of costs
> - Dubious accounting policies such as carrying forward product development costs
> - The implications of involvements in different markets, particularly the overseas market
> - Increased costs bringing, for example, more sales
>
> The discussion on working capital suggests that Y may be suffering some of the signs of over-trading – remember the remedy is more long-term capital.
>
> A conclusion is helpful here.

Profitability

X is the **more profitable** company, both in **absolute terms** and in **proportion to sales** and to **operating capital employed**. This may indicate that X is much better managed than Y, but this is not the only possibility, and a study of the other data shows that Y's profitability, while at present lower, may be more sustainable.

Asset usage

While Y appears to be making worse use of its assets than X, with **asset turnover ratios** lower than X's and falling, this seems to be largely because Y has recently acquired substantial new assets. It may be that within the next few years X will have to undertake a major renewals programme, with consequent adverse effects on its asset turnover ratios.

Sales

A higher percentage of Y's sales are to the home market, while it has still achieved fairly substantial export sales. This suggests that Y could have done better in **exploiting** the **export market**, but also that Y is less exposed than X to **exchange rate fluctuations** and the possible imposition of **trade barriers**. The prospects for the home market appear good, and should give scope for adequate growth. Y has achieved higher growth in total revenue than X over the past three years.

Y is making **sales per employee** about 50% higher than X, and has consistently done so over the past three years. X shows no sign of catching up, despite the fact that its total number of employees has recently fallen slightly. The modest rises in sales per employee over the past three years in both X and Y may be due largely to inflation.

Costs

Y seems to be significantly better than X at **controlling** the cost of sales (49% of sales in Y, and 65% in X), though X has made improvements over the past three years while there has been little change in Y. On the other hand, X's **administration expenses** have been only 6% of sales, while Y's have been 26% of sales. This contrast between the two types of cost suggests that different categorisations of costs may have been used. If we combine the cost of sales and administration expenses, then for X they total 71% of sales and for Y they total 75% of sales. There is thus little difference between the companies, though X has shown improved cost control while Y has not. X has also had **lower selling and distribution costs**.

One must however bear in mind that X will have had a lower depreciation element in its costs than Y, because Y has **recently invested substantially** in non-current assets. Y's costs will also be increased by its **higher salaries**, which may pay off in **better employee motivation** and hence higher sales per employee. On the other hand, Y's costs have been kept down by the carrying forward of an increasing amount of product development costs, an accounting policy which may well be imprudent.

Working capital management

In working capital management, X has the edge. Y has **very high receivables**, and these have recently risen sharply as a proportion of revenue. Y also carries rather more inventory than X, and has very little cash. While both companies have **tolerable current and liquid ratios**, X's are certainly safer. Y achieves a liquid ratio of 1:1 almost entirely by relying on its receivables. If it suffers substantial bad debts, or if the bank should become concerned and call in the overdraft, Y could suffer serious **liquidity problems**. It also depends heavily on trade credit to finance its receivables. While it is sensible to take advantage of **trade credit** offered, Y may depend too much on the continued goodwill of its **suppliers**. This may indicate the **need** for a fresh **injection of equity**.

Conclusion

On balance, X seems to be a sounder company than Y, with better financial management.

3 Cuando

> **Top tips.** Exam questions may involve a discussion of different views being expressed by different directors. Answers on dividend policy should mix the theory (MM) with the practical arguments against MM. This question requires some planning so that you don't repeat in part (c) what you said in part (a). Note that part (a) takes into account the position of the main shareholder; spread of shareholdings will be a significant issue in many dividend questions.

(a) **Chairman's views**

At present the company has only one major shareholder, David Nile, who owns 80% of the shares. The extent to which Mr Nile has been involved in the management of the company is not clear, but it seems likely that he has been **involved in and has approved** previous decisions regarding dividends, probably in response to the investment needs of the company, and perhaps with an eye to his own individual tax position at different times. The **Chairman** is therefore surely correct to point out that the company has not needed to worry about the signals sent by its dividend policy in the past because it has been retaining profits as needed to develop the business.

Chief Operating Officer's views

The **Chief Operating Officer** says that the pattern of dividends has no effect on shareholder wealth, presumably following the theory put forward by Modigliani and Miller (MM) that dividend policy is irrelevant to shareholders because they can make their own adjustments (buying or selling shares) to achieve the level of income they require from their investments.

This may have been true in the case of David Nile, who probably began with a 100% stake and may since have sold 20% of his shares. But on the other hand to retain this stake he must have invested more money in the company in the meantime (in 20X3), given the increase in share capital from 800,000 shares to 1.5 million, so the argument does not really make sense.

Arguments against MM

In any case, there are strong arguments against MM's view that dividend policy is irrelevant as a means of affecting shareholder's wealth.

(i) **Differing rates of taxation on dividends** and **capital gains** can create a preference for a high dividend or one for high earnings retention.

(ii) Due to imperfect markets and the possible difficulties of selling shares easily at a fair price, shareholders might need **high dividends** in order to have funds to invest in opportunities outside the company.

(iii) **Markets are not perfect**. Because of **transaction costs** on the sale of shares, investors who want some cash from their investments should prefer to receive dividends rather than to sell some of their shares to get the cash they want.

(iv) **Information available** to shareholders is **imperfect**, and they are not aware of the future investment plans and expected profits of their company. Even if management were to provide them with profit forecasts, these forecasts would not necessarily be accurate or believable.

(v) As a consequence of imperfect information, companies are normally **expected at least to maintain the same level of dividends** from one year to the next. They are expected to pay a constant dividend or an increased dividend, but not a lower dividend than the year before. Failure to maintain the dividend level would undermine investors' confidence in the future.

(vi) Perhaps the strongest argument against the MM view is that shareholders will tend to prefer a **current dividend** to future capital gains (or deferred dividends) because the future is more uncertain.

Dividend policy in practice

In practice, dividend policy is significant to shareholders and the **Chairman's** view that a listing, putting all of the shares into public hands, will make dividend policy a **more pressing issue** is exactly in line with conventional thinking about dividend policy.

Unexpected changes in dividend payments will have an **effect on the share price**, and to avoid upsetting the market, a company might try to apply a policy of a consistent payout ratio (ratio of dividends to distributable profits for the year).

Companies will often also **'smooth' dividend payments**, ignoring 'temporary' fluctuations in annual profitability. Shareholders might therefore expect to receive dividends from a company that grows each year.

Market expectations can therefore be **a major factor in the formulation of dividend policy**, and listed companies are likely to be extremely reluctant to permit the kind of fluctuations in dividend level that have occurred in the case of Cuando in the past.

(b) **The figures that are available can be analysed as follows.**

	Net profits £'000	Annual growth %	Dividends £'000	Shares In issue '000	Earnings per share £	Dividends per share £	Dividend payout ratio %
20X0	650	–	320	800	0.81	0.40	49.23
20X1	520	(20.00)	150	1,000	0.52	0.15	28.85
20X2	760	46.15	480	1,000	0.76	0.48	63.16
20X3	1,240	63.16	600	1,500	0.83	0.40	48.39
20X4	1,450	16.94	540	1,500	0.97	0.36	37.24

Cuando's earnings have increased steadily apart from a dip in its second year. However, without more detailed information no clear pattern to the growth can be discerned. Most growth was achieved in 20X3.

Earnings per share are typically around 80p with a dividend payout ratio of around 50% of this, but there is no consistent pattern at all. A higher than usual dividend was paid in 20X2, presumably to compensate shareholders for the much smaller dividend in 20X1, but

in the following year, 20X3 (when the most spectacular growth occurred), the dividend fell back again to its 20X0 level. Despite the rise in earnings per share in 20X4 the dividend per share fell once more.

As mentioned in part (a) this policy has presumably been acceptable to the one major shareholder, but when his shares are sold to the public a change seems very desirable on the grounds that shareholders typically expect consistency, at the very least, and prefer steady growth to wild fluctuations for no apparent reason.

(c)   Besides matters already mentioned in this answer there are a number of other factors that affect dividend policy, including the following:

(i)   The purpose of retaining profits should usually be to **invest in new projects**, in order to develop and grow the business. Unless there are profitable investments available to invest in, there should be no reason to retain the profits instead of paying them out as dividends.

(ii)   Companies are **prevented by law from distributing dividends in excess of the distributable reserves** of the company. Broadly speaking, distributable profits are accumulated profits. A loss-making company might therefore find its ability to pay dividends is restricted.

(iii) Dividends have to be **paid in cash** (given that scrip dividends are uncommon). In order to make a dividend payment, a company must therefore **have sufficient free cash flow** to afford to make the payment. It is quite possible for a company to make profits but have insufficient cash to pay a suitable dividend.

(iv)   The board of directors might want to use dividend policy to provide signals to the market about **expectations for future profits and growth**. An increase in dividends could be used to signal optimism about the future. If the signal is well received, the share price could be boosted.

4   PG

(i)   The **current market price** can be found by multiplying the earnings per share (EPS) by the price/earnings (P/E) ratio.

EPS is £3.6/6m = 60p per share

P/E ratio is 15

Market price of shares is $15 \times 60p =$ **£9.00 per share**

(ii)   In order to raise £10,500,000 at a price of 800 pence, the company will need to issue an additional 1,312,500 (£10,500,000/£8.00) shares.

Following the investment, the total number of shares in issue will be 7,312,500 (6,000,000 + 1,312,500).

At this point, the total value of the company will be:

$(6m \times £9) + £10,500,000 = £64,500,000$

The **theoretical ex-rights price** will therefore be £64.5m/7.3125m = **£8.82**.

Problems with calculations

1   The **costs of arranging the issue** have not been included in the calculations.

2   The **market view** of the **quality of the new investment** will affect the actual price of the company's shares.

3   If the **issue** is **not fully subscribed** and a significant number of shares remain with the underwriters, this will **depress the share price**.

4   The effect of the new investment on the **risk profile** of the company and the expected **future dividend stream** could also cause the share price to differ from that predicted.

5   The price of the shares depends not only on the financial performance of the company, but also on the **overall level of demand** in the stock market. If the market moves significantly following the announcement of the issue, this will affect the actual price at which the shares are traded.

(iii)   **Features of a deep-discounted rights issue**

In a **deep-discounted** rights issue, the new shares are priced at a **large discount** to the current market price of the shares. The purpose of this is to ensure that the issue is well subscribed and that shares are not left with the underwriters, and thus this form of issue pricing is attractive when the stock market is particularly volatile. However, the shares cannot be issued at a price which is below their nominal value.

Disadvantage of deep-discounted rights issue

The main drawback to this approach is that a **larger number of shares** will need to be **issued** in order to raise the required amount of finance, and this will lead to a larger dilution of earnings per share and dividends per share.

5   Ducey

> **Top tips.** In part (a) it is helpful to show clearly how the tax-allowable depreciation has been calculated and how they have been allocated over time. In part (b) state clearly the clear assumptions surrounding your choice of interest rate for evaluating the financing alternatives.

(a)   First calculate the NPV cost of the plant if it is acquired using a bank loan. The discount rate to be used will be 13%, this being the approximate after-tax cost of the bank loan (19% × 70%).

Tax-allowable depreciation will be claimed as follows.

All figures £'000

Year	Basis of claim	Value (× 30%)	Claimed in year
1	176 × 25% = 44.00	13.2	2
2	(176 – 44) × 25% = 33.00	9.9	3
3	(176 – 44 – 33) × 25% = 24.75	7.425	4
4	Balance = 74.25	22.275	5

The NPV cost of the project can now be calculated.

Year	Plant £	Tax £	Cash flow £	Disc factor	NPV £
0	(176.00)		(176.00)	1.000	(176.00)
1			0	0.885	0.00
2		13.2	13.2	0.783	10.34
3		9.9	9.9	0.693	6.86
4		7.425	7.425	0.613	4.55
5		22.275	22.275	0.543	12.10
NPV cost of purchase					(142.15)

The NPV cost of leasing the plant can be calculated using the discount rate of 13%.

Year	Lease £	Tax relief £	Cash flow £	Disc factor	NPV £
0	(55.00)		(55.00)	1.000	(55.00)
1	(55.00)	16.5	(38.5)	0.885	(34.07)
2	(55.00)	16.5	(38.5)	0.783	(30.15)
3	(55.00)	16.5	(38.5)	0.693	(26.68)
4		16.5	16.5	0.613	10.11
NPV cost of leasing					(135.79)

The NPV cost of leasing is lower than buying outright using a bank loan and is therefore financially more advantageous to Ducey.

(b)   If the company is in a permanent non-tax paying situation, then the alternative sources of finance can be evaluated on the basis of their **direct NPV costs** excluding tax allowances.

The NPV cost of purchase in year 0 is £176,000.

The NPV cost of leasing can be found by multiplying the annual rental payments in years 1 to 3 by the value of a three-year annuity at 19%, and adding this to the year 0 PV of £55,000. Since the company is not paying tax, it will be unable to receive the tax benefits of any interest payments and therefore the before tax cost of borrowing (ie 19%) will be used to evaluate the lease:

NPV = £55,000 + (2.140 × £55,000) = £172,700.

Leasing is still therefore more financially advantageous than outright purchase.

(c)   Other factors to be considered when the company is making the lease or buy decision include the following:

(i)   **Running expenses**

It is assumed in the calculations that these are the same under the two financing alternatives. However in practice, items such as insurance, maintenance etc may vary.

(ii)   **Current liquidity**

The effect of taking out and servicing an immediate loan of £176,000 on the overall liquidity and borrowing capacity must be considered.

(iii)   **Accuracy of estimates**

The company must be certain that the life of the machine has been estimated correctly at four years. If there is a possibility that the life could be shorter than this then the alternatives should be re-evaluated.

(iv)   **Effect on reported profits**

The effect of the alternatives on the reported profits should be taken into account, since this in turn could affect the dividend policy and therefore the valuation of the company's shares.

(v)   **Change in interest rate**

The calculations assume that the interest rate will be fixed for the life of the machine. If the rate changes then this will have financial implications which should be evaluated.

6 Bases of valuation

> **Top tips.** For this question it is important not only to be able to use the various valuation methods required, but also to know the limitations of each method. In an exam question it is likely that you will need to recommend a realistic purchase price for a company.

(a) (i) Statement of financial position value = £454,100

(ii) **Replacement cost value** = £454,100 + £(725,000 – 651,600) + £(550,000 – 515,900) = £561,600

(iii) **Realisable value** = £454,100 + £(450,000 – 651,600) + (570,000 – 515,900) –£14,900 = £291,700

Bad debts are 2% × £745,000 = £14,900. Bad debts are assumed not to be relevant to statement of financial position and replacement cost values.

(iv) The **dividend growth model value** depends on an estimate of growth, which is far from clear given the wide variations in earnings over the five years.

1 The lowest possible value, assuming zero growth, is as follows:

$$\text{Value} = \frac{£25,000}{0.12} = £208,333$$

It is not likely that this will be the basis taken.

2 Looking at dividend growth over the past five years we have:

20X4 dividend = £25,000

20X0 dividend = £20,500

If the annual growth rate in dividends is g

$$(1 + g)^4 = \frac{(25,000)}{20,500} = 1.2195$$

$$1 + g = 1.0508$$

$$g = 0.0508, \text{ say } 5\%$$

Then, $\text{MV ex div} = \dfrac{\text{Dividend in 1 year}}{0.12 - g}$

$$= \frac{25,000(1.05)}{0.07}$$

$$= £375,000$$

3 Using the rb model, we have:

$$\text{Average proportion retained} = \frac{12,800 + 44,200 + 18,300 + 13,400 + 27,000}{33,300 + 66,800 + 43,300 + 38,400 + 52,200}$$

$$= 0.495 \text{ (say } b = 0.5)$$

$$\text{Return on investment this year} = \frac{53,200}{\text{average investment}}$$

$$= \frac{53,200}{(454,100 + 454,100 - 27,200)/2}$$

$$= 0.1208 \text{ (say } r = 12\%).$$

Then g = 0.5 × 12% = 6%

$$\text{So MV ex div} = \frac{25,000(1.06)}{0.06} = £441,667$$

(v) *P/E ratio model*

Comparable quoted companies to Manon Ltd have P/E ratios of about 10. Manon is much smaller and being unquoted, its P/E ratio would be less than 10, but how much less?

If we take a P/E ratio of 5, we have MV = £53,200 × 5 = £266,000

If we take a P/E ratio of $10 \times {}^2/_3$, we have MV = £53,200 × 10 × $^2/_3$ = £354,667

If we take a P/E ratio of 10, we have MV = £532,000

(b) (i) *The statement of financial position value*

The statement of financial position value should not play a part in the negotiation process. **Historical costs** are **not relevant** to a decision on the future value of the company.

(ii) *The replacement cost*

This gives the cost of setting up a **similar business**. Since this gives a higher figure than any other valuation in this case, it could show the **maximum price** for Carmen to offer. There is clearly no goodwill to value.

(iii) *The realisable value*

This shows the cash which the shareholders in Manon could get by **liquidating the business**. It is therefore the **minimum price** which they would accept.

All the methods (i) to (iii) suffer from the limitation that they do not look at the **going concern value** of the business as a whole. Methods (iv) and (v) do consider this value. However, the realisable value is of use in assessing the risk attached to the business as a going concern, as it gives the base value if things go wrong and the business has to be abandoned.

(iv) *The dividend model*

The figures have been calculated using Manon's k_e (12%). The relevance of a dividend valuation to Carmen will depend on whether the **current retention** and **reinvestment policies** would be continued. Certainly the value to Carmen should be based on 9% rather than 12%. Both companies are **ungeared** and in the same **risk class** so the different required returns must be due to their **relative sizes** and the fact that Carmen's shares are more **marketable**.

One of the main limitations on the dividend growth model is the problem of estimating the **future value of g**.

(v) *The P/E ratio model*

The P/E ratio model is an attempt to get at the value which the **market** would put on a company like Manon. It does provide an external yardstick, but is a very crude measure. As already stated, the P/E ratio which applies to larger quoted companies must be **lowered** to allow for the size of Manon and the non-marketability of its shares. Another limitation of P/E ratios is that the ratio is very dependent on the expected future growth of the firm. It is therefore not easy to find a P/E ratio of a 'similar firm'.

(c) The minimum price which the shareholders of Manon will accept will be the realisable value of the assets, **£291,700**. The **maximum price** Carmen will pay is the earnings basis using a P/E of 10 at **£532,000**.

The dividend basis gives a value of about 5% gives a value of £375,000. This looks optimistic given the lack of dividend growth over the last couple of years.

So the eventual purchase price will probably be in the range £291,700 to £375,000.

7 Perseus

> **Top tips.** If you struggled on either part of this question, you should go back over the material again, as valuation will occur in practically every sitting, often in the compulsory question. Remember that the examiner will never just want you to carry out valuation calculations. You should **always** comment on the methods you use, even if you are not explicitly asked to in the question as you are here.

(a)　(i)　*Net assets basis*

	$m
Freehold land and buildings	104.2
Fixtures and fittings	3.5
Motor vehicles	0.4
Inventory	58.0
Trade receivables	23.4
Cash	21.5
Trade payables	(25.9)
Tax	(5.4)
Bonds	(49.0)
Net assets	130.7

$$\text{Value per share} = \frac{\$130.7m}{50m} = \$2.61 \text{ per share}$$

(ii)　*Dividend yield basis*

$$\text{Dividend per share in Perseus (gross)} = \frac{\$3.3m \times 10/9}{50m} = 7.33 \text{ c}$$

It is assumed that this dividend will remain constant in future years.

Gross dividend yield of Tityus = 2.2%

Adjust upwards for lesser marketability/greater risk of an unlisted company - say 2.6%*

$$\text{Value per share in Perseus} = \frac{\text{Dividend per share}}{\text{Dividend yield}} = \frac{0.073}{0.026} = \$2.81 \text{ per share}$$

*(Alternatively, since this is a very arbitrary adjustment, it would be acceptable to use the unadjusted yield to get a value of $3.22, then add a note to acknowledge that this is likely to be an overvaluation.)

(iii)　*Price/earnings ratio basis*

$$\text{Earnings per share of Perseus} = \frac{\$10.7m}{50m} = 21.4c$$

P/E ratio of Tityus = 20.5

Adjust downwards for lesser marketability/ greater risk of an unlisted company – say 15**

$$\text{Value per share in Perseus} = \$0.214 \times 15 = \$3.21$$

**(A similar note to that at the end of (ii) applies here, with an unadjusted value of $4.39)

(b)   **Net assets basis**

The **net assets (liquidation)** basis is a method of valuation that can be used if the company is to be liquidated and the individual assets sold off to pay the shareholders. If the company is a going concern then the actual business **should be worth** a lot more than the break-up value of the assets, due to the future earnings and cash flows of the business and unrecorded assets such as goodwill. Therefore if the business is to be sold as a going concern then the net asset value is far too low a value. However it can be used as a bottom line figure to give an indication of the absolute lowest figure that could be accepted from a bidder.

Dividend yield basis

The **dividend yield method** of valuation is a conceptually sounder method of valuation for a business that is being valued as a going concern. The dividend valuation model is used to find the **present value of future dividends** based on the shareholders' required dividend yield.

However there are a number of problems with this method. Firstly **a suitable dividend yield** has to be determined. It is possible, as above, to use the published dividend yield of a similar listed company; however when valuing the shares of a private company the dividend yield must be adjusted upwards to reflect the lack of marketability of private company shares and the increased perceived risk compared to a listed company. This adjustment is arbitrary. In addition, the published dividend yield will incorporate an **expected level of growth** (the higher the growth the lower the yield) which may not match growth expectations in the company to be valued.

Secondly a **suitable dividend figure** must be used. This could be the latest year's dividend, an average of a number of past years or an estimate of the actual future dividends.

There is a further problem with the use of the dividend yield for the valuation of an entire company. The dividend yield method is suitable for the **valuation of a small holding** in a company but if the entire company is to be purchased then the new owners may have an entirely different dividend policy and therefore it is the earnings of the company rather than the dividends which are of importance.

Price/earnings method

The price/earnings method of valuation is therefore a good method to use for the purchase of an entire company as it is based upon the last reported earnings of the company.

Again however there are problems with **determining an appropriate price/earnings ratio** and sustainable earnings. The price/earnings ratio of a similar listed company can be used but as with the dividend yield this must be adjusted to reflect the **lack of marketability**, increased risk and difference in growth expectations. This time however the adjustment should be downwards and is again an arbitrary one. The earnings figure that is used could be the current earnings figure, an average of a number of years past earnings or the future earnings that the purchaser expects from the company.

8 Olivine

> **Top tips.** Our answer to part (a)(ii) assumes that the administrative savings have been achieved. Otherwise the answer to (a)(ii) is £(25 + 9.6)m/60m = 57.7 pence per share, and subsequent answers also change.

(a) (i) **The total value of the share offer**

Earnings per share = £25m/40m = £0.625

P/E ratio = 20

Share price = 20 × £0.625 = £12.50 per share

Share offer = 5 shares × (16m shares/4) = 20m shares issued

Value of share offer = £12.50 × 20 million = £250 million

(ii) **Olivine earnings per share**

Earnings = £25m + £9.6m + £2.4m = £37.0m

Number of shares = 40m + 20m = 60 million

Earnings per share = £37.0m/60m = 61.7 pence per share

(iii) **Share price of Olivine**

Earnings per share (part ii) = 61.7 pence per share

Price earnings ratio = 20 × (100 – 5)% = 19

Share price = 19 × £0.617 = £11.72 per share

(b) **Effect on wealth of shareholders**

Olivine shareholders

Original holding = 40m shares @ £12.50 per share = £500m

New share price = £11.72

New share value = 40m shares @ £11.72 = £468.8m

Loss in shareholder wealth = £500m – £468.8m = £31.2m or 6.24%

Halite shareholders

Original earnings per share = £9.6m/16m shares = £0.60

Price/earnings ratio = 15

Share price = 15 × £0.60 = £9.00 per share

Original holding = 16m shares @ £9.00 = £144m

New holding = 20m shares @ £11.72 = £234.4m

Gain in shareholder wealth = £234.4m – £144m = £90.4m or 62.78%

(c) The **market capitalisation** of the separate businesses is (40m × £12.50) + (16m × £9.00) = £644m. When combined the market capitalisation will be 60m × £11.72 = £703.2m so there are benefits to be gained in overall terms.

Effect on share price

The **total share value** of Halite prior to the acquisition is £144 million. However the intended share issue by Olivine of 20 million shares has a value at Olivine's current share price of £250 million. The issue of so many shares to achieve this premium means that there is a small reduction in the size of the earnings per share of Olivine even when the

earnings of Halite and the benefits of the acquisition are taken into account. This reduction in earnings per share together with a 5% reduction in the price/earnings ratio of Olivine after the acquisition would lead to a reduction in Olivine's share price from £12.50 per share before the acquisition to £11.72 per share after the acquisition. The estimate of the revised P/E ratio is possibly too high and needs further scrutiny.

This reduction in share value for Olivine shareholders would **result in a loss in shareholder value** from the acquisition of £31.2 million (6.24%). In contrast the generous premium being considered for the shares of Halite would lead to an increase in the value of the shares held by former Halite plc shareholders of £90.4 million (62.78%).

Beneficiaries of offer

If the proposed offer is made all of the benefit of the acquisition will accrue to the Halite plc shareholders and the Olivine shareholders will suffer a loss in share value. However, the dividend per share for Halite shareholders is likely to be lower in the future than it is at present.

The directors of Olivine might wish to consider a less generous offer than the current premium of £106 million (£250m – £144m) on the purchase of Halite. For example a share-for-share exchange would value the offer at £200 million (16 million shares @ £12.50 per share) thereby still providing a substantial premium to the Halite shareholders but with no loss to the Olivine shareholders.

9 K and H

> **Top tips.** The stages used in (a) are:
>
> - Calculate combined earnings
> - Calculate earnings per share
> - Calculate p/e ratio using share price given in the question
>
> and then comment on the lack of realism, suggesting a better method.
>
> Note in (b) that the 240p estimate is an assumption which should be questioned.
>
> In (c) you have to find out what the excess (premium) on acquisition is, and compare it with the change in earnings that will result from the acquisition. The key to (d) is explaining the significance of the enhancement in size.

(a)

	K	H
Earnings	£5,180,000	£2,340,000
EPS	14.8p	29.25p
Number of shares	35,000,000	8,000,000

An offer of three shares in K for two shares in H would result in the equity of K increasing to 47,000,000 shares.

In order to establish how the estimated post-acquisition market price of K was reached, we must look at **P/E ratios**.

	K	H
Pre-acquisition price	222	322
EPS	14.8	29.25
P/E ratio, pre-acquisition	15	11

The post-acquisition earnings, assuming no synergy or growth, would be (5,180 + 2,340) = £7,520,000 or (÷ 47 million shares) 16p a share.

The estimated post-acquisition share price of K is 240p. On the assumption that the post-acquisition EPS is 16p, the P/E ratio would be 15.

It would therefore seem that the estimated post-acquisition market price of K shares has been derived by applying the **pre-acquisition P/E ratio** of K to an estimated post-acquisition EPS (assuming no profits growth through synergy).

The estimated post-acquisition equivalent market value of an old H share is 1.5 times 240 pence, because three K shares will be exchanged for two H shares, giving a relative value of 3:2 or 1.5.

These estimates cannot be realistic, because it is incorrect to assume that on a takeover where neither company is minuscule relative to the other, the post-acquisition P/E ratio will be the same as the pre-acquisition P/E ratio of the more highly rated company in the takeover.

K is hoping to take over a public company with a **lower P/E ratio** than its own, and its directors must expect K's post-acquisition P/E ratio to fall accordingly.

A better estimate of the post acquisition P/E ratio would be the *weighted average* of their pre-acquisition P/Es as follows:

	Earnings £'000		Market value £'000
K	5,180	(35m × 222p)	77,700
H	2,340	(8m × 322p)	25,760
Combined	7,520		103,460

Weighted average P/E ratio $\dfrac{103,460}{7,520} = 13.758$

Applying this to a post-acquisition EPS of 16p, an estimated post-acquisition market price of K shares would be (13.758 × 16p) 220p each. This would make the post-acquisition equivalent MV of an old H share (220 × 1.5) = 330p.

There would be a very slight gain for H shareholders at the expense of K shareholders, but not much. This is because the share exchange ratio of three for two reflects almost exactly the pre-acquisition market prices per share of 322:222 = 1.45 or nearly 1.50, which is 3:2.

(b)

	£'000
Value of 35 million K shares:	
Estimated post-acquisition value (× 240p)	84,000
Pre-acquisition value (× 222p)	77,700
Gain to K shareholders from acquisition (× 18p)	6,300

K could raise its offer by £6,300,000 without reducing the wealth of its shareholders, but only assuming that the 240p estimate of the post-acquisition share price is correct. This extra value might be offered in **cash** (£0.7875 per share in H) or in **more shares** in K.

(c)   The pre-acquisition market value of K is unchanged at 222p, and so a two for one share exchange offer would value each share in H at 444p as well, compared with its current 322p.

	£'000
Offer value for 8,000,000 shares in H (× 444p)	35,520
Current value of 8,000,000 shares in H (× 322p)	25,760
Excess	9,760

The revised offer would only maintain the wealth of current shareholders if the combined share values of the post-acquisition company were to increase by at least £9,760,000.

It is assumed that the value of the post-acquisition company will be increased by the NPV of the asset disposals, savings in running costs and extra redundancy costs, discounted at K's cost of capital of 14% per year.

Year	Item	Amount £'000	Discount factor @ 14% 14%	Present value £'000
0	Redundancy costs	(3,500)	1.000	(3,500.0)
1	Redundancy costs	(8,400)	0.877	(7,366.8)
1	Fixed asset disposals	7,200	0.877	6,314.4
$1 - \infty$	Savings in running costs	2,750	$(1 \div 0.14) = 7.14$	19,642.9
			Net present value	15,090.5

We might therefore conclude that because of redundancies and rationalisation, the combined value of the post-acquisition companies will increase by about £15,000,000 which is more than the £9,760,000 needed to fund the extra price being offered for their shares to H shareholders. Of the increase in share values, H shareholders would benefit by the first £9,760,000, leaving the remaining £5,240,000 to be shared between all shareholders in the post-acquisition company.

A **two for one offer** should therefore be made.

(d)   Assuming no increase in total post-acquisition earnings, the group will have a fairly low interest cover ratio. The interest cover in the 'old' K is $(12,400 \div 4,431)$ 2.8 times and in the 'old' H is $(5,800 \div 2,200) = 2.6$ times. In the combined company it will be $(12,400 + 5,800) \div (4,431 + 2,200) = 2.75$ times.

Although we do not have statement of financial position details, this low interest cover indicates **high gearing**, and the cost of the existing debt capital might therefore be high.

The takeover will create an **enlarged company**, and because of this, it is fairly reasonable to assume that the **risk of default** will be less than with either of the 'old' companies taken individually. This **reduction in default risk**, if perceived to be significant, might reduce the return that investors in debt capital seek from the company. A reduction in the required return on marketable fixed interest capital would raise its **market value**. In this respect, the acquisition would have some effect on the **market value** of K's debt.

Of course, K's debt might be **non-marketable bank loans** and **overdrafts**, in which case the acquisition would not have any effect on the market value of the debt, since such debt has no market value.

10 Premoco

> **Top tips.** This is a wide-ranging question that requires a good all-round grasp of the factors involved in the acquisition decision. In part (a) set out your ratio calculations clearly and make sure you recognise when there is a need to ungear and gear betas. In part (b) you must comment on each method. In part (c) there is no one right or wrong answer. Follow the question requirements directly in the report.

(a) (i) *Current market values and P/E ratios*

The market value of the company's shares (market capitalisation) is the share price multiplied by the number of shares in issue.

The P/E ratio (price/earnings ratio) is the share price divided by the latest earnings per share.

No figures are available for Carsals, which is a private company.

	Premoco	*Nafco*	*Oiltrans*
Share price (pence)	1,648	675	1,530
Number of issued shares (million)	20	10	12
Total market value of shares (£ million)	329.6	67.5	183.6
Earnings per share (pence)	103	75	85
P/E ratio	16	9	18

(ii) *Cost of equity (k_e) using the CAPM (capital asset pricing model)*

This is given by: $k_e = R_f + (R_m - R_f)\beta_g$

The market return, R_m, is 12% and the risk-free rate, R_f, is 6%. The equity beta factor (β_g) for the first three companies is given directly, but for Carsals it is estimated by degearing the equity beta of a similar quoted company to get the asset beta or ungeared beta, β_u. This is because Carsals has no debt in its capital structure.

The no-tax formula is $\beta_u = \beta_g \dfrac{V_E}{V_E + V_D}$

Thus for Carsals $\beta_u = 1.25 \times \dfrac{80}{80 + 20} = 1.0$

	Premoco	*Nafco*	*Oiltrans*	*Carsals*
Beta factor	1.2	0.9	1.3	1.0
Cost of equity = 6% + (12% – 6%)β	13.2%	11.4%	13.8%	12.0%

(iii) *Prospective market value using the constant growth dividend valuation model*

The formula is $P_0 = \dfrac{d_1}{k_e - g}$ where d_1 (next year's dividend) = $d_0 (1 + g)$.

	Premoco	*Nafco*	*Oiltrans*	*Cars*
Latest dividend per share (d_0) (pence)	31	55	42	1
Expected growth, g	11%	5%	14%	9
Next year's dividend, d_1 (pence)	34.41	57.75	47.88	122
Estimated value per share $d_1/(k_e-g)$ (£)	15.64	9.02	N/A	40.
Number of issued shares (million)	20	10		0.
Total prospective market capitalisation (£m)	312.8	90.2		20

(b)   **Usefulness of the three types of valuation in the acquisition decision**

Summarised values for the four companies

	Premoco £m	Nafco £m	Oiltrans £m	Carsals £m
Current market value	329.6	67.5	183.6	N/A
Prospective market value	312.8	90.2	N/A	20.3
Net asset value	250	60	65	6

(i)   *Current market value method*

1   The **current market value** shows the value of each of the listed companies to its existing shareholders. The efficient market hypothesis (semi-strong form) implies that the market value of each company is the best estimate of its fundamental value, based on public information. Despite criticisms of the EMH, there is a large body of evidence which shows that the **semi-strong form** is substantially correct. However, when making an acquisition decision, Premoco is concerned with the value of each target company to itself, not to that company's existing shareholders. Adjustments may therefore be needed.

2   During the negotiations, information which is not known to the public may emerge. This will cause Premoco to adjust its valuations. Premoco may also have plans for **generating synergy** when it combines a new business with its own (eg by elimination of duplicated assets and costs). This will affect the value of the new business to Premoco. However, extreme caution must be exercised when using estimates of synergy to adjust market values, because the market may already have anticipated the merger taking place and may have increased the price of the target company to allow for possible synergy. This effect can make the market values of companies unreliable if takeover rumours start.

3   Premoco will probably find it necessary to offer a price higher than the **existing market** value in order to induce target company shareholders to sell.

4   There is, of course, no market value for the private company, which cannot be valued by this method.

(ii)   *Dividend valuation method*

The **prospective value based on the constant growth dividend valuation model** is one method of attempting to compute the fundamental going concern value of the business from basic data concerning the company. The model itself is, however, very crude, assuming that dividend growth will be at a constant rate to perpetuity. More complex versions of this model exist where **varying growth rates** can **be postulated**. In particular, the model becomes meaningless if g exceeds the cost of equity and very unreliable when the two figures are close together, as for Premoco itself.

(iii)   *Net asset values*

The **net asset values** of the companies are probably based on **historical** cost, although some oil companies do use a current cost basis for reporting.

1   **Historical cost**

In terms of relevance for an acquisition, historical cost is irrelevant except as an approximation to either net realisable value or current cost.

2   **Current cost**

Current cost, or replacement cost, is useful in showing the cost of setting up a similar business from scratch but it is not a valuation of the business concerned. It ignores goodwill and intangible assets and, if Premoco did decide to set up a competing business from scratch, the original target company would still exist as a competitor.

3   **Net realisable value**

Net realisable values of the business assets are probably the most useful asset figures which can be provided. This is obviously true if the business is acquired to be broken up but NRV asset values are also useful when viewing the business as a going concern: the break-up value of the business shows the worst-case scenario if the business is acquired as a going concern but fails. In other words, it is NRV which should be used as the basis of the 'asset backing' calculation, not historical cost.

(iv)   *Conclusion*

In practice the businesses cannot be valued separately if they are going to be joined together, and a valuation method may well involve a combination of computing the present value of future improved operating cash flows together with the net realisable value of assets which are to be sold. The company will find the 'estimated NPV of the combined organisation' more useful than any of the standalone valuations of the businesses.

(c)   **To:**   David Wong

From: Financial Adviser

Date: 12 November 20X7

Subject: Report on three possible acquisitions available to Premoco

Introduction

I have examined the information which you have supplied to me on the three potential acquisitions and set out my views on the strategic implications of each, bearing in mind your **wish to diversify away from petroleum**. Relevant calculations are shown in the Appendix. I have assumed that the existing market value of Premoco, £329.6 million, is a fair estimate of its true value.

Nafco

(i)   *Price to be offered*

1   On the basis of the financial advisers' figures (see Appendix), the combination will increase equity earnings by £3.9 million and creates added value (synergy) of £114.9 million (29%). The **absolute maximum price** which can be paid for Nafco is £182.4 million, which is £18.24 per share. The minimum that can be offered is the existing market price of £6.75 per share. You should not of course offer the maximum price. If the shareholders of Premoco are to get their fair share of value added from the merger, they should not pay more than 29% more than the current market price per share of Nafco. This gives a price of **£8.71 per share** (£87.1 million in total).

2   A **suggested range for negotiation** is therefore £7 to £9 per share. If your intelligence is correct, Nafco's institutional shareholders would be pleased to accept a reasonable offer from a more up-market firm like yours and there should be no reason to go above the figure of £8.71 unless a competing bid emerges.

(ii)   *Suggested terms of the offer*

1   A price of £87.1 million could be financed substantially by cash in the bank but this would leave no investment funds for improving Nafco's operations. If you wish to pursue the cash route, you will need to borrow over the medium or long term. The gearing of Premoco is not high and borrowing will not be a problem, but you must recognise that **group gearing** will **increase** if this acquisition is made, because Nafco's **debt ratio** is much **higher** than your own.

2   If you intend to borrow, one option is to take up the supplier's offer of cheap loan finance in return for a long-term supply agreement. Acceptance of the offer would reduce Premoco's cost of capital. However, the decision on this source of finance should not be regarded as **part of the acquisition decision**. It is something which needs to be investigated in its own right as it would involve a major **change in strategy** from the existing policy of buying petrol in the open market.

3   The alternative to increasing borrowing is to **issue shares** in Premoco to the shareholders of Nafco (a share-for-share swap). The share price of Premoco (£16.48) is roughly twice the offer price for Nafco, so the terms of the offer would be approximately 1 for 2. This would have the advantage of **keeping gearing low** and would probably be very acceptable to the disaffected institutional shareholders of Nafco, who would be able to retain their investment in the petroleum industry and maintain the balance of their portfolios. However, the transactions costs of share issues are much higher than for borrowing. Share issues become more obviously advantageous for larger acquisitions.

(iii)   *Business implications*

1   The acquisition of Nafco would result in **horizontal integration expanding** the company's operations in **retailing of petroleum** and expanding the company's market share. Large economies of scale could be generated, which accounts for the very high synergy expected from the merger. A choice needs to be made as to whether Nafco's garages should be adapted to run in the same **up-market** way as Premoco's or whether they should concentrate on their existing **low-price** strategy. Whatever the strategy, substantial investment will be needed to improve the image with consumers and hence to improve on the company's existing growth prospects, which are low.

2   The acquisition of Nafco does not in itself represent a **diversification** away from petroleum products and is therefore not what you appear to be looking for at the moment. However, it appears to be a **good buy** if the price can be kept relatively low and there is much **scope for developing convenience stores** on the Nafco sites.

Oiltrans

(i)   *Price to be offered*

Using the same arguments as were put forward for Nafco plc, the **absolute maximum value** of Oiltrans (on the basis of NPV of the combined organisation) is £265.4 million or £22 per share, compared with the current price of £15.30. The added value generated by the merger is 16% which, when added to the current market price, gives £17.75. The suggested **range of prices** for negotiation is **£16** to **£18 per share** but, because the bid is hostile, you might have to be prepared to go higher.

(ii) *Terms of the offer*

1 At £17.75 per share, the total cost of the acquisition is £213 million. This is too large to be financed entirely by cash, and **borrowing** would **increase gearing significantly**. A share issue or a mixture of shares and debt is the most likely route for financing this acquisition. The share-for-share swap would be in the region of 1 for 1 (see tutorial note above) which would mean the issue of 12 million new shares.

2 Since only 10 million shares are available for issue, this would mean that the **authorised share capital** would need to be **increased**, and this in turn would signal to the market that something major was about to happen. To avoid an increase in authorised share capital, the company could offer a **choice of shares or a cash alternative**. In cases like this, the cash alternative is usually less than the equivalent share value because it is less risky.

3 A **further problem** of a large share issue is that existing share ownership of Premoco will become diluted and large shareholders in Oiltrans may become dominant in the combined company.

(iii) *Business implications*

1 The acquisition of Oiltrans would be a **vertical integration** of an **existing supplier** into the company's business. This represents more of a diversification than the acquisition of Nafco and is therefore more in line with your stated strategy but, judging from the figures, less synergy can be created because of the different nature of the two businesses. Oiltrans has significantly higher growth prospects than the existing business of Premoco.

2 Your problem with diversifying into a business of this type is that you **cannot easily demonstrate expertise** and **experience** at managing such companies. In the event of a contested takeover, shareholders will probably back the existing management unless you can demonstrate that they are inefficient in some way. Note that for most large shareholders there is **no benefit** if your company diversifies purely to **reduce risk** because these shareholders will already hold diversified portfolios. Indeed it is quite likely that they already own shares in Oiltrans plc as well as Premoco.

3 If the takeover succeeds, the existing management would probably resign, and we lose their skills which appear to have been a **significant influence** on Oiltrans' success.

4 When two companies of similar size consider merging there is a real problem as to who will end up running the company. The directors of Oiltrans may turn the tables on you by arranging a **counter bid** for the shares of Premoco. Alternatively, to agree bid terms, you will need to decide which directors from both sides should head the combined group.

Carsals

(i) *Price to be offered*

1 The **absolute maximum amount** that could be paid for Carsals (on the basis of NPV of the combined organisation) is £38.4 million, which is £76.80 per share. Our dividend valuation model approach gave a figure of £40.69 per share. Synergy generated by the merger is 5%, so to give your own shareholders their fair share of this gain, the price paid should not be more than £42.72 per share, giving a total price of £21.36 million.

2   The **price paid** would depend on how quickly the **existing major shareholder needs to make the sale** and on **what other offers** he is likely to receive. One major problem is that other car dealers can generate synergy from the acquisition and can therefore afford to pay more than Premoco. Before agreeing the price, you must be sure of the terms of the franchise, in particular the period for which it lasts and the renewal terms.

(ii)   *Terms of the offer*

This company could be purchased using existing cash. However a **share-for-share exchange** could be used as a means of tying in the existing managing director, and solving the problem of appointing a suitable managing director (see below). A generous earn-out arrangement may also persuade the existing managing director to stay on, and reduces the risk of loss of customers.

(iii)   *Business implications*

1   Carsals represents a **complete product diversification** from the existing business but maintains the **same up-market image** in prestige locations. There will be no problems of control arising from the acquisition. The business is predicted to show reasonable growth but there will be **no immediate synergy** available from the business combination. The sort of longer term synergy available is in marketing the superior image for both cars, petroleum and other retail services. In addition there may be scope to sell some **properties**.

2   You will need to appoint a **suitable managing director** from the car sales business if the owner has not groomed a suitable successor. The terms of the franchise must be investigated carefully and, finally, you must be aware that the success of this business depends to a large extent on the continued success of the motor manufacturer.

Conclusions

Despite your wish to diversify, I feel on balance that the opportunity of **expanding the existing business** by the acquisition of Nafco presents much higher wealth-producing opportunities than a contested bid for Oiltrans, which may well drain company resources and come to nothing. The acquisition of Carsals should also be followed up promptly, as a quick purchase may result in a bargain.

Signed: Financial Adviser

APPENDIX

	Premoco £m	Nafco £m	Oiltrans £m	Carsals £m
Total equity earnings	20.6	7.5	10.2	0.8
Existing value of shares*	329.6	67.5	183.6	20.3
Company combination		P+N	P + O	P + C
Sum of existing earnings		28.1	30.8	21.4
Estimated post-merger earnings		32.0	35.0	23.0
Additional earnings predicted		3.9	4.2	1.6
Sum of existing valuations		397.1	513.2	349.9
Estimated NPV of combined organisation		512.0	595.0	368.0
Increase in value from the combination		114.9	81.8	18.1
Maximum price that can be paid for the acquisition**		182.4	265.4	38.4

*Dividend valuation model used for Carsals.

**NPV of combination minus value of Premoco £329.6 million.

INDEX

Note: **Key terms** and their references are given in **bold**

3 E's, 13

Acquisition, 225
Acquisition, 225
Advisers, 174
Agency problem, 11, 27
Agency theory, 11
Allocative efficiency, 260
Alpha value, 193
Arbitrage, 211
Asset turnover, 45
Asset valuation bases, 247

Balanced scorecard, 8
Bank of England, 31
Beta, 279
Beta factor, 190
Beta factor, 190
Big data, 226
Bonds, 116
Bootstrapping, 252
Business risk, 127, 206, 227, 256
Business risks, 5
Business strategy, 27

Calculated intangible values, 264
Capital asset pricing model (CAPM), 189
Capital markets, 169
Capital structure, 203
Capitalisation of earnings method, 266
Capitals, 82
Cash budget, 49
Cash flow hedge, 66
Cash flow valuation methods, 255
Cash forecasts, 49
Cash operating cycle, 47
Cash purchases, 295
Cash slack, 230
Cash surpluses, 56
Chartists, 183
City Code on Takeovers and Mergers, 234, 235
Commercial paper, 115
Comparison with market transactions method, 266
Competition authorities, 29
Competition legislation, 236
Competition regulation, 28
Concentric diversification, 225
Conglomerate diversification, 225
Constraints on financial strategy, 25
Contingency funding, 56
Conversion value, 119
Convertible bonds, 298
Convertible debt, 119
Convertible preference shares, 169
Corporate governance, 12, 28
Cost of capital, 126

Cost of debt, 127
Cost of equity, 278
Cost of preference shares, 188
Cost synergy, 229
Coupon, 116
Credit rating, 26
Creditworthiness, 115
Cum div, 184, 254
Cum rights, 179
Cumulative preference shares, 169
Currency risk, 137
Currency swap, 138, 147
Current ratio, 46

Debenture, 116
Debt and gearing, 45
Debt ratio, 45
Debt/equity, 45
Deep discount bond, 117
Defensive tactics, 234
Demerger, 309
Dilution, 177, 303
Disclosure of financial instruments, 74
Discounted future cash flows, 258
Discounted future cash flows method of share valuation, 255
Diversification, 229
Divestment, 309, 312
Dividend, 99
Dividend cover, 47
Dividend decisions, 23
Dividend growth model, 185
Dividend payout ratio, 48
Dividend policy, 99, 110
Dividend validation on model, 182
Dividend valuation bases, 253
Dividend valuation model, 184, 254
Dividend yield, 47
Double taxation agreement, 41
Drucker's Golden Rules, 307

Earnings per share (EPS), 47
Earnings valuation bases, 249
Earnings yield, 48, 253
Earnings yield valuation method, 253
Earn-out arrangement, 299
Economic constraints, 30
Efficient market hypothesis, 260
EPS before and after a takeover, 301
Equity, 169
Equity share capital, 169
Eurobond, 123
Eurocredits, 123
Eurocurrency, 123
Eurodollars, 123
Ex div, 184, 254
Ex rights, 179
Excess return, 264

Exchange rate, **34**
Exchange rate risk, 35, 37
Exit strategies, 309
Expectations, 33

Failure of mergers and takeovers, 309
Fair value hedge, **66**
Finance lease, **151**
Financial distress costs, 203
Financial objectives, 5
Financial risk, 5, 127, 204, 205, 228, 279
Financial risk disclosure, 70
Financial synergy, 229
Financial targets, 6
Financing decisions, 23, 33
Financing requirements, 56
Fixed charge, 116
Floating charge, 117
Floor value, 120, 249
Flotation, 171, 313
Forecast, **49**
Forecasting exchange rates, 35
Foreign currency cash flows, 277
Foreign exchange constraints, 38, 41
Foreign exchange risk, 124
Foreign subsidiaries, 39
Free cash flow, 256
Fundamental analysis, **182**
Fundamental theory of share values, 182, 185
Funding constraints, 25
Funding deficit, 52

Geared betas, 279
Gearing, 100, 106, 203, 205, 252
Gearing and ungearing betas, 285
Goal congruence, **11**
Going private, 105, 312
Goodwill, **263**
Gordon's growth approximation, 187
Government grants, 277
GRI framework, 79
Growth rate, 186

Hedge accounting, 65
Hedge effectiveness, **65**
Hedge of a net investment in a foreign operation, **66**
Hedged item, **65**
Hedging, **65**
Hedging instrument, **65**
Hire purchase, 155
Historic growth, 186
Horizontal integration, **225**
Human resource accounting, 82

Industry regulators, 29
Inflation, 30, 35
Information processing efficiency, 260
Initial public offer (IPO), **172**

Institutional investors, **113**
Intangible assets, **263**
Integrated reporting, 82
Integration sequence, 308
Intellectual capital, **264**
Interest cover, 46, 207
Interest rate option, 141
Interest rate parity, 36
Interest rate risk, 140
Interest rate swaps, 141
Interest rates, 30
Internal rate of return (IRR), 128
International constraints, 38
International debt finance, 122
Introduction, 174
Inventory days, 46
Investment decisions, 22
Investor relations, 27
Irredeemable, 118
Irredeemable debt, 128
Irrelevancy theory, 102
Issuing house, 172
Jones's Integration Sequence, 308

Leading and lagging, 56
Lease or buy decisions, 156
Leasing, **151**
Legislation, 27
LIBOR, 142
Life cycle, 100
Liquidations, 311
Liquidity, 46, 100

Management buyout, **312**
Management buyouts (MBOs), 115
Management commentary, 74
Managing the debt profile, 137
Market efficiency, 262
Market risk, **189**
Market risk premium, **192**
Market segmentation theory, 33
Market valuation or capitalisation, 249
Market value, 182
Market values, 5, 206
Market-to-book values, 264
Matching, 123
Merger, **225**, 249
Mergers and takeovers, 225, 262
Merging systems, 308
Mezzanine finance, 115, 300
Modigliani and Miller, 102, 210, 284
Monetary Policy Committee, 31
Multinational, 39
Multinational company, **39**

Net assets method of share valuation, 247
Net assets per share, 48
Net operating income, 210, 284
Nominal rates of interest, 31
Nominal value, 169

Non-constant growth, 187
Non-financial objectives, 8
Non-quoted company, 5
Non-systematic risk, **189**
Not-for-profit organisations, 12

Objectives, 5
Offer for sale, 171
Offers for sale by tender, 172
Operating gearing, 46, 206
Operating leases, 151
Operational efficiency, 260
Opportunity cost, 126
Overdrafts, 115
Overseas taxes, 41
Overtrading, 46

P/E ratio, 48
P/E ratio (earnings) method of valuation, 249
Paper bid, 296
Participating preference shares, 169
Payables payment period, 47
Payment methods, 295
Performance analysis, 42
Performance related pay, 12
Placing, 173
Poison-pill, 234
Political risk, 38, 39
Portfolio, 189
Post-acquisition integration, 307
Preference shares, **169**
Premium profits method, 265
Pricing shares, 175
Primary markets, 170
Prior charge capital, **169**
Private equity, 176
Profit margin, 45
Profit maximisation, 5
Prospectus issue, 173
Purchasing power parity, 35

Quick ratio, 46

Random walk theory, 183
Ratio analysis, 42
Rational, 260
Real rates of interest, 31
Receivables collection period, 46
Redeemable debt, 128
Redemption, **117**
Regulation of takeovers, 235
Regulatory bodies, 27
Relief from royalties method, 265
Return on capital employed, 44
Return on equity, 45
Revenue synergy, 229
Reverse takeover, **225**
Rights issue, **177**
Risk, 32, 127, 189, 206

Risk and returns, 190
Risk-adjusted cost of capital, 279
Risk-free rate of return, 127

Sale and leaseback, 155
Scrip dividend, **104**
Secondary markets, 170
Security, 249
Sell-offs, 310
Semi-strong form efficiency, 261, 262
Sensitivity analysis, 55
Share exchange, 296
Share options, 12
Share price, 5
Share price behaviour, 182
Share repurchase, 105
Shareholders, 99
Short-term targets, 6
Short-termism, 175
Signalling effect, 100
Small and medium-sized entities, 125
Spin-offs, 311
Stakeholders, **10**, 237
Statement of financial position based forecasts, 50
Stock market, 5, 171
Strategic approach to takeovers, 228
Strategic financial management, **22**
Strategic fit, 228
Strong form efficiency, 261
Sustainability, 76
Swap, 141
Synergy, **229**
Systematic risk, **189**, 279

Takeover, **225**
Takeover panel, 235
Takeovers by share exchange, 170
Tax exhaustion, 213
Tax inversion, **231**
Tax relief on interest, 129
Tax shield, 26, 284
Taxation, 40, 41, 231, 277
Technical analysis, **183**
Theoretical ex-rights price, 178
Theories of capital structure, 209
Tie-breaker clauses, 41
Traditional view of WACC, 209

Underwriting, 124, 174
Ungeared betas, 279
Unlisted companies, 285
Unquoted company, 233, 251
Unsystematic risk, **189**

Valuation of mergers and takeovers, 301
Valuation using post-merger dividends or cash flows, 304
Value for money, 13

Value of rights, 180
Venture capital, 175, 313
Vertical integration, 225
View of WACC, 210

Warrants, 115, 122
Weak form efficiency, 261
Weighted average cost of capital, 209, 278
White knight, 234

Yield adjusted ex-rights price, 179
Yield curve, 32

Zero coupon bond, 117

Notes

Notes

Notes

Notes

Notes

Review Form – Paper F3 Financial Strategy (01/18)

Please help us to ensure that the CIMA learning materials we produce remain as accurate and user-friendly as possible. We cannot promise to answer every submission we receive, but we do promise that it will be read and taken into account when we update this Study Text.

Name: _____   Address: _____
                                                         _____
                                                         _____

How have you used this Study Text?
(Tick one box only)

☐ Home study (book only)

☐ On a course: college _____

☐ With 'correspondence' package

☐ Other _____

Why did you decide to purchase this Study Text? *(Tick one box only)*

☐ Have used BPP Texts in the past

☐ Recommendation by friend/colleague

☐ Recommendation by a lecturer at college

☐ Saw information on BPP website

☐ Saw advertising

☐ Other _____

During the past six months do you recall seeing/receiving any of the following?
(Tick as many boxes as are relevant)

☐ Our advertisement in *Financial Management*

☐ Our advertisement in *Pass*

☐ Our advertisement in *PQ*

☐ Our brochure with a letter through the post

☐ Our website www.bpp.com

Which (if any) aspects of our advertising do you find useful?
(Tick as many boxes as are relevant)

☐ Prices and publication dates of new editions

☐ Information on Text content

☐ Facility to order books off-the-page

☐ None of the above

Which BPP products have you used?

Text	☑	Passcard	☐
Kit	☐	i-Pass	☐

Your ratings, comments and suggestions would be appreciated on the following areas.

	Very useful	Useful	Not useful
Introductory section	☐	☐	☐
Chapter introductions	☐	☐	☐
Key terms	☐	☐	☐
Quality of explanations	☐	☐	☐
Case studies and other examples	☐	☐	☐
Exam skills and alerts	☐	☐	☐
Questions and answers in each chapter	☐	☐	☐
Chapter overview and summary diagrams	☐	☐	☐
Quick quizzes	☐	☐	☐
Question Bank	☐	☐	☐
Answer Bank	☐	☐	☐
Index	☐	☐	☐

	Excellent	Good	Adequate	Poor
Overall opinion of this Study Text	☐	☐	☐	☐

	Yes	No
Do you intend to continue using BPP products?	☐	☐

On the reverse of this page is space for you to write your comments about our Study Text. We welcome your feedback.

The BPP Learning Media author team can be e-mailed at: cimaqueries@bpp.com

TELL US WHAT YOU THINK

Please note any further comments and suggestions/errors below. For example, was the text accurate, readable, concise, user-friendly and comprehensive?